Redistricting in the New Millennium

Redistricting in the New Millennium

Edited by Peter F. Galderisi

LEXINGTON BOOKS

A Division of
ROWMAN & LITTLEFIELD PUBLISHERS, INC.
Lanham • Boulder • New York • Toronto • Oxford

LEXINGTON BOOKS

A division of Rowman & Littlefield Publishers, Inc.
A wholly owned subsidiary of The Rowman & Littlefield Publishing Group, Inc.
4501 Forbes Boulevard, Suite 200
Lanham, MD 20706

PO Box 317
Oxford
OX2 9RU, UK

British Library Cataloguing in Publication Information Available

Library of Congress Cataloging-in-Publication Data

Redistricting in the new millennium / edited by Peter F. Galderisi.
p. cm.
Includes bibliographical references and index.
ISBN 0-7391-0718-6 (cloth : alk. paper)
1. Election districts—United States. 2. Gerrymandering—United States.
3. Apportionment (Election law)—United States. I. Galderisi, Peter F.
JK1341.R373 2005
328.73'073455—dc22 2004029940

Printed in the United States of America

∞™ The paper used in this publication meets the minimum requirements of American National Standard for Information Sciences—Permanence of Paper for Printed Library Materials, ANSI/NISO Z39.48-1992.

To Holly, my partner, wife, and best friend

Contents

Acknowledgments

In the fall of 2002, a lecture series on "Redistricting in the New Millennium" was held at Utah State University, sponsored by the Milton R. Merrill Endowment at Utah State and the U.C. Berkeley Institute of Governmental Studies. Each participant contributed to this volume, as did several others who were later contracted to write thematic pieces or case studies. Together, these chapters broadly cover the primary issues and concerns raised by the redistricting process, analyzing both the legal and political causes and effects of that process.

This volume was delayed for a number of reasons other than the normal span of time entailed in the production of such an anthology, and speaks to the complexity of the redistricting process itself. Some of the contributors are not only academic researchers, but are also involved in the litigation that inevitably follows each post-Census round of redistricting. Their contributions were deemed essential, however, and more than the normal allotment of time to complete and edit the chapters had to be allocated. The main delay, however, was a function of an editorial decision to wait until a series of pending court cases had been decided (particularly those in Georgia and Texas). Considering that the last U.S. Supreme Court decision on the post-1990 redistricting plans did not occur until 2001, however, the editor finally decided to send the volume to production, knowing that the legal battles had probably not ended, but realizing that to wait for total closure might delay this volume for years. Lest we change the title to *Redistricting in the NEXT Millennium*, these chapters cover the process and outcome of the post-2000 reapportionment and redistricting as of June 2004. The results of the 2004 congressional elections continued the saga laid out by several of the case study authors with little, if any modification. Renewed interest in "depoliticizing" the redistricting process in California and other states simply confirms that redistricting is an issue that will not quickly recede from the political landscape.

Many individuals helped with the conference and preparation of this volume. I would like to thank Natalie Heaton, Melissa Macleod-Young, and Brandee Halverson for managing the budget, taking care of logistics, and attempting to keep me on schedule. My students in the redistricting series workshop helped to focus not only my thoughts, but also the thoughts of the other participants. Two of my students, Rebecca Nelson and especially Angela Nielsen-Redding, provided invaluable and timely editorial assistance. I am especially grateful to the staff at Lexington Books, particularly Serena Krombach, Deborah Justice, Erin Hill-Parks, and Sheila-Katherine Zwiebel for their guidance and endless patience. Douglas Johnson of the National Demographics Corporation spent countless hours redoing chapter 7's maps to bring them up to publication code. Special appreciation is reserved for Lee Brilliant and Sally Okelberry, who, overworked and underpaid, bailed me out of an endless morass of graphics and editorial problems late in the production process. Randy Simmons, as both boss and friend, offered continuous encouragement and assistance. Most of all, I wish to thank my partner and wife, Holly, for her understanding, patience, encouragement, and uncanny ability to keep me sane. This volume, as all else, is dedicated to her.

Figures

Tables

I

INTRODUCTION: REAPPORTIONMENT AND REDISTRICTING—HISTORY AND CONCEPTS

1

Introduction: Redistricting Past, Present, and Future

Peter F. Galderisi and Bruce Cain

THE CHANGING POLITICAL ENVIRONMENT OF REDISTRICTING: A BRIEF HISTORY

Although this volume starts with the "reapportionment revolution" of the 1960s, some of the fairness issues surrounding the process of redrawing political district lines are far from recent. The term "gerrymander" is well known to students of partisan and electoral politics. Although a gerrymander can be constructed for other than partisan purposes (e.g., to promote the representation of individual, minority, or other group interests), the term has since the days of Governor Eldridge Gerry usually denoted the process by which the majority party within a state or other electoral unit draws lines to maximize its representation. That term has even moved beyond U.S. borders to describe the redistricting processes of other nations.[1] The practice of gerrymandering in the United States actually preceded even the 1812 plan from which it takes its name, as the shifting of district boundaries for political advantage occurred with some regularity in states and in the British colonies.

Politics, and the redistricting process through which it is carried out, have always been part of our history. What has changed dramatically in the last four decades, however, has been the frequency with which redistricting and its concomitant political and legal machinations take place. Although the opportunities presented by redistricting have always existed, redrawing political boundaries had generally not been *legally* necessary except under circumstances where reapportionment changed the number of congressional districts within a state (or perhaps in state and local jurisdictions where the number of representatives had changed). Granted, congressional directives and many state constitutions had mandated a rough equality of population among U.S. house and state legislative districts, but that mandate, particularly with regard to state legislative boundaries, was often ignored.[2] That all changed in the 1960s, when a series of court decisions mandated that, under authority of the 14th Amendment, all legislative, and many administrative districts had to be drawn in such a way as to equalize populations within them. Although the motives and means for boundary changes have always been available, the decennial U.S. census now mandates that changes *must* take place unless both population growth and movement remain static. The obvious effect of creating more opportunities to draw district lines is to offer more chances for political mischief of all sorts.

Even opponents of the Supreme Court's abrupt entry into the redistricting thicket in 1963 could not have completely anticipated all the complexities of contemporary line drawing. Of course, office holders and their political parties would predictably try to manage the electoral consequences of running in new district boundaries. And many expected that *Reynolds v. Sims*[3] would weaken the influence of rural areas and strengthen that of the urban and suburban neighborhoods. But these considerations proved to be only the tip of a very large political iceberg. Redistricting ultimately raised many thorny and complex questions about racial and political fairness, incumbency, communities of interest, voter equality, and electoral competition—issues that are still very much in contention today.

To have predicted accurately all that redistricting has become would have required foreseeing much of what the American political system has become as redistricting tends to reflect, as much as affect, the general political environment. Since 1965, the American political system has evolved substantially: a strengthening incumbency advantage, growing political professionalization, rising partisanship, term limits, increasing Court intrusion into political questions, and the reform industry's persistence have all shaped the redistricting process in ways that are reflected in the chapters that follow. To set the stage for these topics, it is useful to lay out the connection between the parallel evolutions of redistricting and the American political system generally.

Professionalization

At the time of *Baker v. Carr*[4] and *Reynolds v. Sims*, politics was a low-tech business and paid consultants vied with volunteers and friends for the job of advising elected officials and candidates. Forty years later, computers and high tech political techniques are commonplace, and the consulting industry has mushroomed in numbers and cost. Computers are widely used in direct mail, opposition research, targeting, and polling at almost every level of election. Even campaign finance disclosure is moving in the direction of instantaneous computerized availability. The new technology creates greater precision when reaching out to voters while the Internet has facilitated grassroots mobilization and fund raising. Consultants have proliferated. Volunteers have been replaced by specialists who can shape the message, measure the progress, and mobilize the "troops" on election day.

The professionalization of American politics generally is mirrored by the professionalization of redistricting. Gone are the political hacks who have worked the neighborhoods for years, replaced by massive computerized data sets containing ten years of precinct returns merged to census tracks and blocs. Now there are multitudes of redistricting consultants who work the computers, high-priced lawyers who advise on the myriad constitutional and legal constraints, moonlighting social scientists who run racial polarization tests and provide expert testimony should the plan end up in court, and in some places, community consultants who set up redistricting hearings and make sure that the right groups are invited to testify. Redistricting has opened up a multimillion-dollar industry for all of these folks in a way that could not possibly have been anticipated by Chief Justice Warren and his colleagues on the Supreme Court in the mid-1960s.

Does professionalization matter? It certainly makes the redistricting process more expensive but apparently it does not guarantee any higher level of fairness or voter satisfaction with the final product. As with modern politics generally, we pay more and enjoy it less. But on the positive side, it means that the rules laid down by the courts are better explained now than in the past to those who have to make the ultimate line-drawing decisions. The nature and tempo of line-drawing negotiations have also changed. Forty years ago, because it was so laborious to consider different alternatives, the initial plan legislators saw was more or less (except for marginal changes) a take it or leave it proposition. Today with the widespread dissemination of redistricting software like Maptitude and the speed of home computers, plans can be generated, analyzed, and disposed of in an afternoon. This makes for potentially greater transparency and more flexible negotiations, assuming the political conditions allow for either.

Incumbency

Incumbency was not invented after 1963, but it became a more significant phenomenon in the seventies. The expansion of district offices, greater effort devoted to constituency service, a more refined art of credit claiming though the use of franking privileges, and the rising cost of elections gave incumbents more advantages than in the past. Underneath all of this was the wider acceptance of politics as a career for elected officials. And since politics was a career, winning became even more important for personal as well as political reasons.

The increasing investment in office holding infected the redistricting process. In countries where there is no residency requirement or expectation, incumbent preferences figure less in the final outcome. But in the United States, a shift in the district boundary that omits the incumbent's house can force the office holder into running for a different seat, or worse, into retirement. Moreover, as Scott Desposato and John Petrocik write about in chapter 3, just the fact that incumbents have to lose familiar areas and acquire new ones can have a destabilizing effect on their future electoral prospects. In most places, legislative incumbents get to vote on their own lines. Even in the reputedly neutral Iowa process, the legislature gets to veto and amend the plans developed by the Legislative Service Bureau.

The growing importance of legislative incumbency and the *Baker v. Carr* mandate that districts have to be redrawn every ten years thus combined to give incumbents a chance to pick their voters—the reversal of the democratic logic of voters choosing their representatives. Fortunately, incumbent preferences are often laden with idiosyncrasy: wanting this restaurant, that amusement park, etc. But most of all, career politicians will generally prefer the district lines that got them elected in the first place, which gives the whole process an inertial force that it might otherwise lack.

Partisanship

Trends in partisanship have also changed in recent decades. Ironically, when partisanship was weakest (in the seventies and eighties), the concern with partisan gerrymanders was the greatest. And now that partisanship has been on the rise, bipartisan plans are the highest priority on the reform agenda. Following the 1981 round of redistricting, the Burton plan in California and the Republican lines in Indiana produced the paradigmatic trouble states. In both cases, the majority party (Democrats in California and Republicans in Indiana) had used the redistricting process to squeeze a few extra districts for themselves. Litigation in this period focused on whether the concept of vote dilution under the 14th Amendment could be extended to include partisan bias. The answer from the Supreme Court in *Davis v. Bandemer*[5] was yes in principle but no as a practical matter. The Court managed to perpetuate this ambiguity in *Vieth v. Jubilerer*[6] when it declined to uphold a political gerrymandering claim under the 14th Amendment but suggested that it might entertain a claim on 1st Amendment grounds.

Ironically, no one was complaining that politics as a whole was too partisan or that the parties were too strong. That did not emerge as an issue until the 1990s. First in the form of congressional polarization and then as the much discussed blue/red electoral divide, the U.S. became more polarized along party lines. The biggest reform concern after the 2001 round of redistricting was that there were too many bipartisan plans: bipartisan plans make seats safer and encourage more ideological representation. Split governments, prevalent now at the state level, produced more bipartisan and pro-incumbent plans, and this created more safely Democratic and Republican seats. Representatives in these areas, not fearing a challenge from the other side, have allegedly become more extreme ideologically, forging a more bitter partisan politics. Twenty years ago, it was thought to be an achievement if the two parties could agree on new district lines. Now it is cause for suspicion.

The Reform Industry and the Courts

The big redistricting breakthrough was made by the Supreme Court. Quite possibly, the states would have gradually reformed themselves, but we will never know for sure. From all the evidence, it appears that Chief Justice Warren reversed his traditional position on the justiciability on reapportionment matters, because he became convinced that the one person, one vote standard was fair.[7] As it turned out, the logic of equality inherent in the 14th Amendment was more powerful and potentially applicable than the courts or anyone else could have imagined. The idea of equally weighted votes morphed into the right to an undiluted vote. Vote dilution claims advanced further in the realm of racial and ethnic representation with the assistance of the Voting Rights Act than they did with respect to partisan fairness. Indeed, the period of the late eighties up until *Shaw v. Reno*[8] was one in which minority plaintiffs and the U.S. Justice Department successfully used the courts to further racial and ethnic representation in rather dramatic ways. But the Court curtailed this activity beginning in 1993 with a series of decisions that ruled that compactness and other traditional districting criteria could not be wholly subordinated to race.[9]

Since *Baker v. Carr*, the state and federal courts have been pulled very heavily into sorting out redistricting disputes. At the most fundamental level, this has involved drawing district boundaries when the states have been unable to do so themselves or when the plans they have designed failed constitutional scrutiny. It is unlikely that Chief Justice Warren imagined such a hands-on level of involvement. But even when the courts have not taken over the task of drawing new lines, they have incrementally defined the districting guidelines for state legislatures and citizen commissions to follow. The courts have become the not-so-neutral referee in many redistricting battles. As Gary Cox argues in this book, the courts' partisan makeup matters and has helped shape plans both directly and indirectly (due to political actors anticipating how courts will react).

The courts' increasing boldness in redistricting parallels its boldness in other political affairs, notably its intervention in the 2000 presidential election. Instead of worrying about whether the courts will acquire a delegitimizing taint by ruling on so-called political questions, a new generation of legal scholars are nudging the courts into ever higher levels of electoral entanglement. Just as the courts prevent economic monopoly, they argue, so the courts should prevent "political lock-ups" that stifle political competition and introduce political bias.[10] As *Bush v. Gore*[11] reveals, even the Supreme Court's judicial conservatives believe in judicial activism when it purports to save the country from political chaos and unfairness.

Hand in hand with a bolder Supreme Court are reform groups pushing the envelope of redistricting change. This has traveled along two fronts. Groups like MALDEF and the NAACP have used litigation to win redistricting rights for their clients, aided by the Voting Rights Act and the Court's openness to 14th Amendment arguments. But citizen groups have also sought to change redistricting procedures and rules through legislation, especially in states with procedures for initiatives and referenda. Voters have adopted through direct democracy state redistricting criteria (usually compactness and community of interest requirements) that go beyond the federal criteria. And in some states, such as Arizona, voters have taken redistricting away from the state legislature and have set up a process that ignores incumbency considerations. In other states, such as California, the referendum has been used to throw out plans that were perceived to be politically unfair. As before, there is no way that the impact of direct democracy on line drawing could have been accurately predicted. Initiative use was low in the 1960s and only rebounded in the following decade. The professionalization of this process and its use as a political tool by interest groups and political parties has evolved considerably since then.

Term Limits

Lastly, no one in political science, and few, if any, in politics, could have predicted the popularity of legislative term limits. But the adoption of term limits has altered the redistricting landscape for state legislatures in critical ways. First, it lessened the incumbent inertia discussed earlier. Since some office holders are now limited to finite terms and cannot run in the redrawn seats, it lessens the aggregate interest in keeping district boundaries as they were. It also shifts the focus more toward the underlying district partisanship since the party cannot count on the incumbency advantage to hold a particular district throughout the decade. This has possibly contributed to the safe seat/high partisanship problem discussed earlier.

In addition, because term limits did not end political ambition and only rechanneled it, redistricting negotiations have become more complex. Incumbents might care less about the boundaries of their existing districts because they are soon to be term limited out of their seats, but they are more likely to have an interest in other congressional or state legislative options. This means that demands for districting arrangements can come from another chamber or from prospective candidates who have an eye on entering the legislature. Along with the heightened access to redistricting data and software by outside groups, term limits have contributed significantly to the general cacophony of redistricting negotiations.

REDISTRICTING: COMPETING GOALS AND STRATEGIES

Perhaps the most historically recognizable redistricting plan is a partisan gerrymander. A partisan gerrymander attempts (although not always successfully) to maximize the number of elected representatives of the majority party. This is usually done by distributing voters in such a way as to minimize wasted votes—that is, those that are above the proportion needed to elect a member of that party. The most logical strategy is to pack opposition party voters into a small number of districts, thus minimizing the number of representatives that that party can elect. An alternative method, particularly when few redrawable districts exist, is to distribute or "crack" minority party voters evenly throughout the jurisdiction so that they never constitute a majority or pose an electoral threat to the majority in any district. The majority party then attempts to redistribute its voters as thinly as possible, reaching as bare a majority in each district as possible to maintain a high chance of electability in each. Usually, some combination of these two strategies is used.

Partisan gerrymanders are, of course, not the only possible outcomes of redistricting. When no single party is in control of the process, or when the process is handed over to courts or independent commissions, redistricting turns out to be bipartisan or incumbent oriented. But even when a single party is in control, individual self-interest does not always follow party lines. Redistricting strategies that maximize the advantage of one party are usually at odds with the goals of incumbent seat holders. As Tom Mann eloquently stated in his volume, *Unsafe at Any Margin*, an incumbent's incentive is to maximize his or her electability.[12] This means increasing the number of constituents likely to be loyal to that incumbent so as not only to guarantee reelection, but also to preempt future challenges by well-known and well-funded opponents. One method to achieve this goal is to increase the proportion of that incumbent's party voters residing within that district (opposite of partisan spreading). Given the fluid nature of voting patterns, and the perceived decrease in the proportion of partisans and their loyalty, many incumbents would rather just maintain their previous boundaries as intact as possible. Voters are tied to an incumbent not only by party, but also by the more personal connections generated by constituent service and contact.

Often, redistricting strategies, whether of the partisan or incumbent kind, get further complicated by personal politics. It is not unusual for a redistricting leader to fashion a district to enhance his or her own electoral chances with less than complete regard to how it affects the party or other incumbents.

This has become especially relevant in states that have imposed term limits for their own legislative chambers, forcing legislators to either retire from politics or run for higher office. Every round of post-Census redistricting also include tales of attempts to fashion districts that would improve if not guarantee the election of a redistricting leader's relative or friend.[13] And it is not unusual for a plan to be created that purposely targets a particularly powerful, combative, or otherwise problematic member of the opposition or, at times, one's own party.[14]

Together with entertaining the concerns of parties and incumbents, redistricting schemes have, since the enactment of the Voting Rights Act of 1965, its 1975 revisions, and especially its 1982 amendments enacted, also had to show concern over the ability of racial and linguistic minority voters to not only cast a ballot, but to have that ballot lead to effective representation for their groups. "Racial gerrymandering," like partisan and incumbent gerrymandering, is not a new concept. For decades, minority voters had had their voting power diluted by a series of at-large and districting schemes purposely designed to minimize the impact of their votes.[15] What the VRA did was to promote redistricting schemes that were at least neutral, if not beneficial, toward minority voting power.

Concerns about race and minority voting outcomes do not, of course, operate in a vacuum. Racial concerns often conflict with incumbent and partisan concerns. Black voters, for example, are the most reliable supporters of the Democratic Party. The creation of a majority-minority district, in which black voters are packed so as to increase the odds of victory for a black, most likely Democratic, representative, often jeopardizes the reelection chances of Democratic incumbents in those surrounding districts from which those minority voters were taken. The creation of those curiously shaped majority-minority districts, such as North Carolina's infamous 12th (1991), was often influenced by a Democratic legislature's desire to meet the perceived standards of the VRA and related Supreme Court decisions, while minimizing the damage to other Democratic incumbents and Democratic legislative strength overall.

Whether discussing partisanship, incumbency, personality, or race, the broader question of the end result of redistricting concerns representation. How are citizens best represented? Is it by electing legislators who share their racial and ethnic characteristics, thereby increasing the odds that minority concerns are advocated? Is it by guaranteeing the reelection of incumbents, thereby increasing the benefits that can be derived from added seniority? Is it by increasing the legislative power of one party, thereby guaranteeing the ability of government to carry out a legislative mandate? The answers to these questions of representation are not clear, nor are the assumptions upon which the answers are based. One fact however is clear. The debate over how citizens are best represented is as old, if not older, than the debate over the adoption of the original U.S. Constitution itself. Federalists and Antifederalists sparred over the meaning of effective representation. Would citizens be best served by defining "communities of interest" in as parochial a fashion as possible (the Antifederalist view), or more widely (as the Federalists envisioned). Are individuals better represented by legislators who share their demographic profiles, or by those who represent such a diverse constituency as to be bound solely by a broader, national interest? It is to these questions, and the history of the U.S. redistricting process, that we now turn.

AN OVERVIEW OF THE CHAPTERS

This volume begins with a historical and theoretical overview of reapportionment and redistricting. In a review of his acclaimed work with Jonathan Katz, Gary Cox discusses the early history of the reapportionment revolution, provides a brief primer on partisan gerrymandering, and assesses the after effects of the *Baker* and *Wesberry* decisions on the level of partisan bias and responsiveness. His essay addresses the crucial role of the courts in reversing a long-standing pro-Republican districting bias, its effects on incumbent safety, and the strategic calculation of challengers. Scott Desposato and John Petrocik follow with a detailed evaluation of how the redistricting process affects the incumbency advantage. In a careful and ingenuous analysis of several data sets, they investigate how the redrawing of district lines brings in new voters, among whom the incumbent has no "personal vote or reputation," both of which anchor independents and weak partisans. The incumbency advantage lost in redistricting is shown to be variable, influenced by levels of partisanship and electoral context and saliency. Richard N. Engstrom provides us with a primary on district geography, discussing whether the contours of a legislative district matter to voters, especially on their desire and likelihood to vote. He discusses how geography can be used in different ways to help define communities of interest and representation. The "compactness" and "conformity to existing geographic boundaries," he asserts, are not related to turnout so much as is "conformity to media markets." In the new millennium, it seems, the flow of information, and therefore the attachment that voters have to the political process, are controlled more by common connection by airwaves than land.

In the second section of this volume, three authors discuss the controversy surrounding the effects of the redistricting process, particularly the subsequent decisions of the courts, on the representation of minorities. David Canon provides a useful history of the constitutional and political issues involved in race and redistricting, especially the implementation of the Voting Rights Act of 1965 and its amendments in 1982. In addressing the courts' foray into the "political thicket" of racial redistricting, Canon argues for judicial restraint. Discussing recent court decisions that loosened "well-defined conditions for standing" and voided black-majority districts, he is especially critical of the courts' neglect of important issues concerning minority representation. Anthony Peacock is also critical of the confusion caused by court decisions. In following the chronology of racial redistricting decisions begun by Canon, Peacock argues that judicial restraint needs to be assisted by the elimination of the VRA when it comes up for renewal in 2007. Interpreting and enacting preclearance provisions of the VRA are both logistically and constitutionally problematic as the VRA conflicts significantly with the Equal Protection clause of the 14th Amendment. Canon and Peacock introduce us to the arguments against racial redistricting jurisprudence from both sides of the ideological aisle, arguments that are currently echoed by a very divided Supreme Court. Florence Adams takes the argument one step further into the new millennium as she addresses the expanding importance of the vote of Hispanics and the inherent tension between satisfying the representative needs of more than just racial minorities and preserving the interests of party and, especially, incumbency. Local redistricting, she argues, has been understudied. These tensions may be more pronounced in redistricting local government jurisdictions where "the shifting balance between white, black, Latino, and Asian populations is most striking."

The third section presents a series of case studies.[16] The section is first introduced by stepping back to overview the post 1990 Southern redistricting plans and their long-term partisan effects. Bernard Grofman and Thomas Brunell update the tale of the gerrymander and discuss a type of redistricting plan they affectionately dub the "dummymander." Due to the perceived need to protect their incumbents, over optimism on how thinly spread they could safely distribute their constituents, and a reluctance to recognize a continuing GOP movement among white southerners, Democrats in a number of states enacted a seemingly partisan gerrymander that, by the end of the 1990s, produced results that benefited the GOP. The post-2000 case studies that follow serve as examples of the different types of redistricting plans that follow each round of redistricting. They collectively address issues of partisanship, incumbent protection, term limits, the strategic constraints and opportunities provided by the lose or gain of seats,[17] court activity, the increasing intervention of national parties and national legislative figures in the redistricting process, and personal rivalries. John Chamberlin takes us to Michigan, home of a classic partisan gerrymander, which resulted in net losses for the Democratic Party in both congressional and state legislative races. Discussing the importance of term limits on the redistricting strategies of those responsible for the process, Chamberlin concludes that "looks can be deceiving" and that a partisan gerrymander can still take place within the ostensibly "nonpartisan" constraints imposed by state statute. Gary Jacobson chronicles the contentious partisan history of California redistricting that, in spite of unified Democratic control of the process, turned into a protection plan for incumbents of both parties in 2001. Having maximized their seats in previous redistricting, Democrats chose not to engage in a potential "dummymander" and produced a plan satisfactory to both parties' incumbents, as well as their national party organizations. Jacobson concludes with a discussion of how the production of more homogenous districts adds not only to the safety of incumbents, but the ideological polarization of legislators of both parties. While Jacobson discusses how one party decided to produce a bipartisan redistricting plan that benefited incumbents of both parties, Barry Burden details how one-party control can result in intraparty conflict, resting more on personal animosities and calculations of future gains than party protection. In Massachusetts, an overwhelmingly Democratic state where the redistricting process should have been fairly straightforward, personality and issue differences between state and congressional legislators almost resulted in a plan that would have dislodged one long-term incumbent. Without concerns about partisan advantage, district loss, nor racial considerations, an otherwise routine round of redistricting quickly degenerated into a Democratic "family feud." Peverill Squire addresses the path of redistricting in Iowa, a state governed by a law that places the drawing of legislative boundaries in nonpartisan hands, bound neither by the promotion of partisan advantage nor incumbent protection. Creating a redistricting pattern where election outcomes are determined by the desires of the electorate, rather than "having them ordained in advance by the cartographical machinations of parties and politicians," Iowa, with only five seats was, in 2002, the home of more competitive congressional races than existed in any other state.

The volume concludes with a summary of the increasingly complicated state of redistricting processes and jurisprudence that we should expect to continue into the new millennium, and an offer of a possible solution. Seth McKee and Daron Shaw introduce us to the concept of "reredistricting"—that is, a modern-day attempt to continue partisan gerrymanders with the assistance and resistance of both state and national legislators and party committees, well beyond the first redrawing of lines. After they provide a general review of the judicial history of redistricting, they detail the torturous, litigious, and sometimes almost comical redistricting process in Texas. After the 2000 census, Texas Republicans sought to reverse the gains made by Democrats in their previously controlled rounds of redistricting. In their analysis they address issues of racial gerrymandering, incumbent targeting, the influence of congressional leadership, the constitutional propriety of redistricting twice in one decade, and partisan gamesmanship. The final forecasted outcome—advantage for the GOP—reads as much like the conclusion of a spy novel than can be found in many fictional best sellers. Like many of the other authors, Richard L. Engstrom also wishes to remove the courts from the political thicket that decades of controversy and political shenanigans have produced. His solution is, however, fairly novel. Rather than alter the balance of judicial and political intervention within our conventional single member districting schemes, Engstrom proposes that elections take place within multimember or other alternate voting systems. Addressing the "misalignment in judicial priorities" of many recent decisions, he outlines how alternate systems can meet constitutional muster while advancing "fair and effective representation," the original goal of the reapportionment cases of the 1960s.

Together, these essays take us through the complicated issues of redistricting, addressing partisan, incumbent, racial, and judicial concerns. They briefly outline the history of the redistricting process, its current contours, and its future prospects. The final history of *Redistricting in the New Millennium* is still to be written. This volume hopes to introduce that final recounting.

We would like to conclude with one final note to our readers. You will undoubtedly be reading this volume after the 2004 elections have concluded and subsequent court cases have been pursued. We trust that the ideas, explanations, and predictions presented in this volume will continue to guide you through the ever-continuing redistricting maze.

NOTES

1. One of us was surprised to hear one visiting Japanese student refer to one of his country's rounds of redistricting as a "Hatamander," named after a one-time Japanese Prime Minister.

2. See, for example, David Butler and Bruce Cain, *Congressional Redistricting: Comparative and Theoretical Perspectives* (New York: Macmillan Publishing, 1992), chapter 2.

3. 377 US 533 (1964).

4. 369 US 186 (1962).

5. 478 US 109 (1986).

6. 124 § Ct. 1769 (2004).

7. Melissa Cully Anderson and Bruce E. Cain, "Venturing onto the Path of Equal Representation: The Warren Court and Redistricting," manuscript, 2/25/04.

8. 113 S.Ct. 2816 (1993).

9. *Miller v. Johnson*, 515 US 900 (1995).

10. Samuel Issacharoff and Richard H. Pildes, "Politics as Markets: Partisan Lockups of the Democratic Process," *Stanford Law Review* 50 (1998): 643, 649.

11. 531 US 98 (2000).

12. Thomas E. Mann, *Unsafe at any Margin: Interpreting Congressional Elections* (Washington, D.C.: American Enterprise Institute, 1983).

13. Perhaps the best example can be found when Philip Burton carved out an extremely favorable district for his brother John as part of the 1982 California redistricting plan.

14. Witness, as example, the California Democratic Party's willingness to sacrifice Gary Condit in its post-2000 redistricting.

15. See, for example, Bernard Grofman, Lisa Handley, and Richard G. Niemi, *Minority Representation and the Quest for Voting Equality* (Cambridge: Cambridge University Press, 1992), and J. Morgan Kousser, *Colorblind Injustice: Minority Voting Rights and the Undoing of the Second Reconstruction* (Chapel Hill, N.C.: University of North Carolina Press, 1999).

16. Many overviews of the post-2000 round of redistricting can be found in the literature. For one excellent analysis, see Sam Hirsch, "The U.S. House of Unrepresentatives: What Went Wrong in the Latest Round of Congressional Redistricting," *Election Law Journal* 2, no. 2 (2003): 179–216.

17. For one example, see Michael Lyons and Peter F. Galderisi, "Incumbency, Reapportionment, and U.S. House Redistricting," *Political Research Quarterly* 48, no. 4 (1995): 857–71.

2

On the Systemic Consequences of Redistricting in the 1960s

Gary W. Cox

Congressional redistricting can have both local and systemic effects. Local effects concern how the new lines affect congressional politics within each particular state that has redistricted—advantaging one party over the other, for example. Systemic effects concern the national level. For example, if one party gains in every state, due to redistricting, its seat share in the House will increase.

In this chapter, I review Cox and Katz's[1] analysis of the systemic effects of redistricting in the United States since the Supreme Court's landmark decisions in *Baker v. Carr* and *Wesberry v. Sanders*. My coverage is, like theirs, limited to congressional elections and focuses on the 1960s.

I begin, in the next section, by describing how the reapportionment decisions affected the congressional redistricting process. I then review some of the basics of partisan gerrymandering, introducing the concepts of bias and responsiveness. This sets the stage for two sections analyzing the consequences of redistricting in and since the 1960s—one concerning systemic partisan effects, one systemic entry effects.

THE REAPPORTIONMENT DECISIONS AND THE REDISTRICTING PROCESS

On March 26, 1962, the Supreme Court issued its decision in the case of *Baker v. Carr,*[2] initiating what has since been known as the reapportionment revolution.[3] The suit was brought by plaintiffs in Nashville, Tennessee, who challenged their state legislature's failure to reapportion despite widespread population shifts that had made urban districts vastly more populous than their rural counterparts. The ramifications of the case were clearly national, because urban and especially suburban Americans were significantly underrepresented in state legislatures throughout the country.[4] Thus, although the Court limited itself to declaring that state legislative reapportionment was justiciable, leaving more specific action in the case to the lower courts, its decision was immediately seen as a revolutionary step—one the Court had repeatedly declined to take (most recently in *Colegrove v. Green*[5]).

The immediate consequence of *Baker* was more litigation: within a year of the decision all but fourteen states were involved in reapportionment suits. The Supreme Court used some of these cases to stake out a clearer substantive position. It had opined in *Baker* that inequalities in district populations—i.e., malapportionment—might constitute a violation of the Fourteenth Amendment's guarantee of equal protection of the laws to all citizens. In *Gray v. Sanders*,[6] handed down in 1963, the Court invalidated Georgia's unit-rule primary elections specifically on the grounds that they did not give all voters an equal voice and thus violated the Fourteenth Amendment. A year later the Court extended its "one person, one vote" principle to cover elections to both houses of all state legislatures (*Reynolds v. Sims*[7]) and elections to the U.S. House of Representatives (*Wesberry v. Sanders*[8]).

The Supreme Court's reapportionment decisions did not simply clarify precedent, however. They also sparked a massive wave of extraordinary redistricting in the mid-1960s. Both state legislative and congressional districts were redrawn more comprehensively—by far—than at any previous time in our nation's history.

The two effects of the Court's ruling just mentioned—making malapportionment justiciable; and sparking a mid-decade burst of redistricting—have been widely recognized. Three other proximal effects, until recently relatively neglected, have been highlighted by Cox and Katz.[9]

Changing the Reversionary Outcome to the Redistricting Process

First, the Court's rulings changed the legal reversion to the congressional redistricting process—in other words, what happens at law if a state fails to enact a new districting statute after a decennial reapportionment of seats. Indeed, this was perhaps the single most important consequence of the Court's decision in *Wesberry*.

Since 1913, the U.S. House has had a fixed number (435) of seats (with minor variations). Since 1929, these seats have been apportioned among the states according to population after each decennial census. It has then been up to each state to define the boundaries of its allotted number of districts. Typically, district boundaries have been established by the passage of a state law, with legislatures and governors bargaining within the confines of the ordinary statutory processes of their respective states.[10] If the governor and state legislature could not agree on a new plan, then the next election was held under a *reversionary plan*—a legally defined default.

Prior to the reapportionment revolution, the reversionary plan was usually the state's current plan. That is, if no new plan could be agreed upon, the current plan continued in force. The only exceptions to this rule arose when a state gained or lost seats pursuant to the decennial federal census. If a state had *gained* seats, the exception was minor: a state could simply elect the new members at large, preserving all the old districts. This was a relatively painless solution that incumbent members of Congress often found preferable to the disruption of their current districts. If a state had *lost* seats in the reapportionment, however, all members had to be elected at large, absent a new districting plan. This was a much less palatable reversionary plan and its unpleasantness explains why the bulk of prerevolutionary redistricting action occurred in states that had lost representation in Congress.

When the current plan was also the reversionary plan (or was the main basis for that plan, as in cases where the state had gained seats), Cox and Katz call the reversion *conservative*. When the reversion was not conservative, they say that it was *radical*. In these terms, prior to the reapportionment revolution all states not losing seats had conservative reversions, while all states losing seats had radical reversions.[11]

Now consider how the entry of the judiciary altered the strategic situation. The role of the courts in the 1960s varied from case to case, but often things played out as follows. First, a federal or state court would declare a state's current districting plan null and void. The court would then give the state a more or less clear and more or less constraining deadline; if the legislature and governor could not agree on a plan by the deadline, the court would impose a plan. Sometimes the plan that the court planned to impose was clear ex ante, sometimes not. But the court's plan was never the preexisting plan. Thus, *all redistricting action in the 1960s took place under threat of a radical reversionary outcome of one kind or another.*

Another important point to note is that all reversions before the reapportionment revolution were *automatic*: a prespecified reversion was to be used when a prespecified condition was met. In contrast, reversions after the reapportionment revolution were *discretionary*: the conditions under which a reversion would be used, and the nature of the reversion itself, were at a court's discretion. Even when the state government produced a new districting plan, a court might decide that the plan produced was unconstitutional and impose its own. Moreover, the plan that a court imposed was restricted only by its interpretation of the relevant judicial criteria.

Increasing the Certainty of Redistricting

In addition to transforming the legal default to the congressional redistricting process, a second important effect of the Court's reapportionment decisions was to make it virtually certain that all congressional districts would be redrawn after each decennial reapportionment. In 1952 and 1962, only 41 percent and 50 percent of all congressional districts were redrawn. In contrast, roughly 98 percent of all districts were redrawn in each of 1972, 1982, and 1992. Thus, the probability that a district would be redrawn after a federal census *doubled* from before the reapportionment revolution (.46) to after (.98).

This doubling was, moreover, largely foreseeable. After *Kirkpatrick v. Preisler*[12] (in 1969), the courts demanded virtually identical populations in each state's congressional districts. Thus, the chances that an existing district would survive the next redistricting intact were very small.

The Courts and Electoral Administration

A final procedural consequence of the courts' decisions had to do with the difference between constitutional validity and administrative convenience. In practice, courts in the 1960s (and after) had not only to decide the constitutionality of a state's districting plan but also to decide what stopgap plan the state would use, in case its plan was declared unconstitutional and there was not enough time to draft and implement a constitutionally valid one before the next election. This necessity to decide the practical administration of elections on a temporary basis opened up another dimension of discretion that, as we shall see, the courts exercised.

A PRIMER ON PARTISAN GERRYMANDERS

The literal output of the redistricting process is a legal description of the boundary lines of each congressional district in the state. But parties care about who wins the various seats at stake, not about lines per se, and so districting plans are usually described in terms of their political rather than literal characteristics. One approach focuses on how boundary lines affect the resultant partisan make up of each district (measured, for example, by the number of registered Republicans and Democrats).[13] Cox and Katz portray the redistricting process as entailing two steps: first, a broad strategic decision about how much partisan bias (denoted λ) and how much responsiveness (denoted ρ) the redistricting plan will entail; second, a particular set of lines that implement the broader strategy.

What are partisan bias and responsiveness? They are features of a redistricting plan that affect (1) how votes translate into seats, and hence (2) the parties' expected seat shares. If party A controls the redistricting process, the standard gerrymandering recipe is to pack as many of party B's supporters in as few districts as possible (creating inefficiently safe districts), while spreading its own supporters evenly across as many districts as possible (creating winnable but not inefficiently safe districts). This strategy ensures that party B pays more in votes for each seat it wins than does party A, which is the same as saying that the redistricting plan engineers *bias* in A's favor.

It is important to note that increasing partisan bias is not the only way a redistricting party might seek to increase its expected seat share. If a party is confident that it will get a statewide majority of votes cast in its favor over the life of a districting plan, another way to increase its expected seat share is to make every district a microcosm of the state. As compared to the packing strategy, this creates more marginal districts, and will thus increase what is typically called the *responsiveness* of the system. Another way to think of the microcosm strategy is that it makes the system more like a winner-take-all election: whoever gets the most votes statewide typically gets the most votes in all the districts (which are microcosms of the state by hypothesis) and, therefore, typically wins all the seats. Given sufficient certainty about its electoral strength, a redistricting party might rationally seek to maximize its expected seat share by maximizing responsiveness, rather than by engineering a bias specifically in its own favor. The high responsiveness strategy runs the risk of giving the "out" party all the seats, should it manage an unexpectedly good electoral showing; but it does not concede any districts at all to the opposition, as the packing strategy does. Finally, note that various compromises between the pure packing and microcosm strategies are possible.

A given districting plan—identified with its associated bias-responsiveness pair, (ρ,λ)—determines how votes will translate into seats. In particular, it determines how big the bonus in seats is that the party winning the most votes gets (via ρ); and whether one party's votes translate at more favorable "terms of trade" into seats than the other's (via λ).

Systemic Partisan Effects

It is easy to see that redistricting can potentially have strong partisan effects in a given state. If a single party controls the redistricting process, it can follow the standard gerrymandering recipe to increase the share of seats that it can expect to win. If partisan gerrymanders consistently benefit the same party in state after state, then there will be a *systemic* partisan gain from redistricting. When can one expect such a gain?

The Conditions for Systemic Partisan Gain

Cox and Katz offer two conditions that must be met before a substantial national partisan gain via redistricting can arise.[14] First, there must be a substantial *imbalance* between the current distribution of partisan control at the state level and the distribution of control reflected in the extant districting plans. In other words, the existing plans must be more favorable (or less favorable) to the Democrats than their current control of states would warrant. This establishes the *possibility* of a substantial net partisan gain. Second, there must be a *correlated dominance of the federal judiciary*, in order for the possible gain to be fully realized. For example, if state Democrats seek to undo past Republican gerrymanders, they must also control the courts that will hear litigation arising from the new plans, in order to succeed.

To explain the first condition more fully, imagine a redistricting in which all the extant plans were written at time t-1 by unified Republican state governments; and all the redistricting is now (at time t) performed by states that are under divided partisan control. The first Cox-Katz condition would be met: there is the potential for a large net Democratic gain nationwide. The old Republican gerrymanders are more favorable to the Republicans than their current control of state governments would warrant.

Whether the Democrats in the hypothetical scenario sketched above realize their potential gains depends crucially on the courts. Prior to *Baker v. Carr*, the legal reversion to the redistricting process was, except in cases where the state had lost seats in the decennial reapportionment, the retention of the old district lines. With this legal state of affairs, old Republican plans could survive any number of bouts of divided government relatively unscathed, as long as such bouts were not combined with a loss of seats at the decennial reapportionment.

During the 1960s, in contrast, most state redistricting actions were undertaken under the supervision of a specific court; and the supervising court largely determined the reversionary outcome. Thus, in the 1960s Republicans (and Democrats) in divided states might suspect that a Democratic supervising court would impose a plan favorable to Democrats, were the contending branches of the state government unable to reach agreement. The relative bargaining power of the parties under divided government was thus completely altered by the *Baker* and *Wesberry* decisions. Even with universal divided control of state government, a substantial net partisan gain could be possible.[15]

In fact, something like the logical possibility just described did play out in the 1960s. First, most of the non-Southern plans' replacements were indeed products of past episodes of unified Republican government (often preserved past their date of origin by the conservative nature of the pre-*Baker* reversionary outcome). At the same time, the Democrats had made substantial recent gains in control of state legislative chambers and governorships. Thus, there was a substantial partisan imbalance between how many extant plans had been drawn by Republicans and how many of the new plans would be drawn by Republicans. Second, the Democrats also dominated the supervising (mostly federal) courts in the 1960s. Cox and Katz[16] report that 74 percent of the non-Southern districts in their study were redrawn under the supervision of a Democratic court, whereas only 12 percent were redrawn under the supervision of a Republican court.[17]

How, precisely, did the courts influence redistricting in the 1960s, and beyond? I emphasize two avenues of influence here.[18] First, a court had some discretion over how strictly it would interpret the Supreme Court's mandate to reduce malapportionment. Second, after a court declared a plan unconstitutional, it had a variety of options regarding the practical issue of what plan the state should use in the next election. I consider these two avenues of influence in turn.

The Court's Discretion, Part I

In this section, I consider how court discretion over the level of allowable malapportionment (precedents removing this discretion do not arrive until 1969) might affect the politics of redistricting. To be specific, consider a Republican state redistricting under the supervision of a Democratic court. The state might fear the court would invalidate its plan, if that plan had *any* malapportionment at all. After all, a traditional plan produced in the usual way by a unified Republican government would be heavily biased against the Democrats. The court could take the high jurisprudential road in invalidating such a plan, citing its positive malapportionment and trumpeting a zero-tolerance standard. At the same time, the court would reap low-road partisan benefits as well: a plan with what it considered bad partisan electoral consequences would be thwarted.

In order to avoid the court's invalidation of its plan, the Republican state could choose from a menu of changes to make its plan more palatable to the Democratic court: it could reduce malapportionment; it could reduce pro-Republican bias; or it could reduce responsiveness. The court would not like malapportionment, on jurisprudential grounds. It would not like pro-Republican bias, as (a majority of) the jurists are Democrats and are presumed to prefer better electoral prospects for Democrats, other things equal. Finally, because the Republicans control the state, their expected vote share is presumably greater than .5, so that Republicans prefer and Democrats do not prefer larger responsiveness values. Thus, the Democratic court would also like to depress responsiveness in the plan enacted, other things equal.[19]

Evidence Regarding Bias

Cox and Katz show that a redistricting plan's bias was systematically related to partisan control of both the state government and the supervising court.[20] Pro-Democratic bias increased as the number of branches of state government controlled by the Democrats increased. More importantly for present purposes, the more Democratic jurists and the fewer Republican jurists there were on the supervising court, the higher the estimated pro-Democratic bias in the resulting plan was, partisan control of state government held constant. Indeed, Cox and Katz's results suggest that a party's addition of one more judge on the supervising panel affected the bias of the resulting plan roughly as much as its addition of one more branch of government. This is a dramatic indication of how much the courts mattered in determining the characteristics of the plan ultimately implemented.

To help convey how important controlling the state government and the supervising court was, consider a state in which the Democrats won 50 percent of the vote (that is, the simple average of the Democratic vote percent across all districts in the state was 50 percent). In such a state, what was the Democrat's expected seat share? Table 2.1 (a reprint of Cox and Katz's table 6.2) provides the answer, as a function of two variables: the number of branches of state government controlled by each party; and the number of judges on the supervising court who affiliated with each party.

As can be seen, in a state redistricted under unified Republican control and the supervision of a court on which two of three judges were also Republican—such as Kansas—the Democrats could expect to get 29.1 percent of the seats for 50 percent of the vote. In contrast, in a state where the roles were reversed (unified Democratic state, two of three judges Democratic), such as Arizona or New Jersey in 1966, the Democrats could expect

Table 2.1. Expected Democratic Seat Share in a State in Which the Democrats Win 50 Percent of the Vote as a Function of Branches and Judges, 1960s

Branches	*Judges**	*Expected Democratic Seat Share*
Unified Republican control (branches = −3)	all 3 Republican (judges = −3)	.234
Unified Republican control (branches = −3)	2 of 3 Republican (judges = −1)	.291
Democrats control 2 of 3 branches (branches = +1)	2 of 3 Republican (judges = −1)	.451
Democrats control 1 branch (branches = −1)	2 of 3 Democratic (judges = +1)	.439
Democrats control 2 of 3 branches (branches = +1)	2 of 3 Democratic (judges = +1)	.525
Unified Democratic control (branches = +3)	2 of 3 Democratic (judges = +3)	.609
Unified Democratic control (branches = +3)	all 3 Democratic (judges = +3)	.677

*three-judge panel assumed
Source: Cox and Katz, table 6.2

to get 60.9 percent of the seats for 50 percent of the vote. This is a very considerable difference in outcomes. Although bias was not itself justiciable at this time (not until *Davis v. Bandemer,*[21] decided on June 30, 1986), states acted as if they expected the courts to be partisan—anticipating and accommodating their presumed partisan preferences.

Evidence Regarding Responsiveness

What about the effect of the courts on the responsiveness of plans? Cox and Katz show that the expected pattern arises: the divided states have the lowest responsiveness, followed by the unified states facing hostile courts, and then the unified states facing friendly courts.

The Court's Discretion, Part II

In addition to some discretion over the allowable degree of malapportionment in the 1960s, supervising courts also faced practical issues for which there were no Supreme Court precedents. If a court declared a state's plan unconstitutional, how would that state's next election be held? Some courts decided to allow the state to use the plan that had just been struck down as unconstitutional. Others chose to impose a new plan. Others required that all members of congress be elected in statewide at-large elections.

Cox and Katz investigate both court decisions on the constitutionality of redistricting plans and court decisions on the usability of such plans. They find that courts with majorities of jurists from the same party as the state government being reviewed, or friendly courts, did not differ from hostile courts on the issue of constitutional validity. However, friendly courts were significantly more likely to allow the use of plans (even unconstitutional ones) than hostile courts. To clarify the substantive size of this effect, consider an example of two plans, both with a fairly high level of malapportionment.[22] If such a plan were reviewed by a friendly court, the estimated probability of acceptance for use would be 0.75. In contrast, if such a plan were reviewed by a hostile court, the estimated probability of acceptance for use would be 0.35. Thus, there was quite a difference in the probability of a plan being allowed for use at the next election in the 1960s, depending on whether the court was friendly or hostile.

The Conditions for Systemic Partisan Gain: Summary

In the post-*Wesberry* polity, there are two facilitating conditions for systemic partisan gain, due to redistricting. There must first be a substantial imbalance between the partisan cast of the existing plans and the current strength of the two parties in the states. This establishes an opportunity for a large fraction of states to redraw lines in a way that will benefit a single party. Second, the would-be redistricting party must also enjoy a preponderance on the courts that will hear and judge redistricting litigation.

In the specific case of the 1960s, these conditions were met. The Republicans had a much better deal in the existing array of districting plans outside the south than their mid-1960s share of state governments would warrant. Moreover, the would-be redistricting Democrats held a preponderance of posts on the mostly federal courts that supervised redistricting actions in the 1960s. The result was a substantial pro-Democratic shift in the distribution of districting plans outside the South, hence a substantial pro-Democratic shift in the translation of congressional votes into seats.

Since the 1960s, the conditions for systemic partisan gain have generally not been met. Analyses of the 1970 and 1980 round of redistricting have found little evidence of net partisan gain. It is not until the 1990 round of redistricting in the south that a large net partisan gain is again observed.[23]

SYSTEMIC EFFECTS ON ENTRY

How Anticipations of Redistricting Help Coordinate Entry

The Supreme Court's decision in *Wesberry* (and *Preisler*) should have abruptly changed politicians' expectations regarding the frequency and inevitability of redistricting. Prior to these rulings, redistricting was infrequent in states that had not lost seats in the decennial reapportionment. After *Wesberry*, in contrast, everyone knew that redistricting would occur at least once every ten years in every state. Moreover, virtually every district would be affected because population shifts over the decade would leave almost no districts close enough to the new state-wide average to satisfy the court's equal-population mandate (especially after *Preisler*).

In actuality, as noted above, the incidence of postdecennial redistricting doubled after *Wesberry*. This doubling provided a stronger focal point in the competition between incumbents and strong challengers. Consider a strong challenger and an incumbent in a district in 1970, 1980, or 1990. Both know that, two years hence, the state will likely redraw the district in which they currently sit. Will the challenger enter? Will the incumbent exit?

If the challenger enters and wins, his investment will immediately be at risk: the district might be redrawn in a way that makes it very difficult to defend. On the other hand, if the challenger waits, he can see if the redistricting brings good news, and enter (or not) after the uncertainty of the redistricting has been resolved. If he waits, gets a favorable redistricting, enters and wins, his investment can be secure against redistricting shocks for up to ten years.[24] Since it is common knowledge that the challenger's incentives to enter just before a redistricting are depressed, the incumbent is more likely to seek reelection and the strong challenger to stay out.

Now consider the race just after a redistricting. The uncertainty about how the district will be redrawn has been resolved. Hence, the new "normal vote" in the district is better known. Moreover, the time to the next redistricting shock is maximal. If the strong challenger thought that national tides would be constant across the coming decade, then he would either enter now, or never. In the real world, of course, there is the possibility of waiting for a particularly large national tide or a scandal. Nonetheless, the natural investment period in a congressional district is, especially after *Wesberry*, ten years. So, the natural or focal point of entry, *ceteris paribus*, is just after a redistricting.

Evidence of a Redistricting Cycle in Entry

The notion that candidates consider the proximity of redistricting, when they decide to enter or exit congressional races, is a natural one mentioned in standard texts on congressional elections.[25] Moreover, if one simply plots the aggregate number of competitive races (as judged by *Congressional Quarterly*) in each year, one finds a substantial downward trend in each reapportionment decade. There were roughly half as many competitive districts in 1990 as there had been in 1982 and, again, roughly half as many competitive districts in 2000 as there had been in 1992.[26]

To test whether the increased certainty of redistricting after *Wesberry* induced a redistricting cycle in entry, Cox and Katz explored when incumbents voluntarily choose not to seek reelection; when experienced challengers choose to enter; and when one observes both a voluntarily exiting incumbent and an entering experienced challenger.

Coordination of Entry

As an initial indication of how the increased certainty of redistricting affected entry, table 2.2 cross tabulates the frequency with which incumbents and strong challengers entered in two periods: 1946 to 1964 and 1966 to 1998. Note two points supported by these figures.

First, in both periods, strong challengers appear less frequently when the incumbent enters; and incumbents appear less frequently when a strong challenger enters. This suggests that strong candidates are avoiding each other.

Second, there is a reduction in the frequency of "crashes" (both the incumbent and a strong challenger entering); an increase in the frequency of cases in which the incumbent enters while the strong challenger stays out; and an increase in the frequency of cases in which the strong challenger

Table 2.2. Non-Southern Incumbents' and Experienced Challengers' Entry Decisions, 1946 to 1964 and 1966 to 1998

	Does an Experienced Challenger Enter?			
Does the Incumbent Seek Reelection?	*1946–1964*		*1966–1998*	
	No	Yes	No	Yes
No (open seat)	67.4%	32.6%	54.2%	45.8%
	(194)	(94)	(207)	(175)
Yes (incumbent-defended seat)	72.1%	27.9%	77.4%	22.6%
	(1,780)	(693)	(2,596)	(757)
Likelihood Ratio $\chi2$	2.77		88.16	

Note: Cell entries are row percentages within the time period given. The numbers in parentheses are the actual number of cases.
Source: Cox and Katz, table 9.1.

enters but the incumbent stays out. Overall, a standard measure of statistical association (the likelihood-ratio χ^2) increases from 2.77 before, to 88.16 after 1966. This large increase suggests considerable improvement in the candidates' ability to coordinate their entries. Increasingly, if one strong candidate entered, the other did not.

The Probability of Voluntary Exit by an Incumbent

In Cox and Katz's analysis of voluntary exit, the independent variable of primary interest is a dummy variable, equal to one for the first election after a state redraws its district lines, zero otherwise. One expects this variable to have a positive coefficient: voluntary exits should be more likely just after a redistricting.

Cox and Katz control for the incumbent party's "normal vote" in each district (by including the incumbent party's vote share in the previous election and whether or not it ran an incumbent). Additionally, they allow a separate intercept term for each party in each year. Finally, they control for the number of terms the incumbent has served and for the number of districts in the incumbent's state. The previous literature has found that incumbents are more likely to exit voluntarily as the number of terms they have served increases and as the number of districts in their state declines.

To assess the differences before and after the reapportionment revolution, Cox and Katz ran the analysis separately for the prerevolutionary (1948 to 1964) and postrevolutionary (1966 to 1998) periods. They find that voluntary exit before *Wesberry* was unaffected by whether the state redistricted. After *Wesberry*, in contrast, voluntary exit was significantly more likely in the first election after a redistricting.[27]

The Probability of Entry by a Strong Challenger

Cox and Katz run a similar analysis of entry by strong challengers and find similar results. After *Wesberry* but not before, strong challengers were significantly more likely to enter in the first election after a redistricting.

Push Outs

Finally, Cox and Katz examine push outs—events in which a strong challenger enters and an incumbent voluntarily exits. One way to view push outs is that the incumbent decides, for reasons unrelated to the strong challenger's intentions, to exit, after which the strong challenger enters. Another way to view them is that the strong challenger makes clear his intention to enter, thereby lowering the incumbent's estimate of her chances of reelection and helping to "push" her out.

Before *Wesberry*, the probability of a push out is unrelated to redistricting. After *Wesberry*, non-Southern push outs are significantly more likely in the election just after a state redistricts.[28]

What Coordination of Entry Means for Measurements of the Incumbency Advantage

As noted at the outset, the "incumbency advantage"—the value in votes to the incumbent party of running the incumbent candidate for reelection rather than a new candidate—increased rather abruptly in the mid-1960s. Why?

To provide an answer, recall that the standard equation used to estimate the incumbency advantage regresses the incumbent party's vote share on (1) the party's lagged vote share, (2) which party holds the seat (Democrats or Republicans), and (3) whether the incumbent candidate appears in the general election or not. The first two independent variables are intended to capture the district's "normal vote." The last then measures how much better a party does when its incumbent seeks reelection.

The potential problem with this procedure is that the incumbent *chooses* to run in the general election or not (cases of death, expulsion, and primary defeat momentarily aside). If incumbents are more/less likely to enter when they have better/worse electoral prospects, then a species of simultaneity bias will afflict conventional estimates of how much the incumbent party gains by running its incumbent for reelection again.

Cox and Katz provide substantial evidence that incumbents are strategic in their entry decisions. In particular, they show that incumbent parties lose significantly more votes when their incumbents decide to retire or run for another office (creating voluntarily open seats) than when they die or are defeated in the primary (creating involuntarily open seats). Moreover, the difference in expected vote losses between these two categories of open seat is especially large after 1966.[29]

It is important to note that the systematically larger vote loss for incumbent parties in voluntarily open seats is inconsistent with the null that there is no simultaneity bias. In both voluntarily and involuntarily open seats, the incumbent party loses the resources of incumbency often thought to drive the incumbency advantage: the perks of office are lost; and the reputation of the incumbent with his or her constituents is lost. There is thus no reason to expect a systematic difference, based solely on an accounting of the resources available to the incumbent party's candidate. The difference is, however, consistent with the idea that voluntary exits by incumbents are partly prompted by poor electoral prospects.

There is other, more nuanced, evidence that supports the idea that incumbents are strategic about when they exit (retire or seek other office). Consider two examples. First, in the 1960s, incumbent party losses after voluntary exit were particularly large in redrawn districts. Put plainly, some incumbents' districts were purposely rendered unwinnable by the redistricting in their states. Recognizing this fact, they left for better opportunities elsewhere. Their party did run someone else in their place but that someone inherited a district with a reengineered (and worse) normal vote. Thus, in redrawn districts, the incumbent party sustained substantial losses when its incumbent exited but much smaller average losses when its incumbent sought reelection.[30]

As a second example, consider the fact that incumbent party losses were larger for the Republicans throughout the period from 1966 to 1994 in involuntarily open seats. One would presume that the majority party (the Democrats throughout 1966 to 1994) had "resources of office" at least as great as those possessed by the minority (Republicans). Thus, it is the Democrats who should be losing more when they lose an incumbent, if resources are the key to explaining the incumbency advantage.

CONCLUSION

Jurisprudentially, the Supreme Court's reapportionment decisions have long been recognized as revolutionary. Administratively, they led to a wave of extraordinary, court-supervised redistricting actions in the mid-1960s whose ostensible purpose was to eradicate the then-massive levels of malapportionment. Politically, however, they seem not to have sparked much change.

Some claimed that court-mandated redistricting in the 1960s favored the Democrats, others, that it favored the Republicans, but the near consensus of the literature has been that redistricting did not produce substantial net gains for either party. Some suspected that redistricting in the 1960s sparked the storied growth of the incumbency advantage but the consensus of the literature is that it did not. Almost everyone expected a substantial change in policy, from a prorural to a more prourban stance, but the near consensus of the literature is that no such change was forthcoming.

There is reason to reject each of these near-consensus opinions, however. *Baker* and its successor decisions permanently altered the redistricting *process* and led to a massive wave of redistricting *action* in the 1960s. The consequences included at least three major changes. First, through a combination of state and court politics, what had been a long-standing pro-Republican bias in the translation of congressional votes into congressional seats abruptly disappeared in the mid-1960s. Second, through the politics of strategic entry, the apparent advantage of incumbency abruptly increased in the mid-1960s. Third, through a variety of not-always-obvious mechanisms, the substantially increased representation of suburban and urban voters led to clear policy shifts in favor of those voters.[31]

NOTES

1. Gary W. Cox and Jonathan Katz, *Elbridge Gerry's Salamander: The Electoral Consequences of the Reapportionment Revolution* (Cambridge, U.K.: Cambridge University Press, 2002).
2. 369 U.S. 186.
3. (Re)apportionment refers to the (re)allocation of seats in the U.S. House of Representatives to the states after each decennial census.
4. Andrew Hacker, *Congressional Districting: The Issue of Equal Representation,* rev. ed. (Washington, D.C.: Brookings Institution, 1964).
5. 328 U.S. 529.
6. 372 U.S. 368.
7. 377 U.S. 533.
8. 376 U.S. 1.
9. Cox and Katz, *Elbridge Gerry's Salamander.*
10. The production of districting plans within the "ordinary statutory process" was especially prevalent in the 1960s, the period of main concern in this essay. Since the 1960s, commissions and other out-of-the-ordinary procedures have been introduced in the redistricting process of several states.
11. Technically, at-large elections were illegal from 1842 until 1872, allowable under certain conditions from 1872 to 1929, then again illegal after 1968. See Kenneth C. Martis, *The Historical Atlas of United States Congressional Districts, 1789–1983* (New York: Free Press, 1982). The legal basis for the reversions noted in the text appears to go back to some court decisions in 1932 (see Apportionment Act. 1982. *U.S. Code.* Vol. 4, sec. 2a, p. 64). For present purposes, it is sufficient to note that the 1941 Apportionment Act repeated the relevant provisions (and that they were not overturned until the 1960s). See Apportionment Act. 1941. *Statutes At Large.* Vol. 55, sec. 1, p. 762.

12. 394 U.S. 526.

13. "Optimal Partisan Gerrymandering," *Political Geography Quarterly* 7, no. 1 (January 1988): 5–22; Michael P. McDonald, "Redistricting, Dealignment, and the Political Homogenization of Congressional Districts" (Ph.D. diss., University of California, San Diego, 1999).

14. Cox and Katz, *Elbridge Gerry's Salamander*.

15. David Butler and Bruce E. Cain, *Congressional Redistricting: Comparative and Theoretical Perspectives* (New York: Macmillan, 1992), 8–9, seem to stipulate unified state control as a precondition for large partisan gains. In the example of the text, however, by hypothesis all the states are under divided government, and yet there is the opportunity for gain.

16. Cox and Katz, *Elbridge Gerry's Salamander*, 97.

17. The remaining cases were from Illinois, where two courts—one Democratic, one Republican—shared jurisdiction.

18. For a more extensive discussion, see Cox and Katz, *Elbridge Gerry's Salamander*, chs. 5–6.

19. For a more nuanced discussion of the motivation of jurists and courts, see Cox and Katz, *Elbridge Gerry's Salamander*.

20. Cox and Katz, *Elbridge Gerry's Salamander*, ch 6.

21. 478 U.S. 109.

22. A "fairly high level" of malapportionment is, in this example, one in which the largest district's population exceeds the average by 12.8 percent (or the smallest falls short of the average by that amount).

23. Cf. Kevin A. Hill, "Does the Creation of Majority Black Districts Aid Republicans? An Analysis of the 1992 Congressional Elections in Eight Southern States," *Journal of Politics* 57, no. 2 (May 1995): 384–401.

24. We say "can" because states have until recently had an unchallenged right to redraw their district lines more than once in a decade, if they so choose.

25. Paul S. Herrnson, *Congressional Elections: Campaigning at Home and in Washington,* (Washington, D.C.: Congressional Quarterly, 1995); Gary C. Jacobson, *The Politics of Congressional Elections*, 4th ed. (New York: Longman, 1997).

26. See Gary C. Jacobson, "Congress: Elections and Stalemate," in *The Elections of 2000,* ed. Michael Nelson, (Washington, D.C.: Congressional Quarterly, 2001).

27. So far as I know, the only other systematic statistical investigation of entry decisions at the district level is the unpublished study of Bruce Larson, Suzanne Globetti, and Marc J. Hetherington, "The Redistricting Cycle and Strategic Candidate Decisions in U.S. House Races," (paper presented at the annual meeting of the American Political Science Association, Washington, D.C., August 31–September 4, 2000). These authors, in an investigation of House elections from 1990 to 1998, find that there is a general downward trend in incumbent retirements and strong challenger entries, as the redistricting cycle progresses from the first election after one redistricting to the last election before the next. As their specification and control variables are considerably different than those of Cox and Katz, yet they find comparable results, their study lends further support to the idea that the redistricting cycle has had strong effects on entry and exit after the reapportionment revolution. As their study does not include any pre-*Wesberry* elections, however, they do not provide additional evidence concerning whether the cycle's impact on entry and exit strength-

ened after the reapportionment decisions. Other studies investigate whether the *extent* of redistricting affects retirement decisions in the first election after the redistricting. See, e.g., John Alford, Holly Teeters, Daniel S. Ward, and Rick K. Wilson, "Overdraft: The Political Cost of Congressional Malfeasance," *Journal of Politics* 56, no. 3 (August 1994): 788–801, and Sean M. Theriault, "Moving Up or Moving Out: Career Ceilings and Congressional Retirement," *Legislative Studies Quarterly* 23, no. 3 (August 1998): 419–33, both of which find that retirement is more likely as the extent to which the incumbent's district was revised increases. Another relevant study is that of Monica Bauer and John R. Hibbing, "Which Incumbents Lose in House Elections: A Response to Jacobson's 'The Marginals Never Vanished'," *American Journal of Political Science* 33, no. 1(February 1989): 262–71. They find that, after 1974, almost all incumbents who lose "do so because of adverse redistricting or a major, personal scandal." Thus, it is not just entry decisions that seem to follow the redistricting cycle; actual outcomes do also.

28. For more on push outs, cf. Jeffrey Lazarus, "Strategic Entry in U.S. House Elections: Assessing the Causes and Effects of Interaction Among Incumbents and Challengers" (Ph.D. diss., University of California, San Diego, 2004).

29. Erik J. Engstrom, and Nathan W. Monroe, "Throwing in the Cards: Term Limits, Strategic Retirement, and the Incumbency Advantage" (paper presented at the annual meeting of the American Political Science Association, Boston, MA, August 28–September 1, 2002) find a similar pattern in California Assembly races, comparing open seats created by term limits to those created by the voluntary exit of an incumbent.

30. This pattern does not bear on conventional measures of the incumbency advantage because such measures routinely exclude freshly redrawn districts. It does, however, illustrate the strategic element in entry.

31. Stephen Ansolabehere, Alan Gerber, and James Snyder, "Equal Votes, Equal Money: Court-Ordered Redistricting and Public Expenditures in the American States," *American Political Science Review* 96, no. 4 (December 2002): 767–93; Mathew D. McCubbins and Thomas Schwartz, "Congress, the Courts, and Public Policy: Consequences of the One Man, One Vote Rule," *American Journal of Political Science* 32, no. 2 (May 1988): 388–415.

3

Redistricting and Incumbency: The New Voter Effect[1]

Scott W. Desposato and John R. Petrocik

Conventional wisdom among office holders and their advisors (and to a lesser extent among political scientists) is that the political consequences of districting plans are predictable.[2] Their confidence rests on the recognition that most voters have a preference for one of the parties, and they invoke that preference in choosing between candidates—the ubiquitous discussion about independent voters and candidate voting notwithstanding. The key to every redistricting among those orchestrating them is to sort voters according to their inferred party preference in a way that (1) maximizes the electoral security of (2) the largest possible number of office holders for their party.

Electoral security is achieved when the district includes enough supporters of a party to provide a high probability that no issue or candidate-induced tide will be so great that it is likely to defeat the incumbent. The largest possible number of office holders is achieved by economically allocating the party's voters. At the margin, electoral security and the number of seats are conflicting goals, but the balance is struck when the dominant party provides the "assurance" of victory to the Nth candidate of the largest possible majority for their party, while providing a "guarantee" of victory to a smaller number from the other party. Minority party incumbents are guaranteed office because, *ceteris paribus*, the redistricting packs minority party supporters together, giving almost all of them substantial majorities. While some number of major party incumbents may face closer contests because their party's electorate is spread across a larger number of districts, most incumbents of the majority party will enjoy easy wins.[3]

The puzzle, and the starting point for this chapter, is that majority party incumbents occasionally do not get that anticipated easy win. Incumbents who should be reelected are not, with the highest turnover occurring in the immediate postredistricting election. Neither fact is new, but our explanation, which has two parts, is different.

First, we argue that there are significant personal vote costs associated with redistricting. After redistricting, incumbents lose part of their incumbency because their district includes new voters in neighborhoods that were previously part of a different district. Among new voters, the incumbent has no personal vote or reputation. These voters were not part of the incumbent's constituency, they were not serviced by his staff, canvassed by his campaign workers in previous elections, and, most importantly, they never had the opportunity to vote for the office holder before.

Republican Elton Gallegly's experience provides a typical example of redistricting's impact. Through the 1990 election, he represented a district (the 21st) that straddled the southeastern border of Ventura and Los Angeles Counties (figure 3.1). Most of his constituents lived in the city of Simi Valley or the western San Fernando Valley part of Los Angeles. Gallegly was given a different constituency for the 1992 election (renumbered to the 23rd district). The new district (figure 3.2) shed all of his Los Angeles County voters and covered nearly all of Ventura County—adding several cities, including Santa Paula. The losses and additions are summarized in figure 3.3. Voters in the left-hatched region were "lost" to the redistricters' pens in 1992. Voters in the cross-hatched area, including the city of Simi Valley, are "old voters" that were in his district in 1990 and remained in his district after the redistricting. Voters in the right-hatched area, covering the city of Santa Paula and the northern and western parts of Ventura County, are "new voters." Prior to 1992 they were represented by 19th district Republican Congressman Robert Lagomarsino. Gallegly, although an incumbent, had no personal vote advantage among Lagomarsino's voters. He had never provided constituency service, was not a regular at community events, and was not regularly mentioned in the community newspaper. Consequently, among new voters Gallegly had effectively lost part of the incumbency advantage: that portion derived from the personal vote.

The second part of our argument focuses on the nature of the personal vote as an incumbency advantage. Specifically, we argue that the value of the personal vote for incumbents varies greatly from year to year and context to context. The existing literature conceptualizes the incumbency advantage as a bonus of approximately 7 percent over the expected normal vote of the district; of that bonus, about 4 percent is the personal vote advantage.[4] We argue that incumbency should not be conceived as a source of an automatic personal vote bonus of a particular magnitude. Rather we believe it provides an anchor that secures weakly partisan voters.

This phenomenon should not affect strong partisans—their vote decisions should be stable and consistent (though not perfectly so), and mostly driven by party identification. But a variable incumbency effect has important implications for the behavior of less partisan voters. In the absence of

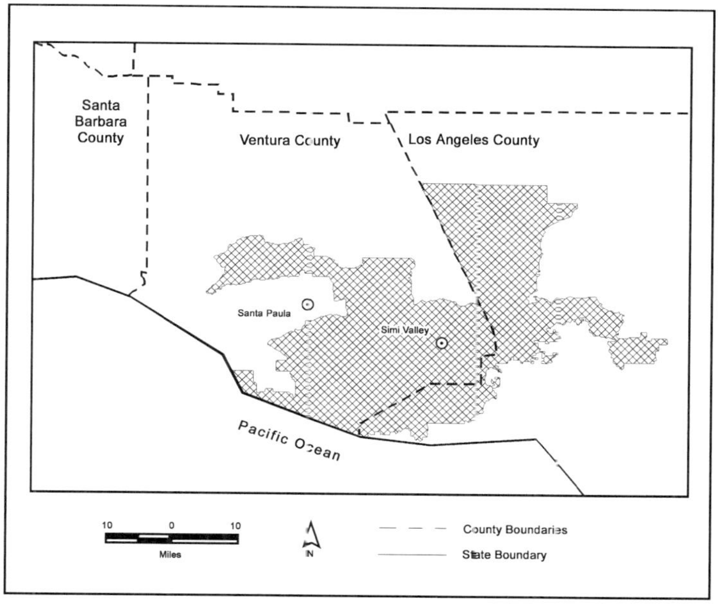

Figure 3.1. Elton Gallegly's 1990 District

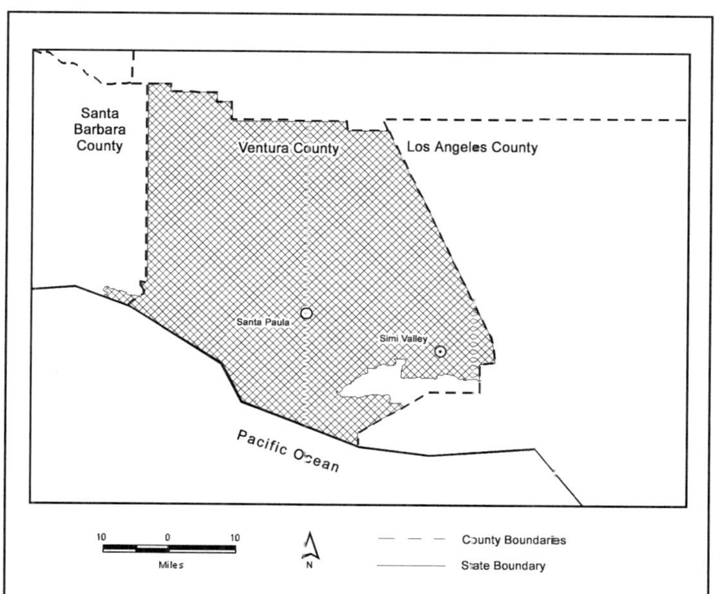

Figure 3.2. Elton Gallegly's 1992 District

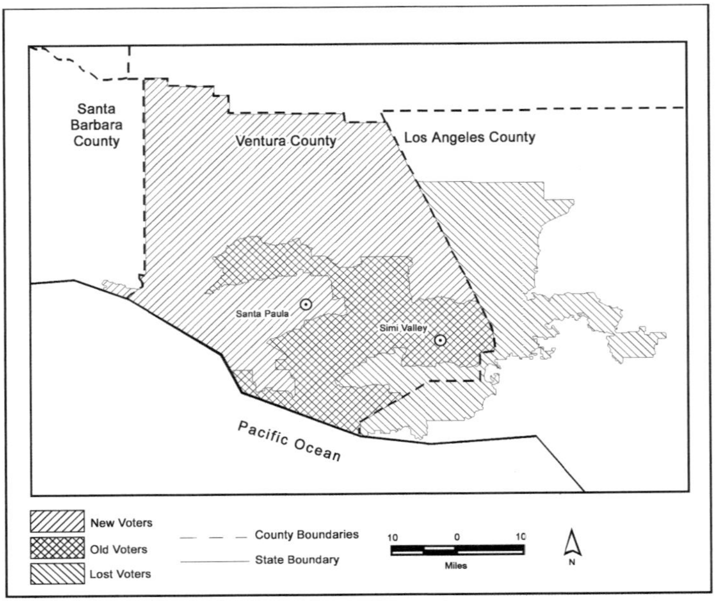

Figure 3.3. New Voters, Old Voters, Lost Voters

incumbency new voters who are less partisan rely on their latent partisanship, the state of the economy, or the voter's opinion of the latest White House scandal. As a result, the personal vote costs of redistricting for an incumbent can vary greatly by context and, therefore, by year. A 4, or 6, or 7 percent incumbency advantage may accurately measure a long-term average—but practically there can be so much year-to-year variance around that figure as to render it purely academic.

The responsiveness of weak partisans to short-term forces is precisely what makes redistricting so dangerous and uncertain for incumbents. Redistricting naturally removes the personal vote portion of the incumbency advantage for the fraction of the electorate that is new, and other factors—partisanship, issues, and personal differences among the candidates—assume greater importance. These short-term forces may work for or against the incumbent. Consequently, the interaction of redistricting and a variable incumbency advantage can produce a healthy margin for an incumbent, or end a career.

We illustrate this formulation in two steps. First, we revisit the notion of the incumbency advantage and propose an alternative conceptualization of the personal vote and its intersection with redistricting. Second, we examine three distinct tests of our formulation, seeking repeated evidence of a variable incumbency advantage and its interaction with redistricting. The first test uses NES survey data for congressional elections from 1980 through

2000. The second looks at the postredistricting elections in the South. The third examines the 1992 and 1994 congressional and state legislative elections in California. The mix of individual voter and election-level data and the variability of the political environments captured by the data provide some assurance that the patterns are not mere coincidence. The results support our argument, showing how redistricting causes a personal vote loss for incumbents that varies across party, context, voters, and election saliency.

PARTISANSHIP AND THE INCUMBENT'S ADVANTAGE

The underlying partisanship of the district is the largest component of the vote. Its exact size varies by office and region, but it exceeded 70 percent of the total vote cast in all but two congressional elections during the last fifty years (see figure 3.4).[5] It has two sources. Its direct component is the voters who choose candidates of their party and never contemplate doing otherwise. Its indirect component arises from the fact that most districts are drawn with effective party majorities. The majority party's candidates, especially

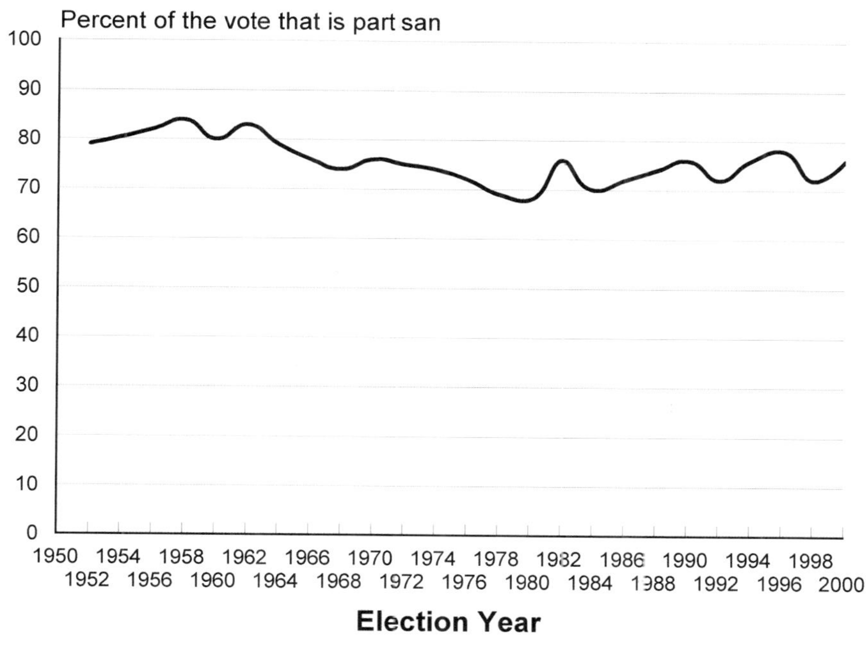

Source: NES surveys for the indicated years

Figure 3.4. Party Voting in Congressional Elections

when they are incumbents, seem assured of reelection. The minority party's candidate, viewed as certain to lose, receives few of the resources needed to mount a strong challenge in a district with a strong party tilt. As a consequence, the incumbent draws weak challengers since the most talented minority party candidates avoid a hopeless effort. All of the things that accompany a weak challenger (less funding, less attention, etc.) push the incumbent in a secure district to a win that exceeds the partisan tilt of the district. Kernell and Jacobson have formulated the latter proposition by considering it as a strategic politician phenomenon.[6]

The 20 percent of the vote contributed by defectors and the 10 percent contributed by core independents in figure 3.4 is the fraction of the vote driven by the personal vote and the political environment.[7] The political environment of the election (strength of top of the ballot candidates, domestic and foreign conditions, and so forth) is a component to the vote that candidates can only hope to exploit or avoid. However, the personal vote is something that office holders work to create for themselves.[8]

Incumbents resolve problems with Social Security, send letters to newly minted Eagle Scouts, attend community events, and expedite passports. They canvass the community, kiss scores of local babies, talk on the radio, and appear in the hometown newspaper. Their reward for these efforts is personal votes conferred by greater familiarity, personal regard, a reputation for competent performance, and deference received simply because the person is the incumbent. Office holders with a smaller partisan advantage are the most in need of personal votes, and the most susceptible to defeat by a short-term tide until they cultivate their own personal votes.

THE VARIABLE INCUMBENT ADVANTAGE

Incumbents' constituency service efforts earn them personal votes among weak partisans and independents. The personal vote moderates the force of short-term political tides and anchors potential drifters to the incumbent. But without the cue of constituency service in an open-seat race or among new voters after redistricting, personal voters' behavior is uncertain. Some may revert to a latent party preference—which may work for or against the incumbent. Others, in the absence of a personal vote orientation, may cast their votes based on the short-term tide of the election, including national political forces, candidate quality, and district specific issues. Again, these forces can work for or against the incumbent's party. But in newly drawn districts and open-seat contests the personal vote is reduced by the fraction of the constituents who have never been represented by the nominal incumbent. Candidates in both types of districts and both parties are more affected by tides. In 1964 the Republicans suffered in the LBJ landslide (following the redistricting triggered by the Supreme Court's one person/one vote decisions); in 1992 and (especially) 1994 it was the Democrats' turn.

Both latent partisanship and short-term forces, we argue, interact with the saliency of the race. Tides push voters and they help campaigns push voters toward or away from a candidate. They prime new issues (as when Democrats reminded voters of the Republicans' unpopular bid to remove President Clinton) or reinforce weak or latent partisanship by running on traditional party issues (tax cuts or welfare spending, for example). The key is that the magnitude of redistricting's personal vote costs varies with the saliency of the considerations that benefit or harm a candidate. When the challenger is well funded and capable of effectively delivering a message, the personal vote matters most—it insulates the incumbent from potentially large short-term effects.

As a consequence of all these variable factors, personal vote losses through redistricting vary with the magnitude of the short-term forces, the fraction of the electorate that is new to the incumbent, the proportion of marginal partisans among the voters, and the saliency of the election for voters.[9] The key concept here is that a personal vote bonus is not 4 percent, or 6 percent, or any other fixed amount. The actual bonus can vary greatly depending on the political environment and other institutional features. Incumbency's personal vote advantage is an anchor that secures less attached voters who would otherwise drift with the political tides.

In every postredistricting election and every open-seat contest, the majority party could have many incumbents and constituencies with a small partisan plurality and, therefore, be vulnerable to a short-term tide. The danger for incumbents is that in spite of their best-laid redistricting plans, new voters are up for grabs. New voters do not have any personal vote relationship with incumbents, they do not know about the legislators' years of loyal service, and they do not remember the speeches at the high school commencement—because all these things happened elsewhere, in the old district lines. These voters are susceptible to short-term political forces. The vote cost of the surge is uncertain, but is moderated or enhanced by the personal vote anchor provided by the constituency.

Three Examples of the Variable Incumbent Advantage

We test our anchor argument with three separate analyses. In the first, we seek evidence of the variable incumbency advantage in national tides. Specifically, we use NES survey data from 1980 through 2000 to compare voter choices in open-seat and incumbent contests in changing political environments and observe the individual behavior that is presumed by the aggregate patterns. The data show the interaction of national tides and incumbency, and support our anchor model of the incumbency advantage over the existing bonus model.

The second test examines redistricting effects on Democratic incumbents in several Southern states in 1992 and 1994. Population changes and efforts to draw more majority-minority districts forced incumbents to run in districts with many new voters in 1992. Because both 1992 and 1994 were marked by strong tides against the Democrats, the large numbers of new voters meant that the Democrats were at great risk because redistricting diminished their personal vote. The data again support our conceptualization of an interaction between incumbency and redistricting, showing how new Southern voters drifted into the Republican party on a realignment tide.

The results from the first two tests, like all district-level analyses, might be the product of other confounding factors. In particular, one could argue that they have nothing to do with the personal vote, but are entirely an artifact of strategic incumbent and challenger behavior.

Our third analysis, therefore, uses a massive, neighborhood-level dataset of electoral returns to control for candidate quality and other district-level variables—and zero-in on the personal vote costs of redistricting. We analyze the effect of the 1991 redistricting in California on congressional and state legislative elections in 1992 and 1994. Because the unit of analysis is subdistrict, we can control for district-level and candidate effects. These data also strongly support our argument. They show that, in the absence of incumbency information, California voters fell back on their partisan alignments, with the magnitude of this retreat varying with the salience of the campaign.

Example 1: Variable Incumbency Influences on Voters

We begin by seeking evidence for a variable incumbency advantage in individual-level behavior. If our conceptualization of the incumbency advantage is correct, two findings should emerge. First, most of the vote should be partisan, immune to incumbency's draw or short-term electoral forces. Second, incumbency should act as an anchor—stabilizing incumbents' vote shares across elections and resisting short-term forces. In contrast, open-seat vote shares should fluctuate dramatically with election-year tides. If we are wrong, and the prevailing "bonus model" is correct, then incumbents' vote shares should also fluctuate with national tides and be a consistent 4 or 5 percent above open-seat results.

Figure 3.5 compares the vote cast for incumbents and open-seat contestants of the same party in contested incumbent and open-seat races in each year.[10] The figure graphs the reported and expected vote for Democrats (top half) and Republicans (bottom half). The left-side figures report the vote when the incumbent sought reelection. The right-side figures report data when the incumbent Democrat (upper-right figure) or Republican (lower-right figure) did not seek reelection. Each graph plots two lines: the reported vote of the respondents and the vote that might have been ex-

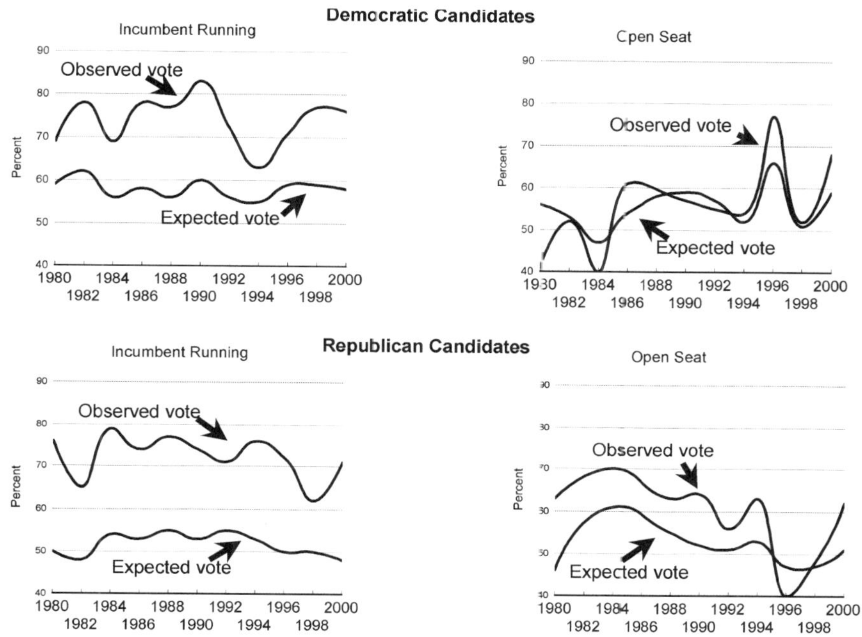

Figure 3.5. Observed and Expected Vote in Incumbent and Open-Seat Races

pected given the respondent's partisanship (their "normal vote") in the absence of short-term forces that caused the electorate to prefer one of the candidates.[11]

The partisan basis of an incumbent's electoral security is apparent in each graph. Majorities in incumbent and open-seat races have a party preference that matches the party of the officeholder (whether that person is the incumbent or the retired incumbent). Respondents from districts represented by a Democrat seeking reelection (the upper left graph) had an average, expected 57 percent Democratic vote. Voters in open Democratic seats (upper right) were, on average, equally Democratic in their party identification, with a 56 percent expected Democratic vote. Those in districts where a Republican sought reelection (lower left graph) had an expected 56 percent Republican vote; those in seats where a Republican was retiring (lower right) had an average 54 percent expected GOP vote. In brief, the candidates in open and incumbent races faced electorates that were, on average, equally supportive of their candidates.

Figure 3.5 provides the raw data for estimating the effect of incumbency on voters. The vote cast for incumbents exceeded the underlying party vote by a significantly larger margin than it exceeded partisanship in open-seat races. Figure 3.6 illustrates this more clearly by calculating the difference between

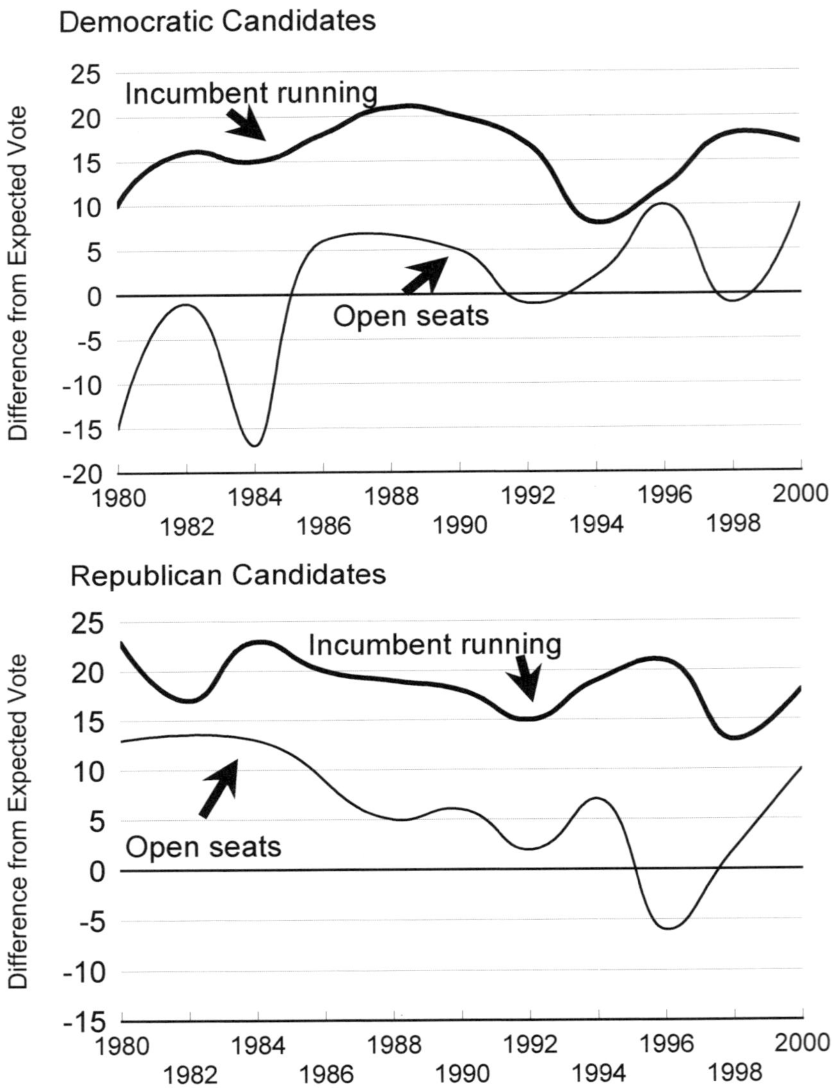

Figure 3.6. Voting in Incumbent and Open-Seat Races

the observed and expected vote for incumbents and the observed and expected vote for the incumbent party's candidate in an open-seat race. The upper graph reports the results for Democrats running as incumbents and Democrats running to succeed a retired Democrat in the open-seat races; the bottom graph reports the vote for Republicans running as incumbents and Republicans running to succeed a retired Republican. The lines report the difference between the observed vote for the candidate and the vote expected if party identification alone dictated the choice. Consider the left-most point on the top graph. The +10 point value is the difference between the reported Democratic vote (69 percent) of respondents and their expected Democratic vote (59 percent) in districts where a Democrat incumbent was seeking reelection. The -15 point value is the difference between the reported Democratic vote (41 percent) of respondents in open-seats and their expected Democratic vote (56 percent).

The difference between these values (25 percentage points reflecting the +10 for incumbent races and the -15 in open seat races) is the incumbent advantage. Voters supported their party's candidates at a rate that exceeded a normal party vote in open-seat races by an average of less than 5 points, but supported incumbents at a rate that was 17 points above their expected party vote—a 12-point advantage for incumbents. This average covers variability that seems related to the magnitude of the short-term surge. In the Republican year of 1994, for example, voters in districts previously represented by a Democrat cast a vote that was only 2 points more Democratic than their party identification. In the Democratic surge of the 1996 contest, voters in open Democratic seats cast a Democratic vote that was 10 points greater than a pure partisan vote. Voters in Republican open-seats behaved in a mirror opposite way. They over supported (relative to their party identification) Republicans running in open seats in 1994 and under supported them in 1996.

This variability, which is significant, contradicts the notion of a stable incumbent advantage. In the 1994 survey, voters gave Democratic incumbents a net 21-point advantage: support for incumbents was 11 points above a straight party vote while the Democratic vote in open-seat Democrats was 10 points below a straight party vote. Voters conferred less of an advantage on incumbent Republicans in 1994, not because they supported them less, but because they supported Republicans running in open GOP seats so heavily. Voters gave virtually no advantage to Democratic incumbents in 1996, because the pro-Democratic surge of Clinton's candidacy gave a boost to Democrats running in open Democratic seats that was virtually equal to the incumbent advantage for Democrats in that year.

The variability of the incumbent's advantage lies in the comparatively greater instability of the vote in open-seat races. Support for incumbents exceeded partisanship, but how much of an advantage the incumbents enjoyed over their colleagues in open-seat races depended on whether open-seat candidates exceeded a straight party vote, which they did in some years but not others. The oscillation seems to vary with conventional interpretations of the election environment for that year. The excess support voters gave to incumbent Democrats shifted from an average of about 20 points for the 1990 through 1994 elections to virtually nothing in 1996 only because of the surge in favor of open-seat Democrats in the run-away Clinton election in 1996. The excess vote for the incumbents increased a couple of points, but the vote for the open-seat Democrats flipped from a 10-point deficit to a 10-point surplus—equal to the excess cast for incumbents. Two-thirds of the return of the 20-point gap in 1998 was contributed by the decline in support for open-seat Democrats. The pattern is repeated for Republican voting. The slight increase in the effect of incumbency on voter choices in 1992 reflects declining support for open-seat Republicans; the increase in the gap from 12 to 21 points between 1994 and 1996 is largely a product of the drop off in support for Republicans in open-seat races as Clinton trounced Dole. The narrowing of the gap again in 1998 was as much a product of an increase in Republican support in the open seats as it is a decline in the GOP vote for incumbents.

In short, every aspect of the incumbent advantage varied across these elections, and for both parties. The first order difference between the observed vote for the incumbent and the vote that might have been expected as a result of the partisanship of the voters oscillated. Moreover, it bears repeating that the variability seems to follow standard interpretations of the party advantage associated with the elections. That is, the difference favored the Democrats when the historical account emphasized a positive election environment for the Democrats. The GOP difference was greater when the milieu of the election had a distinctly pro-GOP bias. Second, as we suggested above, voters in open seats were more likely to cast a purely party vote and more likely to shift their behavior from election to election in concert with the partisan surge of the election. Open seat voters, in brief, were the source of most of the variability in the incumbent's appeal. The incumbent's advantage, viewed through the benchmark provided by party identification, seems quite a bit larger than the conventional estimate.

Example 2: Majority-Minority Redistricting and the Incumbent's Advantage

Our second test examines postredistricting elections in the South. In 1992 and 1994, a significant number of Southern, white, Democratic members of Congress found themselves with many new constituents because African Americans had been removed from their district and packed into new majority black districts in order to ensure the election of African Americans.[12] The average white Democratic incumbent acquired a redrawn district in which about 21 percent of their constituents had been imported from other districts, while the average Republican incumbent had a constituency that was 37 percent new.[13] The bonus model of incumbency would have predicted a loss for incumbents in proportion to the number of new voters they acquired. In this case the Republicans should have fared worse than the Democrats. The reduction in the African American vote played a role in

Democratic losses.[14] In the event, however, the larger factor in the Democrat's greater losses was the interaction of new voters and a short-term anti-Democratic tide.[15]

Figure 3.7 indicates what this coincidence meant for incumbent Southern white Democrats seeking reelection in 1992. These white Democrats were reelected with just fewer than 71 percent of the vote in 1990. The proportion of their district which would be new voters after the redistricting was largely unrelated to the vote in 1990, as the flat line indicates (although, in fact, the relationship was insignificantly positive indicating that Democratic incumbents with the largest margins in 1990 tended to receive slightly more new constituents than average). This line provides a benchmark for determining what happened in 1992 as a function of the proportion of new constituents in the district.[16] The difference between the lines captures the effect of new constituents on the Democratic incumbents.

The typical incumbent's vote declined as the proportion of new constituents increased, but new constituents were a threat to defeat them only when the incumbent received an almost completely new constituency. As figure 3.7 indicates, districts with a 50 percent turnover still averaged a 58 percent Democratic

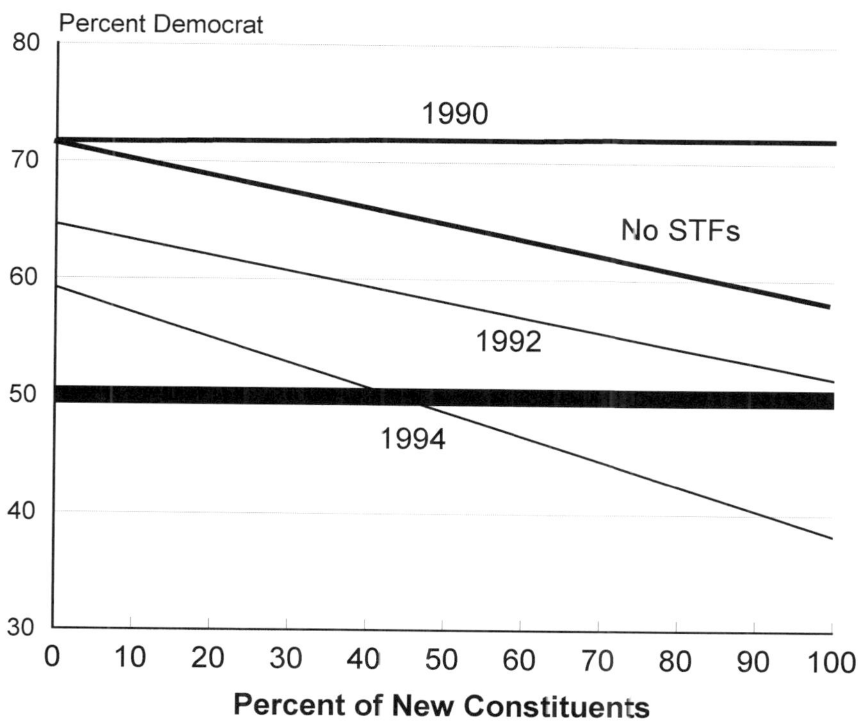

Figure 3.7. New Constituents and the Incumbent's Vote

vote in the 1992 election. The anti-Democratic mood of the election is apparent in the difference between the "1992" line and the line representing the vote in the absence of short-term forces (the "No STFs" line) in figure 3.7 (with the swing defined as the intercept of the regression). A comparison of the 1990 line with the "STF" line indicates how the redistricting might have affected the 1992 vote if there had not been an anti-Democratic swing which depressed the overall Democratic vote by more than 7 percentage points.[17] A Democratic incumbent in 1992 should have expected a vote decline because of a loss in the personal vote, but not defeat.

The more anti-Democratic mood of the 1994 electorate was a Republican high tide that defeated some of the 1992 survivors. Democratic incumbents lost proportionally more votes as a function of new constituents in 1994 than they did in 1992 (the slope was slightly greater). But equally important, the overall Democratic vote declined another five and one-half percentage points (the difference in the regression intercept in 1994 compared to 1992). Coupled with the increased sensitivity of these not-yet-immunized voters to election forces (1994 was the sophomore election, postredistricting), any Democrat with a constituency that was more than 40 percent new had a predicted vote of approximately 50 percent. About twenty Democratic incumbents found themselves in this vulnerable position in 1994, and about half of them were defeated.

Example 3: The Variable Advantage in California

Both of the preceding analyses clearly show a variable incumbency advantage, and demonstrate how the intersection of redistricting, new voters, and a political tide shape an incumbent's advantage. Both analyses, however, are vulnerable to criticisms of endogeneity. Specifically, the observed patterns might reflect the choices of savvy candidates who are deciding to run as a function of the environment of the election (as it is created by redistricting, domestic or foreign events, and so forth). At a minimum, the prospect of significant endogeneity suggests that the personal vote/incumbent effects identified in the previous cases are overstated.[18]

Our third test, that examines elections in 1990, 1992, and 1994 in California, does not have this potential problem, and it allows us to corroborate the variability of the personal vote advantage.[19] This dataset is a particularly rich for examining incumbency effects because, first, the structure of the data allows an analysis that is not likely to be confounded by endogeneity problems. Precinct-level registration and voting data are linked to census blocks by geocoding registered voters according to their addresses in the Statement of Registration. The result is a dataset of approximately 400,000 neighborhood electoral returns. We can precisely distinguish between new and old voters within districts, because neighborhoods new to the district can be distinguished from those previously represented by the incumbent. The neighborhood-level units of analysis allow the proportion of new voters to vary *within* each congressional or state assembly district, thereby assuring that there will be a minimum correlation between the proportion of new voters and interdistrict differences in candidate factors. The incidence of new voters can be separated from the "strategic candidate factors" that potentially confound the estimate of new voter effects. Second, because we have data for state legislative and congressional races for the period from 1990 to 1994, we can estimate the variability of the personal vote advantage in two arenas.

Unlike 1982, when Democratic control of both the state legislature and governor's office led to a Democratic gerrymander, California's 1992 redistricting was relatively bipartisan. The addition of seven new seats (for a total of fifty-two) made it possible that congressional incumbents would face few new voters. The line drawers could have minimized the fraction of new voters for every incumbent shifting voters out of overpopulated districts to create new districts. The redistricting of the state legislature, on the other hand, because its size remained limited to eighty seats, would create a significant number of new voters for many incumbents. As it transpired, the ability of the Republican governor to suppress an ideal Democratic redistricting produced redistricting plans for the state assembly and the congressional delegation that gave incumbents of both parties a large number of new voters in their districts.

Table 3.1 profiles the effects of the 1990 redistricting on incumbents. The relative partisan balance of the average incumbent's district was mostly unchanged. Democratic registration for incumbent Democrats averaged 57 percent before and 55 percent after redistricting. The figures for Republicans were similar: 40 percent and 42 percent. The pattern was slightly different for the state assembly districts. Democratic registration declined 2 percentage points for Democratic incumbents. The average Republican incumbent got a district with only a 40 percent Democratic registration—what they enjoyed in their previous district.

Table 3.1. Democratic Registration before and after Redistricting, 1990 to 1992

	Republican Incumbents	*Democratic Incumbents*
Congressional Districts		
% registered Democrat in 1990	40	57
% registered Democrat in 1992	42	55
% new constituents	30	26
Number of Districts	12	21
State Assembly Districts		
% registered Democrat in 1990	40	59
% registered Democrat in 1992	40	57
% new constituents	53	44
Number of Districts	16	29

More important, incumbents of both parties faced substantial populations of new voters—an average of 27 percent for congressional incumbents and 50 percent for assembly representatives. Several assembly incumbents actually had 100 percent new voters because redistricting had forced a move across the state to seek reelection. On balance the personal vote costs of the redistricting were slightly higher for the GOP. Republican incumbents who sought reelection to Congress in 1992 faced constituencies that were about 30 percent new; Democrat districts had an average 26 percent new population. About 44 percent of the constituents of Democratic state assembly incumbents were new; approximately 53 percent of the constituents of GOP state assembly incumbents were new. These changes, plus the dramatic increase in the number of open seats make the California case an ideal observatory to observe the personal vote costs of redistricting.

The Model

Our anchor model of the incumbency advantage offers several observable implications for these redistricting data. First, all else equal, incumbents should receive a smaller vote share among new neighborhoods than among old neighborhoods. Among new voters, incumbents have lost their personal vote advantage; among old voters, incumbents retain the personal vote they have cultivated. Second, the magnitude of this incumbency effect should vary as a function of the partisanship of the voters: new voters should fall back on their partisanship in the absence of personal vote cues. Third, these incumbency effects should vary with the saliency of the election. All personal vote effects should be substantially smaller when voter information is low.

We use the following model to estimate this formulation of the personal vote costs of redistricting:

$$\begin{aligned} V_{bdy} = {} & B_{0dy}E_{dy} + B_{1y}D_{by} + B_{2py}I_{pdy}D_{by} \\ & + B_{3py}I_{pdy}N_{bdy} + B_{4py}I_{pdy}N_{bdy}D_{by} \\ & + B_{5py}I_{pdy}N_{bdy}Q_{dy} + B_{6py}I_{pdy}N_{bdy}D_{by}Q_{dy} \\ & + \epsilon_{bdy} \end{aligned}$$

where:

- *p*, *y*, *d*, and *b* are subscripts for party of incumbent, year, district, and census block, respectively.
- V_{bdy} is the percentage of the two-party vote received by the Democratic candidate in block *b*, district *d*, year *y*.
- E_{dy} is an indicator variable for district *d* in year *y*.

- D_{by} is the percentage of voters that are registered Democratic in block b and year y.
- I_{pdy} is a set of indicator variables for the presence of an incumbent from party p in district d in year y, coded -1 for Republicans, 0 for Open Seats, and 1 for Democrats.
- N_{bdy} identifies block b as being "new" to the incumbent in district d in year y. New is coded 1 for blocks that were new to an incumbent and 0 for blocks in open districts, all "old" blocks, and for all blocks in the 1990 election—prior to redistricting.
- Q_{dy} is the quality of the challenger in district d and year y, measured using campaign expenditures. To make the expensive congressional races comparable with the less taxing assembly races, we measured challenger quality as the ratio of challenger to incumbent spending. Using raw challenger spending does not change our conclusions, though it makes cross-legislature comparisons more confusing.

The key quantities in the model are B_3 through B_6. The first two, B_3 and B_4, capture the interaction of new voters with partisanship and year—in other words, they capture the difference between new and old voters' behavior, showing the electoral costs associated with new voters. The other key coefficients, B_5 and B_6, capture the interaction of incumbency and challenger quality. Specifically, they allow the personal vote costs of incumbency to vary with challenger quality. Our expectation was that higher challenger quality would increase these costs.

The other coefficients in the model, B_0 through B_2, establish a baseline vote share against which the interactions can be compared. That is, they predict neighborhood electoral returns among old voters where incumbents have the benefit of personal vote cultivation. Specifically, the baseline Democratic vote is modeled as a simple linear function of party registration and incumbency status for each party's candidate.[20] Thus any personal vote impact will be reflected in deviations from the party incumbency baseline, that is, coefficients B_3 through B_6 will be significant.

The model is a fixed-effects regression. This is equivalent to adding a dummy variable for each district in each year to the equation, in this case represented by E_{dy}. Herein lies the advantage of using subdistrict data. Most studies of congressional elections use district-level data and the comparisons that drive their inference are cross district, often reflecting district-level variables such as the quality of a challenger or a scandal with the incumbent. Such idiosyncratic district effects can confound district-level analysis, but our approach controls these factors. The dummy variable for each district controls for the peculiarities of the district, including the crucial variable of candidate quality. What remains are the differences between new and old voters, which we allow to vary across year and party. The estimation uses a linear model because most neighborhoods have registration figures and vote shares between 20 and 80 percent of the registration or vote (although neighborhoods do vary from 0 to 100 percent Democratic registration), where a linear model is reasonable.[21]

Several previous studies have approached the problem similarly. Rush compared electoral returns for New England towns redistricted into other incumbents' districts. He found that "new" towns quickly begin to vote like old towns, suggesting the emergence of a strong personal vote.[22] Banducci and Karp studied the interaction of redistricting and scandal in the 1992 elections.[23] Petrocik and Desposato explored the interaction of new voters, redistricting, and minority majority districts in the South. They found that Democrats' congressional losses in 1992 and 1994 in the South were not the result of "packing" minority voters, but resulted from the intersection of new voters and short-term anti-Democratic tides.[24] Finally, Ansolabehere, Snyder, and Stewart use county-level data and identify as new voters all those in the county when it was shifted to a new incumbent by redistricting.[25]

Our statistical model is similar to Ansolabehere et al., but the design and analysis has several key differences. We trade longevity for detail. They examine an extended time series of county-level data; we use block-level returns from a six-year period, providing depth and detail. Our small and quite homogeneous census block-size neighborhoods provide more precise estimates of the behavior of new voters.[26] Lastly, we use party registration figures to measure the underlying normal vote, rather than relying on lagged votes or average presidential vote shares, which are themselves subject to short-term tides and candidate-quality confounding.

Two practical factors could bias the results *against* our hypotheses. The first is that new voters may have had some personal-vote generating contact with an incumbent. Incumbents have been known to anticipate boundary changes to their districts with a cultivation of voters in areas that they expect to find in their redrawn districts. Certainly voters in "border" neighborhoods may have interacted with or heard of the incumbent, but as we saw in the case of Congressman Gallegly (see figure 3.3), new voters can be relatively far from the old district.[27] We believe that there are only a few cases where this behavior is substantial. The second factor is that incumbents have other nonpersonal vote advantages, including financial resources, prestige, and franking privileges. Clever use of these resources might compensate for the costs of new voters. Regardless, both factors are conservative to our hypothesis test: they work against our hypotheses and should weaken the impact of new voters. Any significant findings are thus quite robust.

The Results

Figures 3.8 and 3.9 show the interaction of redistricting, new voters, and partisanship on the vote share of incumbents in 1992 and 1994. Each graph allows an assessment of the typical incumbent's personal vote costs as a function of the

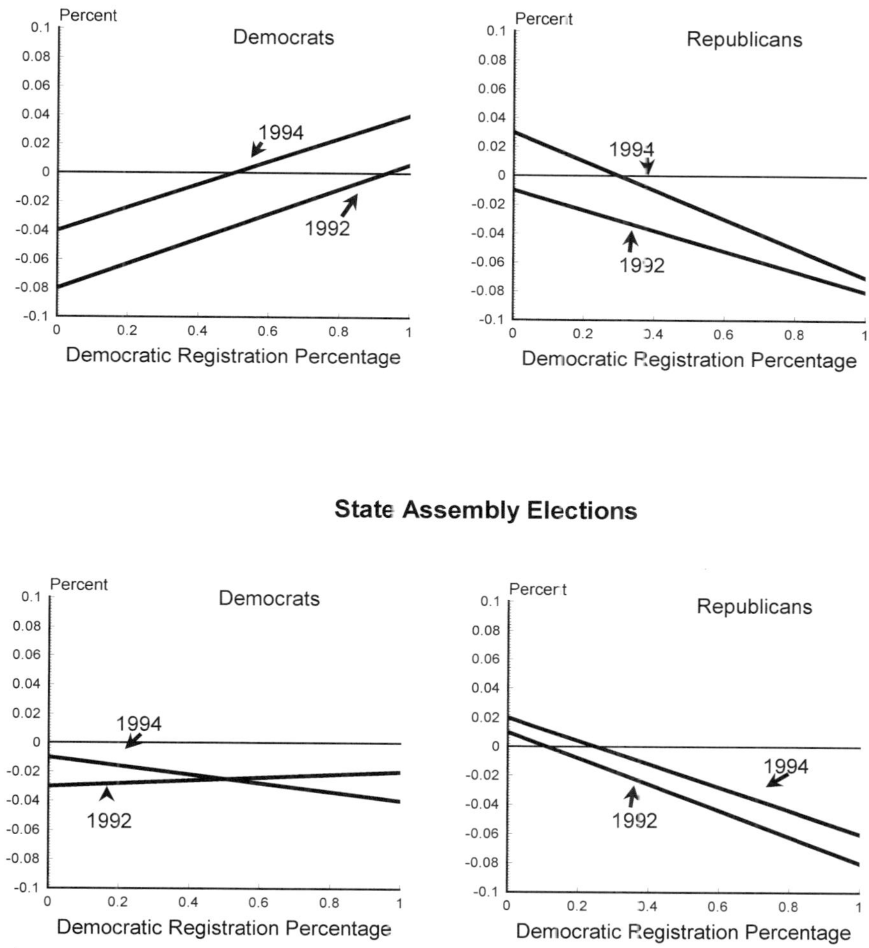

Figure 3.8. New Voters and the Personal Vote: Congressional and State-Assembly Elections of 1992 and 1994

partisan profile of the district. The x-axis in each is the Democratic registration of the neighborhood, *not* the district (see the explanation of the data above); the y-axis is the predicted difference for incumbents among new and old voters (the results from which the calculations are based appear in appendix 2).

The lines compare the choices of new voters in 1992 and 1994 with the neighborhood pattern for 1990. In each graph, the horizontal line represents the baseline vote share an incumbent could expect among old voters (among whom incumbents had no personal vote costs). The lines labeled "1992" and "1994" plot the predicted differences in voting behavior between old and new voters. Specifically, the slopes and intercepts of the 1992 and 1994 lines are calculated using the coefficients from the second half of the appendix 3.2 table—the coefficients that interact with "new neighborhood." For example, the 1992 congressional Democrat line is calculated using the baseline intercept and slopes from appendix 3.2. The intercept of the line (−.09) is the *Incumb*New Voter* coefficient for Democrats in 1992. The slope of the line (.09) is the *Incumb*New Voter*Dem Reg 1992* Democratic estimate. The lines in figure 3.9 use the same approach, but add to the slope and intercept the relevant estimates for challenger quality interactions.[28]

Where the 1992 or 1994 line is below the 1990 (horizontal) baseline, our model predicts that the incumbent loses votes among new voters. Where the 1992 or 1994 line is above the baseline, the model predicts that incumbents perform better than average among new voters. The slopes of the 1992 and 1994 lines show how incumbents' vote losses (or gains) are related to the partisan profile of the district. We hypothesized that, in the absence of incumbency, voters rely on weak partisanship, resulting in higher or lower new voter costs, depending on the partisanship of the new voters (as represented by Democratic registration in the neighborhoods).

The four lines in figure 3.8 allow an examination of the pattern for the congressional and state assembly races for both parties. The first column of graphs in the figure represents the relationships for Democratic incumbents; the second column represents the position of Republican incumbents. We expected new voters to produce a decline in the incumbent's vote relative to the behavior of old voters. We also expected new voters to have their largest effect in the election immediately following the redistricting because, with time, the incumbent would do the things that create a personal vote among his or her new constituents. Finally, we expected the decline to be moderated by the partisanship of the neighborhoods, with the largest losses occurring in neighborhoods with the largest fraction of voters from the challenger's party.

We found all of these things. First, there are significant personal vote costs to redistricting. The 1992 and 1994 lines are below the baseline vote share, indicating that incumbents lose votes among new voters, even holding constant candidate and challenger quality. In the "average" neighborhood (a 50 percent Democratic neighborhood, represented by the center point of the graphs), the new voter cost is approximately 5 percent, the standard incumbency advantage estimate. This simple finding of new voter costs is strong evidence for the incumbency advantage and against Zaller's notion that candidate quality explains the incumbency advantage.[29] If candidate quality were such a powerful force, there should be no systematic difference between the behavior of new and old voters because candidate quality is constant across the new and old neighborhoods. One might conjecture that incumbents choose not to campaign as aggressively among new voters, but why they would systematically ignore all new voters—those most in "need" of campaign attention—is completely unclear and not in keeping with the "wholesale politics" character of California campaigns.

More notable is the variability of the losses. The personal vote advantage of incumbents systematically varies with the partisan strength of the district: reaching about 8 percent in unfriendly neighborhoods and approaching zero in friendly districts. Incumbents can earn votes in unfriendly neighborhoods, but they are personal, not partisan votes. Constituency service and publicity can be worth as much as 8 percent of the vote in an unfriendly neighborhood. For Republicans, this means that as neighborhoods are increasingly Democratic, the expected vote loss among new voters rises. For Democrat incumbents, the inverse pattern appears. Democratic new voter losses are highest where GOP voters are the most numerous. In the absence of the personal vote, voters return to their partisanship, reducing the incumbent's vote share. When the new voters passed to the incumbent are homogeneously supportive of his or her party (at some number above 70 percent registered in the incumbent's party) they seem to simply follow their partisan leaning.

Finally, although the first postredistricting election has the largest new voter effect (as expected), new voter effects persist into the 1994 elections. The 1994 lines are almost uniformly below the baseline horizontal line. New voters continued to cost incumbents votes, even after 2 years of constituency service and personal vote cultivation. There is, however, evidence of a sophomore surge. By 1994, the cost of new voters has fallen in almost all districts (the 1994 lines are almost uniformly above the 1992 lines). Republicans in a median neighborhood (one with 50 percent Democratic registration) lost about 5 percent of the vote among new voters; by 1994 constituency service had reduced this loss to about 2 percent. Democrats' gains in 1994 are similar—their performance among new voters increases by about 4 percent. The implication is that the sophomore surge may largely be an incumbent skill phenomenon, and that the personal vote advantages takes time to develop.

The state assembly pattern does not conform so neatly, although most expectations are met. Incumbents of both parties lost votes among new voters—the 1992 and 1994 lines are consistently below the baseline for both Republicans and Democrats. Vote losses among assembly Republicans match the losses observed by congressional Republicans. In Democratic neighborhoods it reaches about 8 percent in 1992 and 6 percent in 1994. In Republican neighborhoods, personal vote costs largely vanish. Again, the implication is that without the cues provided by the personal vote, the electorate falls back on latent partisanship. Finally, there is evidence of a weak and incomplete sophomore surge in 1994. Republican incumbents performed about 2 percent better among new voters in 1994 than in 1992. Democratic assembly incumbents meet expectations least well. There are consistent new voter costs—about 2 percent—but these do not vary with neighborhood partisanship as expected. Incumbents lose about 2 percent of their predicted vote in both friendly and unfriendly neighborhoods.

As noted above, the reason for examining the California assembly elections is that the electoral dynamics of the professionalized California legislature should parallel what is observed for Congress. Consequently, the flat vote-loss lines for assembly Democrats are a surprise. The difference may reflect the design of the Democratic assembly districts. It may be a residual of the relatively centralized politics of California Democrats (perhaps a declining feature as the era of Speaker Willie Brown recedes further into the past). It may be nothing more than an anomalous spike in an otherwise general pattern if we had more data. In any case we have no explanation for it.

The Effects of Competition on New Voters

Figure 3.9 shows that new voter costs are highest where incumbents face strong challengers (strong by virtue of an ability to fund and wage a campaign or because of a positive short-term tide).[30] The effect, as expected, is strongest in the election that immediately follows a redistricting—before the incumbent has the opportunity to create a personal vote anchor among the new voters. The first column in figure 3.9 shows the new-old voter differences where incumbents faced relatively underfunded challengers. The second column shows districts that had strong challengers.[31]

Personal vote costs vary with challenger quality. The relationship between voter partisanship and new voter costs is significantly stronger for Democratic incumbents facing competitive challengers than those facing weak challengers. Democratic incumbents who faced a competitive challenger lost about 15 percent of their expected vote share in 1992 and 8 percent in 1994, in unfriendly neighborhoods (0 percent Democratic). In contrast, Democratic incumbents facing weak challengers lost less than 5 percent of the vote in both years in unfriendly neighborhoods. The impact of competitiveness for Republican incumbents is similar. In 1994, the cost of new voters rises dramatically where there are competitive challengers. Competition had weaker effects on GOP incumbents in 1992.

Competition in the State Assembly Races

The interactions between challenger quality and new voter costs in the California state assembly races were largely unsystematic. Some of the interaction coefficients for the state assembly are not significantly different from zero, and the observed patterns are unstable. In some contexts, competitiveness seems to increase new voter costs (Republicans, 1994); in others the reverse is apparent (Democrats, 1992 and 1994). We speculate that this difference has several possible sources. First, the low salience of state legislative offices may limit the ability of these incumbents to create a very substantial personal vote despite resource similarities. Alternatively, the difference may be aberrant; after all, not every data point exactly fits a pattern. Replications in other legislatures, especially if the design contrasts bod-

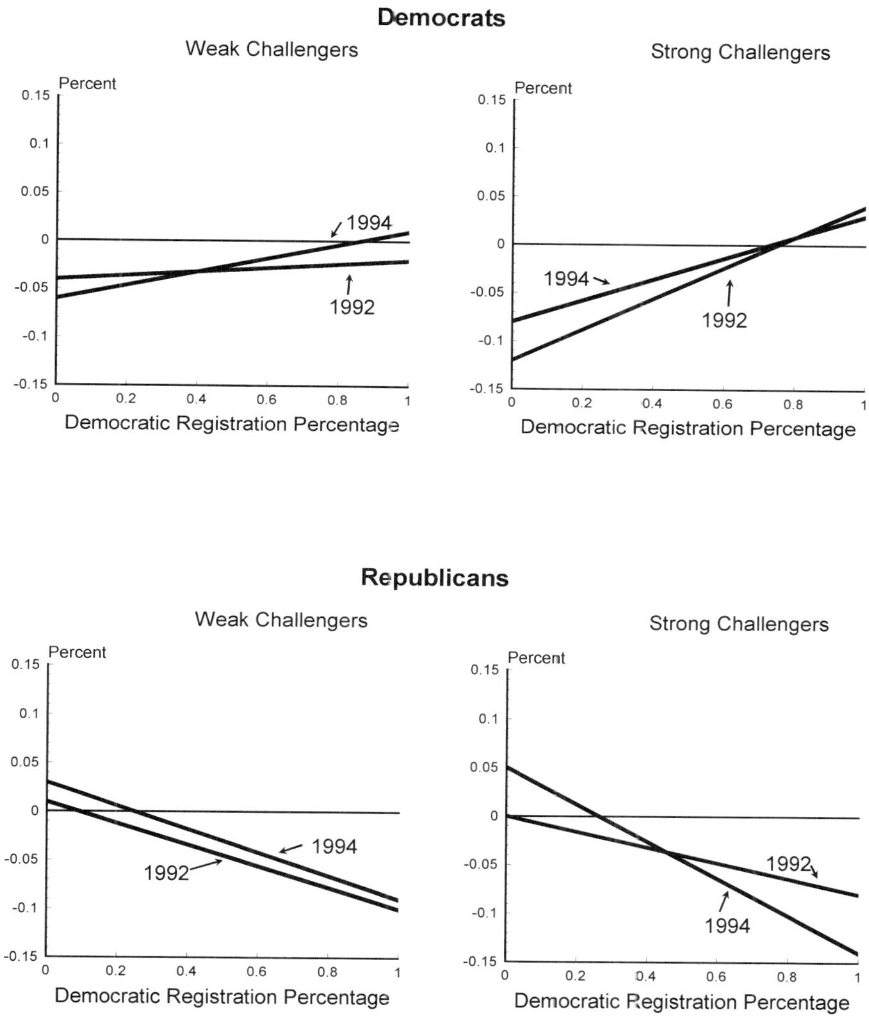

Figure 3.9. Competition and the Personal Vote: Congressional Elections of 1992 and 1994

ies that give members the resources that permit developing personal votes compared to those that do not, may smooth out the pattern. Finally, assuming the pattern is general, we may be observing differences that may be peculiar to short-term California politics, e.g., the end of a strong Speaker era in California politics. Some elaboration and replication of this study in more states—not just at the congressional level—will further our understanding of incumbency.

CONCLUSION

In this chapter we formulated and tested a model of the personal vote costs of redistricting. Not unexpectedly, we observed significant vote costs to redistricting. The inevitable boundary shuffles associated with redistricting means that incumbent legislators often face significant numbers of new voters after redistricting. Our analysis demonstrates that legislators lose part of their incumbency advantage, and expected vote share, among these new voters.

But more importantly, we demonstrated that the existing "bonus model" of incumbency should be reformulated. Incumbents facing new voters don't simply lose the stable 6 or 7 percent bonus that incumbency provides because incumbency is not a bonus. Rather, incumbency is an anchor that stabilizes the votes of the less partisan. When redistricting cuts these voters loose from their old representative, their behavior depends on their underlying partisanship, the saliency of the election, and short-term political tides. Our analysis has shown that the interaction of these factors can produce a personal vote advantage as large as 15 points or none at all. The average seven-point incumbency advantage is an average, and not a bonus on which incumbents can depend.

APPENDIX 3.1: NOTES ON THE DATA

For the California study, we used block-level electoral and census figures for the November elections of 1990, 1992, and 1994. For each census block, the votes cast for national and state elections and voter referendums, registration figures for all political parties, and basic census demographics are reported. There are over four hundred thousand census blocks in the State of California, each with an average population of about one hundred.

The data are compiled by the Institute for Governmental Studies at the University of California, Berkeley. They collect precinct-level electoral returns and registration figures statewide. There are approximately forty thousand voting precincts and thirty thousand electoral precincts in the state; hence there are approximately ten census blocks per precinct. The precinct-level registration and voting data is tied to census blocks by geocoding registered voters according to their addresses in the Statement of Registration.

We compiled the data from the Southern states by matching TIGER digital map files into Census tapes to precisely identify which census blocks had been moved from one incumbent's district to another's from 1990 to 1992. The TIGER files included a variable for each census block that identified both the 102nd (1990) and 103rd (1992) congressional district of the block. We matched the TIGER files to census population data, then aggregated the population values in new and old blocks up to the district level to calculate the percentage "new" and "old."

APPENDIX

Table 3.2. Fixed-Effects Models of Democratic Vote Share Congressional and Assembly Elections, 1990 to 1994

		Congress		*Assembly*	
		Coefficient	*SE*	*Coefficient*	*SE*
Baseline Vote Variables					
Democratic Reg.	1990	0.81	0.01	0.80	0.01
	1992	0.57	0.00	0.57	0.00
	1994	0.52	0.00	0.54	0.00
*Incumb*Dem. Reg.*					
Republicans	1990	0.18	0.01	0.10	0.01
	1992	0.10	0.00	0.08	0.00
	1994	0.14	0.00	0.17	0.01
Democrats	1990	−0.02	0.01	−0.11	0.01
	1992	−0.05	0.00	−0.05	0.00
	1994	0.03	0.00	0.08	0.00
New Voters Effects					
*Incumb*New Voter*	1992	0.01	0.00	0.01	0.00
Republicans	1994	0.04	0.00	0.02	0.00
Democrats	1992	−0.09	0.00	−0.03	0.00
	1994	−0.07	0.00	−0.01	0.00
*Incumb*New Voter* Dem. Reg*					
Republicans	1992	−0.10	0.01	−0.08	0.01
	1994	−0.16	0.01	−0.08	0.01
Democrats	1992	0.09	0.00	0.01	0.00
	1994	0.10	0.00	−0.03	0.01
R^2		0.79		0.80	
N		734,250		717,842	

Competition and Predicted New Voter Costs Fixed-Effects Models of Democratic Vote Share Congressional and Assembly Elections, 1990 to 1994

		Congress Coefficient	Congress SE	Assembly Coefficient	Assembly SE
Baseline Vote Variables					
Democratic Reg.	1990	0.81	0.01	0.80	0.01
	1992	0.57	0.00	0.57	0.00
	1994	0.52	0.00	0.54	0.00
*Incumb*Dem. Reg.*					
Republicans	1990	0.18	0.01	0.10	0.01
	1992	0.12	0.00	0.12	0.01
	1994	0.18	0.01	0.17	0.01
Democrats	1990	−0.02	0.01	−0.11	0.01
	1992	−0.05	0.00	−0.08	0.00
	1994	0.04	0.00	0.10	0.01

(continued)

Table 3.2. (continued)

		Congress		Assembly	
		Coefficient	*SE*	*Coefficient*	*SE*
*Incumb*Dem Voters* Challenger Qual*					
Republicans	1992	−0.10	0.01	−0.24	0.02
	1994	−0.14	0.02	−0.20	0.14
Democrats	1992	0.00	0.01	0.10	0.01
	1994	−0.04	0.00	−0.22	0.02
New Voters Effects					
*Incumb*New Voter*					
Republicans	1992	0.01	0.00	0.05	0.00
	1994	0.03	0.00	0.02	0.00
Democrats	1992	−0.03	0.00	−0.07	0.00
	1994	−0.06	0.00	−0.03	0.00
*Incumb*New Voter* Challenger Qual.*					
Republicans	1992	−0.04	0.01	−0.25	0.01
	1994	0.05	0.01	−0.05	0.08
Democrats	1992	−0.23	0.01	0.13	0.01
	1994	−0.04	0.00	0.25	0.02
*Incumb*New Voter* Dem. Reg.*					
Republicans	1992	−0.11	0.01	−0.16	0.01
	1994	−0.11	0.01	−0.07	0.01
Democrats	1992	0.00	0.01	0.07	0.00
	1994	0.07	0.00	0.01	0.01
*Incumb*New Voter* Challenger Qual.* Dem. Reg.*					
Republicans	1992	0.08	0.02	0.50	0.03
	1994	−0.20	0.03	−0.12	0.19
Democrats	1992	0.41	0.02	−0.16	0.01
	1994	0.09	0.01	−0.45	0.03
R^2		0.79		0.80	
N		734,250		717,842	

NOTES

1. This chapter is a revision and reassessment of three previous articles: John R. Petrocik and Scott W. Desposato, "The Partisan Consequences of Majority-Minority Districting, 1992–1994." *Journal of Politics* 60 (August, 1998): 613–33; Scott W. Desposato and John R. Petrocik, "The Variable Incumbency Advantage: New Voters, Redistricting, and the Personal Vote," *American Journal of Political Science* 47, no.1

(January, 2003): 18–32; and John R. Petrocik and Scott W. Desposato, "Incumbency and Short-Term Influences on Voters," *Political Research Quarterly* 57, no. 3 (September, 2004): 363–73.

2. See extended commentary: Kousser, Morgan J., "Estimating the Partisan Consequences of Redistricting Plans, Simply," *Legislative Studies Quarterly* 21, no. 4 (1996): 521–41.

3. Usually redistricting is less optimal for the majority than this textbook description implies. Because the smaller party can affect this process only at the margin, the decennial districting drama is typically bipartisan by its conclusion: minority party incumbents accept a safe seats for themselves as compensation for acquiescing to a small number of seats for their party.

4. See Ansolabehere, Snyder, and Stewart (2000), for an extended discussion of the methods for measuring and estimates of the incumbency advantage and personal vote.

5. The percentages in the figure are the fraction of the reported vote that is composed of Democrats who voted for the Democratic candidates and Republican identifiers who reported a vote for a Republicans candidate. Democrats and Republicans who defected and all independents sum to the proportion that provides the nonparty vote. See also Petrocik (1989) and Bartells (2000).

6. Jacobson, Gary C. and Samuel Kernell. *Strategy and Choice in Congressional Elections* (New Haven: Yale University Press, 1996).

7. However, this could interact with party identification.

8. For classical statements see: Cain, Bruce, John Ferejohn, and Morris Fiorina. *The Personal Vote* (Cambridge: Harvard University Press, 1987). Fiorina, Morris. *Congress, Keystone of the Washington Establishment* (New Haven: Yale University Press, 1989). Yiannakis, Diana E. "The Grateful Electorate: Casework and Congressional Elections," *American Journal of Political Science* 25 (1981): 568–80.

9. Saliency has several dimension. The two that are relevant here are how many voters are aware of the candidates and whether they become linked to the issues in the contest. Both dimensions are in play in the typical Senate race. Voters are less likely to know the candidates in House and state assembly elections and consciously use contemporary issues to differentiate them. The average state legislative race is below the campaign radar of most voters.

10. Incumbents facing new voters still have some incumbency tools at their disposal including institutional privileges, better financing on average, and the prestige and publicity that come with being a member of the United States Congress. After redistricting, incumbents only lose their personal vote advantage—not the other components of incumbency.

11. The normal vote provides an out-of-sample estimate of the effect of partisanship that is not confounded by the correlation between party ID and the vote that is a function of the short-term forces of the election. These values are a reformulation of the original concept articulated by Converse (1966). See Petrocik, John R. "An Expected Party Vote: New Data for an Old Concept," *American Journal of Political Science* 33, no. 1 (1989): 44–66.

12. This section is drawn from Petrocik and Desposato (1998).

13. These averages don't fully capture the party disparity. Almost 40 percent of Democrat incumbents had districts with less than 10 percent new constituents. Of

that fraction, 70 percent (28 percent of the total) had fewer than 5 percent new voters. By contrast, almost half (48 percent) of the Republicans received districts in which 30 percent or more of their constituents were new; most of that group (34 percent of the total) were given districts in which more than half of their constituents were new to them.

14. This proposition has a long history, see, for an example: Brace, Kimball, Bernard Grofman, and Lisa Handley. "Does Redistricting Aimed to Help Blacks Necessarily Help Republicans?" *Journal of Politics* 49 (February 1987): 143–56. Banducci, Susan A., and Jeffrey A. Karp. "Electoral Consequences of Scandal and Redistricting in the 1992 House election," *American Politics Quarterly* 22 (January 1994): 3–26. Hill, Kevin A. "Does the Creation of Majority Black Districts Aid Representation? An Analysis of the 1992 Congressional Elections in Eight Southern States," *Journal of Politics* 57 (May 1995): 384–401. Lublin, 1995a, 1995b.

15. The new voters were made all the more significant by the shifting partisanship of Southern whites. Incumbency had provided a large bonus that the short-term GOP tide and new voters stripped away. See Petrocik and Desposato (1998).

16. Appendix 1 in Petrocik, John R. and Scott W. Desposato. "The Partisan Consequences of Majority-Minority Redistricting in the South, 1992 and 1994," *Journal of Politics* (1998).

17. On the far left side of the graph, the "No STF" line meets the mean vote in 1990 reflecting the probability that an incumbent with an unchanged electorate should do equally well in two elections occurring in similar political environments.

18. One could even argue, as does Zaller (1998) that there is no incumbency advantage. He proposes a "prizefighter" model of political competition that is sufficient to explain the observed incumbency advantage observed both in election returns and in survey data. He argues that elections are battles of skill between candidates, and uses simulations to produce an apparent incumbency advantage where there is none. His formulation ignores that underlying partisanship of districts that "eliminates" the prospects of challengers in most districts. We doubt its validity, but the general point is worth noting—the vote share that is estimated as an incumbent advantage has many nonindependent—endogenous—qualities.

19. The data are compiled by the Institute for Governmental Studies at the University of California, Berkeley. IGS collects precinct-level electoral returns and registration figures statewide. The precinct-level registration and voting data is tied to census blocks by geocoding registered voters according to their addresses in the Statement of Registration. See McCue, 1994, for more details.

20. The district-year fixed effects (discussed below) preclude the inclusion of a simple dummy variable for party-incumbency status.

21. We also tried to estimate a nonlinear model, specifically an extended-beta binomial model (see Palmquist, 1998). But after twelve hours working on a dataset of approximately 800,000 observations, the estimation routine had not yet completed its first iteration. As an alternative, we also tried a simple logit transformation of the original data. This is not entirely appropriate, since the data reaches its natural bounds of 0 and 1, but the results of this crude proxy to a better nonlinear model concur with the linear model's conclusions.

22. Rush, Mark E. *Does Redistricting Make a Difference? Partisan Representation and Electoral Behavior* (Baltimore: Johns Hopkins University Press, 1993).

23. Banducci, Susan A., and Jeffrey A. Karp, "Electoral Consequences of Scandal and Redistricting in the 1992 House Election." *American Politics Quarterly* 22 (January 1994): 3–26.

24. Petrocik, John R. and Scott W. Desposato. "The Partisan Consequences of Majority-Minority Redistricting in the South, 1992 and 1994," *Journal of Politics* (1998).

25. Ansolabehere, Stephen, James M. Snyder, Jr., and Charles Stewart, III. "Old Voters, New Voters, and the Personal Vote: Using Redistricting to Measure the Incumbency Advantage," *American Journal of Political Science* 44 (2000): 17–34.

26. Their approach leaves out urban areas—where a substantial share of the districts is located—because district lines rarely correspond to county boundaries. This analysis includes urban and rural areas, precluding any bias that might arise because of urban-rural differences. Although our data are specific to California and the patterns may not generalize to the nation, we think that they probably are representative and we cannot offer a reason for believing they are different given the "professionalized" politics of California's national and state-level politicians.

27. Although new and old voters could be in the same media market, that may not help awareness. Urban media with multiple elections rarely provide much coverage to legislative candidates while local media may have very narrow readership markets. From the Gallegly example, Simi Valley and Santa Paula, though close, are served by different local newspapers.

28. The 0 to 100 percent range in the figures is correct. Many of the neighborhood (census block) units of analysis are homogeneously Democratic or Republican. Although proportionately few, there are several thousand cases at the limit of the range.

29. Zaller, John R. "Politicians as Prize Fighters: Electoral Selection and Incumbency Advantage," in *Party Politics and Politicians*, ed. John Geer. (Baltimore: Johns Hopkins University Press, 1998), 128–85.

30. We use money to index competition because the ability to raise funds is usually the best index of competitiveness. Although prior political experience makes a candidate an effective campaigner for reasons other than fundraising prowess, money measures most of what prior office experience captures with regard to the strength of a candidate's campaign.

31. A weak challenger district is one where a challenger spent just 5 percent of the incumbent's total spending. More than half of all challengers in 1992 and 1994 spent significantly less than this. Strong challenger districts are those where challenger spending was 40 percent of incumbent spending. About 80 percent of House incumbents and 90 percent of assembly incumbents faced challengers that were much weaker than this.

4

District Geography and Voters

Richard N. Engstrom

In the 1990 round of congressional redistricting many state legislatures created electoral districts that critics labeled as "bizarre." These districts, and the critical attention they received, brought questions about district geography to the forefront of the redistricting debate. Several commentators have argued that state legislatures should abide by what they term "traditional districting principles." Those principles dictate that electoral districts respect the preexisting political landscape, and that districts be geographically compact and contiguous.[1]

Many redistricting plans adopted in the 1990s disregarded the stipulations that districts be compact and respect preexisting political boundaries, and several scholars have been critical of the practice of drawing these geographically irregular districts. Ely, for example, points out that residents will be aware of the results built into the strangely shaped district and will find that "the selfactualizing power of the franchise is significantly reduced" when the process looks tainted and manipulated.[2] Thernstrom and O'Conner in the *Shaw* opinion also express concern that irregular districts can marginalize voters and send an undesirable message to constituents about the value and impact of their participation.[3] Grofman has described an electoral district that winds and sprawls in unpredictable ways as "cognitively demanding," and therefore a hindrance to citizen participation in the political life of the district.[4] These critics of modern districting practices imply that district geography can impact the incentives that district residents have to participate in the district's politics.

A few empirical investigations of congressional districts have shed some light on the relationship between district geography and voters. Campbell,

Alford, and Henry determine that when congressional districts and media markets share populations, citizens are better able to recognize and recall House candidates' names.[5] Niemi, Powell, and Bicknell construct a measure of the extent to which cities contain one, two to three, or four or more congressional districts and find that recall and recognition is related to district-city congruence.[6] In an earlier study, I investigated the effect of district compactness on participation and found that compactness is positively related to citizen voting in congressional elections.[7]

These studies demonstrate that how districts are placed in their environments can affect citizens. Yet the two studies focusing on district conformity with existing boundaries limit their attention to how district characteristics affect citizen familiarity with candidate names. While this is important, it ignores an issue that is prominent in the debate over redistricting among academics and in the courts: how district characteristics impact the incentives for citizen participation. We still do not know the extent to which district conformity to important boundaries can encourage or discourage citizens from participating in electoral politics. Also, revisiting the question of district conformity using more recent data is appropriate given that the state of electoral district geography has changed so dramatically in recent years. Districts today wind across the landscape in ways that were not imagined in the 1970s (when the districts investigated in the above studies were in place), and it is this state of affairs that has led to the recent controversies over district boundaries. My earlier (2000) compactness study does investigate how district geography relates to citizen voting, and makes use of data from more recent congressional districts, but investigates neither the mechanisms through which district geography might impact voters, nor the effects of other aspects of traditional districting principles (such as congruity with existing boundaries).

In short, social science has brought little empirical evidence to bear on the question of the relationship between electoral district boundaries and citizen participation. To the question "is citizen engagement in the political process facilitated by the application of traditional districting principles?" we have much speculation, but little real evidence. This study is designed to address that question.

In this paper, I integrate geographic measures of recent district boundaries into models of voter participation to create tests of the relationships between electoral district characteristics and citizens. This approach directly addresses the question of whether or not geographic characteristics of electoral districts have the consequences posited in discussions of contemporary majority-minority districting practices. In particular, it provides a means for testing assertions about relationships between districting arrangements and citizen participation.

ELECTORAL DISTRICTS AND VOTERS

Understanding the impact of electoral district boundaries on citizens requires that we analyze the relationship between citizens' context and their behavior. District shape is an example of what Books and Prysby call a "global" context (that is, a measurement of the nature of the environment itself, rather than an aggregation of individual-level features or behaviors).[8] The mechanism through which global and other categories of context can affect individual-level political behavior lies in its ability to impact the environment in ways that affect the information to which citizens are exposed, as well as the opportunities that citizens have to find people with whom they can exchange information about the decisions they face on election day.

Geographic characteristics at issue in the debate over traditional districting principles can influence the information environment of citizens of electoral districts. In the case of a district's degree of compactness, not knowing where a district takes an unexpected right turn means not knowing who in the immediate area is, and is not, in the district. This confusion about district boundaries can lead to confusion about which legislative race to pay attention to and who among one's neighbors is also in the relevant district. By keeping an electoral district compact, boundary confusion is minimized and citizens are better able to focus on the correct political information and find other constituents with whom to discuss the district's politics. This leads to hypothesis one:

H_1: More compact districts will be associated with higher voter turnout.

Similarly, district conformity with other boundaries is also an important element of a district's geography that might change the information environment for citizens. Fenno observes that "members of Congress thrive where some sense of community already exists."[9] When districts fragment preexisting boundaries, it is more difficult to take advantage of the community's potential as an information pathway. When districts conform to preexisting boundaries, political information is easier to come by, making participation easier for citizens. Thus, a second hypothesis:

H_2: Districts with a higher degree of conformity to preexisting political boundaries will be associated with higher voter turnout.

District geography can conform not only to community boundaries, but also to areas that contain shared sources of political information. Citizens get a great deal of their political information from media sources, particularly local media sources.[10] Nielsen Media Research compiles information on the local television viewing habits of Americans and groups them into "Designated Market Areas"—commonly called media markets. Media markets are composed of counties with populations that rely on the same local media outlets. We can expect a district's relationship with a region's local media markets to have an effect on political participation. Districts that conform to media markets should simplify information acquisition in districts, which in turn should improve participation. This leads to a third hypothesis:

> H_3: *Districts with a higher degree of conformity to media market boundaries will be associated with higher voter turnout.*

METHODS

Measurement

The assertions I make about the impact of district geography on citizens focus on two particular geographic characteristics: compactness and congruity. The first is a statement about an area's shape, and the second is a statement about the relationship between the district boundaries and other boundaries in the environment. These two concepts require different approaches to measurement.

Compactness

Measures of compactness are based on the approach of comparing the shape under investigation to that shape which is perfectly compact: a circle. A circle has unique features that justify its use as a compactness standard. Most importantly, a circle minimizes the distances between points within its perimeter. In the context of electoral districts, it can be said that the more compact (or "circle like") a district, the closer the far-flung parts of the district are to the other points in the district. It is important to note that it is not feasible to demand perfectly compact districts. Simple geometry would not allow a state to create a district plan made up of circular districts without leaving empty spaces of state land out of the plan. Nonetheless, using a compactness measure will allow us to measure the extent to which a district is irregular (one simply has to accept that all districts are irregular to some degree). For the purposes of this study, I will use a standard[11] perimeter-based measure of the geographic compactness of electoral districts:

Compactness = district X's area / area of a circle with the same perimeter as X

Congruity

Measuring how congruous a shape is with other shapes in its environment is not particularly straightforward. The goal is to find a measure that produces high scores when sets of boundaries overlap. District boundaries that are perfectly congruous with county boundaries would share those boundaries perfectly. When boundaries are not shared, a degree of incongruity exists. The congruity measure must account for the fact that the degree of incongruity between two sets of boundaries can be affected by at least two things: a district falling entirely within another set of boundaries and not touching those boundaries, and a district and another set of boundaries crossing one another.

Unfortunately, the empirical literature on redistricting has largely neglected the question of how to measure the extent to which district boundaries geographically conform to other preexisting boundaries, despite the concept's importance in theoretical discussions of districting issues. The congruity measure presented in this study draws insight from a measure developed by Campbell, Alford, and Henry.[12] The Campbell et al. measure focuses on population characteristics of congressional districts rather than geographic characteristics. Yet the procedure they use to establish how each county population in a media market overlaps the district population is a very sophisticated general approach to determining congruence. I have adapted their approach to measuring population overlap to develop an appropriate measure of geographic congruity.

The measure I develop identifies the extent to which congressional district and county boundaries overlap. Though my intention at this point is to describe the measurement of congruity in general, some readers may wonder if district-county congruity is a good measure of how well districts conform to preexisting political communities. City boundaries exist as an attractive alternative, for example. I use a measure of district-county congruity for several reasons. First, county boundaries are easier to locate at a resolution and in a form useful in an analysis of geography (particularly in a national study). Second, unlike county boundaries, municipal boundaries often change from year to year as new developments are annexed. Those changes complicate not only the analysis, but also the idea that many cities' boundaries are "preexisting" in a realistic sense. Also, counties have been, and continue to be, used as guides for electoral districts. Counties have local governments, representatives, and the other trappings of a political community, and are thus definitely preexisting communities of interest when a redistricting plan is being crafted in the legislature. The fact that district-county congruity scores are relatively high (reported below) also lends credence to the idea that counties are preexisting political communities that play an important role in the redistricting process.

Determining district-county congruity requires two approaches. When one district is entirely contained within a county, the measurement of congruity between district and county is simple: district area is divided by county area.

$$\textit{Congruity}_1\text{: area of district/area of county}$$

The resulting quotient will report the proportion of the county covered by the district. The higher the congruity score, the closer the two sets of boundaries approach congruity. When district and county boundaries align perfectly, this procedure will report a congruity score of 1.

When a district extends into two or more counties the measure must be calculated differently. In this case, the following calculation is performed:

Congruity$_2$:

$$\frac{\sum \left(\frac{C \cap D_{1\ldots n}}{C_{1\ldots n}} * C \cap D_{1\ldots n} \right)}{D}$$

$C \cap D$ = Areas of county–district intersections
C = Areas of counties
D = District area

This procedure calculates the area of intersection between each district segment and its relevant county, and determines the proportion of the county that each intersection occupies. It then weights these individual values according to the areas of the intersected portions of the districts. The sum of these values is then divided by the district area. This produces an overall score that has the same properties as the simpler index calculated when a district is entirely contained within a county.[13] A district with a boundary that is perfectly aligned with a set of counties produces a congruity score of 1.

I apply this new geographic congruity measure to two relationships. To measure the extent to which district boundaries conform to preexisting political boundaries, I measure the degree of conformity between electoral districts and county boundaries. To measure the extent to which district boundaries conform to areas that share media outlets, I measure the degree of conformity between electoral districts and media market boundaries.

Data

Using MapInfo Geographic Information System software, digital maps of the electoral districts used in the 1994, 1996, and 1998 congressional elections were overlaid with county and media market maps. These separate maps include all changes to districts that occurred between each election. A program written in MapBasic (MapInfo's programming language) was then run on the maps to measure (as outlined above) the degree to which the districts are compact and the extent to which they conform to county and media market boundaries.

Measures used to assess citizens' attitudes and behaviors in districts with varying geographic characteristics are taken from the 1994, 1996, and 1998 National Election Studies. These include reported *Turnout*, simply the reported turnout of NES survey respondents,[14] and a set of control variables. The control variables serve to account for many known influences on turnout that can exist at various levels in different electoral districts. By controlling for these variables' influence on voting, we can determine the independent effect the variables of interest have on the dependent variable. The control variables can be divided into two categories: individual-level influences and district-level influences. Variables describing individual-level characteristics such as *Income*, *Age*, *Education*, *Race*, *Gender*, and the *Strength of respondents' party affiliation* are standard control variables commonly used in models of voter behavior. District-level variables describing the competitive nature of the election in each district include whether or not the district's *House seat is open*, if a candidate is *Unopposed*, the amount of *Campaign Spending* in the congressional race, and the balance of campaign spending between the challenger and the incumbent (*Spending Difference*), and are taken from the *Almanac of American Politics*.[15] Finally, the variables of interest: district *Compactness*, *Conformity to county boundaries*, and *Conformity to media market boundaries* are merged to NES respondent data. The resulting dataset includes each respondent's individual-level data as well as variables describing characteristics of each respondent's electoral district. These data are used to estimate the relationship between district geography and citizen voting behavior.

RESULTS

Compactness

The first hypothesis is that district compactness is related to citizen voting behavior. The compactness measure in this data set ranges between a minimum score of .01 and a maximum score of .77. North Carolina's 3rd congressional district has a score of .01, and as figure 4.1 shows, it is remarkably noncompact (which is not surprising given how the district winds around itself and sprawls outward, with portions of the district extending away from its geographic center). The state of Wyoming, on the other hand, has a compactness score of .77 (indicating that Wyoming's regular, nonsprawling features make it

North Carolina's 3rd Congressional District

Wyoming

Figure 4.1. Geographic Compactness

the most compact congressional district in the nation, though it isn't circular enough to warrant a perfect compactness score); Figure 4.1 shows that this congressional district cannot be said to sprawl or wind around in an irregular shape. The districts associated with the respondents in the National Election Study between 1994 and 1998 have an average compactness score of .2580 and a standard deviation of .1305.

The question is: are these varying degrees of compactness related to differences in turnout behavior? The first column of table 4.1 presents the results of a model of voter turnout. Once factors such as income, age, party strength, and the competitive conditions in the districts' elections are accounted for in a logistic regression analysis, we find that compactness exhibits a random relationship with voter turnout. The control variables in this model behave as would be expected. For example, a well-known positive and significant relationship exists between voting and income; that is,

Table 4.1. Electoral District Geographic Characteristics and Voting

	Model 1 *Compactness*	*Model 2* *Conformity*	*Model 3* *Media*	*Model 4* *Full*
Income	.0517**	.0516**	.0528**	.0524**
	(.0063)	(.0063)	(.0063)	(.0063)
Education	.2372**	.2374**	.2394**	.2371**
	(.0165)	(.0166)	(.0166)	(.0166)
Age	.0428**	.0429**	.0430**	.0428**
	(.0024)	(.0024)	(.0024)	(.0024)
African American	.2011*	.1843	.2042*	.2062*
	(.1205)	(.1203)	(.1201)	(.1209)
Female	−.0616	−.0625	−.0619	−.0607
	(.0752)	(.0751)	(.0752)	(.0752)
Party Strength	.0069	.0066	.0063	.0071
	(.0189)	(.0189)	(.0189)	(.0189)
Party Contact	1.1457**	1.1493**	1.1512**	1.1523**
	(.0970)	(.0969)	(.0970)	(.0971)
Open Seat	−.0533	−.0570	−.0432	−.0280
	(.1233)	(.1232)	(.1233)	(.1238)
Unopposed	−.3938*	−.4150**	−.4180*	−.3899**
	(.1132)	(.1122)	(.1122)	(.1137)
Campaign Spending	.0019	.0029	.0015	.0019
	(.0072)	(.0072)	(.0072)	(.0073)
Spending Difference	.0024	.0012	.0047	.0062
	(.0124)	(.0124)	(.0125)	(.0125)
Compact	.3784			.3446
	(.2947)			(.3003)
County Conformity		.0056		−.2458
		(.1253)		(.1545)
Media Market Conformity			.4827**	.6975**
			(.2250)	(.2766)
Constant	−5.5779**	−5.4878**	−5.6336**	−5.5608**
	(.2946)	(.3069)	(.2940)	(.3126)
N	4098	4098	4098	4098
Chi square	1002.057	1000.405	1005.038	1008.506
	(.0000)	(.0000)	(.0000)	(.0000)
% Predicted Correctly	72.45%	72.25%	72.35%	72.25%
% Reduction of Error	13.75%	13.44%	13.58%	13.44%

*P < .10 **P < .05

people with higher incomes tend to vote more often. The fact that the income variable is positive and significant in this model reiterates that relationship. Though the variable of interest in this analysis, compactness, is positively related to voter turnout, it is not statistically significant in the model. Therefore, we cannot be confident that the relationship between voting and district compactness is anything more than random. The model does not support the argument that district compactness systematically impacts voter turnout.

Compactness, the geographic characteristic that has so concerned scholars and political commentators, does not seem to discourage citizens from participating in the political process. Noncompact districts, in this analysis, do not lead to discouraged, nonparticipatory citizens. Because compactness is not significantly related to voter turnout, it is difficult to conclude that district compactness has the kinds of real-world effects often alleged in discussions of redistricting practices.

Conformity with County Boundaries

The second hypothesis is that the extent to which electoral district boundaries conform to existing county boundaries will be related to citizen turnout. Citizen participation in elections should be easier in districts with boundaries that conform to county boundaries, and we should find higher levels of citizen participation in districts with high levels of district-county congruity. Using a measure of district congruity that indicates the extent of the district-county overlap, I test to determine if district conformity with existing boundaries is related to voter turnout.

The measure of district conformity with counties in this data set ranges between scores of .01 and 1 in districts associated with NES respondents. California's 32nd congressional district has a score of .01, and as figure 4.2 shows, its boundaries have very little relationship with county boundaries. Iowa's district 3 follows county lines perfectly, and thus has a conformity score of 1. The districts in the data set have an average county conformity score of .7210 and a standard deviation of .3059.

As the high average conformity score indicates, most districts conform remarkably well to county boundaries. It is obvious that those who draw district boundaries commonly use county lines as a guide. Nevertheless, the data in the analysis does show that congressional districts vary quite a bit in the degree to which they conform to county boundaries. Are these varying degrees of conformity systematically related to turnout?

Column 2 of table 4.1 shows that district conformity to county boundaries is not systematically related to voter turnout. Once we account for many of the variables that are related to turnout, we find that people who live in districts with a greater degree of conformity to county boundaries are no more

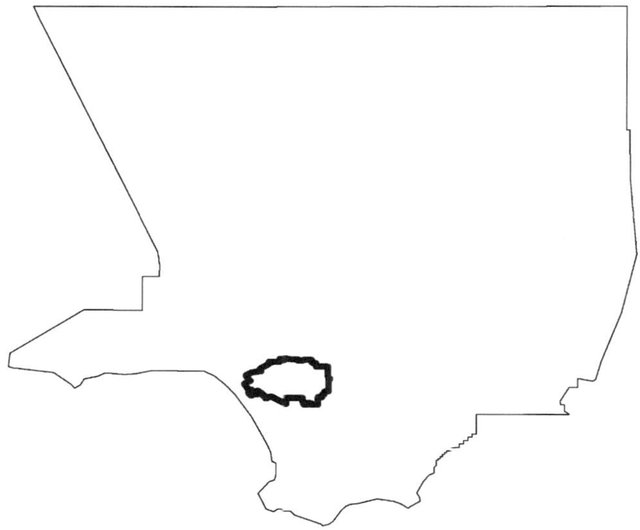

California's 32nd Congressional District in Los Angeles County

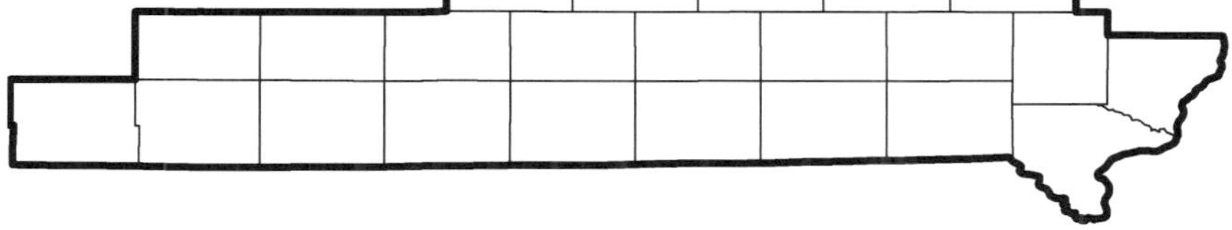

Iowa's 3rd Congressional District and Its Constituent Counties

Figure 4.2. District-County Congruity (district lines in bold)

likely to turn out to vote than are those in districts with a lesser degree of conformity to county boundaries. This does not support the assertion that citizens are demonstrably harmed when electoral districts fail to conform to existing political boundaries, at least when existing political boundaries are defined as counties.

Conformity with Media-Market Boundaries

Geographic communities of interest may refer to areas with a shared political identity, but there is more to a community than identity. Some geographic areas share sources of information. The geographic layout of these areas that share media sources can also impact if and how people participate. The third hypothesis I test is that district conformity to media market boundaries is related to citizen turnout. It is predicted that there will be higher levels of voter turnout in districts that conform to media-market boundaries. The measure of district conformity with media markets ranges between scores of .01 and .94. New Jersey's 10th congressional district has a score of .01, and as figure 4.3

New Jersey's 10th Congressional District in Its Media Market

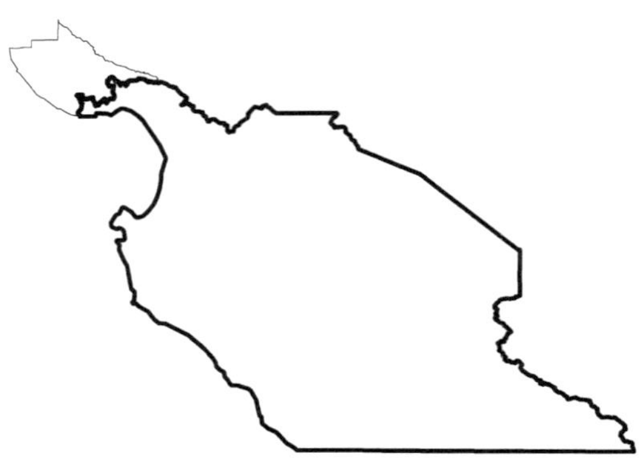

California's 17th Congressional District in its Media Market

Figure 4.3. District-Media Market Congruity (district lines in bold)

shows, its boundaries have very little relationship with media-market boundaries. No congressional district in the data set maps perfectly onto a media market; however California's 17th congressional district follows media market lines remarkably accurately, with the exception of a small area in the north where the media market extends outside of the district. This district thus has an understandably high conformity score of .94. The districts in the data set have an average media-market conformity score of .2047 and a standard deviation of .1704. Do varying degrees of media-market conformity significantly correlate with turnout?

Column 3 of table 4.1 shows that, as predicted, district conformity to media-market boundaries is systematically related to voter turnout. Accounting for other factors that influence turnout, we find that people who live in districts with greater levels of conformity to media markets are more likely to turn out to vote than those in districts with lower levels of conformity to media-market boundaries.

In sum, district geography is systematically related to citizen voting behavior, though it is interesting that compactness and conformity to existing political boundaries do not play the central roles one might expect given their prominence in the literature. What seems to matter is the extent to which districts map onto media-market boundaries.

Full Model

For purposes of comparison, I run a final, complete model of the relationship between district geography and citizen voting tendencies. This model includes all three geographic variables investigated in this project: district compactness, district conformity to county boundaries, and district conformity to media-market boundaries. The model, presented in the fourth column of table 4.1, verifies the conclusions above. Compactness and county congruity are not systematically related to citizen voting behavior. The coefficient for county congruity is actually in the wrong direction in this model, further indicating that political boundaries are not as essential to participation as might otherwise be argued. Media-market congruity, on the other hand, is properly signed, and significantly related to voter turnout.[16]

How Does Media-Market Conformity Matter?

As noted by Books and Prysby, contextual variables and their behavioral consequences are appropriately explained using intervening variables.[17] What is the mechanism through which these differences in district-media market relationships translate into differences in voter behavior? District geography can create difficulties in obtaining information about the candidates and the election. When information is difficult to find, we expect the increased information costs to result in lessened attentiveness to the campaign. One might expect, then, that variations in district-media market conformity might affect how much information individuals have received about the campaign. The name of the campaigns' candidates is an essential piece of information campaigns attempt to get out to potential voters. When district boundaries and media-market boundaries conform to one another, information is easier to gather and we can therefore expect citizens to be more informed about campaigns in high-conformity districts than they are in low-conformity districts. We might expect, then, that if district-media market conformity affects the information environment for citizens, then citizens' ability to recall candidates' names would be related to how well their electoral districts conform to media markets:

H_4: Districts with a higher degree of conformity to media market boundaries will be positively associated with citizens' ability to recall candidates' names.

Initial analysis of the relationship between candidate recall and the vote indicates that candidate recall is a significant predictor of whether or not citizens choose to vote, and thus is a potential intervening variable linking district-media market conformity and voting. As Table 4.2 shows, candidate recall is positively related to people's tendency to vote. If district-media market congruity is systematically related to citizen ability to recall candidate names, this explanation may account for the relationship between district-media market congruity and voting.

My expectation is that district-media market conformity will be positively related to citizens' ability to recall candidates' names. Table 4.3 shows that district-media market conformity is positively and significantly related to citizens' ability to accurately recall candidates' names. The more a district conforms to its media environment, the more likely it is that citizens are able to recall the names of candidates running for office in that district.

DISCUSSION

Figure 4.4 summarizes the overall findings from this analysis. District compactness is shown to have no relationship with citizens' tendency to vote. Despite numerous assertions among scholars and political observers, compactness does not seem to have significant consequences for citizen voting participation, contradicting many of the concerns in the redistricting literature. This finding contradicts my previous finding linking congressional district compactness and voter turnout in the 1994 congressional elections.[18] It

Table 4.2. Candidate Recall and Voting

Income	.0569**
	(.0120)
Education	.2559**
	(.0319)
Age	.0383**
	(.0048)
African American	.6693**
	(.2978)
Female	−.0244
	(.1441)
Party Strength	−.0162
	(.0341)
Party Contact	.9794**
	(.1718)
Open Seat	.2165
	(.2339)
Unopposed	−.1571
	(.2406)
Campaign Spending	−.0165
	(.0124)
Spending Difference	.0555**
	(.0252)
Candidate Recall	.4383**
	(.1551)
Constant	−5.2497**
	(.5854)
N	1649
Chi Square	225.961
	(.0000)
% Predicted Correctly	83.57%
% Reduction of Error	1.5%

is possible that the different time frame in this study is responsible for that difference. Citizen confusion and information levels affected by noncompact districts could well be time dependent. By incorporating election years later in the decade in this study, the data here may contain more cases where citizens are no longer confused by the election districts to which they have become more accustomed. It is also possible, of course, that the peculiarities of the 1994 election in general made that year a special case in terms of voter turnout. Nonetheless, this study finds no relationship between district compactness and citizen turnout.

Conformity to existing political boundaries (counties) is also found to be unrelated to voter behavior. People do not demonstrate a greater tendency to vote when their electoral districts conform to this other important political boundary in their environment. This geographic characteristic of electoral

Table 4.3. District-Media Market Congruity and Candidate Recall

Income	.0001
	(.0100)
Education	.0875**
	(.0244)
Age	.0017
	(.0035)
African American	−.5390**
	(.2107)
Female	−.3102**
	(.1114)
Party Strength	−.0257
	(.0259)
Party Contact	.2693**
	(.1180)
Open Seat	−.5665**
	(.1768)
Unopposed	−.3997**
	(.1821)
Campaign Spending	.0324**
	(.0109)
Spending Difference	−.0055
	(.0193)
Media Market Conformity	.6791**
	(.3276)
Constant	−.5436
	(.4402)
N	1686
Chi Square	78.019
	(.0000)
% Predicted Correctly	70.76%
% Reduction of Error	0%

districts fails to demonstrate the consequences for citizens assumed by many who argue for the value of traditional districting principles.

District conformity to media-market boundaries, however, proves to have important and systematic consequences for voter participation. The greater the district-media market conformity, the more likely citizens are to be informed about the candidates, and therefore the more likely citizens are to vote on election day.[19]

The substance of this relationship is demonstrated in table 4.4. In this table's first row, we can see the likelihood of a person voting when residing in districts with various levels of district-media market conformity. The probability of a person voting in a district with an average level of conformity to media markets is 60.3 percent. The table clearly shows that as a person

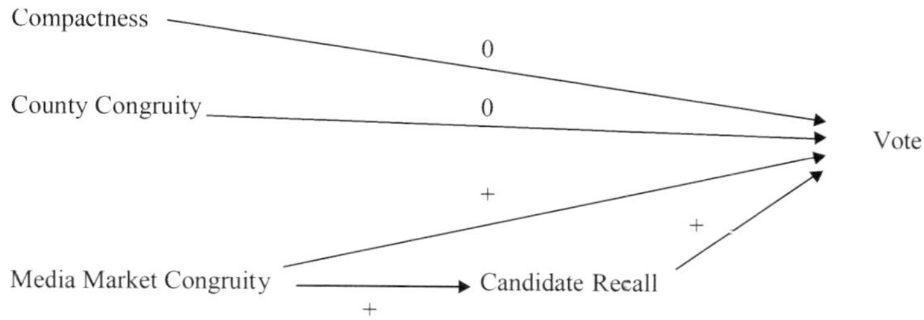

Figure 4.4. District Geography and Voting

moves from districts with low conformity scores to districts with high conformity scores, their associated probability of voting increases. For example, a person moving from a district that can be characterized as typical among nonconforming districts (one standard deviation below the mean), to one that displays typically high levels of conformity (one standard deviation above the mean) increases his or her probability of voting by 3.93 percent. Moving from a typically nonconforming district to one that is exceptionally conforming (two standard deviations above the mean) increases that person's chances of voting by over 5.5 percent.

Interestingly, the implications of this study for voting in districts that have been deemed "gerrymandered" by the court system are by no means straightforward. Several districts have bizarre boundaries, yet occupy relatively large portions of media markets and thus have correspondingly high district-media market conformity scores. Even districts that were thrown out by the Supreme Court as unconstitutional actually would not concern someone whose goal was to respect media market boundaries. A good example would be Texas's 18th district, which sprawled in a very irregular fashion, yet occupied a large share of the Houston media market. It had a district-media market conformity score of .26, several points above the overall average of .2. We would actually expect this "gerrymandered" district to have turnout levels that were enhanced by its geography, despite its irregularities. Nonetheless, in most cases districts ruled to be unconstitutional gerrymanders have low district-media market conformity scores. The famous North Carolina 12th, for example, has a conformity score of .01, as does New York's 12th ("Bullwinkle") district. Both would improve the likelihood of citizens' voting (by over 2 percent) if they were redrawn to conform to their respective media-market environments even to average levels.

Table 4.4. Probability of Voting and Knowing Candidates' Names at Various Levels of District-Media Market Congruity

	−2 s.d	*−1 s.d.*	*Mean*	*+1 s.d.*	*+2 s.d.*
Voting	.5630	.5832	.6030	.6225	.6416
Candidate Recall	.6191	.6459	.6791	.6969	.7208

As reported above, the reason for the relationship between district-media market congruity and voting seems to be that district-media market congruity has an impact on citizen information levels. Citizens in districts that conform to media-market boundaries are more likely to know the names of candidates running for office in their districts. The substantive interpretation of that finding is presented in the second row of table 4.4. Here we see that the likelihood of a respondent knowing the name of a candidate in his or her congressional race is 67.91 percent in districts with an average level of district-media market congruity. Those chances increase as district conformity to media-market boundaries increases, however. In fact, citizens in districts that are typically nonconforming to media markets (one standard deviation below the mean) are 5 percent less likely to know the names of candidates than those in districts that are typically conforming to media markets. The difference between the chances of a person in a typically nonconforming district and one in an exceptionally conforming district knowing the names of candidates is roughly 7.5 percent.

These findings reinforce previous research arguing that district-media market relationships play an important role in citizens' ability to gather information about candidates in congressional elections.[20] It extends these findings by demonstrating that such relationships have implications for both citizen information gathering and for voter participation. It also makes use of a measurement of geographic conformity that is more advanced than measures used in previous research. It challenges previous findings, based on a more limited set of data, linking district geographic compactness to voter turnout.[21] The findings in this project address the question of whether or not the drawing of electoral district lines can affect citizen political behavior. The answer is, yes it can.

Yet these findings show that the relationship between district geography and voters is more subtle than many believe. Compactness and conformity to existing political boundaries are not, perhaps, as essential to the healthy functioning of democracy as some claim. However, there are important and theoretically reasonable relationships between district geography and electoral behavior. Media markets, rarely discussed in analyses of redistricting questions, seem to play a role worthy of our attention. This finding blends nicely with others' who have "produced arguments that generally moved the contextual effects literature toward behavioral and informational interdependence as opposed to arguments rooted in shared social characteristics."[22] Electoral districts can usefully be thought of as more than a collection of individuals with particular racial and partisan profiles. District geography, and how it interacts with other aspects of the environment, has implications for important and basic political activities like information acquisition and voting.

Electoral district lines could have implications beyond citizens' decisions to vote. Cleaner district-media market relationships should make it easier for challengers to get their names out to potential voters, therefore increasing their chances of defeating incumbents. Limiting the number of fractional media market areas in a district could also make campaigning less costly. Though the location of media markets may not possibly be the main criteria for drawing electoral district boundaries (other factors, most notably population, would have to be considered first), it may be that those who draw electoral district lines would serve democracy well if they paid greater attention to where sources of information lie on the electoral district maps they construct.

NOTES

1. David Butler and Bruce Cain, *Congressional Redistricting: Comparative and Theoretical Perspectives* (New York: Macmillan, 1992). Arend Lijphart, "Comparative Perspectives on Fair Representation: The Plurality-Majority Rule, Geographical Districting, and Alternative Electoral Arrangements," in *Representation and Redistricting Issues,* ed. Bernard Grofman, Arend Lijphart, Robert McKay, and Howard Scarrow, (Lexington, Mass.: Lexington Books, 1982). Bernard Grofman, "Criteria for Districting: A Social Science Perspective," *UCLA Law Review* 33 (1995): 77–184.

2. John Ely, "Standing to Challenge: Pro-Minority Gerrymanders," *Harvard Law Review* 111, no. 34 (1997): 576–95.

3. Abigail Thernstrom, "By Any Name, It's a Quota," *New York Times,* 7 December 1994. Also see O'Connor's opinion in *Shaw v. Reno,* 509 U.S. 630 (1993).

4. Grofman, "Criteria for Districting," 1985, and Bernard Grofman, "Would Vince Lombardi Have Been Right if He Had Said 'When It Comes to Redistricting, Race Isn't Everything, It's the Only Thing?'" *Cardoza Law Review* 14 (1993): 1237–76.

5. James E. Campbell, John R. Alford, and Keith Henry, "Television Markets and Congressional Elections," *Legislative Studies Quarterly* 9 (1984): 665–78.

6. Richard Niemi, Lynda W. Powell, and Patricia L. Bicknell, "The Effects of Congruity between Community and District on Salience of U.S. House Candidates," *Legislative Studies Quarterly* 11 (1986): 187–201.

7. Richard N. Engstrom, "Electoral District Compactness and Voters," *American Review of Politics* 21 (2000): 383–96.

8. John Books and Charles Prysby, *Political Behavior and the Local Context* (New York: Praeger, 1991).

9. Richard F. Fenno, *Home Style: House Members in Their Districts* (New York: Harper Collins Publishers, 1978): 236.

10. Stephen Hess, *Live From Capitol Hill!* (Washington, D.C.: Brookings Institution, 1991). Peter Clarke and Susan H. Evans, *Covering Campaigns: Journalism in Congressional Elections* (Stanford: Stanford University Press, 1986).

11. Richard Niemi, Bernard Grofman, Carl Carlucci, and Thomas Hofeller, "Measuring Compactness and the Role of a Compactness Standard in a Test for Partisan and Racial Gerrymandering," *Journal of Politics* 53 (1990): 1155–79.

12. Campbell, Alford, and Henry, "Television Markets," 665–78.

13. The multicounty formula produces the same result as the single county formula when only one county is involved. In the one county case, the county-district

intersection and the district area are the same, and therefore cancel each other out. For example, if the district size were 5 square miles (in the denominator), the county-district intersection would also be 5 square miles (in the numerator). The remaining terms in the equation essentially reduce to district size divided by county size, the formula for a single district-county overlap. Note that the fact that it is a single county-district intersection makes the summation sign irrelevant.

14. It is true that voter turnout is typically overreported in NES surveys, but analyses have shown that this overreporting is distributed in a manner that is sufficiently unbiased to allow for its use in voter turnout models. Ruy A. Teixeira, *The Disappearing American Voter* (Washington, D.C.: Brookings Institution, 1992). Lynn Ragsdale and Jerrold G. Rusk, "Who Are Nonvoters? Profiles from the 1990 Senate Elections," *American Journal of Political Science* 37 (1993).

15. Michael Barone and Grant Ujifusa, *The Almanac of American Politics 1996* (Washington, D.C.: National Journal, 1996). Barone and Ujifusa, *The Almanac of American Politics 1998* (Washington, D.C.: National Journal, 1998). Barone and Ujifusa, *The Almanac of American Politics 2000* (Washington, D.C.: National Journal, 2000).

16. To control for the possibility that the media-market conformity measure might be serving as a surrogate for population density, another model was estimated that included population per square mile as an independent variable. With population density controlled for, the relationship between media market-district conformity and voting was unchanged.

17. Books and Prysby, *Political Behavior and the Local Context*, 111.

18. Engstrom, "Electoral District Compactness."

19. The data used in this project consist of a pooled cross-section, and therefore was subjected to an additional set of analyses using data clustered by district. Those analyses confirmed the results reported above, finding positive and significant relationships between district-media market conformity and voting and between district-media market conformity and candidate recall.

20. Campbell, Alford, and Henry, "Television Markets." Niemi, Powell, and Bicknell, "Effects of Congruity," 1986.

21. Engstrom, "Electoral District Compactness."

22. Edward G. Carmines and Robert Huckfeldt, "Political Behavior: An Overview," in *A New Handbook of Political Science*, ed. Robert E. Goodin and Hans-Dieter Klingemann (Oxford: Oxford University Press, 1996), 231–32.

II

RACE AND REDISTRICTING IN THE OLD AND NEW MILLENNIA

5

Race, Redistricting, and the Courts[1]

David T. Canon

The Supreme Court is typically reluctant to address "political questions."[2] However, in 1993 the Court jumped into the "political thicket" of racial redistricting in its seminal decision *Shaw v. Reno*. This case questioned the constitutionality of black-majority districts and subsequent decisions over the next ten years refined the boundaries within which race could be considered in drawing district lines. However, uncertainty remains about exactly how race can be used: race cannot be the predominant factor in drawing a district, but it may be *a* factor, especially if it is difficult to disentangle the competing influences of race and party. This uncertainty and the absence of any clear-cut principles virtually require that every case be analyzed independently; this means that racial redistricting will remain a contested and heavily litigated area of the law well into the twenty-first century. Indeed, the courts' role in redistricting now appears to be a permanent fixture on the American political landscape rather than a decennial event that lasts a couple of years. The litigation from the 1990s' round of redistricting nearly overtook the next set of cases. There were only five days separating the last case from the 1990 reapportionment and redistricting (April 18, 2001) and the first case from the current round (April 23, 2001)!

This chapter will situate the topic of racial redistricting and the courts within the historical, contemporary, and broader political contexts. First, the chapter will provide a brief summary of the historical and legal background on race and redistricting.[3] Second, I will review the recent cases involving racial redistricting, starting with *Shaw v. Reno*. Finally, I will address two aspects of the broader political implications. I discuss the links between my work on the representation of racial interest in the U.S. House and the current legal debates. Integrating the representational consequences of black majority districts would further muddy the unclear waters by raising a set of factors that thus far has not come into play in the *Shaw*-type cases. However, these consequences provide the empirical basis for the argument made by Justice Breyer and others, that white plaintiffs do not suffer any particularized harm and therefore do not have standing to sue. Finally, I also show how these issues are related to broader debates about the proper role of the Court within the political system (activism and restraint) and about a jurisprudence of originalism versus "active liberty."

HISTORICAL AND LEGAL BACKGROUND OF RACIAL REDISTRICTING

The First Century of the Battle for Voting Rights

The goal of empowering African Americans through the creation of black-majority districts is rooted in a century-long struggle to give blacks the right to vote. The 15th Amendment to the Constitution, adopted on March 30, 1870, guaranteed "the right of citizens of the United States to vote shall not be denied or abridged by the United States or any State on account of race, color, or previous condition of servitude." In the Reconstruction era blacks in the South gained considerable political power through institutions such as the Freedmen's Bureau and the Union League, with substantial help (some would argue manipulation and exploitation) from the Radical Republicans. Between 1869 and 1901, twenty different blacks served a total of 41 terms in the U.S. House, and two blacks served a total of eight years in the Senate—all of them from the South. However, after 1879, there was only token representation of blacks in Congress, with no more than three being elected in any given Congress.[4] When federal troops withdrew and the Republican party abandoned the South,[5] blacks were almost completely disenfranchised through the imposition of residency requirements, poll taxes, literacy tests, the "grandfather clause," physical intimidation, other forms of disqualification, and later the white primary.[6] While these provisions purported to be race neutral on their face, their impact fell disproportionately on black voters. The most transparent of these was the grandfather clause, which V.O. Key explains, "provided an exception to the literacy test that could be taken advantage of only by illiterate whites."[7] Many states also had "understanding" or "good character" exceptions to the literacy tests, which gave election officials substantial discretion over who would be allowed to vote. The collective impact of these obstacles to voting was to virtually eliminate black voting; for example, only 6 percent of blacks were registered to vote in Mississippi in 1890 and only 2 percent were registered in Alabama in 1906.[8]

After the last post-Reconstruction black left the House in 1901, it was 72 years until another black represented a Southern district in Washington (Barbara Jordan from Texas). Blacks were not concentrated in large enough numbers outside the South to elect a black to Congress (and most whites were not willing to support blacks in the first part of the twentieth century), thus no blacks served in Congress between 1901 and 1929. Between 1929 and 1945 one black served in the House (from Chicago) and one more black member was added in 1945 from New York City. Through 1969, no more than six blacks served in Congress at the same time.[9]

The Voting Rights Act of 1965 (VRA) changed this legacy of political exclusion by eliminating direct obstacles to minority voting in the South such as discriminatory literacy tests and other voter registration tests. The VRA is often cited as one of the most significant pieces of civil rights legislation passed in our nation's history.[10] In an address to Congress on March 15, 1965, President Johnson compared the critical events at Selma, Alabama, that helped provide the impetus for passage of the VRA, to the American Revolution and the Civil War. He cited all three as moments when "history and fate meet at a single time in a single place to shape a turning point in man's unending search for freedom."[11] After its passage, President Johnson hailed the VRA as a "triumph for freedom as huge as any ever won on any battlefield."[12] Even critics of the 1982 amendments to the VRA recognize the significance of the initial legislation; one such critic claims that the "passage of the act was an event that transformed American political life."[13]

The statistics on the explosion in black participation in the South after the passage of the VRA are familiar, but bear repeating. The most dramatic gains came in Mississippi where black registration increased from 6.7 percent before the VRA to 59.8 percent in 1967. As Davidson notes, "The act simply overwhelmed the major bulwarks of the disenfranchising system. In the seven states originally covered, black registration increased from 29.3 percent in March 1965, to 56.6 percent in 1971 and 1972; the gap between black and white registration rates narrowed from 44.1 percentage points to 11.2."[14]

The central parts of the VRA are Section 2 and Section 5. The former prohibits any state or political subdivision from imposing a voting practice that will "deny or abridge the right of any citizen of the United States to vote on account of race or color." The latter was only imposed on "covered" jurisdictions with a history of past discrimination that must submit changes in any electoral process or mechanism to the federal government for approval.[15] Changes may either be "precleared" by the Department of Justice (DOJ), or approved by the federal district court for the District of Columbia. Most states use the preclearance option because the judicial route is more time consuming and costly.

Despite the gains in access to the polls, blacks faced more subtle forms of discrimination, including changing electoral practices such as shifting from district to at-large elections or redrawing district boundaries to dilute black voting power. An important Supreme Court case, *Allen v. State Board of Elections* (1969) held that "the preclearance provisions were applicable, not only to changes in laws directly affecting registration and voting, but all changes 'which alter the election law of a covered State in even a minor way.'"[16] As *Allen* was applied, covered practices not only included literacy tests and other practices that directly restricted access to voting, but also actions such as switching from single-member to at-large elections, switching from elective to appointive office, qualifications for independent voters and write-in votes, redistricting, and annexation or other voting practices that could *abridge* the right to vote based on race or color.[17] Redistricting cases were primarily of the former type, while the vote dilution cases typically involved the types of practices outlined in *Allen*.

While litigating vote dilution involved many complex issues, fairly clear standards were laid down by the Court in *White v. Regester* (1973) and *Zimmer v. McKeithen* (1976) in a "totality of circumstances" approach to proving vote dilution.[18] This relatively settled approach to vote dilution cases was turned on its head in 1980 when the Court upheld a multimember district plan that appeared to favor white politicians, arguing that minority voters' 14th Amendment protections were not violated unless it could be shown that district lines were *intentionally* drawn to dilute the votes of minorities (*City of Mobile v. Bolden*). This was a major departure from precedent and placed a much greater burden on plaintiffs trying to prove a voting discrimination claim.

The 1982 VRA Amendments

With sections of the VRA set to expire and pressure from the civil rights community building against the *Bolden* decision, in 1981 Congress started to tackle the first major revision of the Act since 1975. A division of labor developed between the House and the Senate with the House focused on extending Section 5 preclearance and amending the bailout provisions (which would allow states to no longer be covered by Section 5) and the Senate working on Section 2 modification. The division was somewhat accidental because the significance of the Section 2 changes were not recognized or debated in the House, as "potential opponents were asleep at the switch."[19] By the time the bill moved to the Senate, the Section 2 changes became the focus of Orrin Hatch's Subcommittee on the Constitution. Opponents of extending the VRA and expanding its coverage thought they were in a strong political position with Republican control of the Senate (53 to 47) and a Republican president. However, Henry Hyde's (R-IL) attempts to water down the Section 5 changes and Hatch's efforts in the Senate did not prevail. The final version of the bill sailed through Congress with a twenty-five-year extension of Section 5 preclearance, tough "bailout' provisions, and language in Section 2 that restored the results standard to prove a vote dilution claim.[20]

The part of this debate that is most central to this chapter concerned the amended portion of Section 2. The changed version reads:

> (a) No voting qualification or prerequisite to voting standard, practice, or procedure shall be imposed or applied by any State or political subdivision in a manner which results in a denial or abridgement of the right of any citizen of the United States to vote on account of race or color . . . (b) A violation of subsection (a) is established if, based on the totality of circumstances, it is shown that the political processes leading to nomination or election in the State or political subdivision are not equally open to participation by members of a class of citizens protected in subsection (a) in that its members have less opportunity than other members of the electorate to participate in the political process and to elect representatives of their choice. The extent to which members of a protected class have been elected to office in the State or political subdivision is one circumstance which may be considered: *Provided*, That nothing in this section establishes a right to have members of a protected class elected in numbers equal to their population.[21]

The seemingly subtle change of Section 2 from "deny or abridge the right of any citizen of the United States to vote on account of race or color." to "which results in a denial or abridgement of the right of any citizen" effectively wiped out the *Bolden* decision. The Senate Judiciary Committee report explained the reasons for this change: requiring plaintiffs to prove the intent to discriminate undermined the original legislative intent of Section 2, *Bolden* "marked a radical departure from both Supreme Court and lower federal courts' precedent in voting discrimination cases,"[22] and the intent test of *Bolden* placed an undue burden upon plaintiffs and "asks the wrong question."[23] The report also defended the amended Section 2 saying that proportional representation would not be required, at-large representation would not be automatically suspect, and that the results test is a "well-defined standard" that will "provide ample guidance to federal courts."[24]

Thornburg v. Gingles

The first Supreme Court decision to apply the amended VRA clarified some issues, but left a great deal of confusion. The unanimous verdict obscures a fractured decision with four separate opinions; there was no agreement among more than four justices on any specific part of the decision (see table 5.1). The heart of the 1986 decision, authored by Justice Brennan, established the "three *Gingles* prongs" by winnowing the nine factors that could be used to demonstrate a discriminatory result. The decision struck down parts of the 1984 North Carolina state legislative redistricting, holding that a minority group can claim discrimination under Section 2 if "First, the minority group [is] able to demonstrate that it is sufficiently large and geographically compact to constitute a majority in a single-member district. . . . Second, the minority group [is] able to show that it is politically cohesive. . . . [And] third, the white majority votes sufficiently as a bloc to enable it . . . usually to defeat the minority's preferred candidate."[25]

The decision greatly pleased voting rights advocates because it upheld the results standard over the more difficult burden of proving intent. However, Justice O'Connor argued that the Court went too far in elevating the election of preferred candidates and vote polarization as the critical tests, saying that the Court created "the right to a form of proportional representation."[26] While the *Gingles* prongs do not require proportional representation, officials in the DOJ responsible for enforcing the Voting Rights Act under its preclearance provisions interpreted these actions as a mandate to create majority-minority districts. In some cases (Georgia and North Carolina especially) the DOJ seemed to be imposing proportional representation on the states.

While there was little consensus among the lower courts on the details of applying *Gingles*, there was strong agreement within state legislatures that the decision required the creation of black-majority districts whenever possible. State legislators feared that a failure to create black-majority districts when the three *Gingles* prongs were present could result in vote dilution lawsuits. This led to the creation in 1992 of 15 districts that were drawn to help elect African Americans and ten districts that were to provide opportunities for Latino House candidates.

The *Shaw* Revolution

The relatively orderly process of elaborating and refining the host of questions raised by *Gingles* came to an abrupt end with the landmark decision *Shaw v. Reno* (1993) which held that bizarrely shaped black-majority districts violated the rights of white voters if they were created racially motivated and ignored traditional districting practices. Justice O'Connor, in the most widely quoted passage of the decision, argued that the challenged reapportionment plan:

> bears an uncomfortable resemblance to political apartheid. It reinforces the perception that members of the same racial group—regardless of their age, education, economic status, or the community in which they live—think alike, share the same political interests, and will prefer the same candidates at the polls. We have rejected such perceptions elsewhere as impermissible racial stereotypes.[27]

The decision departed from recent precedent by creating a new basis for making a voting rights claim under the "equal protection" clause of the 14th Amendment (also note that table 5.1 shows that the key decisions went from

Table 5.1. Summary of Major Court Cases on Minority Districting

Case	*Vote*	*Majority Opinion*	*Concurring*	*Dissent*
Thornburg v. Gingles 6/30/86	9–0	Brennan, Marshall, Blackman, Stevens, and White	White, O'Connor and Burger Powell and Rehnquist	Stevens, Marshall, and Black (on only one of the five districts; the court was unanimous on four of the five, 6–3 on the 5th)
Growe v. Emison 2/23/93	9–0	Scalia	—	—
Voinovich v. Quilter 3/2/93	9–0	O'Connor	—	—
Shaw v. Reno 6/28/93	5–4	O'Connor, Rehnquist, Scalia, Kennedy, and Thomas	—	White—Blackman and Stevens, Blackman, Steven, Souter
Shaw v. Hunt 6/13/96	5–4	Rehnquist, O'Connor, Scalia, Kennedy, and Thomas		Stevens—Ginsburg and Breyer, joined as to Parts II, III, IV, and V. Souter—Ginsburg and Breyer joined
Miller v. Johnson 4/19/95	5–4	Kennedy—Rehnquist, O'Connor, Scalia, and Thomas, joined	O'Connor	Stevens,Ginsburg—Stevens and Breyer, joined; Souter joined except as to Part III-B
Bush v. Vera 6/13/96	5–4	O'Connor,—Rehnquist and Kennedy, joined	O'Connor, Kennedy, Thomas—Scalia, J., joined	Stevens— Ginsburg and Breyer Souter—Ginsburg and Breyer
Hays II v. U.S. 6/29/95	9–0	O'Connor—Rehnquist, Scalia, Kennedy, Souter, Thomas, Breyer	Breyer I Souter, Stevens, Ginsburg	
Ambrams v. Johnson 6/19/97	5–4	Kennedy—Rehnquist, O'Connor, Scalia, Thomas joined	—	Breyer—Stevens, Souter, Ginsburg joined Thomas—Rehnquist, Kennedy, Scalia, joined
Easley v. Cromartie 4/18/2001	5–4	Breyer—Ginsburg, O'Connor, Souter, Stevens joined		

consensual nine to zero verdicts to conflictual five to four decisions). While *Shaw* did not reverse *Gingles* or *Beer v. United States* (no retrogression standard), it applied a different standard than was used in decisions such as *Growe v. Emison*, where a few months earlier O'Connor said, "[T]he State may create any district it might desire, so long as minority voting is not diluted."[28] Similarly in *Voinovich v. Quilter* the Court held that "the state may concentrate the minority vote even if it does not have to do so to correct or prevent a violation of minority voting rights."[29] *Shaw* also did not adhere to a ruling in *United Jewish Organizations of Williamsburgh, Inc. (UJO)* v. *Carey* (1977) that strict scrutiny did not apply and the districts were valid even though the State "deliberately used race in a purposeful manner" to create majority-minority districts.[30] A majority of the Court also held that the intentional creation of majority-minority districts does not produce an equal protection claim, unless the districting diluted the majority's voting strength. Justice O'Connor argued in *Shaw* that *UJO* did not apply because the North Carolina case did not involve a vote dilution claim. However, Justice Ginsburg challenges that view in her *Miller* dissent:

> Nor is *UJO* best understood as a vote dilution case. Petitioners' claim in *UJO* was that the State had "violated the Fourteenth and Fifteenth Amendments by *deliberately revising its reapportionment plan along racial lines*." Petitioners themselves stated: "Our argument is . . . that the history of the area demonstrates that there could be—and in fact was—*no reason other than race* to divide the community at this time."[31]

Justice O'Connor clearly erred in arguing that the plaintiffs in the *Shaw* case brought "an analytically distinct claim (from the plaintiffs in *UJO*) that a reapportionment plan rationally cannot be understood as anything other than an effort to segregate citizens into separate voting districts on the basis of race without sufficient justification."[32] In fact, as Justice Ginsburg points out, that is precisely what the *UJO* plaintiffs claimed, at least in part.

While the extent to which *Shaw* deviated from precedent is somewhat disputed, there is no disagreement that the decision created a new basis for challenging the constitutionality of a voting district. O'Connor's decision notes that *Shaw* "warrants different analysis" than previous voting rights cases. Prior to *Shaw*, there were only two bases upon which to challenge a district: "one person one vote" and vote dilution. The U.S. District Court noted in *Shaw v. Hunt* (the remand from *Shaw v. Reno*) that, "Until *Shaw*, no majority opinion of the Supreme Court had held that a state redistricting plan that did not cause concrete, material harm to the voting strength of an identifiable group of citizens in one of these two ways could nonetheless be challenged under the Equal Protection Clause on the grounds that it impermissibly took race into account in drawing district lines."[33] This new analysis emphasized "traditional districting practices" for the first time, citing the importance of compactness, contiguity, and respect for political subdivisions (respect for "communities defined by actual shared interests" was added in *Miller*). Or in O'Connor's words "we believe that reapportionment is one area in which appearances do matter."[34] Richard Engstrom suggests that these criteria, which have no basis in the constitution or federal statute, create a confusing "conceptual thicket" to compound the difficulties posed by the "political thicket" of redistricting that for decades the Court was loath to enter.[35]

Even those who see the landmark decision as a reasonable compromise recognized the problematic nature of the decision itself. Bernard Grofman argues that *Shaw* steers a course between "premature optimism that will lead to the elimination of safeguards vital to the continuing integration of minorities into American electoral politics, and an unrealistic pessimism that insists we will never get beyond judging people by the color of their skin," yet notes the decision is "somewhat muddled."[36] Paul Peterson calls the decision "logically incoherent," but sees it as "politically correct" because it does not try to impose racial classifications on the political process.[37] The critics of *Shaw* are far less charitable. Morgan Kousser says, "It is true that the abstract, deeply ambiguous, and often unreflective opinion suggested only vague and unworkable standards that have led to much-heightened judicial intrusions in the political process, and that it encouraged a cruelly ironic interpretation of the 14th and 15th Amendments, an interpretation surely unintended by their framers, that aims to undermine the sharpest minority gains in politics since the First Reconstruction."[38]

Shaw's Progeny

Subsequent decisions expanded the scope of judicial scrutiny. *Miller v. Johnson* (1995) established that congressional districts were unconstitutional if race was the "predominant factor" in their creation while moving away from the importance of the appearance of the district. Bizarrely shaped districts were no longer a threshold requirement for an equal protection claim. As Justice Ginsburg pointed out in her *Miller* dissent, this was a dramatic shift from the relatively proscribed language of *Shaw*: "[In *Shaw*] the Court wrote cautiously, emphasizing that judicial intervention is exceptional: '[S]trict [judicial] scrutiny' is in order, the Court declared, if a district is 'so extremely irregular on its face that it rationally can be viewed only as an effort to segregate the races for purposes of voting'"[39] *Miller* also held that compliance with Section 5 preclearance was not an adequate reason for creating a black-majority district, even when the Justice Department insisted that additional black-majority districts be added. *Abrams v. Johnson* (1997) upheld the dismantling of two of Georgia's black-majority districts that followed the *Miller* decision, even though the state legislature had shown a clear preference for keeping one of those two districts during the redistricting process. This decision signals that the courts are becoming increasingly activist in this area of litigation, rather than allowing the elected officials to settle the issue.[40]

Bush v. Vera (1996) established that protecting incumbents was not a strong enough reason to dislodge race as the predominant factor when both motivations were present. The Court recognized incumbency protection as a legitimate end of redistricting, and thus categorized *Vera* as a "mixed motive" case; however race was seen as predominant and thus the district was subjected to strict scrutiny. This logic is problematic.[41] While race may have been predominant in determining that one or more black-majority districts would have to be created in Georgia, Texas, and North Carolina, in the latter two states incumbency protection dictated the actual shape of the district. For example, the infamous I-85 district in North Carolina was largely a product of incumbency protection. The Republican plan that called for a more compact district could have been drawn across the southern tier of counties. Texas also produced some of its irregularly shaped districts to protect incumbents, but the Court rejected this alternative "compelling state interest" because the state legislature improperly used black voters as proxies for Democratic voters (*Bush v. Vera*). In other words, even if the districts were oddly shaped to protect incumbents, race predominated because the state legislature assumed that blacks would vote Democratic! The only bright spot for advocates of the districts was *Hays v. Louisiana* (1995) when the Court narrowed the scope of standing, noting that a plaintiff must reside in the challenged district in order to file a 14th Amendment claim.

Justice O'Connor realized that this string of decisions left state legislatures potentially "trapped between the competing hazards of liability."[42] After affirming the constitutionality of the VRA and its amendments she stated, "I believe that States and lower courts are entitled to more definite guidance as they toil with the twin demands of the Fourteenth Amendment and the Voting Rights Act."[43] Thus in an unusual separate concurring opinion (she also wrote the plurality opinion), O'Connor laid out the following steps to determine whether a given district would survive judicial scrutiny. First, the plaintiffs have to prove that race was the predominant factor in creating the black-majority district by showing that traditional districting principles were subordinated to race. Violation of compactness, contiguity, communities of interest, or traditional political boundaries do not satisfy the burden of proof faced by the plaintiffs unless they can show that this neglect is predominantly due to race.[44] For example, in the district court case *Moon v. Meadows* the state of Virginia attempted to show that some irregularities of district lines (compactness) and splitting of precincts (respect for political boundaries) were caused by nonracial considerations such as protecting incumbents and splitting two shipbuilding yards between two districts. Despite these arguments, the district court ruled that race was the predominant factor in the creation of the 3rd district.

The second step of the process requires that if the predominance of race is established, the district comes under strict scrutiny and the burden of proof shifts to the state to demonstrate that the district was "narrowly tailored" to achieve a compelling state interest other than race. One important aspect of O'Connor's concurring opinion in *Vera* is that compliance with Section 2 can be a compelling state interest if the *Gingles* preconditions are met and if the state does not violate traditional districting principles in the creation of the district for predominantly racial reasons.

While this may sound like a relatively straightforward procedure, there are practical difficulties and important political implications posed by the *Shaw* decisions. For example, Justice Breyer in his *Abrams v. Johnson* (1997) dissent points out:

> Legislators, for example, may ask just what the words "predominant racial motive" mean. The question has no obvious answer because racial motives (here efforts to include some additional African-American voters in a particular district) *never* explain a predominant portion of a district's entire boundary (most of which inevitably reflects county lines, other geographical features, and sometimes even a discriminatory history); yet those motives *always* predominate in respect to those voters (whether few or many) whom the legislature, with consciousness of race, places for that reason in one district rather than another. . . . [A] legislator might reasonably wonder whether he can ever knowingly place racial minorities in a district because, for example, he considers them part of a "community already there; because he thinks doing so will favor the Democrats (or the Republicans); because he wants to help an African-American incumbent; because he believes doing so will encourage participation in the political process by racial minorities in whom historical discrimination has induced apathy; because he believes that doing so will help those same voters secure representatives that better reflect their needs and desires; or simply because he wants to see more racial minorities elected to office in a Nation that has become increasingly diverse."[45]

Tellingly, the Court has made no effort to define its core principle—race as the predominant factor—in a fashion that would help answer Justice Breyer's questions.

The last case of the 1990s' round of redistricting, *Easley v. Cromartie* (2001), started to sort out some of these ambiguities. For the first time in the *Shaw* line of cases, Justice O'Connor voted with the liberals and upheld an African American influence district. At issue was an incarnation of the infamous "I-85 district," the target of *Shaw v. Reno* (the North Carolina 12th). This was the fourth time that the district was before the Supreme Court. This version of the district had been pared back to 47 percent black voting age population, but the federal district court still found that race was the predominant factor in the creation of the district. The Supreme Court disagreed, saying that the lower court decision was "clearly erroneous" because it had not proven that race rather than partisan motivations was dominant. The majority opinion pointed out that "racial identification correlated highly with political affiliation" and that the state legislature was attempting to create districts that protected incumbents and were reliably Democratic.[46] Given that about 95 percent of African Americans in North Carolina register in the Democratic Party and about 97 percent vote Democratic, a district that may *appear* to have been created for racial reasons could have been drawn for partisan reasons. The Court said, "Those attacking the district have the demanding burden of proof to show that a facially neutral law is unexplainable on ground other than race."[47] That burden was not met.

Easley v. Cromartie does not provide definitive guidance on how to balance the Voting Rights Act's requirement to provide minority voters an equal opportunity to elect candidates of their choice and the *Shaw* line of cases' prohibition against race as the predominant factor in creating districts. However, if map drawers respect traditional districting principles and balance partisan and racial motivations so they are clearly complementary or even indistinguishable from one another, African American districts are likely to pass constitutional muster. Given the lack of "bright line" distinctions, congressional and state legislative districts will be decided on a case-by-case basis and litigation in this field is not likely to dissipate any time soon. Indeed, by the end of 2002, 36 states had already had to deal with more than 100 redistricting cases in state and federal court since 2001 and many of these involved race.

One other legal issue still before the Court is "retrogression," the prohibition in Section 5 of the Voting Rights Act against eroding "the position of racial minorities with respect to their effective exercise of the electoral franchise."[48] Defining this concept in the current climate of racial redistricting is very complex. If the percentage of African American voters is reduced in a given district does that constitute retrogression even if the opportunity to elect candidates of choice may be enhanced in the adjoining districts? This is precisely the question that has come up with the evolving interaction between party and race in the most recent round of redistricting. In the previous decade Republicans and black Democrats often worked together to create black-majority districts, even if the districts may have harmed some white Democratic incumbents. In the most recent round, black state legislators were much more likely to work with white Democrats to try to preserve and even expand the number of Democratic districts by shifting some African American voters out of black-majority districts. This was most evident at the state legislative level in New Jersey and Georgia, but it also happened at the congressional level in several states including Missouri and Georgia.[49] In New Jersey the issue was not raised as "retrogression" because the state is not "covered" by Section 5 of the Voting Rights

Act. Instead, plaintiffs in *Page v. Bartels*[50] made a Section 2 argument that blacks' voting power was being diluted and that their 14th and 15th Amendment rights were being violated by spreading black voters across four districts instead of three. Table 5.2 shows the changes in the voting age population of the four relevant districts. Thus, while African American voters lost voting power in three districts (especially the 27th), they gained an "influence district." African American state legislators testified that they could win in the new districts and the federal district court upheld the new districts.

The Supreme Court addressed this issue more explicitly in the context of Section 5 and retrogression in the case *Georgia v. Ashcroft*. In this instance the district court upheld the new U.S. House districts and the lower house of the state legislature, but struck down the state senate district plan saying that it failed the retrogression test by reducing large black majorities to just under 50 percent. Georgia's attorney general, Thurbert Baker, defended the districts before the Supreme Court saying that, "Section 5 cannot constitutionally require the drawing of supermajority minority legislative districts in order to create safe seats, rather than seats that afford minorities equal opportunities to win."[51] The Supreme Court agreed with the state of Georgia and "vacated and remanded" (this is, overturned and sent back) the district court decision because it had considered too narrow a range of factors in determining that the districting plan was retrogressive. The Supreme Court established a new standard of retrogression in which an increase in the number of "influence districts" could offset the loss of safe black-majority districts if the overall plan enhanced, or at least did not undermine, the representation of black interests.

Despite the flurry of litigation following the most recent round of redistricting, as of 2002, no *Shaw* plaintiffs have been successful and few Section 2 litigants have prevailed. Thus, the legal disputes surrounding racial redistricting are starting to reach some type of uneasy equilibrium. Why? Part of the reason is the state legislators who draw the district lines are adapting to the new legal standards. In the 1990s, state legislators did not *think* they were doing anything wrong by creating the black-majority districts, so they did not attempt to hide their motivations. Indeed, many states believed they were compelled to create the districts based on the 1982 VRA Amendments and

Table 5.2. Redistributing Black Voters in New Jersey

	Original Districts			*New Districts*		
	White	*Black*	*Hispanic*	*White*	*Black*	*Hispanic*
District	*(Voting Age Population)*			*(Voting Age Population)*		
27	31.4%	52.8%	9.4%	58.0%	27.5%	6.6%
28	20.4%	57.4%	16.8%	30.3%	48.3%	14.0%
29	20.9%	48.2%	26.2%	22.5%	39.2%	33.2%
34	76.8%	3.9%	11.3%	48.2%	35.3%	9.8%

Thornburg v. Gingles. But then the rules of the game changed in midstream with the *Shaw* line of cases. Now that state legislators are aware that race cannot be the predominant factor it will be much more difficult for plaintiffs to prove that a district "is unexplainable on ground other than race." Even the "smoking gun" email in the *Cromartie* case, in which a state legislative staffer mentioned that he "moved Greensboro Black community into the 12th, and now need[ed] to take about 60,000 out of the 12th" was not seen by the Supreme Court as compelling evidence that race predominated.[52]

BROADER POLITICAL IMPLICATIONS

Racial Representation, Responsiveness, and Legal Standing

The *Shaw*-type cases raise important questions concerning representation, but ironically the Court's majority opinions have almost completely ignored these issues. My research is specifically linked to this body of law in two areas: responsiveness of elected officials and standing. Responsiveness was not included in the Senate report's first seven factors that could be used to show that blacks did not have an equal opportunity to participate. However, it was one of the two additional factors in the Senate report and Sen. Robert Dole (R-KN) mentioned it as an important consideration when asked by Sen. Orin Hatch (R-UT) how he would define "equal opportunity to participate." Dole responded, "Typical circumstances include a history of official discrimination, racist campaign tactics, racial polarity in voting, *unresponsiveness of elected officials*, and the use of voting practices or procedures which enhance the opportunity for discrimination."[53] In *Rogers v. Lodge* (1982) the Court cited "representatives who were 'insufficiently responsive' to the distinctive needs of minority citizens" as one reason for striking down the at-large system of representation in Burke County, Georgia.[54] More recently, the plaintiffs in *Moon v. Meadows* (1997) tried to show that white politicians were just as responsive to blacks as black politicians, and that blacks would lose representation with a black-majority district (the same point developed by Lublin and also Cameron, et al.).[55] This was an unusual argument because lower courts (the 5th and 11th Circuits) have held that while evidence that white politicians are unresponsive to black voters may be useful in proving a Section 2 claim, demonstrating responsiveness is not probative because vote dilution may exist for other reasons.[56] Furthermore, white plaintiffs in the *Shaw*-type cases are making equal protection rather than vote dilution claims and they have not been required to offer evidence of responsiveness. However, my research could aid defendants in *Shaw*-type cases whose districts come under strict scrutiny. My evidence that white representatives are not as responsive to black constituents as black representatives could help establish a Section 2 justification for the creation of a black-majority district under a "totality of circumstances" analysis that demonstrates blacks did not have an equal opportunity to participate.

While responsiveness has no probative value in determining a vote dilution claim, it is relevant for the debate concerning standing. Vigorous dissents from Justices Ginsburg, Stevens, Souter, Blackman, White, or Breyer in nearly every decision have developed the importance of representation and responsiveness through the topic of standing. My central argument, which is shared by most of the dissenters, is that white voters did not suffer any "cognizable harm like dilution of the abridgement of the right to participate in the electoral process."[57] Therefore, white plaintiffs should not have standing to sue unless they can demonstrate a particularized harm. There is no harm because white voters *are* adequately represented by blacks. As my book *Race, Redistricting, and Representation* shows, whites were the pivotal voters in many districts and were able to elect the representatives of their choice. I also show that black representatives are responsive to white voters and spend most of their time on issues that are important to all constituents in their district. Justice O'Connor's assertion in *Shaw* that, "When a district obviously is created solely to effectuate the perceived common interests of one racial group, elected officials are more likely to believe that their primary obligation is to represent only the members of that group, rather than their constituency as a whole,"[58] is simply wrong (and was asserted by the Court without any empirical evidence). Furthermore, the current approach taken by the Court ignores differences in the types of African American candidates who are elected and the type of representation they provide to the white and black communities. Clearly a moderate like Mike Espy was very acceptable to the white voters of the Mississippi Delta, while they probably would not be as supportive of a radical former Black Panther. By ignoring differences within the African American community, a majority of the Supreme Court is guilty of racial stereotyping that they claim is represented by the districts they reject.

The Court majority has argued that white plaintiffs have standing because they suffer two types of concrete harms: "stigmatization" that occurs from the general classification by race in the racially gerrymandered districts and "representational harms" that occur when black politicians focus their attention on black constituents (*Shaw v. Reno* 1993; *Hays v. Louisiana* 1995). For example in *Moon v. Meadows* (1997), one of the plaintiffs asserted, "I have been stigmatized by the fact that the Virginia General Assembly classified voters according to race and segregated us, to the extent it was practicable. . . . Additionally, the tortured construction of the Third District has made my job as the Republican Chairman of the Third Congressional District exceedingly difficult."[59] However, they did not provide evidence to support either claim and they have not been required to do so by the Court, which assumes that the harm flows from the simple act of classification and that the other harms *may* occur.

Critics of *Shaw* assailed this new basis for standing.[60] Rep. McKinney quotes a *New York Times* editorial noting that the white plaintiffs in her district had their "feelings hurt."[61] Arthur Baer testified before a House Subcommittee Roundtable on Voting Rights:

> In *Shaw* . . . there was no allegation of vote dilution on white voters. That is, there was no harm to them. So it is an extraordinary case, because essentially it is unique in terms of creating standing for a group without injury. We had never had ideological standing before. This is essentially ideological standing.[62]

Morgan Kousser is blunt in his attribution of the motivation behind this expansion of standing, "In *Shaw v. Reno* the Court majority blatantly ignored their own broadly stated standards on standing in order to get to an issue that they wanted to decide."[63] David Kairys proposed a provocative "dual system thesis" in which one set of standards applies to black plaintiffs in discrimination and equal protection cases and another applies to white plaintiffs.[64] While Kairys takes the argument further than I would, there are clearly different criteria for standing and burdens of proof in the pre- and post-*Shaw* cases.

Other "standing" cases outside the area of voting rights also have great relevance. In *Lujan v. Defenders of the Wildlife* (1992) the Court established clear guidelines for standing: plaintiffs have suffered an "injury in fact" that is "concrete and particularized" and "'actual or imminent,' not 'conjectural' or 'hypothetical.'"[65] In *Allen v. Wright*, Justice O'Connor wrote for a six-person majority in denying standing to plaintiffs who were claiming an "abstract stigmatic injury."[66] However, in *Shaw*, the stigmatic injury was sufficient for standing, as the simple classification of people based on race was held to be unconstitutional.

Karlan and Levinson point out that this is a "radical proposition." They continue, "If racial classification is itself the injury, then a wide range of government activities—from juror selection questionnaires to police descriptions of fleeing suspects to much of the census—may also be presumptively unconstitutional."[67] Justice Stevens makes the same point concerning the census in his dissent in *Shaw v. Hunt* (1996) and goes on to criticize the constitutional grounds for standing used in the *Shaw*-type cases:

> Given the absence of any showing, or, indeed, any allegation, that any person has been harmed more than any other *on account of race*, the Court's decision to entertain the claim of these plaintiffs would seem to emanate less from the Equal Protection Clause's bar against racial discrimination than from the Court's unarticulated recognition of a new substantive due process right to "color-blind" districting itself. Revealed for what it is, the constitutional claim before us ulti-

> mately depends for its success on little more than speculative judicial suppositions about the societal message that is to be gleaned from race-based districting. I know of no workable constitutional principle, however, that can discern whether the message conveyed is a distressing endorsement of racial separatism, or an inspiring call to integrate the political process. As a result, I know of no basis for recognizing the right to color-blind districting that has been asserted here.[68]

The dubiousness of the stigmatic claim is further supported by noting its unique application in racial redistricting cases. In the early segregation cases cited in *Miller*[69]—*New Orleans City Park Improvement Assn. v. Detiege* (1958), *Gayle v. Browder* (1956), *Holmes v. Atlanta* (1955), *Mayor and City Council of Baltimore v. Dawson*, (1955), and *Brown v. Board of Education* (1954)—classification by race was not allowed, but the context was entirely different than current redistricting cases. These cases were challenges to the Jim Crow laws that segregated the races in public parks, buses, golf courses, beaches, and schools respectively. Blacks were clearly stigmatized by being *excluded* from participation because of their race. It is not clear why whites are stigmatized by being *included* in a district with large numbers of blacks.[70] Unlike blacks in the 1950s, whites are able to fully participate in the political process. Justice Stevens develops this argument in his *Shaw II* dissent:

> Even if race-based districting could be said to impose more personal harms than the so-called "stigmatic" harms that *Hays* itself identified, I do not understand why any voter's reputation or dignity should be *presumed* to have been harmed simply because he resides in a highly integrated, majority-minority voting district that the legislature has deliberately created. Certainly the background social facts are not such that we should presume that the "stigmatic harm" described in *Hays* and *Shaw I* amounts to that found cognizable under the Equal Protection Clause in *Brown* v. *Board of Education,* where state-sponsored school segregation caused some students, but not others, to be stamped with a badge of inferiority on account of their race.[71]

The basis for standing moves to even shakier ground when considering the more tangible "special representational harms" referred to in *Shaw* and *Miller*. Bernard Grofman, writing before the *Shaw* decision, explains why the precedents cited by the Court, such as *Adarand v. Pena* (1995) and *Richmond v. Croson* (1989), in which white contractors were denied business because of minority set-aside programs, are inappropriate in the context of voting rights:

> The nature of the remedy for minority vote dilution *does not require injury to innocent parties* as is the case, for example, in those situations where the future job prospects of whites may be threatened as a result of having been fired by a firm, which is found to have been discriminating against blacks. The only

> possible losers when minority districts are created are the white *incumbents* whose districts will be severely reconfigured . . . and these white incumbent legislators have no "right" to their seats. As the majority cannot be said to have a right to elect *all* the candidates, white *voters* are being denied no entitlement when minority vote dilution is remedied, and white voters' rights to elect candidates of choice remain unimpaired.[72]

Even Abigail Thernstrom, who supports the general reasoning of the Court in the *Shaw* cases, agrees with Grofman's argument about white politicians, "Whites denied medical school admission as a consequence of minority preference have been arguably denied a right; those disadvantaged by a change in electoral rules cannot make that claim. There are no 'objective' criteria for elected office—no equivalent of the Medical College Aptitude Test. A white denied a seat on a city council cannot claim entitlement on the ground of 'merit.'"[73] Indeed, the Court has never used the 14th Amendment to "strike down a racial classification which has had no tangible consequences," other than in the *Shaw* cases.[74] The link to standing is developed by Justice Stevens:

> To prove the representational harms that *Hays* holds are needed to establish standing to assert a *Shaw* claim, one would think that plaintiffs should be required to put forth evidence that demonstrates that their political representatives are actually unlikely to provide effective representation to those voters whose interests are not aligned with those of the majority race in their district. Here, as the record reveals, no plaintiff has made such a showing. Given our general reluctance to hear claims founded on speculative assertions of injury, I do not understand why the majority concludes that the speculative possibility that race-based districting "may" cause these plaintiffs to receive less than complete representation suffices to create a cognizable case or controversy.[75]

Perhaps plaintiffs have not presented evidence of representational harm for one simple reason: it does not exist. As my research has demonstrated, African American members of Congress adequately represent whites.[76] While space limitations preclude an extensive review of my evidence, I will briefly address the question of how a House member's race affects the quality of representation on racial issues. Black members of Congress tend to balance their representational efforts between nonracial issues, which are of interest to white voters and black voters alike, and racial concerns that are more central to their black constituents (this is especially true for black members that I label practitioners of the "politics of commonality," but even those who practice a "politics of difference" spend a majority of their time on nonracial issues). Whites, on the other hand, tend to spend an overwhelming majority of their time on nonracial issues. This important point is explained, in part, by the institutional pressure of a majority-rule institution. White representatives from districts that are 30 to 40 percent black *can* largely ignore their black constituents, and many do. Black representatives from districts that are 30 to 40 percent white cannot ignore their white constituents *because they are operating in an institution that is about 86 percent white and a nation that is 82.5 percent white.* Therefore, even the most race-conscious members of the Congressional Black Caucus (CBC) spend a majority of their legislative efforts on nonracial issues.

Race matters in the U.S. House of Representatives, both at the institutional and individual level. At the institutional level, the CBC is highly cohesive but increasingly diverse. It is a strong supporter of black interests but instrumental in helping mainstream Democratic Party positions succeed. CBC members provided the pivotal votes on crucial legislation in the 103rd Congress, serve on a broader array of committees, and play an increasing role in the leadership. The common wisdom holds (both among academics and House members) that there is a tradeoff between cohesion and dispersion. As a group becomes more diverse and its interests more dispersed, its cohesion and ability to speak with one voice declines.[77] In one sense, this is obviously true. More diverse groups will not be as cohesive by definition. However, it does not necessarily follow that diversity and cohesion cannot peacefully coexist *across a range of issues*. For many members of the CBC, it makes sense to break with the CBC and work with the Democratic leadership on one piece of legislation, while simultaneously speaking out for minority interests on another. Furthermore, it does not make sense to measure the success of the CBC by only examining racial issues or general ideological ratings, such as LCCR, ADA, or COPE scores. Black constituents have identical preferences to whites over a broad array of nonracial interests[78] and black members distribute their efforts and time over a broad range of concerns. Most importantly for the policy debates surrounding black majority districts, the CBC *can* have its voice heard in a majority rule institution. My analysis of 2,751 bills in the 103rd Congress showed that bills that had a black sponsor had a significantly higher chance of making it through the legislative process than those that did not and that the margin of victory on roll call votes did not vary substantially across racial, part racial, and nonracial issues.

The individual-level analysis provided strong confirmation of my supply-side theory, which is rooted in the racial coalitions that are formed during the member's initial election to the House, by demonstrating significant differences across the types of representational styles. Commonality members were more likely to serve in the leadership, slightly more moderate in their roll call behavior, less likely to emphasize race in their speeches on the floor and in their sponsorship and cosponsorship of legislation, and more likely to cosponsor bills that were successful in the legislative process than "difference" members. This broad range of evidence emphasizes the value of moving beyond an exclusive focus on roll call voting as the primary tool for examining racial representation.

While I found systematic differences among black members, even larger differences between white and black members were found. Blacks were disproportionately represented on committees that addressed black interests, their speeches touched on racial issues more frequently than whites, and a far greater proportion of the bills they sponsored and cosponsored had racial content. This is strong evidence against the "no racial difference" hypothesis. While white members certainly *can* represent black interests, as Carol Swain has shown, on average, the white members in the 103rd Congress who represented districts that were at least 25 percent black did not show much interest in racial issues.[79] This argument is consistent with Grofman, Handley, and Niemi's assertion, "[A]lthough we recognize that white liberal legislators may vote similarly to their black counterparts on roll call votes, this does not mean that they have the same commitment to a leadership role on civil rights or on economic issues of concern to the black community."[80] At the same time, however, blacks did not ignore broader nonracial interests: 49 percent of the 3,722 speeches the members of the CBC made on the House floor in the 103rd Congress, 58 percent of the 411 substantive bills they sponsor, and about 63 percent of the 11,620 cosponsorships by CBC members did not have anything to do with race.

Finally, there is one important methodological point: my analysis stacks the deck in favor of the "no racial difference" hypothesis and against my argument that race matters by only including the members of the 103rd Congress who represented districts that were at least 25 percent African American (plus Gary Franks and Alan Wheat, two CBC members who represented districts that were less than 25 percent black). That is, if differences between white members and black members in terms of racial representation are found in this subset of districts in which members should be the most sensitive to racial issues, it is extremely likely that even greater differences would be found if all districts were examined.

Racial Redistricting and the Role of the Supreme Court

Debates concerning the broader role of the courts within our political system focus on two topics: judicial restraint or activism and strict or loose construction of the Constitution and statutes. The former revolves around whether the courts should defer to the elected institutions by rarely striking down their actions (restraint) versus taking a more aggressive role in ruling laws and actions of Congress and the president unconstitutional (activism). The latter refers to whether a justice attempts to follow the meaning of the text of a law or the Constitution, without regard to contemporary sentiments and values (strict construction) versus a more pragmatic or "living" interpretation of the documents (loose construction). The current Supreme Court is a very activist court that tends to be strict constructionist, but both of these central tendencies can vary by the topic. With regard to racial redistricting, the Court has clearly been activist (striking down the actions of state legislatures), but it has not followed the dictates of strict construction. I will elaborate these points below and make an argument for judicial restraint in the area of racial redistricting, based on the concepts of "political questions" and Justice Breyer's notion of "active liberty."

The Supreme Court typically avoids "political questions" that are better left to the elected branches. John Marshall discussed this basis for judicial restraint in the landmark case *Marbury v. Madison*:

> The province of the court is, solely, to decide on the rights of individuals, not to inquire how the executive, or executive officers, perform duties in which they have discretion. Question in their nature political, or which are, by the constitution and laws, submitted to the executive, can never be made in this court.[81]

Of course, in *Marbury* the Court did *not* defer to the elected branches, but instead established the practice of judicial review. However, Marshall took a very deferential position when the question at hand was clearly political and no overriding constitutional issues forced the Court to intervene. The "political question" doctrine was first applied in *Foster v. Neilson*, in 1829, when the Court refused to resolve an international boundary dispute because the decision must be made by the representative institutions. Typical areas the courts are reluctant to enter include foreign affairs (most recently the Court refused to hear a challenge to the constitutionality of the war in Iraq), legislative process, and separation of powers issues.

However, there are no absolute criteria for defining a political question and the Court has put itself at the center of important political issues that it could have ducked. Critics of *Bush v. Gore*, the case that gave the 2000 presidential election to George W. Bush, such as Jeffrey Rosen and Steven Calabresi argue that the Court should not have agreed to hear the Florida case because the state legislature and the U.S. Congress had clear constitutional and statutory authority to resolve disputes over the electors from Florida.[82] In the area of redistricting, the Court consistently avoided the "political thicket" until in *Baker v. Carr* (1962) the Court ruled that the large population differences between legislative districts in urban and rural areas violated the equal protection clause of the 14th Amendment. As noted above, a similar logic was used with race and equal protection in *Shaw v. Reno* (1993) even if the constitutional underpinnings of the case are not as clear (because of the distinction between benign and invidious racial classification and the lack of traditional standing by white plaintiffs).

While the "political question" doctrine does not unambiguously require judicial restraint for racial redistricting, it provides a strong argument for that result. The legal questions surrounding racial redistricting are inextricably intertwined with policy and partisan politics and also do not have a clear constitutional or statutory mandate for action. Indeed, it is difficult to imagine a set of criteria that are more political than those concerning redistricting: partisan bias, incumbency protection, and communities of interest are inherently political. Other redistricting criteria are more objective, such as compactness, contiguity, split municipalities, and respect for natural geographic boundaries, but decisions about how to draw district lines will always involve political battles. For example, it may be possible to argue that one plan is "better" than another because it only splits 43 municipalities rather than 75. But the key *political* question will be which municipalities are split. When these various criteria have to be balanced against the two factors that have received closer judicial scrutiny—equal population and race as the predominant factor—many additional political judgments and tradeoffs have to be made. The legislature is better equipped to deal with these political questions than the courts.

Justice Stephen Breyer in his James Madison Lecture at the New York University Law School provided a comprehensive basis for judicial restraint that is grounded in the notion of "active liberty." He said:

> To focus upon that active liberty, to understand it as one of the Constitution's handful of general objectives, will lead judges to consider the constitutionality of statutes with a certain modesty. That modesty embodies an understanding of the judges' own expertise compared, for example, with that of a legislature. It reflects the concern that a judiciary too ready to "correct" legislative error may deprive "the people" of "the political experience and the moral education that come from . . . correcting their own errors." It encompasses that doubt, caution, prudence, and concern—that state of not being "too sure" of oneself—that Learned Hand described as the "spirit of liberty." In a word, it argues for traditional "judicial restraint."[83]

When applied to racial redistricting, Breyer relies on the distinction between invidious and benign (or positive) discrimination. The former prevents a minority from participating in the political process. "By way of contrast," Breyer says, "affirmative discrimination ordinarily seeks to enlarge minority participation in that self-governing democracy. To that extent it is consistent with, indeed furthers, the Constitution's basic democratic objective. That consistency, along with its more benign purposes, helps to mitigate whatever lack of equal respect any such discrimination might show to any disadvantaged member of a majority group."[84] Therefore, he argues, the racial classification that white plaintiffs are concerned about in the *Shaw*-type cases would not be subject to strict scrutiny, while electoral practices that would dilute black voting power would. With positive discrimination, the legislatures should be given more latitude to craft political solutions to difficult questions of representation.

Ultimately, the solution to the legal and political quagmire is judicial restraint. As Justice Souter points out in his *Bush* dissent, the Court has confused the issue without resolving anything and the political process had been making some progress with one of the nation's most persistent problems. The most recent redistricting cases reviewed here demonstrate that confusion surrounding the legal principles persists. A more positive argument for restraint is rooted in the historical role that congressional districts built around ethnic neighborhoods played in assimilating European immigrants into our political culture. Justice Souter notes, "The result has been not a state regime of ethnic apartheid, but ethnic participation and even a moderation of ethnicity's divisive effect in political practice."[85] Black-majority districts put in place in 1992 and the black-influence districts that replaced them could have that same integrative impact if the Court would abandon its "failed experiment" of judicial activism in this area.

CONCLUSION

A major shift in how the Supreme Court applies the 14th Amendment to congressional redistricting has left the status of black-majority districts in serious doubt. State legislatures have been told that it is possible to consider race as a factor when drawing district lines, but not as the predominant factor. To reach this position, the Court loosened well-defined conditions for standing, while moving toward a color-blind theory that ignores history and the distinctiveness of voting rights law when compared to other areas of civil rights law, such as affirmative action and discrimination. Unlike the white plaintiffs in *Bakke* (medical school admissions), *Adarand,* and *Croson* (minority contracting "set-aside" programs), or *Wygant* (considering race or seniority in laying off teachers) white voters were not harmed by being placed in black-majority districts. Justice O'Connor noted the hypothetical representational harms that come from the district, but no such harms have been demonstrated, even though they are claimed in some of the *Shaw*-type cases.

Thus, the motivation for the challenges to the black-majority districts boils down to an extremely thin conception of "stigmatic harm." One must look only as far as the dictionary to see what a distortion of language and the law this is. The archaic definition of stigma is "a mark burned into the skin of a criminal or slave; a brand." The current definition is "a mark or token of infamy, disgrace, or reproach." Stigmatize is "to characterize or brand as disgraceful or ignominious."[86] The use of the term by white plaintiffs in this context is certainly ironic (Justice O'Connor also used the language of slavery and racism in *Shaw* by noting the parallels to "political apartheid"). Slaves in this country were literally stigmatized. Their offspring were effectively "branded" by the Jim Crow laws in the century that followed the Civil War. It is difficult to see how white voters, who participate fully in the political process and dominate the political system at the national level ("virtual" representation), are branded as "disgraceful or ignominious" or suffer a mark of "infamy, disgrace, or reproach" by being placed in black-majority districts.[87]

Furthermore, the notion of an individual right to color-blind districting[88] does not mesh with the group-based focus of the politics of drawing district lines and the history of the Voting Rights Act. State legislators make precise calculations, based on census data that is aggregated by demographic groups, about the political consequences of separating groups of voters in various ways. Districting decisions cannot avoid group-level analysis.[89] Similarly, vote dilution claims under the VRA are based on patterns of group-level behavior (racial bloc voting and the ability to participate in the political process as the member of a group). As Karlan and Levinson note, "only a group of voters can suffer dilution from districting. A lone voter cannot."[90]

A meaningful basis for evaluating the constitutionality of black-majority districts must be rooted in an assessment of their consequences. Do they dilute a group's voting power? Do they restrict a group's ability to elect candidates of their choice and participate fully in the political process? Do voters suffer representational harms such as those endured by black constituents in the pre-VRA era, (or, in the language of the 1982 Senate report, are elected leaders unresponsive to a group of constituents)? The answer to all of these questions for the white plaintiffs in the *Shaw*-type cases is an unequivocal *no*. First, no claims of vote dilution have even been made by white plaintiffs. Second, white voters often elect their preferred candidate. Critics of the black districts, such as Thernstrom, have argued that black support of white candidates should be considered in determining candidates of choice.[91] By the same logic, the courts should consider white support for black candidates and recognize that white voters were pivotal in choosing many of the black representatives who were elected in 1992, and thus are electing *their* candidates of choice. Unless the parallel logic is applied in both contexts, there is an implicit argument that whites can represent blacks, but blacks cannot represent whites. Third, as Justices Stevens and Souter note, the white plaintiffs have never provided any evidence of representational harms; indeed, these harms do not exist. Given this reality, it is difficult to see how the 14th Amendment "equal protection" complaints can be sustained.[92] When black plaintiffs bring a lawsuit under the Section 2 of the VRA, concrete harms must be demonstrated. It seems only fair that white voters should bear the same legal burdens.

I have no illusions that the federal courts will suddenly alter the standards used to evaluate the constitutionality of a given district. I am convinced that the predominance of race in creating the districts and strict scrutiny will prevail given the current composition of the Court. I am sympathetic to the reasons that the Court would not want to open this can of worms—it is difficult to determine whose interests are being represented and who is being ignored. However, the current array of concepts is as difficult to define and measure as "responsiveness" and standing: Was race the predominant factor in drawing the district lines? If so, is there a Section 2 liability (that is, was there racial polarization, voting cohesiveness, district compactness, and denial of candidates of choice)? Why should the courts privilege one type of question over another, especially when in other areas of 14th Amendment law plaintiffs *have* been required to show specific discrimination, rather than generalized patterns of discrimination (*Richmond v. Croson* 1989) and specific harm rather than vague, generalized stigmatic harm (*Adarand*, *Bakke*)?

The important questions of representation and democracy have not been addressed by the Court's majority in the racial redistricting cases. *Candidates of choice, opportunity to participate, and vote dilution matter because representation matters.* If white politicians and black politicians were completely interchangeable in terms of representation, the fairness of the process would be much less important. However, my research shows that black and white politicians are not interchangeable. Most white representatives from black-influence districts do not spend much time representing their black constituents, while most black members of Congress spend a substantial proportion of their time representing white constituents.[93]

NOTES

1. This chapter is a revision and expansion of chapter 2 of my book *Race, Redistricting, and Representation: The Unintended Consequences of Black-Majority Districts* (Chicago: University of Chicago Press, 1999).

2. "Political questions" do not have any core constitutional issues and typically are better addressed by the elected institutions.

3. The reader should be warned that this is only a very brief overview. There is a comprehensive literature on the Voting Rights Act, its amendments, and the subsequent legal controversies that may be consulted for more in-depth treatments. Consult: Donald Strong, *Negroes, Ballots, and Judges: National Voting Rights Legislation in the Federal Courts* (University, Al.: University of Alabama Press, 1968); Howard Ball, "Racial Vote Dilution: Impact of the Reagan DOJ and the Burger Court on the Voting Rights Act," *Publius: The Journal of Federalism* 16 (1986), 29–48; Abigail Thernstrom, *Whose Votes Count? Affirmative Action and Minority Voting Rights* (Cambridge, Mass.: Harvard University Press, 1987); Pamela S. Karlan and Peyton McCrary, "Without Fear and Without Research: Abigail Thernstrom on the Voting Rights Act," *Journal of Law and Politics* 4 (1988): 751–77; Frank Parker, *Black Votes Count* (Chapel Hill, N.C.: University of North Carolina Press, 1990); Bernard Grofman, Lisa Handley, and Richard Niemi, *Minority Representation and the Quest for Voting Equality* (Cambridge: Cambridge University Press, 1992); Chandler Davidson and Bernard Grofman, eds., *Quiet Revolution in the South : The Impact of the Voting Rights Act, 1965–2000* (Princeton, N.J.: Princeton University

Press, 1994); Bernard Grofman, "*Shaw v. Reno* and the Future of Voting Rights," *PS: Political Science and Politics* 28 (1995): 27–36; J. Morgan Kousser, *Colorblind Injustice: Minority Voting Rights and the Undoing of the Second Reconstruction* (Chapel Hill, N.C.: University of North Carolina Press, 1999); Tinsley E. Yarbrough, *Race and Redistricting: The Shaw-Cromartie Cases* (Lawrence, Kans.: University Press of Kansas, 2002). This list is very limited. A Lexis search on the term "racial gerrymandering" produced 270 law review articles between 1983 and 1997 and several hundred more have been added since then; about 200 of these were directly related to racial redistricting and the Voting Rights Act. Other useful sources are the symposia in several leading law journals on the future of the Voting Rights Act and racial redistricting: *American University Law Review* (Fall, 1994); *Michigan Law Review* (December, 1993; February, 1997); *Rutgers School of Law-Camden Rutgers Law Journal* (Spring, 1995), *Stanford Law Review* (May, 1995), and *Texas Law Review* (June, 1993).

4. Congressional Research Service. "CRS Report for Congress: Black Members of the United States Congress, 1789–1989." (Washington, D.C.: Library of Congress, 1989).

5. Richard M. Valelly, "National Parties and Racial Disenfranchisement," in *Classifying by Race*, ed. Paul Peterson. (Princeton, N.J.: Princeton University Press, 1995), 188–216.

6. Chandler Davidson, "The Voting Rights Act: A Brief History," in *Controversies in Minority Voting: The Voting Rights Act in Perspective,* ed. Bernard Grofman and Chandler Davidson (Washington, D.C.: The Brookings Institution, 1992). V. O. Key Jr., *Southern Politics.* (New York: Vintage, 1949), 531–675. Frank R. Parker, *Black Votes Count.*

7. For example, the Louisiana grandfather clause read, "no male person who was on January 1, 1867, or at any date prior thereto, entitled to vote under the Constitution of the United States, wherein he then resided, and no son or grandson of any such person not less than twenty-one years of age at the date of the adoption of this Constitution, . . . shall be denied the right to register and vote in this State by reason of his failure to possess the educational or property qualifications." Grandfather clauses, as they applied to voting, were ruled unconstitutional in 1915. See V. O. Key Jr., *Southern Politics*, 538, 556.

8. Davidson, "The Voting Rights Act: A Brief History,"11.

9. Congressional Research Service. "Black Members of the United States Congress, 1789–1989."

10. Drew S. Days, III, "Section 5 Enforcement and the Justice Department" in *Controversies in Minority Voting: The Voting Rights Act in Perspective*, ed. Bernard Grofman and Chandler Davidson (Washington, D.C.: The Brookings Institution, 1992), 52. Frank R. Parker, *Black Votes Count*, 1.

11. Cited in *Congressional Record*, October 22, 1965, 28354.

12. Quoted in Senate, *Voting Rights Act Extension, Report of the Subcommittee on the Constitution of the Committee on the Judiciary*, no. J-97-417, 97 Congress, 2nd Session (Washington, D.C.: Government Printing Office, 1982), 4.

13. Timothy O'Rourke, "The Voting Rights Paradox and the 1982 Voting Rights Act Amendments," in *Controversies in Minority Voting: The Voting Rights Act in Per-*

spective, ed. Bernard Grofman and Chandler Davidson (Washington, D.C.: The Brookings Institution, 1992), 86. See also Abigail Thernstrom, *Whose Votes Count?*, 1.

14. Davidson, "The Voting Rights Act: A Brief History," 21.

15. The original "covered" jurisdictions were the six states of the deep South, 26 counties in North Carolina, Alaska, and one county in Arizona. States in which less than 50 percent of the voting age population either registered or voted in the 1964 presidential election and had various discriminatory prerequisites for voting as of November 1, 1964, were subject to Section 5 preclearance. States and jurisdictions could "bailout" from coverage if they could prove the absence of discriminatory practices. The list of covered states has evolved with various bailouts and the addition of other jurisdictions in the 1970, 1975, and 1982 Amendments. There are currently 22 states that have at least some covered jurisdictions.

16. Senate, *Voting Rights Act, Hearings before the Subcommittee on the Constitution of the Committee on the Judiciary*, no. J-97-92, 97 Congress, 2nd Session (Washington, D.C.: Government Printing Office, 1982), 1073.

17. Senate, *Voting Rights Act Extension*, 6–9.

18. See Lani Guinier, "The Triumph of Tokenism: the Voting Rights Act and the Theory of Black Electoral Success," *Michigan Law Review* 89 (1991): 1091–1101, for a discussion of the evolution of court decisions on vote dilution; See also Evelyn Elaine Schockley, "Voting Rights Act Section 2: Racially Polarized Voting and the Minority Community's Representative of Choice," *Michigan Law Review* 89 (1991): 1039–45; and Gregory G. Ballard, "Application of Section 2 of the Voting Rights Act to Runoff Primary Election Laws," *Columbia Law Review* 91 (1991): 1150–56, for an explanation of the necessary conditions to establish a claim of vote dilution.

19. Thernstrom, *Whose Votes Count?*, 83.

20. The House version passed 385–24; the Senate version passed 85–8 and the House passed the Senate version by unanimous consent; President Reagan signed the bill into law on June 29, 1982.

21. Title 42 of the U.S. Code, Section 1973b.

22. After reviewing the case law and noting that the *White* and *Zimmer* standards were used in nearly 50 vote dilution cases in the 1970s, the committee report concludes, "the prevailing standard in voting dilution was the 'results' test and intent was not a prerequisite" (Senate, Voting Rights Act Extension, 23). Despite this overwhelming evidence, Hatch strenuously argued that *Bolden* did not create a new intent standard (Senate, *Voting Rights Act, Hearings*, 33–35).

23. Senate, *Voting Rights Act Extension*, 16–27, 36–39, quotes from p. 16.

24. Senate, *Voting Rights Act Extension*, 16–27, 36–39, quotes from p. 16. The "results test" that determined that black voters had an equal opportunity to participate in the political process was to be ascertained by the set of factors outlined in *White* and *Zimmer*. This included factors such as the whether black candidates had been elected to public office, whether campaigns included racial appeal, whether candidate-slating procedures denied access to minority candidates, and whether there were lingering effects of discrimination in education, employment, and health. See Senate, *Voting Rights Act Extension*, 28–29.

25. *Thornburg v. Gingles*, 1986, 50–51. The *Gingles* case concerned multimember districting, but the three conditions were applied to single-member districts in *Growe*

v. Emison (1993). See Grofman, Handley, and Niemi. *Minority Representation*, ch 5. for a discussion of the lower court decisions that applied *Gingles* to single-member districts.

26. *Thornburg v. Gingles* 1986, 90.

27. *Shaw v Reno,* 1993, 2827.

28. Quoted in *CQWR* (6 March 1993), 538.

29. Quoted in *CQWR* (6 March 1993), 538.

30. Reference is to p. 165, *United Jewish Organizations of Williamsburgh, Inc. (UJO)* v. *Carey* (1977). Strict scrutiny is the most rigorous standard applied by the courts to determine whether group-based classifications are permissible. Typically, racial classifications must be justified by the state under the standard of strict scrutiny. Very few policies survive strict scrutiny (the internment of Japanese Americans during World War II is one of the few exceptions). Weaker standards apply to gender (intermediate scrutiny) and age. Thus, for example, it is permissible to deny twenty-year-olds the "right" to drink alcohol, but it would not be permissible to distinguish between twenty-year-old women and men, or whites and blacks, when establishing drinking laws. Similarly, some classifications based on gender would be allowed (separating men and women in military barracks), but not race.

31. Ginsburg's dissent in *Miller*, p.12, note 11, internal citations omitted, emphasis in original.

32. *Shaw v. Reno,* 1993, 2830.

33. Lexis, 11102, 10.

34. *Shaw v. Reno,*1993, 2827.

35. Richard L. Engstrom, "Voting Rights Districts: Debunking the Myths," *Campaigns and Elections* (April 1995): 323–24.

36. Bernard Grofman, "*Shaw v. Reno*" 34, 29.

37. Paul E. Peterson, "A Politically Correct Solution to Racial Classification," in *Classifying by Race,* ed. Paul E. Peterson (Princeton, N.J.: Princeton University Press, 1995), 16.

38. Kousser goes on to note that "the fears of liberals and the hopes of opponents of the voting rights revolution have been exaggerated." However, it is clear that he sees serious flaws in the *Shaw* decision. See J. Morgan Kousser, "*Shaw v. Reno* and the Real World of Redistricting and Representation," California Institute of Technology Working Paper #915, (1995), 1.

39. *Miller v. Johnson*, 1995, slip op., 6.

40. Many critics have argued that judicial activism is one of the greatest failings of the *Shaw* decisions. Christopher Eisgruber argues, ". . . this judgment (*Shaw v. Reno*) is empirically contingent in a way that makes it appropriate for legislative, rather than judicial, resolution. That is why I think *Shaw* is a monster: not because I agree with the policy it declared unconstitutional (I don't), but because the Shaw Court wrongly interfered with legislative discretion to treat America's most severe and most intractable problem, the problem of racial inequality," quoted in Christopher L. Eisgruber "Ethnic Segregation by Religion and Race: Reflections on *Kiryas Joel* and *Shaw v. Reno,*" *Cumberland Law Review* 26 (1996): 525.

41. *Vera* also is inconsistent with *Wright v. Rockefeller* (1964), in which the Court held that even though racial motivation was evident in the drawing of district lines,

the districts did not violate the 14th Amendment because other motivations were evident in the process as well. See Jeanmarie K. Grubert, "The Rehnquist Court's Changed Reading of the Equal Protection Clause in the Context of Voting Rights," *Fordham Law Review* 65 (1997): 1841.

42. Quoting *Wygant* v. *Jackson Bd. of Ed.,* 1986.

43. *Bush v. Vera* 1996, 2, slip op.

44. *Bush v. Vera* 1996, 1969.

45. Internal citations omitted, p. 13.

46. *Easley v. Cromartie*, 2001, 1453.

47. *Easley v. Cromartie*, 2001, 1454.

48. 425 U.S. at 421.

49. David T. Canon, Forthcoming, "Race and Parties in Congressional Redistricting," in *Representation, Redistricting, and Congressional Policy Making,* ed. Neil Pinney and George Serra.

50. 155 F Supp 2nd 346, 2001.

51. Linda Greenhouse, "Supreme Court Takes Case On Black Voting Districts," *New York Times,* 18 January 2003, 12(A).

52. *Easley v. Cromartie*, 121 S.Ct., 1464.

53. Senate, *Voting Rights Act, Hearings*, 81, emphasis added.

54. Pamela S. Karlan and Dayrl J. Levinson, "Why Voting Is Different," *California Law Review* 84 (1996): 1210.

55. David Ian Lublin, *The Paradox of Representation: Racial Gerrymander and Minority Interests in Congress* (Princeton, N.J.: Princeton University Press, 1997). Charles Cameron, David Epstein, and Sharon O'Halloran, "Do Majority-Minority Districts Maximize Substantive Black Representation in Congress?," *American Political Science Review* 90 (1996): 794–812.

56. Grofman, Handley, and Niemi, *Minority Representation*, 43–44.

57. Souter dissent in *Shaw* 1993, slip op. 5.

58. *Shaw v. Reno*, 529.

59. Plaintiffs Answers to the First Interrogatories, 1 April 1996, 2–3. *Moon v. Meadows.*

60. In the pre-*Shaw* cases there are two relevant lines of cases for the issue of standing: those that established the "judicially cognizable injury" in redistricting and vote dilution cases, and those that address standing more generally. *Davis v. Bandemer*, a partisan gerrymandering case, established that plaintiffs suffer no injury if they receive "adequate representation" or "virtual representation." The Court held that supporters of the losing candidate are represented adequately "by the winning candidate and . . . have as much opportunity to influence that candidate as other voters in the district." Virtual representation is provided by representatives elected from other districts. Racial vote dilution cases, such as *White v. Regester* (1973), *Rogers v. Lodge* (1982), and *UJO* (1977), established a heavy burden of proof that had to be met showing that plaintiffs did not have an equal opportunity to participate in the political process and that they were not being represented. See Karlan and Levinson, "Why Voting Is Different," 1209–11.

61. Cynthia McKinney, "The Politics of Geography," *Emerge* (Dec/Jan 1996): 63.

62. House of Representatives, "Voting Rights Roundtable, House Subcommittee on Civil and Constitutional Rights, Committee on the Judiciary," May 11, 1994, mimeo.

63. Kousser, "*Shaw v. Reno* and the Real World," 12.

64. David Kairys, "Unexplainable on Grounds Other than Race," *American University law Review* 45 (1996): 746 (summary table).

65. Jack Pritchard, "*United States v. Hays*: A Winnowing of Standing to Sue in Gerrymandering Claims," *Mercer Law Review* 47 (1996): 957.

66. *Allen V. Wright*, 1984, 3327.

67. Karlan and Levinson, "Why Voting Is Different," 1214.

68. *Shaw v. Hunt*, 1996, slip op. 6–7.

69. *Miller*,1995, slip op. 8.

70. Karlan and Levinson, "Why Voting Is Different," 1214.

71. Stevens dissent in *Shaw v. Hunt*, slip op., 10, citations omitted.

72. Bernard Grofman, "Would Vince Lombardi Have Been Right if He Had Said: 'When It Comes to Redistricting, Race Isn't Everything, It's the *Only* Thing'?," *Cardozo Law Review* 14 (1993): 1246, emphasis in original.

73. Thernstrom, *Whose Votes Count?*, 242.

74. Karlan and Levinson, "Why Voting Is Different," 1214.

75. Stevens dissent in *Shaw v. Hunt*, slip op., 9, citations omitted.

76. Canon, *Race, Redistricting, and Representation,* especially chapters 4 and 5.

77. Robert Singh, *The Congressional Black Caucus: Racial Politics in the U.S. Congress* (Thousand Oaks, Calif.: Sage Publications, 1998), 135–38, 166.

78. Canon, *Race, Redistricting, and Representation*, 26–31.

79. Carol M. Swain, *Black Faces, Black Interests: The Representation of African Americans in Congress* (Cambridge, Mass.: Harvard University Press, 1993).

80. Grofman, Handley, and Niemi, *Minority Representation*, 135.

81. *Marbury v. Madison* (1803), 1 Cr. 137 at 170.

82. In Bruce Ackerman, *Bush v. Gore: The Question of Legitimacy* (New Haven: Yale University Press, 2002).

83. http://www.supremecourtus.gov/publicinfo/speeches/sp_10-22-01.html

84. http://www.supremecourtus.gov/publicinfo/speeches/sp_10-22-01.html

85. Souter dissent in *Bush*, 1996, slip op.27.

86. *American Heritage Dictionary*.

87. See Souter's dissent in *Vera* (1995, slip op.9-10) for an eloquent discussion of the contextual differences between the subjugation of blacks and the placement of whites in black-majority districts. See Erving Goffman, *Stigma: Notes on the Management of Spoiled Identity* (New York: Simon and Schuster, 1963) for an interesting contrast to *Shaw's* use of the term. Goffman examines the lives of truly stigmatized people—drug addicts, prostitutes, people with physical deformities, and exmental patients—who do not conform to the "normal" expectations of society. It is difficult to see how the concept can be stretched to fit white plaintiffs.

88. The Court did not entirely adopt the colorblind view, noting that "race conscious" districting may be constitutional. However, the Court did recognize the individual-level basis for the constitutional challenge to the districts in *Shaw II*, (1996, 64 U.S.L.W. at 4443).

89. Souter dissent in *Vera* 1996, 3–5, slip op. Also see Samuel Issacharoff, "Groups and the Right to Vote," *Emory Law Journal* 46 (1995), 869–83.

90. Karlan and Levinson, "Why Voting Is Different," 1204, note 16.

91. Thernstrom, *Whose Votes Count?*, 225.

92. Of course, in some of these instances a majority of whites would have voted against the black Democratic nominee (when white Republicans are included). Thus, if all whites are considered, the black representative may not be the whites' candidate of choice. However, this does not contradict the reality that white voters were pivotal in the nomination and thus the election of more than half of the newly elected blacks in 1992.

93. Canon, *Race, Redistricting, and Representation,* chapter 4.

6

From *Beer* to Eternity: Why Race Will Always Predominate under the Voting Rights Act

Anthony A. Peacock

The Supreme Court's June, 2003 decision, *Georgia v. Ashcroft*,[1] was a stark reminder of why Sections 4 and 5 of the Voting Rights Act (VRA)[2] should be allowed to lapse in 2007 when they are set to expire. Independently of the cost of the litigation to the state of Georgia, which was significant, the dispute between the parties in *Ashcroft* demonstrated that the VRA has long since ceased to be a remedy for problems of discrimination and is now little more than a bald entitlement program for liberal Democrats. Democrats, however, are not the only ones guilty of using the act for partisan advantage. Republicans have been equally culpable, utilizing the act to "pack" Democratic loyalists into "safe" minority electoral districts, thus "bleaching" surrounding districts for Republican capture. *Ashcroft* provides a case in point.

What was at issue in the high court's decision was the extent to which the Democrat-controlled state legislature could maximize minority and Democratic representation in the state senate without violating the provisions of Section 5 of the VRA. Ironically the act may have stood in the way of black members of the Georgia Assembly and their Democratic allies by requiring the Democrats to create senate districts that contained more Democratic voters than were necessary to reelect Democratic incumbents. The Democrats apparently realized that what they were proposing was not likely going to be precleared by the Republican controlled U.S. Department of Justice. Accordingly, they sought preclearance from the D.C. District Court, the only other alternative but one that was more dilatory and expensive. Predictably, the Bush DOJ objected to the Georgia senate redistricting plan, claiming that the Georgia legislature had failed to create the number of majority-minority districts (MMDs)[3] necessary to comply with the "retrogression" test established by the U.S. Supreme Court in *Beer v. United States* (1976).[4]

The Bush administration's DOJ may have raised the objections purely as a matter of legal principle but it was just as likely that it was exercising the same brazen utilitarian calculations the Democrats had engaged in creating the plan. The tea leaves were not hard to read: a victory for the plaintiffs meant that black and Hispanic Democrats in the South would be able to hold Republican dominated states hostage to increased Democratic capture of electoral seats in future redistricting. Republican legislatures that failed to provide these seats would be immediately branded with the scarlet letter of "racist" for having failed to provide those districts to which minorities were entitled under the act. Democrats had already been swift to accuse Texas Republicans of having engaged in precisely such tactics during the redistricting fiasco of 2003, when Democratic senators fled the state twice to avoid voting on redistricting plans proposed by the Republicans.[5] By holding Democrats in Georgia to the more rigid test of retrogression the DOJ was proposing, such unsavory political outcomes for Republicans might be reduced in the future.

But why should states covered by Section 4 of the VRA have to continue meeting the *Beer* retrogression test anyway? The test was developed in the mid-1970s to address the problem of states in the Old South that had recently been forced to renounce racism. Was it still necessary to impose the same severe restrictions on states in the New South a quarter century later, particularly when there was no evidence of invidious discrimination against blacks by the jurisdictions covered by the act?

In this chapter, I investigate this question with the intent to illustrate the difficulties courts and the DOJ have had interpreting *Beer*, both before and after the post-2000 redistricting. The chapter begins with a brief review of the *Beer* ruling and the construction of Section 5 that the Court struggled with throughout the 1970s and early 1980s. Even in the early years *Beer* was not an easy case to administer and the Court generated muddled rulings on the meaning of retrogression. The second section follows the construction of Section 5 through the 1990s, with particular emphasis on the Court's response to the racial maximization policies imposed on states by the DOJ. The transformation of the VRA into an instrument of racial identity politics had already begun in the 1970s. It was consummated in the 1990s.

One of the results of the disputes that took place over that decade was that states would be left guessing just how Section 5 might be administered following the 2000 census, a problem aggravated by *Easely v. Cromartie* (2001)[6] where the Court appeared to reverse course on its earlier race and redistricting rulings. The Justice Department's 2001 Redistricting Guidance, examined later in this chapter, was an attempt by the DOJ to clarify questions jurisdictions covered by the VRA might have following the 2000 census. However, the Guidance still left a host of questions unresolved. It did make clear, however, that the *Beer* retrogression test still applied to jurisdictions covered by Section 4, even if precisely how it was to be applied would again be the subject of litigation. The fourth section of the chapter provides a brief summary of how states reacted both to the 2001 Redistricting Guidance as well as to the DOJ's and the courts' preclearance mandates post-2000. The emphasis at the end of this section is on the district court's interpretation of *Beer* and the retrogression test in *Georgia v. Ashcroft*. The penultimate section of the chapter reviews the U.S. Supreme Court's interpretation of that test in the same case, an interpretation that, according to Justice Souter, was so ambiguous it would invite arbitrary preclearance decisions in the future as well as more litigation.

The principal theme of this chapter is that *Beer* created a formalistic rule that could not accommodate the complexities of representational government or the changes in Southern politics that occurred over the decades of its application. By creating what amounted to yet another racial entitlement, *Beer* would work to facilitate the incorporation of a new multiculturalist ethos into American republicanism, one in which racial and ethnic differences were defined "not merely as sources of identity and of mutual interest but as legally determinative categories that provide[d] a legitimate foundation for claims to political rule."[7] Application of the *Beer* rule, throughout its history, would require race-based redistricting in either moderate or severe form. As occurred with other civil rights initiatives, the VRA would provide racial and ethnic interest groups with an institutional core through which they would be encouraged to regard their policy preferences as matters of legal "right,"[8] leading the VRA to become a model of what Theodore Lowi has referred to as "interest group liberalism."[9] Like many other civil rights initiatives, the VRA became an instrument of racial identity politics, setting the act—specifically Section 5—on a collision course with the laws of equal protection. In the 1990s this collision took place in a raft of cases that dominated the Supreme Court's docket throughout the decade and into the new millennium. As it turned out, not much changed post-2000 As Justice Kennedy emphasized in his separate concurring opinion in *Georgia v. Ashcroft*, the conflict between the Equal Protection Clause and the administration of Section 5 continues to this day. The chapter concludes that the VRA, once the consummate civil rights initiative fortifying American republicanism, now threatens that republicanism as much as any other federal mandate.

BEER AND THE RETROGRESSION TEST

Beer v. United States was the offspring of earlier Supreme Court decisions that had failed to resolve the meaning of Section 5 of the VRA. Sections 4 and 5 of the 1965 act were originally designed to be complementary provisions. Section 4 used a formula (voter turnout in the 1964 presidential election less than 50 percent and use of a literacy test) that applied the VRA to those states in the South with the worst history of racial discrimination in voting. Section 5 required that those states covered by Section 4 have any changes to voting practices or procedures "precleared" by either the DOJ or the United States District Court for the District of Columbia. States applying for preclearance had to prove that a proposed voting change will "not have the *purpose* and will not have the *effect* of denying or abridging the right to vote on account of race or color."[10] In *Allen v. State Board of Elections* (1969)[11] the Court determined that this broad language in Section 5 warranted a broad construction of what was protected by the VRA. In that case, the majority announced that minorities protected by the act not only had the right to cast a ballot but the right to an undiluted or "effective" vote as well. The Court, however, failed to address the specific meaning of purpose and effect in Section 5 since the lower courts had failed to determine whether the statutes at issue presented evidence of either.[12]

In *Beer* the Court took up this question, addressing for the first time the meaning of "effect" under Section 5 in the context of redistricting. What was at issue was the city of New Orleans' post-1970 redistricting plan. Justice Stewart, attempting to decipher the meaning of Section 5, enlisted the 1965 congressional House Report as a guide for interpreting the meaning of preclearance: "'Section 5 was a response to a common practice in some jurisdictions of staying one step ahead of the federal courts by passing new discriminatory voting laws as soon as the old ones had been struck down.'"[13] The 1975 House Report on the seven-year extension of the VRA had simplified the interpretation of Section 5 to assessing whether the ability of minorities to elect their candidates of choice was "'*augmented, diminished, or not affected* by the change affecting voting.'"[14] Stewart interpreted this to mean that "the purpose of § 5 had always been to ensure that no voting procedure changes would be made that would lead to a retrogression in the position of racial minorities with respect to their effective exercise of the electoral franchise."[15] When the new retrogression test was applied to New Orleans's redistricting proposal, the city had little difficulty meeting the test: at least one, if not two, members of the city council would be elected by blacks, whereas under the benchmark plan of the 1960s, only one member had any prospect of being so elected. Retrogression would therefore not occur under the new plan.

Although *Beer* imposed a retrogression test for Section 5 preclearance in redistricting, both earlier and later cases suggested that a different standard, one of proportional representation based on race, applied under the "effects" component of Section 5. In *City of Richmond v. United States* (1975), for instance, the Court had emphasized that in annexation cases in which the percentages of blacks in a city were reduced, the annexing city could overcome Section 5's proscribed "effects" by ensuring proportional representation of blacks postannexation.[16] In *United Jewish Organizations of Williamsburg, Inc. v. Carey* (*UJO*, 1977),[17] decided only one year after *Beer*, the Court interpreted *Beer* and *City of Richmond* to imply "that the Constitution does not prevent a State subject to the Voting Rights Act from deliberately creating or preserving black majorities in particular districts in order to ensure that its reapportionment plan complies with § 5."[18] The Court was even more emphatic in terms of what was permissible: "Unless we adopted an unconstitutional construction of § 5 in *Beer* and *City of Richmond*, a reapportionment cannot violate the Fourteenth or Fifteenth Amendment *merely because a State uses specific numerical quotas in establishing a certain number of black majority districts*."[19] Quotas then were permissible exceptions to the Constitution if they were used to comply with Section 5.

Throughout the 1970s, the Supreme Court had made it clear that the "purpose" and "effect" prongs of Section 5 required independent burdens of proof: jurisdictions petitioning for preclearance had to establish that proposed electoral changes were devoid of both discriminatory intent and discriminatory effect. In *City of Rome v. United States* (1980), the Court affirmed that "[b]y describing the elements of discriminatory purpose and effect in the conjunctive, Congress plainly intended that a voting practice not be precleared unless both discriminatory purpose and effect are absent."[20] Proof of discriminatory effect, in a word, was sufficient for a VRA violation and for a denial of preclearance. Moreover, as the Court suggested in *Beer*, Congress had reaffirmed the conjunctive language of Section 5 when it extended the VRA for an additional seven years in 1975.[21]

In *Rome*, however, there was a hitch. The Court had to resolve how an effects test that was independent of discriminatory purpose could be tied to the constitutional authority under which Congress had passed Section 5. If jurisdictions proved lack of discriminatory intent, as the city of Rome had before the district court, what precisely did the additional proof of nondiscriminatory effect amount to? What was the specific wrong that was being remedied once lack of intentional discrimination had been proved and what did the Court's denial of preclearance to the city of Rome imply for the purposes of the VRA's temporary provisions? If Rome had established lack of discriminatory intent as the animating purpose for the electoral changes at issue, what did adding the additional requirement of overcoming disparate impact do to help realize the act's objectives? And just what did the Court think these objectives were?

Skeptics of separate burdens of proof for purpose and effect in Section 5 had accepted Justice Harlan's observations in *Allen* that in 1965 effect and purpose were complementary concepts, "close to interchangeable terms," the former simply being "circumstantial evidence of the latter."[22] The purpose and effect language of Section 5 had to be understood in the context of the section's "prophylactic remedial structure": Since Section 5 applied only after a finding of liability under Section 4, it was reasonable for Congress to ensure that any electoral practices that might be susceptible to abuse be prohibited.[23] In *Rome*, as in *Beer*, the Court made precisely this argument: "Congress could rationally have concluded that, because electoral changes by jurisdictions with a demonstrable history of intentional racial discrimination in voting create the risk of purposeful discrimination, it was proper to prohibit changes that have a discriminatory impact."[24]

The problem with this argument was that the rationale the Court offered for Section 5 no longer applied. The "risk of purposeful discrimination" could hardly persist where the city had proven lack of purposeful discrimination. In cases such as this, what was the point of requiring proof of nondiscriminatory effect once the prophylactic role of Section 5, specifically, the nondiscriminatory impact component, had become irrelevant? What did the majority's additional mandate of compliance with nondiscriminatory impact mean?

According to Justice Rehnquist, dissenting, the majority's decision carried a number of implications. First, to the extent the disparate impact of the electoral changes at issue was the result of racial bloc voting, the Court was permitting Congress to redress *private*, not *governmental*, discrimination. This Congress could not do under either the Fourteenth or the Fifteenth Amendments. Second, prohibiting all practices that had a disparate impact would not enhance Congress' attempt at prohibiting purposeful discrimination since there was no discriminatory conduct at issue nor any future discriminatory conduct—such as the discriminatory application of literacy tests—that would be prevented by the Court's decision. What then was the policy rationale for such a mandate if it was not a pure entitlement to representation on the basis of race? Finally, the Court's requirement that the local government "structure its political system in a manner that most effectively enhances black political strength" was "premised on the assumption that white candidates will not represent black interests, and that States should devise a system encouraging blacks to vote in a bloc for black candidates."[25] The Court had proposed a dangerous ideological platform, one that identified race with political interest. Descriptive representation had become the underlying rationale for preclearance. If this was not what the majority's decision meant, it was hard to fathom what else its reasoning could have implied. The VRA was well on its way to becoming an instrument of racial identity politics.

THE LEGACY OF *BEER*

The controversies over the meaning of Section 5 throughout the 1970s and 1980s highlighted the new meaning of political equality second-generation voting rights issues had engendered. The transition from first to second generation questions in VRA law marked the beginning of a move away from fundamental rights questions of ballot access, on which there was virtually no disagreement, to contentious second-order policy questions regarding fair electoral process, on which there was virtually no agreement. It also marked a move away from a republican to a democratic theory of representation, the preference for a descriptive model of representation that would increasingly identify race with political interest. In retrospect, the trajectory of this development was predictable given the rationalization and bureaucratization of the representative process precipitated by the VRA and the dominance of political and legal professionals in the development of VRA law.

The VRA has become a paradigm of what Ward Elliott referred to in 1974 as "executive-judicial democracy."[26] Not only have the judiciary and the Civil Rights Division of the Department of Justice become naturally allied constituencies, charged equally with the task of giving operational meaning to a host of opaque enforcement mechanisms under the act,[27] but also up until 1993 the two branches of government operated uniformly to transform American republicanism through imposition of a singular vision of representation that identified voters' race with their political interests.[28]

In 1993, the amicable relationship between the DOJ and the U.S. Supreme Court began to unravel. That year, the Supreme Court released *Shaw v. Reno*,[29] a case that, in contrast to *UJO*, gave renewed significance to the Fourteenth Amendment. In *Shaw*, the Court was not concerned with racial discrimination so much as with the balkanizing effects of race-based redistricting.[30] As Justice O'Connor demurred on behalf of the Court, the bizarrely contoured North Carolina congressional districts at issue (CD 1 and CD 12) bore "an uncomfortable resemblance to political apartheid," reinforcing "the perception that members of the same racial group—regardless of their age, education, economic status, or the community in which they live—think alike, share the same political interests, and will prefer the same candidates at the polls."[31] In *Miller v. Johnson* (1995),[32] the Court clarified that it was not the bizarre shape of the North Carolina congressional districts that rendered them constitutionally suspect. Rather, it was the racial classifications they embodied. In other words, *Shaw* and *Miller* were not voting rights cases so much as race classification cases finally applying to voting rights the same antidiscrimination principle that had been applied for decades to segregated schools, juries, swimming pools, beaches, and other public facilities.[33]

Shaw and *Miller* were also consistent with *Richmond v. Croson* (1989)[34] and *Adarand v. Pena* (1995),[35] which affirmed the principle of racial reciprocity: that it did not matter what race the complainants were; anytime a state classified citizens by race, whites as well as blacks could sue, demanding the imposition of strict scrutiny on the jurisdiction at issue.[36] The proposition by critics of *Shaw* and *Miller* that whites should only be allowed to succeed or be permitted standing in racial redistricting cases if they can demonstrate "particularized harm" (which the critics deny whites can do) not only misconceives the constitutional issue but is tantamount to advocating the resurrection of the notorious separate but equal doctrine from *Plessy v. Ferguson* (1896).[37] The critics in essence contend that jurisdictions should be free to separate the races into racially defined districts so long as there is no demonstration of harm, particularly harm to whites. Understandably, the majority in *Miller* rejected this line of reasoning and adopted a more principled approach to equal protection, one requiring plaintiffs to demonstrate discriminatory intent, which was the usual test applied in equal protection law.[38] In *Miller*, the threshold question became whether "race was the *predominant factor* motivating the legislature's decision to place a significant number of voters within or without a particular district."[39]

Shaw and *Miller* were principled equal protection decisions that followed a long line of precedents. However, their belated recognition of the applicability of the laws of equal protection to racial redistricting undermined the keystone to the VRA. As the facts in *Shaw* and *Miller* made clear, the remedy of choice in preclearance cases was the same as it was in Section 2 cases: the creation of MMDs. Yet as Justice Thomas highlighted in *Bush v. Vera* (1996), anytime MMDs are created, race will necessarily predominate: "it means that the legislature affirmatively undertakes to create a majority-minority district that would not have existed but for the express use of racial classifications—in other words, a majority-minority district is created 'because of,' and not merely 'in spite of,' racial demographics." The resulting redistricting will necessarily constitute a racial gerrymander.[40] How then can the remedy of choice in VRA controversies, MMDs or even minority-influence districts (MIDs) be squared with the laws of equal protection?[41]

The simple answer is they cannot. The Court avoided this eventuality in *Easley v. Cromartie* (2001)[42] by skirting around the harsher implications of *Shaw* and its post-*Shaw* rulings. *Easely* was the fourth and last installment of North Carolina's 1990s redistricting woes to reach the high court. There, Justice O'Connor sided with the Court's four more liberal members. In an opinion written by Justice Stephen Breyer, the majority held that the third reconfiguration of Congressional District 12 was the product of a political, not racial, gerrymander. Signaling a retreat from the Court's earlier attempts to rein in race-conscious affirmative action, *Easley* took the rare step of overruling a district court's factual findings that North Carolina's 1997 congressional redistricting was based on race-driven criteria. The dissenting justices complained that by holding that the lower court's findings were "clearly erroneous," the Supreme Court had undermined the Court's longstanding measure of appellate review.

For our purposes, the more significant feature of the decision is that it may have had the effect of moderating the Court's earlier critique in *Miller* regarding the DOJ's administration of the VRA. In *Miller*, Justice Kennedy had chastised the DOJ for imposing on the state of Georgia a "max-black" congressional redistricting plan conceived and advocated by the ACLU.[43] As Kennedy noted, "the Justice Department's implicit command that States engage in presumptively unconstitutional race-based districting brings the Voting Rights Act, once upheld as a proper exercise of Congress' authority under § 2 of the Fifteenth Amendment . . . into tension with the Fourteenth Amendment."[44] The question following *Miller* was whether this admonition would temper the DOJ's administration of Section 5. Now the question was: would *Easley* effectively undermine any such tempering by indicating that the Court would turn a blind eye to racial redistricting taken to comply with the VRA in the future?

THE JUSTICE DEPARTMENT'S 2001 REDISTRICTING GUIDANCE

Prior to *Easely*, in January, 2001 the DOJ had released its guidelines for redistricting under Section 5 of the act. The 2001 Redistricting Guidance made clear that not much had changed since the 1990s. Although the Guidance was issued in response to the confusion generated by the effects of *Shaw v. Reno* and subsequent cases on VRA enforcement,[45] the "nonretrogression" rule established in *Beer v. United States* still governed. The Supreme Court reaffirmed the *Beer* holding in *Reno v. Bossier Parish School Board* (*Bossier II*, 2000)[46]: jurisdictions covered by Section 5 had the burden of proving "that a proposed redistricting plan does not have the purpose or effect of worsening the position of minority voters when compared to that jurisdiction's 'benchmark' plan."[47] Benchmarks determined to be unconstitutional pursuant to the Court's holding in *Shaw v. Reno* and its progeny could not serve as such for purposes of retrogression analysis. However, this did not prevent racial maximization policies post-2000 because of how the DOJ construed the meaning of intent under Section 5.

In *UJO*, the Court's construction of Section 5 had amounted to a county-wide requirement that approximated proportional representation based on race.[48] Although *Beer* required that jurisdictions comply with the nonretrogression rule, not proportional representation, two developments in the 1980s would change this. First, the Court's decision in *Thornburg v. Gingles* (1986), which construed the 1982 amended Section 2 for the first time, provided for a right to roughly proportional representation for legally recognized minority groups that were sizeable, compact, and cohesive.[49] Second, in 1987, the DOJ adopted a regulation that required the Justice Department to refuse preclearance to any jurisdiction that proposed electoral changes which might be "free of discriminatory purpose and retrogressive effect" but that nonetheless constituted "a clear violation of amended Section 2."[50] In other words, Section 5 preclearance analyses were to be guided by potential Section 2 actions and, by implication, the *Gingles* standard of proportional representation. Managing to work its way around the nonretrogression rule,[51] the 1987 regulation was one of the principal reasons the DOJ was able to demand racial maximization policies on jurisdictions covered by the VRA in the early 1990s.

In *Reno v. Bossier Parish I* (1997)[52] the Supreme Court ruled that the DOJ's 1987 regulation was invalid. Nevertheless, this did not mean that the Justice Department would not demand racial maximization post-2000 since it had also construed failure to maximize minority districting in the 1990s as tantamount to intentional discrimination under Section 5.[53] In the 2001 Preclearance Guidance, the DOJ cautioned that although *Bossier II* (and *Bossier I*) precluded denying preclearance on grounds that a redistricting plan violated Section 2, this did not prevent the department from bringing subsequent legal challenges on this basis, as well as on other bases.[54] Given, on the one hand, the vast array of factors considered when assessing whether or not a proposed redistricting plan will have a retrogressive purpose or effect[55] and, on the other, that the meaning of "effective exercise of the electoral franchise" is generally assessed in terms of how a proposed plan will affect "the opportunity of minority voters to elect candidates of their choice,"[56] there would be a strong incentive on the part of jurisdictions post-2000 to increase minority representation in any new redistricting plan.

As was the case in the 1990s, interest groups would continue to play a significant role in the preclearance process since when assessing retrogression, the department would consider not only plans actually proposed by the submitting jurisdiction but also "alternative plans presented or made known to the submitting jurisdiction by interested citizens or others."[57] As much as the ACLU's relationship with Justice was chastised in *Miller v. Johnson*,[58] both it and other public interest groups would continue to be significant players in preclearance applications.

One final difficulty the 2000 census posed for redistricting originated in the opportunity it provided respondents to identify themselves for the first time with more than one racial category. In 1997, the Office of Management and Budget decided to use multiple race reporting in federal statistical systems. This decision was incorporated into the 2000 Census. The OMB's guidelines concerning how to allocate and aggregate data on race in civil rights enforcement required that multiple race respondents who indicated that they were both white and one of the other five race categories relevant to VRA enforcement would be allocated to the minority race. If respondents indicated that they belonged to multiple race categories, these responses would be allocated alternatively to each racial category recognized under the act. The 2001 Redistricting Guidance anticipated that the multiple race responses from the 2000 census and their effect on VRA administration would be small.[59] This would prove to be wrong, as the state of Georgia would soon learn.

REDISTRICTING LITIGATION UNDER THE VRA FOLLOWING THE 2000 CENSUS[60]

Although it may still be too early to conclusively determine the overall effects of the DOJ's enforcement of the VRA on jurisdictions covered by Section 4 of the act, there have been some interesting developments, which may, at this time, allow for at least some tentative conclusions. Although the longest of my analyses will involve the case of Georgia, cases from other jurisdictions also serve to highlight some of the ongoing difficulties with redistricting preclearance applications in the new millennium. Perhaps the most notable overall effect of the DOJ's enforcement criteria has been their ambiguity. Given the numerous factors that must go into retrogression analyses and the possibility of differing judgments about what these mean, jurisdictions have spent significant political and legal capital trying to anticipate what will pass muster with Justice and what will not. This guesswork has been further complicated by the unpredictable approach to preclearance applications taken by federal and state courts, one more element making the preclearance process both difficult and expensive to manage.

In *In re 2001 Redistricting Cases*,[61] the Alaska Supreme Court rejected the state Redistricting Board's drawing of a house district to comply with Section 5 of the VRA. In order to keep the Native American population in one district—District 6—at a sufficiently high number, the board had to reduce the population of another district—District 40. As a result, the latter district had a negative deviation from the equipopulous districting standard of 6.9 percent. This produced, further, a maximum statewide population deviation of 12 percent.[62] The court rejected the board's stated goal of attempting to avoid retrogression under Section 5 of the VRA since the 2001 Redistricting Guidance precluded population deviations exceeding 10 percent to achieve this objective.[63] As the dissent pointed out, however, the deviation in District 40 was the lowest possible deviation given the board's attempt to comply with other state constitutional requirements, such as respecting socioeconomic integration. In fact, the total statewide deviation of 12 percent was the lowest deviation of any redistricting plan in the history of Alaska,[64] a state notoriously difficult to remap. In addition, it is noteworthy that the DOJ emphasized that the 2001 Guidance, on which the majority in this case was relying, was "not legally binding."[65]

The moral of the story in the Alaska case was this: when combined with other state objectives, such as compliance with state constitutional requirements, meeting the retrogression test and the criteria of the DOJ's Guidance can be highly unpredictable. This was demonstrated by the different approaches to the facts of the case taken by the original trier of fact, on the one hand, and the appeals court, on the other. The state Redistricting Board had made a convincing case to the superior court judge charged with hearing the complaint in the original instance only to fail before the state supreme court on appeal.

The 2001 Redistricting Guidance suggests that criteria other than equipopulous districts "may need to give way to some degree to avoid retrogression." The DOJ listed county, city, and precinct boundaries, protecting incumbents, preserving partisan balance, and requiring district compactness, as examples of criteria that may have to give way to accommodate nonretrogression.

In the case of North Carolina, the criterion that had to give way in order to accommodate Section 5 was the boundaries of the state's counties. This, at any rate, is what the government alleged. Following North Carolina's nightmarish redistricting battles of the 1990s, the state was able to preclear its state legislative redistricting post-2000 in fairly short order. On February 11, 2002, the DOJ approved the state's house and senate redistricting plans. Less than a week later, however, Judge Knox Jenkins of the Johnston County Superior Court ruled that the precleared plans violated the state's constitutional requirement mandating the preservation of whole counties. North Carolina's 2001 redistricting plan divided 51 of 100 counties into different senate seats and 70 of 100 counties into different house seats. The government said it had to do so because it had to comply with the VRA and the constitutional requirement of one person, one vote. But, on appeal, the North Carolina Supreme Court did not buy the argument. "The 2001 legislative redistricting plans," the court declared, "violate the WCP [Whole County Provision] for reasons unrelated to compliance with federal law."[66] In particular, the counties were divided primarily for reasons of partisan advantage and incumbency protection. Evidence filed suggested that following the 2001 redistricting, 30 of 50 senate seats (60 percent) would be uncontested in the November 2002 general election. Similarly, 71 of 120 house seats (59 percent) would be uncontested in the general election. Although the North Carolina Supreme Court affirmed Judge Jenkin's ruling, it emphasized that compliance with the VRA's nonretrogression principle placed limitations on the state's whole county constitutional requirement: minority electoral opportunities could not be retrogressed to satisfy the requirements of the state constitution. After Judge Jenkins threw out a second set of redistricting plans offered up by the General Assembly in May, 2002,[67] proceeding to draw maps of his own, the DOJ precleared Jenkin's redistricting plans July 12, 2002. The North Carolina Supreme Court denied a subsequent appeal of Jenkin's original ruling.

Louisiana challenged the 2001 Redistricting Guidance itself in a complaint filed in the D.C. District Court, January, 2002.[68] The complaint alleged that the Guidance represented "an unlawful expansion of the scope of the Attorney General's Section 5 review authority."[69] The issue concerned the benchmark that was proposed for assessing retrogression in the case of the state's house redistricting plan. The state argued that either its 1981/1982 plan or its "first" 1991 redistricting plan, rejected by the DOJ on Section 5 grounds, should serve as the benchmark.[70] The state's complaint against Justice was that its objection to Louisiana's 1991 plan was illegal. The only legitimate grounds on which the DOJ could object to Louisiana's redistricting was that it resulted in retrogression of the minority vote. Yet the basis for the DOJ's objection was not retrogression but racial maximization. The DOJ's demand for an additional four house MMDs "overwhelmingly reflected the predominance of [a] racial motive," one that Section 5 did not warrant.[71]

The specific problems with the 2001 Guidance, according to Louisiana, were threefold. First, it sought to retain as the benchmark for retrogression analyses any redistricting plan that had not been found by a court to be unconstitutional. This applied even to those plans for which there was strong evidence that race predominated in the construction of a district in contravention of the Equal Protection Clause. The 2001 Guidance emphasized that "a jurisdiction is not required to address the constitutionality of its benchmark plan when submitting a redistricting plan and the question of whether the benchmark plan is constitutional will *not be considered* during the Department's Section 5 review."[72] According to Louisiana, this position was inconsistent with the U.S. Supreme Court's opinion in *Abrams v. Johnson* (1997).[73] There the Court declared that "Section 5 cannot be used to freeze in place the very aspects of a plan found unconstitutional."[74] Whether the Court's statement in *Abrams* authorized the rejection of a benchmark not specifically "found" unconstitutional in a judicial proceeding was not answered by the Court. Nevertheless, it was Louisiana's position that the Attorney General's intention to persist in using, as Section 5 benchmarks, plans which on the evidence appeared to be unconstitutional racial gerrymanders had "the potential to require maintenance of minority-majority districts that were created to cure a Section 5 objection that the Attorney General did not have the authority to interpose."[75]

Louisiana's second objection concerned the DOJ's statement that where it was not clear whether a proposed redistricting plan would have a retrogressive effect, the department would focus on whether the legislature "intended to reduce minority voting strength, either now or in the future." The state's specific complaint here was that both *Beer* and *Bossier II* proscribed a review of legislative intent. The focus had to be solely on "effects." What was at issue in retrogression analyses was "backsliding," a purely factual determination "based upon an analysis of voting patterns and election history."[76] A review of legislative intent would not advance such an inquiry. Accordingly, neither the VRA nor its supporting case law gave the attorney general the authority to request "information related to the process by which the redistricting plan was adopted or the intent of the decision makers individually or as a group." Therefore, "such [a] request represents an unconstitutional intrusion on the rights and responsibilities that the Tenth Amendment of the United States Constitution has reserved to the States."[77]

Louisiana's final objection concerned the disclaimer that the 2001 Redistricting Guidance was "not legally binding." This may have seemed innocuous enough but its legal significance was that jurisdictions could not challenge the guidelines prior to submitting a voting change to Justice, even where the guidelines promoted a procedure that was legally suspect. If the guidelines had been enacted as regulations, such a challenge would be available. The implications of the difference between utilizing guidelines rather than regulations were that a jurisdiction could not get preclearance under the VRA in the most economical and time efficient way, secure in the knowledge that what the Justice Department was demanding was an approach consistent with case law and the Constitution. Louisiana apparently wanted to avoid the lesson jurisdictions learned in the 1990s: that compliance with DOJ mandates did not necessarily mean compliance with the law or inoculation against lawsuits that could drag on for years.

Florida, Texas, and Georgia, the last three states to be examined here, also suffered dilatory and costly litigation in connection with preclearance compliance in the 1990s.

In the case of Florida, the DOJ interposed a Section 5 objection to the state's house redistricting plan on July 1, 2002. The department alleged that house district 101 was retrogressive respecting Hispanic voters. To correct this, the court adopted a plan that was identical to the state house's March 2002 plan rejected by the DOJ save for three districts (76, 101, and 112). These three districts were modified to meet the DOJ's objection. Importantly, the court rejected a proposal by a group of plaintiffs that sought to modify eleven to twelve districts in the state house plan. The court emphasized that its Section 5 remedies should be tailored to modify the state's original redistricting proposal as little as possible.[78]

Litigation over Texas' redistricting focused on three cases, one involving the state's congressional redistricting plan, the other two the state's house and senate redistricting plans. These cases, like others in the 2000s, again revealed the power of interest group liberalism driving VRA litigation. In all three cases, many of the key moving parties, in addition to elected officials and the DOJ, were minority litigation groups.

In the congressional case, *Balderas v. Texas* (*Balderas I*, 2001),[79] a three-judge federal district court had to create the state's redistricting map because an earlier state court-drawn map was vacated by the Texas Supreme Court for constitutional irregularities (see McKee and Shaw, this volume). Although the court set aside districts to comply with Section 5 of the VRA, the congressional map is not directly relevant to my analysis here because there was no DOJ objection at issue. However, the case is interesting for two reasons. First, it highlights the partisan nature of Section 5 entitlements under the VRA. As Judge Patrick Higginbotham noted in relation to the court's attempt to produce a congressional delegation roughly proportional to the statewide breakdown of party voting: "It must be understood that any plan necessarily begins with a Democratic bias due to the preservation of protected majority-minority districts, all of which contain a high percentage of Democratic voters."[80] This has been a longstanding feature in Section 5 enforcement. As we will see in the case of Georgia, every federal and state MMD and MID created by the state post-2000 was to benefit the Democrats.

The second important feature from *Balderas I* was that it illustrated how Section 5 has created incentives to institutionalize race-conscious distinctions and for facilitating racial conflict in entitlements. A significant part of *Balderas I* addressed the demands of Latino and black groups which had sought MMDs and MIDs beyond those to which Hispanics and blacks were already entitled under the VRA. The court rejected these claims on grounds they would have involved the court in a "raw political choice."[81] It further noted what a number of political scientists who testified in the case had alluded to: that "[t]he Latino and African-American plaintiffs . . . present competing positions, reflecting a political reality that they are competitors in the political process. This competition finds expression in an absence of cohesive voting between Latinos and African-Americans at the point in which it is meaningfully measured, the Democratic primaries."[82]

Balderas II, dealing with Texas's House of Representatives, did involve an objection from the Justice Department filed November 16, 2001. (The DOJ had earlier precleared the state's senate plan in October, 2001.) Justice's preclearance denial in *Balderas II* centered on the Texas Legislative Redistricting Board's having retrogressed Hispanic voting power in South and West Texas. The court responded first to the complaints of Hispanic groups which sought the creation of further MMDs under Section 2 of the VRA, noting that to accommodate these demands would have risked retrogression in existing Latino MMDs.[83] The court also rejected a request from plaintiffs and House Speaker Pete Laney to create MIDs. Again, the court reiterated that it had "no power to address such claims."[84] The court also refused to create a black opportunity district in Tarrant County which would have relied upon a coalition of Latino, Asian, and black populations because there was insufficient evidence of political cohesiveness among these groups, as required by *Thornburg v. Gingles* (1986).[85] The court did alter the state's house redistricting to accommodate the objections of the DOJ under Section 5. It qualified, however, that the court's plan was a "judicial plan, and while it unavoidably bears some resemblance to plans submitted by the parties in certain areas, it is entirely of our own making. Therefore it is not subject to the preclearance requirements of Section 5 of the Voting Rights Act."[86] The Court met the DOJ's objections by raising the level of Spanish surnamed registered voters in each of the districts at issue. Interestingly, the court did not specify how, precisely, it distinguished a Spanish surnamed registered voter from a non-Spanish surnamed registered voter.

It is worth noting that in both the congressional and house lawsuits in Texas, as well as in *Balderas III*, a lawsuit challenging Texas's senate redistricting that was heard *after* the DOJ had precleared the plan and in which *all* of the plaintiffs' claims were dismissed for presenting "no meritorious challenge,"[87] the court ordered that all court costs be paid by the state of Texas. Why the court did not impose cost consequences on the losing plaintiffs not acting on behalf of the state or its representatives was not explained but such a policy might go a long way to discouraging unnecessary lawsuits in future. In addition, in *Balderas III*, plaintiffs and the Texas NAACP again invited the court to recognize a right of minorities to MIDs, a claim the court declared it had "no warrant"[88] to recognize but that indicates the direction in which minority grievance groups are likely to push Section 2 and Section 5 litigation in future.

The case of Georgia presents the most interesting and significant set of facts. Rather than seeking preclearance from the DOJ for its post-2000 congressional and state redistricting plans, the state decided to obtain a declaratory judgment from the D.C. District Court, a curious and potentially dilatory move. The likely reason for the state's action was that the Democratic leaders of Georgia realized that their plan would not be precleared by the DOJ since they had defined retrogression under the *Beer* rule in an unusual and potentially illegal manner.[89]

As it turned out, the state did not have much better luck before the district court. On April 5, 2002, the court granted preclearance for Georgia's congressional and house legislative plans, but denied preclearance for the state's senate plan. It did so because it disputed the state's compliance with the benchmark plan against which retrogression was to be measured.

Georgia v. Ashcroft[90] is interesting for a variety of reasons. First, it highlights the exceedingly technical and speculative nature of Section 5 evidentiary investigations. As both the majority and concurring/dissenting opinions emphasized, the analysis of retrogression is "fact intensive and must carefully scrutinize the context in which the proposed voting change will occur."[91] Most of the district court decision centered, first, on what evidence should be primary, expert or lay witness testimony, and, second, on which of the two experts, the state's Professor David Epstein or the federal government's Professor Richard Engstrom, provided the more compelling evidence. The evidentiary issues focused, as almost all preclearance cases do, on the voting patterns of racial groups, specifically, whites and blacks. As it turned out, neither Professor Epstein nor Professor Engstrom provided sufficient evidence for the court to make the determinations it sought to make regarding retrogression. Nevertheless, Engstrom presented evidence of racial polarization in the existing senate districts, even if he did not compare the benchmark districts with the proposed districts.[92] This was sufficient to raise a presumption of retrogression, which the state (having the burden of proof) failed to rebut. Accordingly, the state's application for preclearance was denied.

The second issue of interest in *Ashcroft* concerned the legal question of what constituted "retrogression" for the purposes of a Section 5 analysis. As the majority noted, "The Supreme Court has never comprehensively defined 'retrogression,' nor has it engaged in any detailed discussion of what constitutes an 'effective exercise of the electoral franchise' by minority voters."[93] The majority and the DOJ argued that retrogression occurred where there was any diminution of minority voting strength relative to the benchmark senate districts. Judge Oberdorfer, dissenting on this score, and the state of Georgia, argued that retrogression occurred only where there was less electoral opportunity for minorities vis-à-vis benchmark districts—that is, the state could reduce minority populations in benchmark districts relative to earlier benchmark numbers as long as minorities retained an equal opportunity to elect their candidates of choice. In this way, minorities could be "unpacked" from MMDs, where their votes had been "wasted" in earlier elections.[94] These residual minority votes could be reallocated to districts where they could help elect additional candidates of the minority's choice.

In this case, the additional candidates elected would be Democrats. It is not difficult to see why. During the Georgia General Assembly's 2001–2002 session, the 34 of 180 representatives who were black and the 11 of 56 senators who were black were all Democrats.[95] There were no black Republicans. The state had argued that by enhancing the prospect of electing Democrats to government this would enhance black political strength. "One of the reasons given by African American senators for aligning their interests with those of the Democratic Party was that, should the Democratic Party cease to be in the majority in the State House and State Senate, all existing African American chairs of the committees would be lost."[96] How did this consideration factor into the calculus of effective representation for the purposes of retrogression? The short response is that it did not—at least not for the majority of the court.

Although every Republican in the Georgia Assembly voted against the state house and senate redistricting plans in 2002, only one black representative and one black senator voted against them.[97] Blacks were well represented on the Senate Reapportionment Committee (comprising 6 of 24 members) and on the House Reapportionment Committee (comprising 6 of 29 members).[98] In addition, Robert Brown, a black senator from District 26, was both the vice chairman of the Senate Reapportionment Committee and chair of the subcommittee that drafted the senate plan itself. The majority leader of the Senate was black, as was the chair of the rules committee.[99] Given these facts, why did the court not pay greater heed to the overwhelming desire of black legislators to approve the senate redistricting plan when considering whether the plan had the purpose or effect of "denying or abridging the right to vote on account of race or color" (the Section 5 test)?

The reason was the specific problem of the meaning of retrogression, which as we saw earlier the majority of the court defined as any reduction in minority voting strength relative to the benchmark plan. Although black legislators may have overwhelmingly approved the Georgia senate redistricting plan, this was irrelevant to the legal question of whether there was retrogression.

The problem of what was meant by retrogression raised the further question of how to define a district as majority-minority. The three standard measures used in such analyses have been total population, voting age population, and registered voters. The dispute between the majority and dissent in *Ashcroft* involved the last two categories. The majority and DOJ assessed retrogression with emphasis on black voter registration, rendering Georgia's senate redistricting five MMDs short of meeting the preclearance requirements. Judge Oberdorfer and Georgia, by contrast, emphasized the more standard measure of black voting age population (BVAP), which resulted in increasing the number of MMDs from twelve to thirteen, thus meeting (and exceeding) the retrogression test.

This latter issue was further complicated by the new census data and the question of how to calculate BVAP. How to tally up multiple race respondents under the new Census was not easy. It would prove to be yet one more source of division between the majority and Judge Oberdorfer and between the DOJ and Georgia.

According to the DOJ, respondents who self-identified as black or as black and white would be counted as black. Those who identified as black in combination with another nonwhite racial or ethnic group were excluded from the BVAP. By contrast, Georgia included in the BVAP all those voters who identified themselves as either exclusively black or as black in combination with some other racial or ethnic group. How one counted black voters made a significant difference. Using the DOJ's method, Georgia's senate plan was retrogressive. Using Georgia's method, it was nonretrogressive. The majority accepted the DOJ's method of counting. Judge Oberdorfer accepted the state of Georgia's.

The dispute about how to count multirace respondents highlighted a final problematic area in the science of preclearance law. As Judge Orberdorfer observed: "Georgia presented unrefuted testimony from Dr. Roderick Joseph Harrison, former chief of the Racial Statistics Branch at the U.S. Census Bureau, that the Department's allocation rule is not justified as a matter of statistics, empirical evidence, or other considerations, such as communities of interest."[100] The state of Georgia's Jurisdictional Statement before the U.S. Supreme Court was even more emphatic: "Inexplicably, the DOJ contended at one point that it might be appropriate to count, as 'blacks,' those multiple-race responders who responded both black and white, but not persons who responded as black and any other race."[101]

In addition to the above objections, Oberdorfer also took issue with the majority on a host of other matters. First, the majority placed too much reliance on the testimony of Professor Engstrom. Engstrom focused excessively on voting patterns in local elections to the disregard of statewide elections and ignored the effects of white crossover voting in the districts at issue.[102] Second, the majority adhered too strictly to earlier black voting percentages in benchmark districts. The effect of this was to disregard the change in black/white voting patterns that may have taken place over the years intervening between the benchmark plan and the proposed plan.[103] Third, the majority depended excessively on statistics for assessing voting behavior. As Oberdorfer emphasized, the U.S. Supreme Court had highlighted that such statistics were problematic because of "the 'inherently uncertain' nature of voting behavior data,[104] and already outdated census data."[105] Finally, the majority gave preference to evidence from the declarations (affidavits) of lay witnesses over the witnesses' deposition testimony. The latter tended to provide more comprehensive and reliable evidence since it allowed witnesses to explain themselves. In addition, deposition testimony represented "the witnesses' own words, rather than the adoption of statements at least partially prepared by the counsel."[106]

Georgia v. Ashcroft illustrated as well as any other post-2000 redistricting case the inherent difficulties of preclearance applications and the nature of the vision adopted by the DOJ in the administration of such applications. The dispute between the majority and minority in *Ashcroft* was as much a dispute over, on the one hand, the meaning of retrogression and the risk of excessive federal oversight of a traditionally sacred state prerogative—redistricting—as it was a dispute, on the other hand, of the extent to which racism still dominates Georgia politics. Two passages from Judge Oberdorfer's opinion highlight each of these elements of the dispute. The first passage introduced his analysis of the meaning of "retrogressive effect":

> Today, we face an unprecedented, yet not unforeseen, challenge: to assess whether a deliberate reduction of black supermajorities, undertaken with the endorsement of African-American legislators with the reasonable expectation that these bare majorities, in combination with meaningful white crossover voting, would have the effect of enhancing or preserving minority voting strength statewide, is nonetheless retrogressive because it reduces the BVAP in three contested Senate districts to just above fifty percent.[107]

Oberdorfer's second statement was made in the context of his critique of Professor Engstrom's use of local election data to generalize across senatorial district contests:

> The lower rates of white crossover in local elections may be specific to those pockets of the Senate district, may be specific to the office, or may be less statistically accurate due to smaller number of precincts available for analysis. Any of these explanations are more plausible than a theory that white voters who refuse for racist reasons to support black candidates for local office would nonetheless vote to elect black candidates to more powerful and prestigious statewide positions.[108]

In support of this last statement, Oberdorfer continued in a footnote:

> A comparison of the 16.6 percent white crossover rate in the district attorney election in Bibb County, and the 46.9 percent white crossover rate in the election for state Attorney General is illustrative. It may be that there is a cohort of white voters in Georgia who will not support a black candidate for county district attorney simply because they are racists. However, it is implausible to assume that a significant portion of those white racists would turn around and support a black candidate for state Attorney General.[109]

Oberdorfer's dissenting remarks highlighted that the proposition frequently underlying VRA disputes, that racial bloc voting necessarily implies racism, may be a dubious one. In jurisdictions where whites tend to vote Republican and blacks tend to vote Democrat, racial polarization will occur in virtually every contested election in which whites and blacks vote. Such polarization is not inherently blameworthy. Beyond the obvious partisan divide, there may be many other nondiscriminatory reasons for racially polarized voting. VRA law and the pathologies of litigation however may tend to preclude the discovery of such explanations. To say nothing of other things, where social scientists are retained by parties who have a legal and political agenda and who want to win not lose, there will be strong incentives to present evidence in a way that promotes partisan advantage.

GEORGIA V. ASHCROFT BEFORE THE U. S. SUPREME COURT

Georgia's long-awaited resolution of its redistricting woes came only three days after the Supreme Court released its seminal affirmative action decisions in *Grutter v. Bollinger* (2003)[110] and *Gratz v. Bollinger* (2003).[111] Perhaps this explains why *Ashcroft* generated so little public commentary. In the context of the VRA, however, the decision was significant.

Justice O'Connor emphasized on behalf of the majority in *Ashcroft* that the case addressed for the first time the specific meaning of the last part of the *Beer* rule: the meaning of "effective exercise of the electoral franchise."[112] Importantly, the Court rejected the district court's interpretation of retrogression and effectively adopted Judge Oberdorfer's interpretation. O'Connor stressed that the assessment of retrogression had to be more comprehensive than the district court allowed, focusing excessively as it did on senate districts 2, 12, and 26, and on whether black voters could elect their candidates of choice in designated MMDs. Rather, Section 5 analyses had to incorporate all potentially "relevant circumstances, such as the ability of minority voters to elect their candidate of choice, the extent of the minority group's opportunity to participate in the political process, and the feasibility of creating a nonretrogressive plan."[113] O'Connor implored that in "assessing the totality of circumstances, a court should not focus solely on the comparative ability of a minority group to elect a candidate of choice."[114] This seemed to conflict with the Court's earlier Section 5 case law where the ability of minorities to elect their candidate of choice was the central feature of *Beer* retrogression analyses. The DOJ's own 2001 Redistricting Guidance highlighted this fact, as did the dissent in *Ashcroft*. Justice O'Connor however disagreed, declaring that under the *Beer* rule, states had a choice between the *descriptive* or *substantive* representation.

> In order to maximize the electoral success of a minority group, a State may choose to create a certain number of "safe" districts, in which it is highly likely that minority voters will be able to elect the candidate of their choice. . . . Alternatively, a State may choose to create a greater number of districts in which it is likely—although perhaps not quite as likely as under the benchmark plan—that minority voters will be able to elect candidates of their choice.[115]

In the former case, minorities mirroring the racial characteristics of the majority of voters in the district would probably be elected, thus providing more descriptive representation. In the latter case, coalitions of voters that could more readily achieve the electoral objectives of the designated minority could be formed more easily, thus providing more substantive representation. In either case, Section 5 did not mandate one method of redistricting over another. "Either option 'will present the minority group with its own array of electoral risks and benefits,' and presents 'hard choices about what would truly 'maximize' minority electoral success.'"[116]

O'Connor emphasized twice in consecutive paragraphs—and again later in the case—the importance of maximizing the electoral success of minority groups. In both instances she cited *Thornburg v. Gingles*, in the last case paraphrasing from the decision. *Gingles* involved vote dilution under Section 2, not retrogression under Section 5. What, precisely, then was O'Connor saying? Were Section 5 cases now to be governed by some sort of racial maximization standard rather than retrogression? Or was the retrogression test met if jurisdictions maximized minority voting strength? In either case, was the Court not departing from earlier Section 5 case law?

O'Connor seemed to be saying that states were free to use whatever theory of representation they preferred—descriptive or substantive representation—but that the goal was maximization of minority political power. In addition, she emphasized that political power—"the power to make and pass laws"[117]—was central to assessments of effective minority representation. This meant that considerations other than minority numbers in electoral districts were germane to retrogression analyses. What legislative leadership positions, political influence, and power minority candidates would enjoy post-election were significant factors, as were the opinions of minority incumbents elected from the districts created by the VRA.[118]

Social science evidence would also be of increasing importance, not only for courts but also for administrators and legislators attempting to calculate retrogression. It was social science evidence that had undermined the importance of MMDs in the first place and that had introduced MIDs and coalitional districts as alternatives to MMDs. With more options available to jurisdictions regarding how to avoid retrogression, social science would also be critical in meeting the evidentiary burden Section 5 applications would henceforth require. Again, O'Connor stressed the importance of maximization: "[V]arious studies," she remarked, "have suggested that the most effective way to maximize minority voting strength may be to create more influence or coalitional districts."[119] Retrogression analyses in future would then have to be based on empirical evidence that was up-to-date and that could calculate how minority electoral success might be most effectively maximized. The increased rationalization of the representational process that had begun with the reapportionment cases and that would be refined through the various generations of VRA jurisprudence was entering it seemed yet another phase. But did it imply "fairer" representation for minority groups or the reduction of the use of race in the calculus of effective representation under the VRA?

According to members of both the majority and minority in *Ashcroft*, the answer to these questions was "no." Regarding the question of the use of race, even members of the majority had difficulty with the Court's decision. The irony of its reasoning was not lost on Justice Kennedy. Like Justice Thomas, Kennedy had joined the Court's opinion only because it was consistent with earlier precedents and no constitutional issue had been raised in the case. But that said, Kennedy had his reservations:

> As is evident from the Court's accurate description of the facts in this case, race was a predominant factor in drawing the lines of Georgia's State Senate redistricting map. . . . Race cannot be the predominant factor in redistricting under our decision in *Miller v. Johnson*. . . . Yet considerations of race that would

> doom a redistricting plan under the Fourteenth Amendment or § 2 seem to be what save it under § 5. . . .
>
> There is a fundamental flaw . . . in any scheme in which the Department of Justice is permitted or directed to encourage or ratify a course of unconstitutional conduct in order to find compliance with a statutory directive.[120]

Justice Thomas sounded an equally dour note in his separate concurring opinion. Even though he too had joined the majority, his brief remarks referenced his own earlier opinion in *Holder v. Hall* (1994).[121] Thomas's concurring opinion in *Holder* was one of the longest concurring opinions in Supreme Court history and the most penetrating indictment of the Court's VRA jurisprudence dating back 25 years. In a lengthy examination of the VRA's history, Thomas had excoriated his colleagues for their decades long misguided adventures in vote dilution jurisprudence. The *Allen* decision, Thomas proclaimed, had committed the Court to assessing questions of "effective representation," a dubious enterprise that had forced the Court to engage in questions of political theory and that ultimately resulted in the Court adopting an arbitrary, illiberal theory of representation, one that could not have been better designed to exacerbate racial cleavages throughout the country. Vote dilution jurisprudence under Section 2 and Section 5 of the VRA had divided the electorate into race-based "political homelands."[122] Georgia's 2001 senate redistricting plan, Thomas indicated, was destined for a similar legacy, making the same pernicious assumptions about racial minorities: "that members of racial and ethnic groups must all think alike on important matters of public policy and must have their own 'minority preferred' representatives holding seats in elected bodies if they are to be considered represented at all."[123]

Just how closely *Ashcroft* followed earlier precedents was an open question. In Justice Souter's dissenting opinion, joined by Justices Stevens, Ginsburg, and Breyer, Souter made clear that he thought *Ashcroft* was an aberration that had broken with earlier case law. In particular, the Court had unmoored Section 5 from any kind of practical or administrable concept of minority influence in retrogression analyses.[124] Once a jurisdiction moved from MMDs to minority influence or coalitional districts, Souter asked, what guarantee was there that nonminority voters would vote along with protected minorities, thus preserving the latter's effective representation? In addition, since calculating effective representation would now consist of something more than merely assessing the ability of minorities to elect their candidates of choice, how precisely was this to be done? Retrogression analyses would now involve such assessments as what committee assignments minorities might get postelection (and what were the most powerful of these assignments), which incumbents might be reelected and how would their reelection affect party and minority fortunes, what sort of preelection promises had been made to minority political groups, and a rash of other considerations.

Souter was particularly concerned that basing measurement of retrogression on minority incumbents' approval of a redistricting plan, as occurred in *Ashcroft*, would turn out to benefit minority incumbents rather than minority voters. Such approval by minority incumbents was "'far more probative of a lack of retrogressive *purpose* than of an absence of retrogressive *effect*.'"[125] The problem of a lack of cognizable standards by which to measure retrogression, however, remained the central problem with *Ashcroft*. Expanding the scope of "effective representation" under the *Beer* rule meant that any coherent standard of retrogression was being undermined.

> Indeed, to see the trouble ahead, one need only ask how on the Court's new understanding, state legislators or federal preclearance reviewers under § 5 are supposed to identify or measure the degree of influence necessary to avoid the retrogression the Court nominally retains as the § 5 touchstone. Is the test purely ad hominem, looking merely to the apparent sentiments of incumbents who might run in the new districts? Would it be enough for a State to show that an incumbent had previously promised to consider minority interests before voting on legislative measures? Whatever one looks to, however, how does one put a value on influence that falls short of decisive influence through coalition? Nondecisive influence is worth less than majority-minority control, but how much less? Would two influence districts offset the loss of one majority-minority district? Would it take three? Or four? . . . The Court's "influence" is simply not functional in the political and judicial worlds.[126]

The majority's decision was particularly problematic when considering the burden of proof in preclearance applications. The "unquantifiable standard" that the Court had now made the measure of retrogression analyses meant that the outcomes of preclearance applications would be arbitrary. If a "serious burden of persuasion" remained on states, their reliance on the novel theory of influence now being propounded by the majority would likely guarantee that they would lose such applications since minority influence would be "too amorphous for objective comparison" to allow conclusive findings of nonretrogression. However, placing an onerous burden on states was the less likely scenario in future. The more likely outcome would be deference to states, allowing them to satisfy their burden through an "unquantifiable influence" that could "be equated with majority-minority power." If that occurred, Section 5 would "simply drop out as a safeguard against the 'unremitting and ingenious defiance of the Constitution' that required the procedure of preclearance in the first place."[127] For this last point, Souter quoted *South Carolina v. Katzenbach* (1966),[128] the Court's original decision upholding the constitutionality of Section 5 as an extraordinary measure for extraordinary times.

Souter's dissent raised a host of important and compelling points. He was certainly correct that the majority's new retrogression test was an ambiguous one that would be difficult, if not impossible, to apply in the future, virtually guaranteeing arbitrary outcomes and unnecessary litigation. What factors would count toward enhancing potential minority political power was anyone's guess. In addition, there was little assurance that respecting the wishes of minority incumbents would guarantee that minority voter interests would also be respected, however one might calculate these. Indeed, it was a serious question whether protecting incumbent interests of any sort—minority or otherwise—was consistent with sound democratic practice.

The more important point, however, was whether Sections 4 and 5 of the VRA still had any relevance to twenty-first-century American politics. Souter's invocation of *South Carolina v. Katzenbach* and his suggestion that the state of Georgia or any other jurisdiction covered by Section 5 was today engaged in "unremitting and ingenious defiance of the Constitution" had a melodramatic but empty ring to it. No one in the case was even remotely suggesting the existence of invidious discrimination against blacks by the Georgia Democrats. To the contrary, the Georgia legislature had made every attempt to accommodate black politicians and the Georgia Black Caucus in the state's post-2000 redistricting. Critics might say that this was precisely because the legislature had to comply with the VRA, but even in the absence of the act, could anyone seriously suggest, as Souter seemed to be, that the political circumstances of twenty-first-century Georgia were in any way similar to those of South Carolina in the mid-1960s? Or that the state of Georgia was today engaged in "unremitting and ingenious defiance of the Constitution"? Could *any* jurisdiction covered by Section 5 in 2003 be accused of "unremitting and ingenious defiance of the Constitution"? If not, what did this imply about the relevance of Section 5 to present day American politics? Ironically, it was the VRA, not the Georgia Democrats, or even the state's Republicans, that stood in the way of black Democratic political interests post-2000, a fact that the majority in *Ashcroft* appeared to recognize but refused to explicitly acknowledge.

In the context of the *Beer* rule and the VRA more generally, *Ashcroft* is important, among other reasons, because it represents the first time the Court has recognized the breadth of the calculations necessary to assess "effective representation" under Section 5. This was evident in its acknowledgment that both substantive and descriptive representation could be pursued to avoid retrogression. The factors that determine how effectively voters are represented are so numerous as to be virtually incalculable—a point made by the dissenting justices in *Baker v. Carr* (1962)[129] and *Allen v. State Board of Elections*. How effectively an individual or group is represented depends on what particular standard or widget in the kaleidoscope of representational phenomena one uses as the measure of "effectiveness." If office holding is the standard, then election to office becomes the measure of effectiveness. But as Lani Guinier has pointed out, mere election to office is "tokenism" if it does not translate into policy outcomes for minority groups.[130] And those outcomes are determined by a litany of factors, many of which are intangible and have nothing to do with elections. Elections and methods of electing representatives obviously may be relevant to questions of how effectively individuals and groups are represented. But equally obviously, they may also be highly irrelevant.

Two examples might suffice to illustrate the point. Both Section 5 and Section 2 vote dilution law operate roughly on the basis of what Robert Higgs has referred to as the "Political Redistribution Thesis," the idea that voters are "highly knowledgeable and narrowly self-interested and [that] elected officials [are] sensitively responsive to clear messages sent them by the voters."[131] If this is not the assumption of VRA jurisprudence then it makes little sense focusing so much attention, as courts and administrators do, on the connection between constituent voting preferences and who gets elected. As Higgs points out, as plausible as the informed voter thesis may be in some circumstances, it tends to be undermined by the empirical evidence. "To assume that the typical voter is completely ignorant would approximate the truth more closely. An authority on public opinion has reported that Americans can name their astrological sign more readily than they can name their representative in Congress." The incongruence between constituent interests and the actions of elected officials has resulted in numerous well-known anecdotes, a number of which are amusing, as the widely recounted confession of David Stockman, Ronald Reagan's first budget director, reveals:

> "I went around and cut all the ribbons . . . and they [the electorate] never knew I voted against the damn programs." Congressman Pete McCloskey made the same point in recalling his first congressional victory. A post election survey, intended to demonstrate the victorious candidate's mandate, revealed, as McCloskey put it, "that 5 percent of the people voted for me because they agreed with my views; 11 percent voted for me even though they disagreed with my views, and 84 percent didn't have any idea what the hell my views were."
>
> In sum, one has many good reasons to agree with Joseph Schumpeter's assessment: "The freely voting rational citizen, conscious of his (long-run) interests, and the representative who acts in obedience to them, is this not the perfect example of a nursery tale?"[132]

The problem of the noncorrespondence between constituent interests and the actions of representatives, which constitutes the core assumption underlying Section 5 and Section 2 law, goes a long way to revealing the limitations of current assessments of effective representation under the VRA.

A second example also illustrates how the narrow rationalism characteristic of the adjudication and administration of voting rights tends to disregard the political context in which state and federal policy is formed. Consider the complaint of VRA critics who contend that when assessing questions of effective representation for minority interests, one has to factor in not merely the electoral but more importantly the nonelectoral factors that bear on race issues in America. Critics of the VRA have complained for decades that the evolution of the act into a racial spoils system occurred through intimidation, misrepresentation, and deception. Civil rights groups and their supporters denounced opposition to broadening and extending the act, as early as 1975, as tantamount to race prejudice and the pursuit of politically exclusionary policies.[133] Regardless of what one thinks the reality is here, the noninstitutional influences on the formation of policy points up that there is more to the effective representation of minority interests than simply tallying up the correlation between racial votes and who gets elected. Guinier herself—no conservative—points this out. If one accepts the conservative thesis that race is the affectation of the American Left and that racial identity politics already overwhelms American politics to an unhealthy degree, the VRA is simply aggravating a perennial problem rather than curing those diseases incident to American republicanism. The question for today's VRA is not whether race will predominate or not in the administration and adjudication of the act. It is rather in what sense it has come to predominate.

CONCLUSION

The remarks of Judge Oberdorfer in *Ashcroft* and the other cases examined in the last two sections raise questions about the continuing relevance of the VRA's temporary provisions—and perhaps even its permanent provisions—to American politics. The costs of preclearance are significant. In the case of Georgia, \$1.4 million was allocated in 2003 for attorneys' fees to cover the expenses of *Ashcroft* through the appeal before the Supreme Court. In addition, the state had to hire three outside attorneys (special assistant attorneys general) to assist with the case.[134] As of December 2003, the three outside attorneys had cost the state over \$1,050,000. This figure did not include the time the state's in-house lawyers and paralegals had to spend on *Ashcroft*, which was in excess of 1600 hours.[135] And the litigation was still ongoing in early 2004. On the other side of the country, the city of Santa Paula, California, with a population of 28,600, paid an attorney \$700,000 to comply with a Justice Department request to move from an at-large city council electoral system to a districting system. The cost per resident of the attorney's fees was \$24.50.[136]

Although the concerns for enhancing minority representation were an understandable objective in the late 1960s in the face of racist attempts to impede the minority vote, *Georgia v. Ashcroft* and the other post-2000 cases were not cases involving invidious discrimination on the part of state legislators. In the *Balderas* house case, for instance, the court summarily dismissed an allegation of intentional discrimination without comment, suggesting there was no serious issue here.[137] Allegations of discrimination post-2000, like the 1990s, typically identify "discrimination" with a denial of racial entitlements or racially maximized representation. To the extent that they do, the post-2000 redistricting cases provide further evidence that the VRA has ceased to be an equal opportunity, antidiscrimination measure and has followed the course of other civil rights initiatives, hardening into yet another instrument of racial identity politics, epitomizing what Hugh Davis Graham has described as the evolution from the *economic* regulatory state of the early Progressive and New Deal eras to the more comprehensive *social* regulatory state of the Great Society and beyond.[138] But what kind of regulatory state does the VRA represent? Do we really want to condone a political system in which problems of retrogression are remedied by counting up Spanish surnamed registered voters and allocating these individuals to electoral districts on that basis, as was done in the *Balderas* litigation?

Advocates of race-based districting have denied the existence of evidence that the VRA promotes racial antagonism. But both empirical and anecdotal evidence strongly suggests otherwise.[139] In 2003 and 2004, for instance, Texas Republicans were accused of being racist and antiminority for failing to create black and Hispanic congressional districts under the VRA. These allegations, made by Democrats and minority groups, were widely reported over the period of a year in the national news media. Yet the federal court that heard these groups' complaints dismissed them all, pointing out what was apparent to everyone, including the Democrats: that what was at issue was not race prejudice but partisan politics.[140] Yet it was the VRA that provided the vehicle for the inflammatory allegations of racism—the playing of the "race card"—that defenders of racial redistricting claim the act does not facilitate. As the court noted in *Session v. Perry*, the purely partisan nature of the Texas Republicans' congressional redistricting plan was agreed to not only by the Democrats' own expert witness but by the Texas House Democratic Caucus and congressional Democrats John Lewis, Chris Bell, Sheila Jackson Lee, Martin Frost, and Nick Lampson, all of whom filed a brief in *Vieth v. Jubelirer*[141] conceding that "'[t]he newly dominant Republicans . . . decided to redraw the state's congressional districts *solely* for the purpose of seizing between five and seven seats from Democratic incumbents.'"[142]

Perhaps then it is time to reconsider the efficacy of Sections 4 and 5 of the VRA. Consider what is likely on the horizon if the temporary provisions are extended in 2007. The amorphous retrogression test established in *Ashcroft* will likely mean that Republican-controlled states covered by Section 4 will pursue descriptive representation for minorities while Democrat-controlled states will pursue substantive representation. In either case, Justice Souter's assumption in *Ashcroft* that courts and the DOJ will probably be deferential to states in preclearance applications is a dubious proposition. It has certainly not proven to be the case with the VRA so far. Too much is at stake. Nothing less than the allocation of political power between the major parties is at issue in the redistricting controversies VRA litigation addresses. One can be certain, for instance, that in Republican controlled states covered by the act, Democrats will file lawsuits in future anytime the substantive representation of minorities is not maximized There is little to lose with such challenges and *Ashcroft* will invite, not discourage, litigation because parties litigate cases where the law is ambiguous. And as Justice Souter rightly emphasized, the *Beer* retrogression test following *Ashcroft* is highly ambiguous.

In his separate concurring opinion in *Ashcroft*, Justice Kennedy suggested that Section 5 remains a "fundamentally flaw[ed]" provision, inviting the DOJ to pursue or encourage "a course of unconstitutional conduct in order to find compliance" with the section. The Court in 2003 had the opportunity to expunge the politics of race and racial identity, as well as its corollary, the judicial and administrative micromanagement of state electoral processes, from the VRA. It missed the opportunity. The consequence will be that race will continue to predominate under the act as it has for the last generation. And a statute that once stood as much as any other to fulfill the promise of American republicanism now stands as much as any other to undermine it.

NOTES

1. 123 S.Ct. 2498.
2. 79 Stat. 439, as renumbered and amended, 42 U.S.C. 1973c.
3. A majority-minority district is typically an electoral district in which roughly 65 percent of the voting age residents are a recognized minority under the VRA.
4. 425 U.S. 130.
5. Texas Democratic Senator Judith Zaffirini said that according to nine minority senators in the state, the congressional redistricting map originally passed by the Texas Senate September 23, 2003 was "discriminatory." "Texas Senate Gives Tentative OK for Map," Natalie Gott, Associated Press Writer, findlaw.com (9-24-2003). When the redistricting plan was passed during a third special legislative session October 12, 2003 Zaffirini was again quoted by the Associated Press as remarking that "the map would disenfranchise millions of minority voters." April Castro, "GOP Pushes through Texas redistricting," *Salt Lake Tribune*, 13 October 2003, A8.
6. 532 U.S. 234.
7. Anthony A. Peacock, "The Voting Rights Act and the Politics of Multiculturalism: The Challenge to Commercial Republicanism at Century's Turn," in *Courts and the Culture Wars*, ed. Bradley C.S. Watson (Lanham, Md.: Lexington Books, 2002), 167, 168.

8. See Jeremy Rabkin, *Judicial Compulsions: How Public Law Distorts Public Policy* (New York: Basic Books, 1989), xi.

9. Theodore J. Lowi, *The End of Liberalism: The Second Republic of the United States*, 2nd ed. (New York: W.W. Norton & Company, 1979).

10. Emphasis added.

11. 393 U.S. 544.

12. 393 U.S. at 572, opinion of the Court.

13. 425 U.S. at 140.

14. 425 U.S. at 141, emphasis in original.

15. 425 U.S. at 141, emphasis in original.

16. Summarizing *City of Richmond* in *United Jewish Organizations of Williamsburg, Inc. v. Carey* (1977), the Court wrote: "the proscribed 'effect' on voting rights can be avoided by a postannexation districting plan that 'fairly reflects the strength of the Negro community as it exists after the annexation' and which 'would afford [it] representation reasonably equivalent to [its] political strength in the enlarged community.'" 430 U.S. 144, 160, citing *City of Richmond v. United States*, 422 U.S. 358, 370–371.

17. 430 U.S. 144.

18. 430 U.S. at 161.

19. 430 U.S. at 162, emphasis added.

20. 446 U.S. 156, 172.

21. 446 U.S. at 172–73.

22. Abigail M. Thernstrom, *Whose Votes Count? Affirmative Action and Minority Voting Rights* (Cambridge: Harvard University Press, 1987), 26–27.

23. James F. Blumstein, "Defining and Proving Race Discrimination: Perspectives on the Purpose v. Results Approach from the Voting Rights Act," *Virginia L. Rev.* 69 (1983): 633, 682–83. See also, Richard K. Scher, Jon L. Mills, and John J. Hotaling, *Voting Rights and Democracy: The Law and Politics of Districting* (Chicago: Nelson-Hall Publishers, 1997), 48–49.

24. 446 U.S. at 177.

25. 446 U.S. at 218, dissenting opinion.

26. Ward E. Y. Elliott, *The Rise of Guardian Democracy: The Supreme Court's Role in Voting Rights Disputes, 1845–1969* (Cambridge: Harvard University Press, 1974), 241.

27. See Timothy G. O'Rourke, "The 1982 Amendments and the Voting Rights Paradox," in *Controversies in Minority Voting*, ed. Bernard Grofman and Chandler Davidson (Washington, DC: Brookings Institution, 1992) 85, 87.

28. See Peacock, "Politics of Multiculturalism."

29. 113 S.Ct. 2816 (1993).

30. Abigail Thernstrom, "More Notes from a Political Thicket," *Emory Law Journal* 44 (1995): 911, 916.

31. 113 S.Ct. at 2827.

32. 115 S.Ct 2475.

33. See James F. Blumstein, "*Shaw v. Reno* and *Miller v. Johnson*: Where We Are and Where We Are Headed," *Cumberland Law Rev.* 26 (1996): 503, 504–505.

34. 488 U.S. 469.

35. 515 U.S. 200.

36. Blumstein, "*Shaw v. Reno* and *Miller v. Johnson*," 505.
37. 163 U.S. 537.
38. See, for instance, *Washington v. Davis*, 426 U.S. 229 (1976), *Village of Arlington Heights v. Metropolitan Housing Development Corporation*, 429 U.S. 252 (1977), and *City of Mobile v. Bolden*, 446 U.S. 55 (1980). See also, Blumstein, "*Shaw v. Reno* and *Miller v. Johnson*," 506–508.
39. 115 S.Ct at 2488, Kennedy, J., opinion of the Court, emphasis added.
40. *Bush v. Vera*, 517 U.S. 952, 1001, Thomas, J., concurring.
41. Even MID's have the object of securing the election of a race-preferred candidate.
42. 532 U.S. 234.
43. *Miller v. Johnson*, 115 S.Ct. at 2491–93.
44. 115 S. Ct. at 2493.
45. Federal Register/Vol. 66, No. 12/Thursday, January 18, 2001/Notices, 5412, hereinafter "Guidance" or "Redistricting Guidance."
46. 528 U.S. 320.
47. Guidance, 5412.
48. 430 U.S. at 169, Brennan, J., concurring opinion.
49. *Thornburg v. Gingles*, 106 S.Ct. 2752, 2787, O'Connor, J., concurring opinion.
50. See C.F.R. ' 51.55(b)(2) (1994), originally adopted by the DOJ in 1987.
51. See Daniel H. Lowenstein, "Race and Representation in the Supreme Court," in *Voting Rights and Redistricting in the United States*, ed. Mark E. Rush (Westport, Conn.: Greenwood Press, 1998), 49, 62–63.
52. 520 U.S. 471.
53. Lowenstein, "Race and Representation in the Supreme Court," 63.
54. Guidance, 5412.
55. Guidance, 5413:

> These factors include whether minority voting strength is reduced by the proposed redistricting; whether minority concentrations are fragmented among different districts; whether minorities are overconcentrated in one or more districts; whether available alternative plans satisfying the jurisdiction's legitimate governmental interests were considered; whether the proposed plan departs from objective redistricting criteria set by the submitting jurisdiction, ignores other relevant factors such as compactness and contiguity, or displays a configuration that inexplicably disregards available natural or artificial boundaries; and, whether the plan is inconsistent with the jurisdiction's stated redistricting standards.

The fact that minorities can be neither fragmented nor overconcentrated in districts suggests that the Guidance factors do not so much promote Section 5 retrogression as Section 2 racial maximization.

56. Guidance, 5413.
57. Guidance, 5413.
58. In *Johnson v. Miller* (1994), the court demurred that "the considerable influence of ACLU advocacy on the voting rights decisions of the United States Attorney General is an embarrassment." As the court elaborated,

> The ACLU and Reps. Brooks and McKinney were concerned only with racial percentages. They could afford such a narrow focus. The General Assembly leadership was concerned

> with passing redistricting legislation affecting all Georgians, and contended with numerous factors racial, political, economic, and personal. As the lawmaking body for the entire state, the General Assembly could *not* afford such a narrow focus. Consequently, its submissions reflected many influences, and the ACLU's reflected only race. (*Johnson v. Miller*, 864 F. Supp. 1354, 1368 (S.D.Ga. 1994), emphasis in original)

59. Guidance 5414.

60. The following analysis of case law benefited greatly from "Redistricting Cases: the 2000s," http://www.senate.leg.state.mn.us/departments/scr/redist/redsum2000/redsum2000.htm. The "Redistricting Cases" provides an excellent, comprehensive guide to redistricting litigation following the 2000 census. I utilized the outline of the cases provided in the "Redistricting Cases" but the analysis of the case law is my own.

61. Alaska Supreme Court No. S-10504 (Order No. 39 - March 21, 2002).

62. Alaska Supreme Court No. S-10504 (Order No. 39 - March 21, 2002), 9.

63. Guidance,5413.

64. *In re 2001 Redistricting Cases* at 24.

65. Guidance, 5412.

66. *Stephenson v. Bartlett*, No. 94PA02 (N.C. April 30, 2002), 1, 11.

67. *Stephenson v. Bartlett*, No. 1 CV 02885 (Superior Court, Johnston Co., May 31, 2002).

68. *Louisiana House of Representatives v. Ashcroft*, (D.D.C. complaint).

69. *Louisiana House of Representatives v. Ashcroft*, 36.

70. *Louisiana House of Representatives v. Ashcroft*, 8–9.

71. *Louisiana House of Representatives v. Ashcroft*, 10–11.

72. Guidance, 5412–13, emphasis added.

73. 521 U.S. 74.

74. 521 U.S. at 97.

75. *Louisiana House of Representatives v. Ashcroft* at 30.

76. *Louisiana House of Representatives v. Ashcroft* at 31.

77. *Louisiana House of Representatives v. Ashcroft* at 32.

78. *Martinez v. Bush*, Case No. 02-20244-CIV-JORDAN and *Maurer v. Florida*, Case No. 02-10028-CIV-JORDAN (S.D. Fla. July 9, 2002).

79. *Balderas v. Texas*, Civil Action No. 6:01CV158 (E.D. Tex. November 14, 2001), hereinafter *Balderas I*, 1. Although the three *Balderas* cases discussed in this and the next paragraphs all have the same civil action number, they were released on separate dates and dealt respectively with challenges to Texas's congressional, house, and senate redistricting plans. I refer to these respectively as *Balderas I*, *Balderas II*, and *Balderas III*.

80. *Balderas I*, 9.

81. *Balderas I*, 13.

82. *Balderas I*, 12.

83. *Balderas v. Texas*, Civil Action No. 6:01CV158 (E.D. Tex. November 28, 2002), hereinafter *Balderas II*, 1, 6.

84. *Balderas II*, n.14.

85. *Balderas II*, 7.

86. *Balderas II*, 8.

87. *Balderas v. Texas*, Civil Action No. 6:01CV158 (E.D. Tex. November 30, 2001), hereinafter *Balderas III*, 11.

88. *Balderas III*, 7.

89. See Response of Interveners to Georgia's Jurisdictional Statement to the United States Supreme Court, at 1–2:

> In Georgia, the legislative and executive branches are controlled by the Democratic Party and have been since 1865. When Appellant entered the redistricting process this decade it was clear that Appellant could either (1) preserve minority voting strength and sacrifice the political strength of the Democratic Party or (2) sacrifice minority voting strength and preserve the political power of the Democratic Party. Appellant chose the latter.
>
> However, because Georgia redistricting is subject to Section 5 preclearance, Appellant was required to prove there had not been any "retrogression" or worsening of minority voters' opportunities to exercise their voting rights. Using the traditional retrogression analysis methods of the Department of Justice and voting rights experts, Appellants could not succeed. Therefore, Appellant rejected the administrative preclearance process and sought a declaratory judgment in the United States District Court for the District of Columbia.

90. 195 F. Supp. 2d 25.

91. 195 F. Supp. 2d, at 76, Sullivan, District Judge, opinion of the court; also quoted by Oberdorfer, District Judge, concurring in part and dissenting in part, 103. My discussion of Judge Oberdorfer's opinion below focuses on his dissenting remarks. Thus, I refer to his opinion throughout as "dissenting."

92. 195 F. Supp. 2d, at 86.

93. 195 F. Supp. 2d, at 74.

94. See, 195 F. Supp. 2d, at 77 and 96 opinion of the court:

> The State argues that all three redistricting plans were drawn with the intent to maintain and bolster the Democratic control of the State House and Senate. In order to reach these goals, Democratic legislators sought to "unpack" majority black districts, and to increase Democratic voting strength throughout the State. The testimony of State Democratic legislators reflects a belief that African American votes, which generally heavily favor Democrats, are "wasted" in districts with high percentages of African American voters.

95. 195 F. Supp. 2d, 39.

96. 195 F. Supp. 2d, 42.

97. 195 F. Supp. 2d, 41. In its Jurisdictional Statement before the U.S. Supreme Court, the state of Georgia remarked:

> In the Senate, only one African American Senator (S.D. 2) voted against the Senate plan . . . and she did so simply because of her personal desire for a district exactly as she wanted it, which ignored the fact that 56 Senate districts had to be drawn with no one incumbent getting just what they wanted. One African American House member also voted against the House plan. . . . Such near unanimous support is a rarity in any political endeavor. (At 11n2)

98. 195 F. Supp. 2d, at 40.

99. 195 F. Supp. 2d, at 42.

100. 195 F. Supp. 2d, at 120, n.72, dissenting opinion.

101. Jurisdictional Statement, 2, n. 1.

102. *Georgia v. Ashcroft*, 195 F. Supp. at 108–112 and 123–126, Oberdorfer, S.D.J., dissenting opinion.

103. 195 F. Supp. 2d, at 121–123.
104. 195 F. Supp. 2d, at 127, citing *Easley v. Cromartie*, 532 U.S. at 247 (2001).
105. 195 F. Supp. 2d, at referring to *Abrams v. Johnson*, 521 U.S. at 100–101 (1997).
106. 195 F. Supp. 2d, at 128–129.
107. 195 F. Supp. 2d, at 118–119.
108. 195 F. Supp. 2d, at 125.
109. 195 F. Supp. 2d, at 125 n.80.
110. 123 S. Ct. 2325.
111. 123 S. Ct. 2411.
112. 123 S. Ct. at 2511 (2003).
113. 123 S. Ct. at 2511.
114. 123 S. Ct. at 2511.
115. 123 S. Ct. at 2511.
116. 123 S. Ct. at 2511–2512.
117. 123 S. Ct. at 2513.
118. 123 S. Ct. at 2513.
119. 123 S. Ct. at 2512–2513.
120. 123 S. Ct. at 2517, Kennedy, J., concurring opinion.
121. 114 S. Ct. at 2581.
122. 114 S. Ct. at 2598.
123. 114 S. Ct. at 2597.
124. 123 S. Ct. at 2518.
125. 123 S. Ct. at 2523.
126. 123 S. Ct. at 2519.
127. 123 S. Ct. at 2520.
128. 383 U.S. 301.
129. 369 U.S. 186.
130. Lani Guinier, "The Triumph of Tokenism: The Voting Rights Act and the Theory of Black Electoral Success," *Michigan Law Rev.* 89 (March 1991): 1077.
131. Robert Higgs, *Crisis and Leviathan: Critical Episodes in the Growth of American Government* (New York: Oxford University Press, 1987), 12.
132. Higgs, *Crisis and Leviathan,* 14–15, quoting Joseph A. Schumpeter, *History of Economic Analysis* (New York: Oxford University Press, 1954), 429.
133. Keith Bybee, *Mistaken Identity: The Supreme Court and the Politics of Minority Representation* (Princeton, N.J.: Princeton University Press, 1998), 52. See also, Thernstrom, *Whose Votes Count*, 79–136.
134. My source for these figures is an email dated April 4, 2003, from Bryan Tyson, aide to Georgia Representative Lynn Westmoreland.
135. I obtained the December 2003 information from Dennis Dunn, Deputy Attorney General for the state of Georgia, in a telephone conversation Wednesday, January 14, 2004. The specific figures Mr. Dunn provided me were as follows. The state spent $1,050,894.01 on the three outside attorneys. $834,973.50 of this figure was spent on fees, $199,783.81 on expenses, and $16,136.70 on other miscellaneous costs. A small portion of these latter expenses and costs included expenditures by the Attorney General's office for such things as meals, lodging, and transportation to Washington D.C. but the majority of the costs were incurred by the outside attorneys.

136. My source for these figures are two emails dated October 28, 2002, from Douglas Johnson, a senior analyst at the National Demographics Corporation.

137. *Balderas v. Texas*, Civil Action No. 6:01CV158 (E.D. Tex. November 28, 2002), at 7.

138. See Hugh Davis Graham, "Voting Rights and the American Regulatory State," in *Controversies in Minority Voting*, 177. See also, Hugh Davis Graham, *The Civil Rights Era: Origins and Development of National Policy, 1960–1972* (New York: Oxford University Press, 1990), esp. 362–65.

139. As Paul M. Sniderman and Thomas Piazza concluded in their survey of attitudes toward race-conscious policies over ten years ago:

> Politics shapes as well as reflects public opinion as the politics of affirmative action painfully demonstrates: whites have come to think less of blacks, to be more likely to perceive them as irresponsible and lazy merely in consequence of the issue of affirmative action being brought up. . . . The new race-conscious agenda has provoked broad outrage and resentment. Affirmative action is so intensely disliked that it has led some whites to dislike blacks—an ironic example of a policy meant to put the divide of race further behind us in fact further widening it. (Paul M. Sniderman and Thomas Piazza, *The Scar of Race* [Cambridge: Belknap Press of Harvard University Press, 1993], 109)

140. See *Session v. Perry*, 298 F. Supp. 2d 451 (E.D. Tex., 2004).

141. 241 F. Supp. 2d 478 (MD Pa. 2003), on appeal to the U.S. Supreme Court.

142. 298 F. Supp. 2d, at 472, emphasis added.

7

Minorities and Representation in the New Millennium

Florence P. Adams

The Voting Rights Act of 1965 was aimed to correct discrimination against blacks in the American South; although the Act was later expanded to cover Hispanics and other minorities, the principal political focus and the bulk of the litigation continued to be on blacks all the way through the 1990s. As I have argued elsewhere,[1] I believe that the focus in the twenty-first century will be increasingly on Hispanic representation in the West and Southwest, that many of the most interesting and fateful redistricting issues in the new century will be decided in states that are experiencing rapid growth of Hispanic population, and that much of the controversy will be found at the local level of government and in political struggles among minorities in these states. I have previously argued,[2] also, that the political science literature on redistricting, which has emphasized legal and statistical questions, should turn closer attention to the practical political consequences of legal rulings and to the results of applying statistical standards. In the first section of this chapter, therefore, I compare the radically different approaches used to redistrict state legislative and congressional seats in Arizona, Florida, and California, looking to the treatment of minority populations in each case. In the second section, I illustrate the issues confronting local jurisdictions as they seek to comply both with court decisions and new Justice Department regulations. And in the third, I raise some questions and attempt some conclusions, again focusing on actual situations and political struggles in Arizona, Florida, and California.[3]

STATE LEGISLATIVE AND CONGRESSIONAL REDISTRICTING

Arizona

The graphic at figure 7.1 shows the population growth in Arizona between the 1990 and 2000 Census; the graphic at figure 7.2 shows the percentage increase of minority groups in Arizona from 1990 to 2000.[4] Though all groups grew in raw numbers, only Hispanics grew as a percentage of the state's population, increasing from less than one-fifth to more than one-fourth.[5] The graphic at figure 7.3 shows the distribution of Hispanics in the Phoenix area as of the 2000 Census. In Arizona, however, Hispanics are not the only significant minority: there are Navajo, Hopi, and other Native Americans concentrated in and around reservations throughout the state; and in Phoenix, there is a concentration of black population (see figure 7.4).

Arizona has thirty legislative districts from which are elected two members of the state house and one member of the state senate. In the case of the house, the top two vote getters win seats. By 2000, there were twelve Hispanic members of the state house and state senate. Most of these Hispanics had found seats in the legislature in part because of term limits and in part because of increased political organization in the Hispanic community. It must be said, however, that the redistricting of 1992, which was conducted by incumbents in their own interest and to assure the continuation in power of the Republican Party, did very little to assist increased minority representation. Following

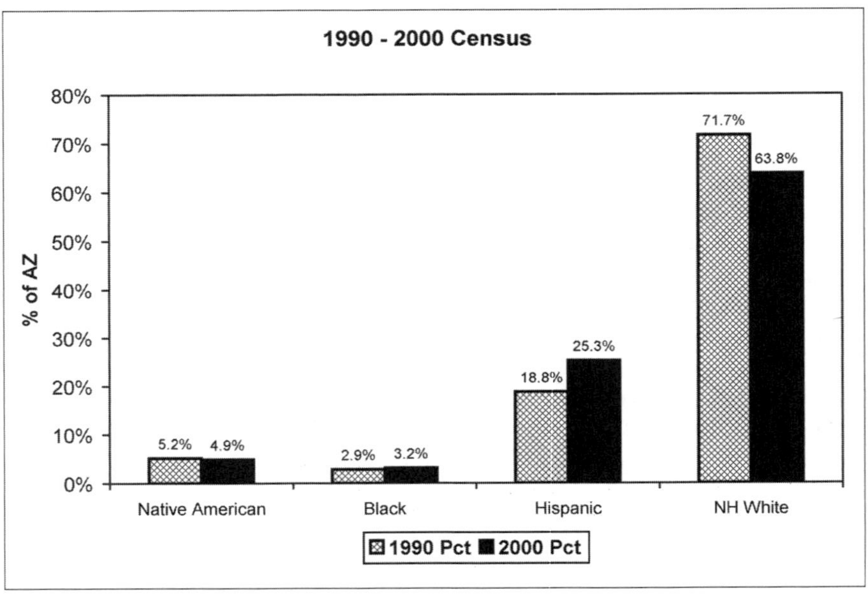

Figure 7.1 Population Growth in Arizona between the 1990 and 2000 Censuses

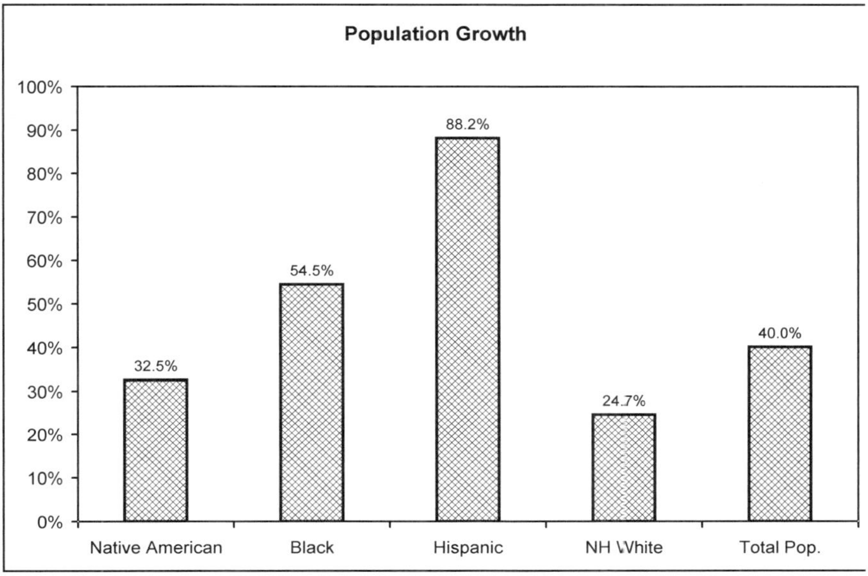

Figure 7.2. Percentage Increase of Minority Groups in Arizona from 1990 to 2000

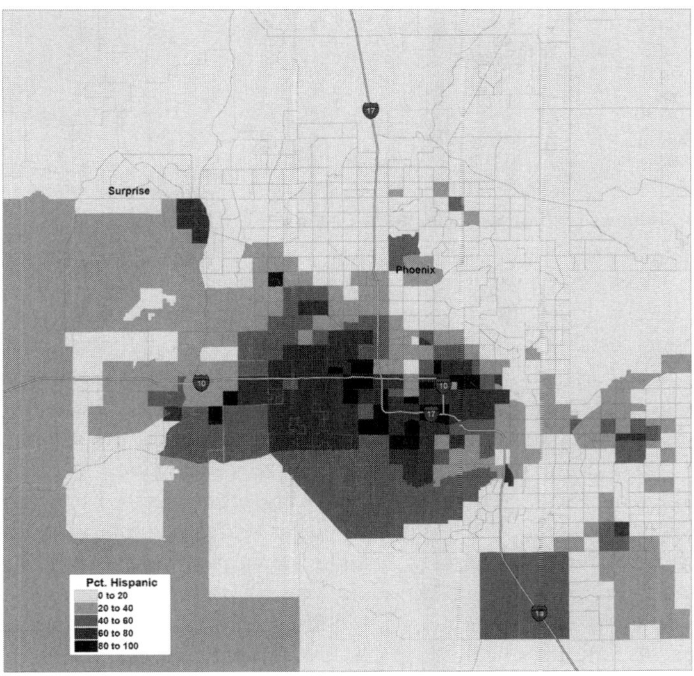

Figure 7.3. Hispanics in the Phoenix Area, 2000 Census

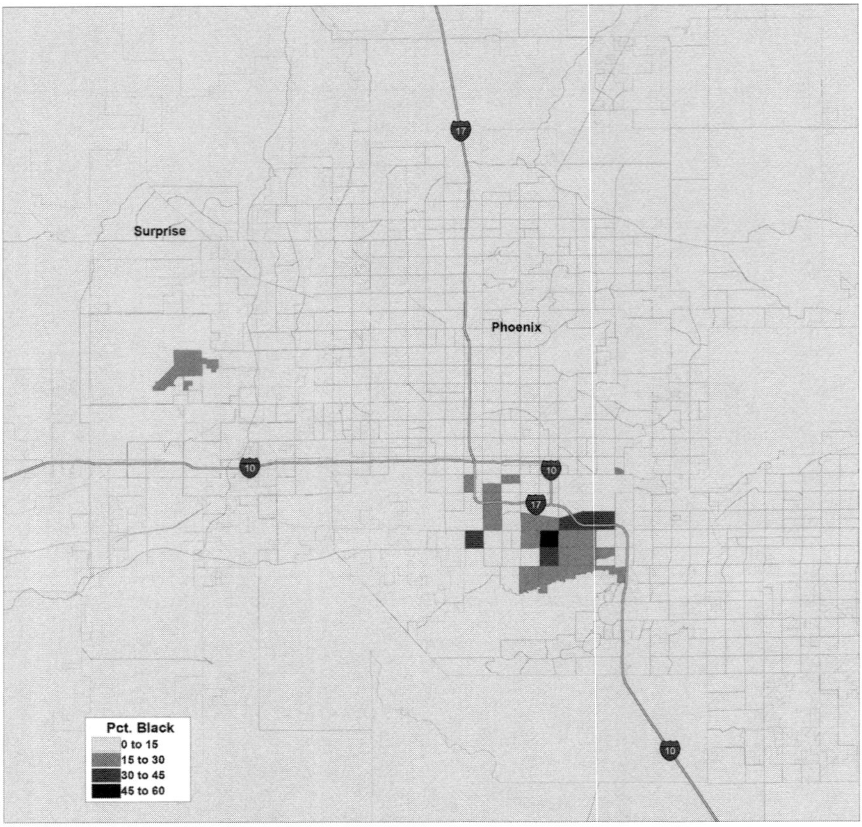

Figure 7.4. Blacks in Phoenix Area, 2000 Census

a commission-style redistricting, described below, and the 2002 elections, the state legislature added three more Hispanics to its ranks. Arizona now has eight congressional seats, up from six in the last decade by virtue of reapportionment. In the last decade, only one member of the delegation was Hispanic. Again, as a result of the commission redistricting, after 2002, there are two.

In 1998, in good part because of public reaction against the redistricting of 1992, the voters of Arizona qualified and passed a statewide initiative, Proposition 106,[6] which took redistricting out of the hands of the legislature and placed it in the hands of a five member redistricting commission. The initiative was financed in large part by a single individual, who became the chairman of the Democratic Party. The elements of Proposition 106 included the legally mandated criteria (equal population and adherence to the Voting Rights Act) and all the so-called "good government" criteria. Following is the actual language of the Proposition:

A. Districts shall comply with the United States Constitution and the United States Voting Rights Act;
B. Congressional districts shall have equal population to the extent practicable, and state legislative districts shall have equal population to the extent practicable;
C. Districts shall be geographically compact and contiguous to the extent practicable;
D. District boundaries shall respect communities of interest to the extent practicable;
E. To the extent practicable, district lines shall use visible geographic features, city, town and county boundaries, and undivided census tracts;
F. To the extent practicable, competitive districts should be favored where to do so would create no significant detriment to the other goals.[7]

The first five goals (A through E) were all preceded by the word "*shall*"; then, the Proposition added goal "F," stating that the commission "*should*" consider competitiveness if to do so did not constitute a "significant detriment to the other goals." In addition, the commission was allowed to use party registration and voting history data only to test maps for compliance with the stated goals; and it was forbidden to identify or consider "the places of residence of incumbents or candidates."[8]

The minority groups approached the Independent Redistricting Commission (IRC) with some degree of apprehension in 2001 for there were neither Hispanic nor Native American nor black members (although the commission did act to appoint a Hispanic executive director and Hispanics formed the majority, also, of the IRC staff). The most active and potent minority groups to appear before the commission were, first, an Hispanic group, the Arizona Minority Coalition for Fair Representation, headed by Mary Rose Wilcox, a Latina Maricopa County supervisor and former Phoenix councilwoman; and, second, the Navajo, a tribe with more than one hundred thousand members and a multistate political base.

Early in the process, tensions between the Hispanic interests and those of the Democratic Party leadership made their appearance. The charts at figure 7.5 give insight into the problem. Statewide, Republicans have a 5.3 percent registration advantage, but if you exclude the ten majority-minority legislative districts, Republicans have a 16.8 percent registration advantage. Mary Rose Wilcox and the coalition insisted repeatedly on the importance of concentrating Hispanic population to assure majority status in as many of the new districts as possible.

Understanding the thrust of the Supreme Court decisions of the late 1990s, the coalition avoided characterizing the Hispanics as a racial community but insisted, instead, on the social, cultural, and economic ties that bound them together. Meanwhile, however, the Democrats presented a very different

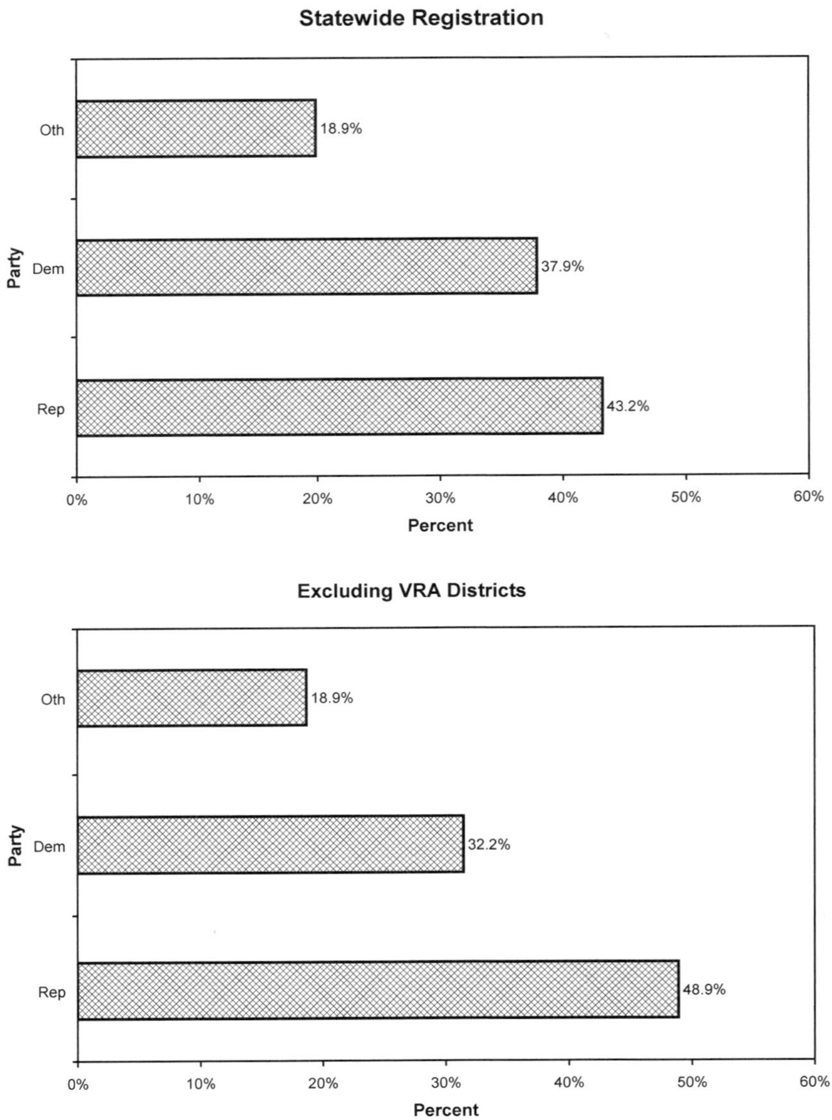

Figure 7.5 Party Registration in Arizona

plan. The contrast between the two plans was marked. Figures 7.6 and 7.7 depict the alternative configurations of districts in Maricopa County. A moment's thought is sufficient to explain the differences. The priority for the Hispanics was to increase the number of those Hispanics elected to the legislature, an aim that they believed was best served by focusing districts

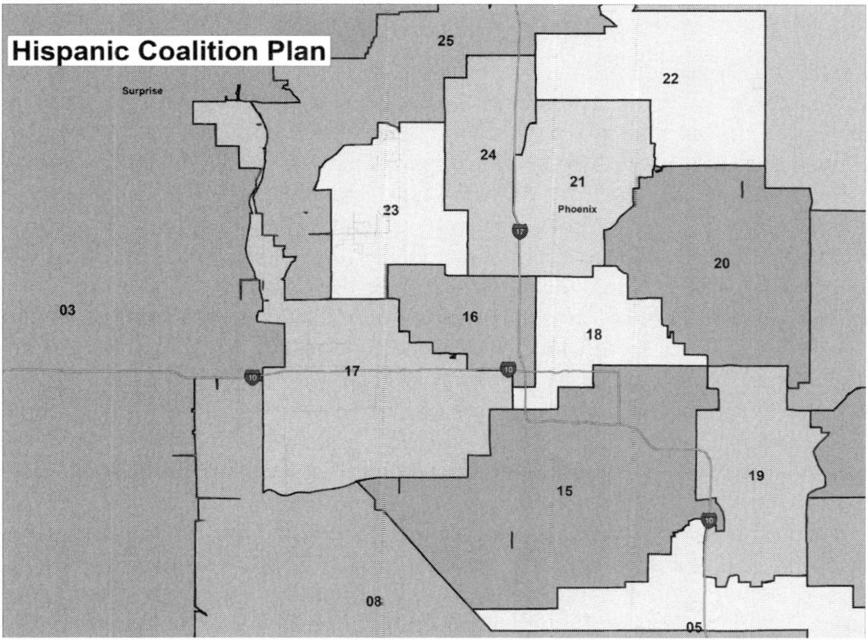

Figure 7.6. Districts Concentrate Hispanic Population in LDs 8, 15, 16, 17, and 18

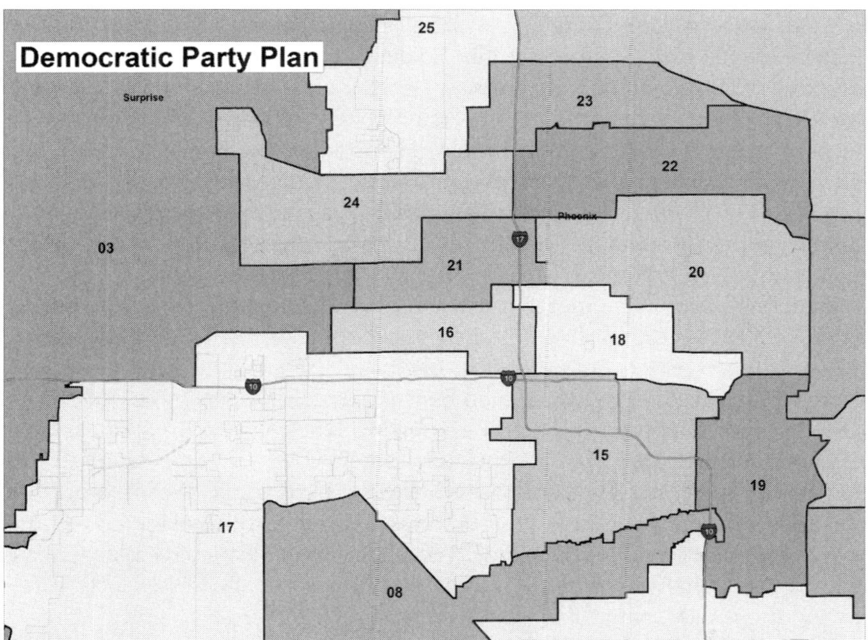

Figure 7.7. Horizontal Districts Distribute Democratic Voters

within the Hispanic community sufficient to constitute a voting majority of each such new district. The aim of the Democratic Party, by contrast, was to maximize the number of Democrats, regardless of ethnicity, that would be elected to the legislature. To serve this partisan goal, the Democrats' plan distributed Hispanics, the majority of whom are reliable Democratic voters, among a much larger number of districts to assure the election of Democrats. Another point of difference, of course, is that the Hispanic plan provided for significantly fewer competitive districts than the Democratic plan. After all, to concentrate 50-plus percent Hispanics in a district is generally to assure that it is massively Democratic in registration and in voting behavior. From the perspective of the white Democratic Party leadership, ethnically representative districts constituted a waste of Democratic voting power. Although the Republican leadership stayed shrewdly quiet as this contest between plans developed, there was no doubt that GOP strategists preferred the Hispanic approach to redistricting.

The commission adopted a compromise plan. With Minority Coalition support, they created districts that were less than the benchmark required by the Justice Department. At the October 14, 2001, hearing of the commission, the lawyer for the coalition, Democrat Aaron Kizer, said, "We have nine districts. You lived up to your end of the bargain. We'll live up to our end."[9] With the support of the Minority Coalition, the plan should have breezed through Justice Department preclearance; but the honeymoon was soon over. Democratic leaders convinced the Minority Coalition to join in a lawsuit against the adopted plan. Meanwhile, the Justice Department objected to the plan and one may reasonably assume that this may have been due to the failure of the Minority Coalition to lend their promised support to the plan. The Court then intervened, appointed a special master and the commission was forced back into session to further concentrate Hispanics into the minority districts.[10]

Redistricting also had a significant effect on Arizona's black population concentration in Phoenix. Following the 1990s redistricting, blacks were able to elect one state house member to each of two districts—legislative districts 22 and 23. Although the black voting age population of these two districts was only 8 percent and 13 percent respectively, the area had a long-term and very popular black city council member in the person of Calvin Goode, who had succeeded in organizing and energizing black voters. In spite of their registration edge, Hispanics did not turn out to vote, so blacks were able to win seats in this area. By the 2001 redistricting both black districts were significantly underpopulated, so the commission merged the black concentrations of legislative districts 22 and 23 into legislative district 16. Blacks were able to elect only one member to the state house in the 2002 election following the redistricting.

Arizona's redistricting of 2001 and 2002 gives abundant proof of the tensions between the aspirations of Hispanic groups and the aims of Democratic Party strategists. The effectiveness of Arizona's Independent Redistricting Commission in balancing the various goals of Proposition 106 will become clearer when the current litigation is settled. What is beyond doubt, however, is that the commission was able to meet many of the needs of Hispanic groups without paying attention to the concerns of individual incumbents. In the next two sections we will consider states in which incumbent concerns in redistricting were given much higher priority.

Florida

Florida's legislature, controlled for 120 years by Democrats, fell to Republican majorities in the mid-1990s (the senate in 1994 and the state house in 1996). This power shift is traceable to the 1992 redistricting which, although controlled by Democrats, set in motion a train of events favorable to the GOP. The Democratic leadership in both houses approached the redistricting in time-honored ways, using it to advance their own careers, reward supporters, and punish opponents.[11] Under pressure from the U.S. Department of Justice, however, the Democrats created several districts with supermajorities of blacks and Hispanics. The first three black lawmakers elected to Congress from Florida since reconstruction—Representatives Alcee Hastings, Carrie Meek, and Corinne Brown—were elected in DOJ-approved districts, and representative Lincoln Diaz-Balart became the second Cuban American elected to Congress from Florida. These minority gains, resulting primarily from an alliance between Republicans and blacks in pursuit of Voting Rights Act goals, created concentrations of loyalist Democratic black voters, thus reducing Democratic margins of victory in neighboring districts, several of which ultimately fell to Republicans. At the same time, the growth of the Hispanic population, dominated by loyalist Republican-voting Cuban Americans, also added to GOP strength.

Thus, Republicans soon found themselves in power in Tallahassee. Quickly, they abandoned their commitment to redistricting reform and prepared themselves for the 2001 reapportionment.[12] In partisan terms, their aim was to increase the GOP advantage in Florida's congressional delegation from 15 to 8 to 18 to 7; and in the legislature they hoped for 26 senate seats and 82 state house seats. As in past Democratic-controlled redistrictings, the personal interests of the leaders were given considerable priority: Speaker Tom Feeney and State Representative Mario Diaz-Balart (brother of Lincoln and chairman of the redistricting unit) managed to draw congressional seats for themselves; and losers in Republican intraparty struggles found themselves without districts or severely disadvantaged, as did several Democrats. Nevertheless, the Republican leadership clearly understood their party's long-term strategic stakes in the redistricting. The threat of a potential return to power of the Democrats was much on their minds: both U.S. senators from Florida were

Democrats; registered Democrats outnumbered registered Republicans 42 percent to 39 percent; two Democratic-backed education initiatives had won voter approval; and, above all, there was the dramatic Bush-Gore cliff-hanger election of November 2000.

The partisan stakes in the 2001 redistricting became clearest in the court challenges to the Republican plan in the following year. In June of 2002, attorneys for Democratic Congressman Peter Deutsch, Hialeah's Democratic mayor, Raul Martinez, and the Reverend Victor Curry, a black community leader from Miami, claimed before a three-judge federal panel that the Republican plan had illegally concentrated Democrats, discriminated against non-Cuban Hispanics and unfairly reduced the influence of black voters in Miramar and Miami-Dade.[13] Attorneys for the Republicans argued that the official plans sought to be fair to two minority communities—both blacks and Hispanics—and that if the judges chose to bolster black voting strength it would be at the cost of a Hispanic seat.

The judge ruled in favor of the Republican congressional and state senate plans but against the state house plan. In July, the court was faced with deciding how to adjust the Republican plan for the state house in order to satisfy a Justice Department complaint of retrogression. The focus was house district 101, which DOJ claimed gave 6,000 Hispanic voters in Collier County less political influence than they had possessed under the 1992 plan. A relatively minor change was made by the Republican leadership and the plan won court approval in July of 2002.

Lying behind and helping to explain the political maneuverings in the Florida redistricting were important demographic trends, particularly those affecting the Hispanic community, where Puerto Ricans and Central Americans had rapidly increased their numbers in the 1990s. Cuban Americans remained politically preeminent among Hispanic groups; but competition from these other Democratic-leaning Hispanic groups threatened their power. According to the 2000 Census, Cubans had dropped from 45 percent to 30 percent of Florida's Hispanics.

Florida's Hispanic community had become considerably more diverse, with Mexican, Puerto Rican, and "Other Hispanic" populations showing growth of nearly twice the rate of the Cuban population (Figure 7.8). The increasing diversity within the Hispanic community helped to increase the state's total diversity as well: Non-Hispanic whites dropped from 81 percent of the state's population in 1990 to 65.4 percent in 2000. Cubans, at 5.2 percent of the total population, showed no percentage increase from 1990 to 2000; however, non-Cuban Hispanics rose from 6.8 percent in 1990 to 11.6 percent in 2000. Total black, Asian, and others (all non-Hispanic) rose from 7.2 percent to 18.8 percent of the state's population.

Although Florida's non-Cuban Hispanic population is spreading throughout the state, particular growth can be noted in Orlando and Broward coun-

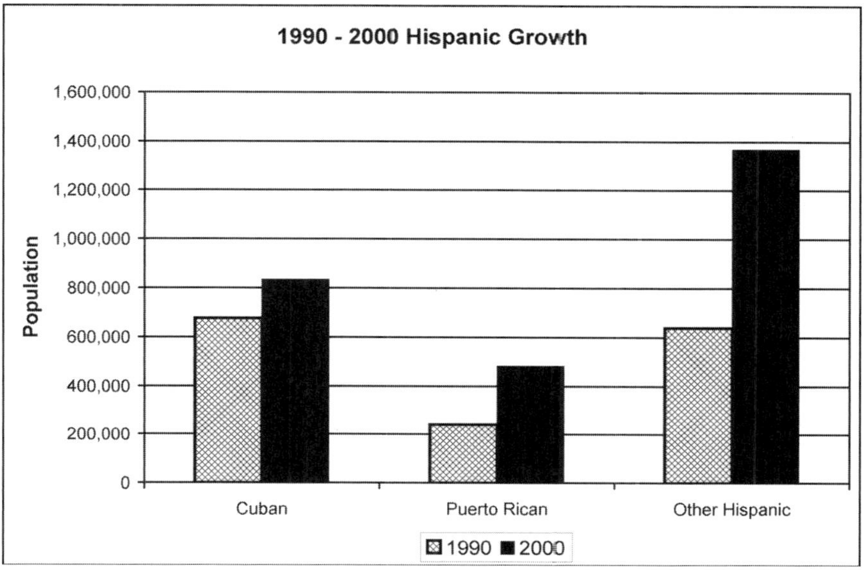

Figure 7.8. Florida Population Trends

ties. Cubans remain concentrated in Miami-Dade. A consequence of these trends is that Republican (Cuban) dominance of Florida Hispanics is waning: although Miami-Dade Hispanics are still dominated by Cuban Republicans, Hispanics in other parts of the state are heavily Democrat.

It should be noted, also, that naturalized citizens in the immigrant population are growing faster than the noncitizen population, although the noncitizen population remains larger (55 percent) than the naturalized citizen population (45 percent). This trend, also, has the potential to diminish Republican and Cuban dominance of the Hispanic vote.

The Hispanic growth in Florida could have justified the creation of a fourth Hispanic-dominated state senate seat; however, this district would have had to be created in the non-Cuban Hispanic areas of Orlando and Broward counties. The Cuban Hispanics still had enough clout to prevent this from happening, while holding onto their three seats in Miami-Dade. Florida did add one Hispanic seat to its congressional delegation and, thanks to redistricting chair Diaz-Balart, the Cuban Americans were able to capture it as well.

There is little doubt that the Florida redistricting of 2002 fits the classic definition of a partisan gerrymander: Republicans increased or solidified their advantage both in the state legislature and the congressional delegation. The traditionally strong relationship between the Republicans and Florida's Cuban American community meant that, by and large, the two pursued the same goals in redistricting and could jointly exploit territory in Democratic districts. Moreover, the higher voting propensity of Cuban Americans meant that no supermajority districts had to be created in order to achieve Cuban American representation. We must turn now, however, to a state where Hispanics found themselves dealing with an incumbent protection gerrymander.

California

In 1992, Republican Governor Pete Wilson, rejecting the redistricting plans advanced by Democratic majorities in both houses of the California State Legislature, forced the process into the courts. The court plans, which "nested" assembly and senate districts, pleased neither party and discomfited a number of incumbents.[14] The division between the parties was remarkably even, both in the legislative houses and in California's congressional delegation. In the assembly, for example, Democrats found themselves with thirty safe seats, the Republicans with twenty-nine, and the remaining twenty-one were competitive.

In 2002, the Democrats controlled not only the legislature but also, in the person of Gray Davis, the executive; many, therefore, expected a harsh partisan gerrymander; but in fact, redistricting took a very different turn. Some Washington Democratic Party leaders did indeed hope to use the redistricting to win additional seats to help return the U.S. House to their control; but most Democratic congressional incumbents in the delegation were more interested in securing their own districts. Some state Republicans and a few national Republican leaders (notably Congressman Bill Thomas, chairman of the House Ways and Means Committee) thought GOP interests would best be served by another competitive redistricting, to be achieved either in the courts or by initiative; but the White House and most House Republicans in the delegation (led by David Dreier, chairman of the House Rules Committee), fearing the risk to GOP control of the House in a renewed partisan struggle over redistricting, preferred the status quo and a "sweetheart" redistricting. Perhaps most important, California's volatile electoral tides had thrust the Democrats into a position of such dominance in 2001—control of fifty of eighty assembly seats, twenty-six of forty state senate seats, and thirty-two of fifty-two congressional seats—that only slight gains could have been achieved from a partisan gerrymander and, then, only at the risk of "overreach," the classic cause of party reversals in the election following redistricting.

For all these reasons, the 2001 redistricting took the form of a bipartisan or incumbent gerrymander. Nearly all Democratic incumbents and nearly all Republican incumbents approved the final plans. As the senate Democratic redistricting consultants phrased it in an article in the *California Journal*, the plans ended "a decade long partisan war by garnering unprecedented bipartisan support."[15]

Instead of the usual partisan warfare over redistricting, the plans pitted white Democrats against Mexican Americans—the Democratic leadership against the Mexican American Legal Defense and Education Fund (MALDEF)—in a kind of internecine conflict. The Democratic staff referred to MALDEF's litigation against the official plans as "little more than a political smear directed toward the leadership of the State Legislature."[16] MALDEF, however, saw in incumbent protection, as practiced by the Democratic staff and consultant, a threat to minority voting rights. In an article in the *California Journal*, a MALDEF representative noted that:

> Minority communities in congressional districts, approved by the California Supreme Court in 1991, were calculatedly divided to protect incumbents. The residents of the previous box-shaped congressional district in northeast San Fernando Valley were separated into two oddly shaped districts for no other reason than that they were Latino voters. . . . Similarly, the residents of the Logan Heights community of San Diego were moved into a neighboring non-Latino congressional district for no other reason than that they were Latino voters who pushed Latino registration above the comfort level for an Anglo incumbent. The incumbents were protected; the voters were divided. . . . When legislators will not protect voting rights, it falls upon voters to protect those rights in court.[17]

Latino population growth and its implicit threat to white Democratic incumbents had come to the fore in the first draft of the congressional map. Drawn by veteran Democratic consultant Mike Berman (brother to Congressman Howard Berman) the congressional map had increased the Latino percentage in Congressman Brad Sherman's district from 20 percent to 52 percent while decreasing the Latino percentage in Congressman Berman's district from 65 percent to 40 percent. Sherman, claiming that he had been stabbed in the back, succeeded in forcing a redraft of the map better to equalize the number of Latinos in the two districts—36.5 percent in Sherman's congressional district and 55.6 percent Latino in Berman's district. It was this redrawn map that drew the ire of MALDEF and that became the focus of litigation in *Cano v. Davis*.[18]

MALDEF claimed that the districts diluted Latino voting power, thereby limiting the ability of Latinos to elect candidates of their choice. They emphasized that the use of minority populations to shore up the districts of white incumbents was a classic racial gerrymander.

In deciding *Cano v. Davis*, the court said that the districts in question "do not constitute a threshold showing of bizarreness that would support an inference that the districts are racially gerrymandered."[19] The three-judge panel (all Democratic appointees) made their summary judgment against MALDEF (an unusual approach in a voting rights case) basing their decision "on the absence of a necessary *Gingles* precondition, precondition three."[20] Plaintiffs, decided the court, could not provide evidence of racial bloc voting:

> Although the existence of historical discrimination is a factor . . . the *Garza* findings shed little light on whether the voters of SD 27 presently vote as a bloc

against Latino candidates. The only evidence in the record that is probative of this issue is the outcome of recent elections in the area that comprise SD 27. . . . In Los Angeles County, whites and other non-Latinos are currently far more willing to support Latino candidates for office than in the past."[21]

The Supreme Court affirmed their decision.

The *Cano* case illustrates the tensions between the self-interest of Democratic incumbents and the drive for ethnically represented districts. The incumbents of the two congressional seats under challenge both have strong records of supporting Latino interests; what was at issue here is whether these districts should have been drawn in such a manner as to provide a greater opportunity for Latinos to elect one of their own. Although the districts in question are not "bizarrely drawn" (at least compared with those struck down by the Court in *Shaw v. Reno*), they could, in fact, easily have been drawn so that one had a significantly higher Latino population as well as a more compact shape (figure 7.9).

Although the Democratic leadership could point to the fact that redistricting created a new Latino congressional district (CD 39), the gain was much less than Latino activists thought they deserved and far less than they felt their population justified. The tensions between the Democratic leadership and the Latino community may not have been exhausted in *Cano v. Davis* as suggested in the conclusion of this chapter.

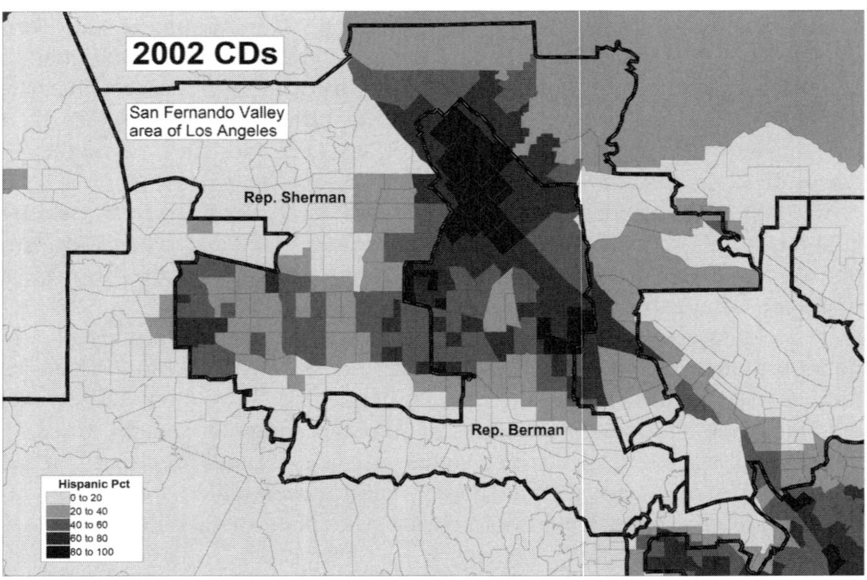

Figure 7.9. Sherman and Berman Districts, California

ISSUES AT THE LOCAL LEVEL

Undoubtedly other political science studies will shed much further light on the issues raised in the redistrictings of state legislatures of Arizona, Florida, and California. Only a handful of political science studies, however, deal with local redistrictings, even when such redistrictings raise the most troubling questions of minority representation and influence. In this section, therefore, the focus is primarily on local governmental redistrictings.

Demographic change is typically much more dramatic at the local rather than the state level. For example no states experience a double or tripling of total population, which was the case during the 1990s in Surprise and Peoria, Arizona. Moreover, it is at the local level that the shifting balance between white, black, Latino, and Asian populations is most striking.

Another factor is that the Justice Department developed regulations to guide the 2001 redistrictings for Section 5 jurisdictions. This affected all the local jurisdictions in Arizona and four counties in California. These regulations stated that, "The last legally enforceable redistricting plan in force for a Section 5 covered jurisdiction is the 'benchmark' against which a new plan is compared.[22] . . . A proposed plan is retrogressive under the Section 5 'effect' prong if its net effect would be to reduce minority voters' effective exercise of the electoral franchise when compared to the benchmark plan."[23] Further, the regulations noted, "The most current population data are used to measure both the benchmark plan and the proposed redistricting plan."[24] If a retrogressive plan was submitted to the DOJ, it became the burden of the submitting jurisdiction to prove that a less-retrogressive plan could not be drawn. Meanwhile, the courts were picking away at the Voting Rights Act by limiting bizarrely shaped districts, ruling that race alone was not a valid criterion for drawing districts, delving further into the Voting Rights Act vs. Equal Protection thicket, and generally making it more difficult for jurisdictions to meet the retrogression standard set by the DOJ regulations.

Surprise, Arizona

Surprise moved to a six-district electoral system with an at-large mayor in 1998 and used data from the 1995 Maricopa County mid-decade census to draw its districts.[25] Hispanics comprised 45.99 percent of the 10,737 persons counted in that census, making it possible for the city to draw two 80 percent-plus Hispanic districts in the old town area of Surprise (District 4—84.25 percent Hispanic, 80.28 percent Hispanic voting age; and District 5—83.28 percent Hispanic and 78.95 percent Hispanic voting age). The total population of the city of Surprise according to the 2000 Census was 30,848 persons, an increase of 23,132 persons since 1990 and 20,111 persons since 1995. Of the 30,848 total, only 7,148 persons (23.29 percent) were reported as Hispanic in origin. The old town area exhibited very little growth between 1995 and 2000, as is typical of older downtown areas. Meanwhile, District 2 to the northwest of the old town area experienced dramatic growth. The map at figure 7.10 depicts the Hispanic concentration in the old town area with an overlay of the districts as drawn in 1998. The chart at figure 7.11 demonstrates graphically the dramatic growth in District 2 and the lack of growth in Districts 4 and 5 (both underpopulated by around 60 percent).[26] The city looked at two possibilities in the 2001 redistricting: one was to draw two minority "influence" districts at the 40 percent level; the other was to collapse Districts 4 and 5 into one minority district. The city chose the latter option creating an 80 percent Hispanic voting age population district in District 4. Their plan also included a finger from a newly constituted District 5 that removed the non-Hispanic incumbent from the new majority-minority district. The Justice Department precleared the city's plan after ascertaining that there was no alternative to the retrogressive plan.

Peoria, Arizona

Peoria moved to a district system in March of 1989, when the voters approved an amendment to the city's charter requiring council members to be elected from six districts. Districts were developed in 1989 and 1990 using the 1985 Maricopa County mid-decade census, redrawn in 1991 following

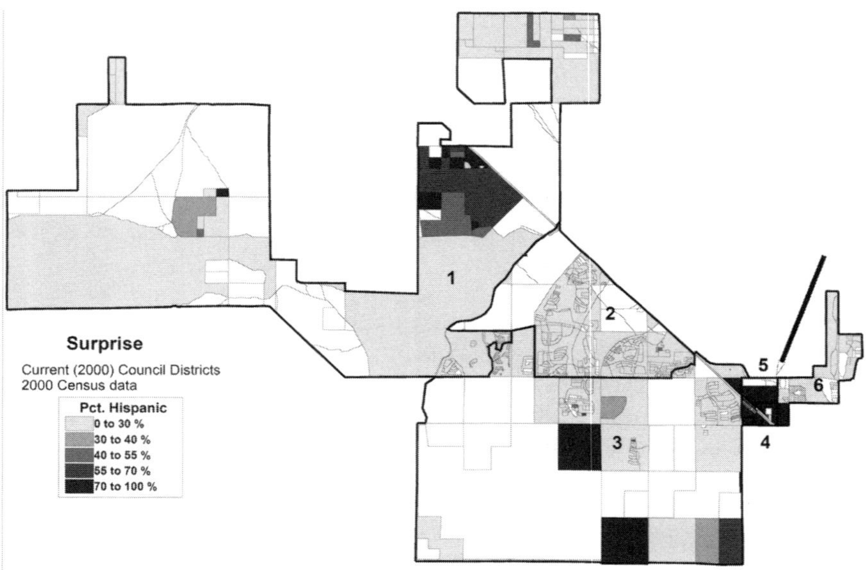

Figure 7.10. Hispanic Concentration in the Old Town Area, 2000 Census

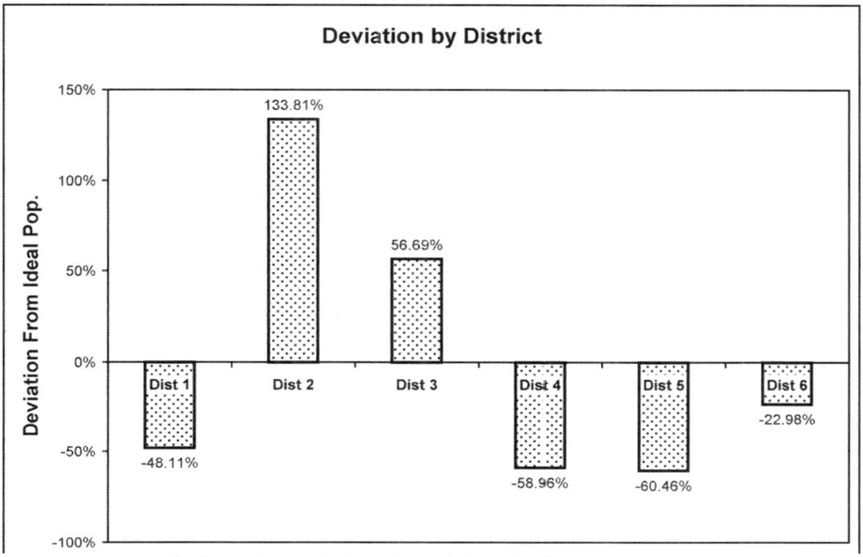

Figure 7.11. Unbalanced Population Growth by District

the 1990 Census, redrawn again in 1996 based on numbers in the Maricopa County 1995 mid-decade Census and in 2001 following the release of the 2000 Census.

In 1985, Peoria's population stood at 28,765 persons, of whom 5,034 (17.5 percent) were Hispanic. Although, like Surprise, there was a concentration of Hispanics in the old downtown area, unlike Surprise, there were large numbers of Hispanics dispersed throughout the city. It proved impossible to create a majority-minority Hispanic district; however, because a Hispanic incumbent councilmember, who had previously been elected at large, lived in the district, a Hispanic percentage of 36.55 percent was sufficient to create a district that could elect him. Support of the plan by the Hispanic incumbent and other members of the Hispanic community, led the Justice Department to preclear the plan, even though it was possible to create a bizarrely shaped 44 percent Hispanic district.

By 1990, Peoria's population had nearly doubled, but the Hispanic population had shrunk as a percentage of the total to 15.5 percent. Although the policy had not yet been translated into regulations, the Justice Department was using the 1990 Census infused into the current districts as the basis on which to judge redrawn districts. They pursued this policy in spite of the fact that the Hispanic district under the new census was severely underpopulated. With an election coming up, Peoria wished to avoid a DOJ objection and the council passed a nearly 42 percent district that was most bizarrely shaped. The district became even more contorted following the 1995 mid-decade census, at which time the city's population had grown by a further 25,000 persons, while the Hispanic percentage of total population remained the same as it had been in 1990—around 15.5 percent. The district redrawn following the 1995 census was just over 41 percent Hispanic.

By the year 2000, Peoria had more than doubled its 1990 population (49,926 to 108,364 persons); moreover, an increasingly widely dispersed Hispanic population still represented only 15.4 percent of the total. By the time of the 2001 redistricting, the new Justice Department regulations regarding retrogression were in place; however, due to a number of factors, including extensive redevelopment of the downtown area, the Hispanic district, even though underpopulated by almost 3,000 persons, had a benchmark of only 38.37 percent total Hispanic and 35.01 percent Hispanic voting age. Even so, the city was unable to meet the benchmark and it sent a minority influence district to the Justice Department that was 37.05 percent Hispanic and 33.63 percent voting age Hispanic. To achieve these percentages it was necessary to underpopulate the district by 4.9 percent. The Justice Department saw no alternative but to accept the plan without objection.

Glendale, Arizona

On February 9, 1988, Glendale, Arizona voters passed Proposition 100, a Charter Amendment authored by Glendale Citizens for a Responsive Government. The Charter Amendment required Glendale to elect a six-member council by district rather than at-large. Moreover, in 1991, the council passed an ordinance setting out the guidelines for redistricting the council district boundaries and reserving the right to redistrict every five years if the mayor and council determined that the districts were not reasonably equal in population. Glendale's original districts under the Charter Amendment were drawn in 1988; the city was redistricted in 1992 (using the 1990 census) and in 1996 (using the 1995 Maricopa County mid-decade census); and the council redistricted following the release of the 2000 Census in April 2001.

Glendale's population, reported in the 1985 Maricopa County mid-decade census, was 122,400; 19,600 (16 percent) were Hispanic. Like Peoria, Glendale had a rather dispersed Hispanic population; however, roughly one-third of that population was concentrated in the city's old downtown area, making it possible to create a 36.4 percent minority influence district there. By 1990 Glendale had 23,334 Hispanics (15.3 percent) out of a total population of 152,091 persons. In the 1990 redistricting of Glendale, the concept of retrogression became a significant factor. Already hard-pressed to maintain a 36.4 percent Hispanic district due to the fact that the district, according to the 1990 Census, was underpopulated by 3,500 persons, the Justice Department attempted to require the city to use a benchmark percentage for the Hispanic district of 41.95 percent (the percentage of the district when infused with the 1990 Census numbers). Although the Justice Department ultimately backed down, this was the first instance of what was ultimately to become a DOJ regulation regarding retrogression and benchmarks that this author/consultant had encountered.

By the year 2000, Glendale had nearly doubled its 1985 population and its Hispanic population had actually grown in percentage terms to almost one-quarter of the city's population. Although some dispersal continued, significant numbers of Hispanics moved across the border from Phoenix and settled in the southern and western portions of the city around the old downtown and around Luke Air Force Base. As its charter allowed it to do, Glendale districts were redrawn following the 1995 mid-decade census. The trend of Hispanics moving across the border from Phoenix continued. The Hispanic population achieved in the minority district in the 1996 redistricting was 42.5 percent; when the 1996 DOJ-approved minority district was infused with the 2000 Census population, the benchmark became 52.66 percent—a majority of Hispanics (although just under a majority, 47.39 percent, voting age Hispanics); moreover, a second south Glendale district was now 36.51 percent Hispanic. The city now had two benchmarks to meet and did so quite easily by simply not changing the districts at all. The growth in south Glendale made it unnecessary to add any population to either district.

Mesa, Arizona

In May of 1998, by passage of Proposition 100, the citizens of the city of Mesa replaced their at-large system of electing six council members with a by-district system; the mayor is still elected at large. The first district lines were drawn using the mid-decade census of 1995, the latest official count that was then available. In the wake of the 2000 Census, the city redrew the districts to bring them into conformity with the new population data.

The April 2000 Census population statistics reported Mesa's population at 396,375. Although there had been nine annexations to the city since the Census was taken, only two of them were populated. The annexations added 1,385 persons to the city's base Census population making a total figure of 397,760 persons. The city had added more than 100,000 persons since 1990, 40,000 of whom were added since 1995. In 2000, 78,473 persons or 19.73 percent were of Hispanic origin (16.77 percent voting age). This percentage was up from 10.9 percent in 1990 (6.5 percent voting age) and 15.46 percent at the mid-decade in 1995 (12.99 percent voting age). So, unlike Surprise, Mesa experienced a percentage increase in its Hispanic population. Mesa was faced with a different phenomenon: the Hispanic population was becoming increasingly less concentrated.

Infusing the 2000 Census population into the most recently DOJ-approved districts (those created using the 1995 mid-decade census), District 4, which had been only 34.27 percent Hispanic (30.18 percent Hispanic voting age) had a total Hispanic population of 47.64 percent and an Hispanic voting age population of 43.66 percent. These became the benchmarks. The district was underpopulated by 5,866 persons, so the challenge was to maintain the benchmark while adding 5,866 persons in order to meet the one person, one vote standard. Although none of the other currently existing districts had a very large Hispanic population, it was noted that current District 1 had a Hispanic total population of 24.77 percent and a Hispanic voting age population of 20.96 percent, and that District 3 had a Hispanic total population of 19.2 percent and a Hispanic voting age population of 16.49 percent. Further questions arose. Can these be considered influence districts? Must the benchmarks in these districts be maintained? Given the distribution of the Hispanic population in Mesa, it was not possible to maintain the Hispanic population levels in all these districts; moreover, maintaining the benchmark population in at least two of the districts involved some regrettable distortion of district lines, and population deviations of a level higher than the city wished. The overall Hispanic percentage in District 4 in the final DOJ-approved plan was 47.84 percent and the voting age Hispanic population percentage was 43.67 percent, slightly exceeding the benchmarks of 47.64 percent and 43.66 percent respectively. Although a potential Hispanic candidate was active in the redistricting process, she chose not to run in the newly strengthened district; a second viable candidate attempted to have his neighborhood included in the district but, because it was a demographically mixed neighborhood, including it would have reduced the Hispanic percentage below the benchmark.

CONCLUSIONS

The detailed descriptions of the local redistrictings set out in the preceding sections will have raised more questions than conclusions in the mind of the reader. The questions do not focus primarily on the authority charged with redistricting. In two of the local jurisdictions, Mesa and Surprise, a commission or advisory committee was used; in the other two, the council was the responsible body; but it is hard to see that this made much difference to the outcome of the redistrictings or to minority interests. Perhaps incumbent survival is a less important stake for local officials, and significantly less at odds with minority group aspirations, than in statewide redistrictings. The questions, instead, center on practical, logistical issues and especially the problems of meeting DOJ regulations.

The law is clear that one cannot intentionally divide a minority population; but is that only if a majority district can be created? Basic good government districting would dictate that no self-identified community be divided unnecessarily; but do we need to maximize so-called "influence" districts? Should other good government criteria be taken into consideration—natural and manmade geography, compactness, contiguity, neighborhoods—and how should they be balanced against the effort to preserve minority influence? Should an influence district be 40 percent? 35 percent? 30 percent? If minority population is maximized, what happens when the Anglo population continues to grow faster than the minority population?

"Retrogression" in the degree of concentration of minority population presents several questions: For example, how is retrogression calculated in areas of shrinking minority population or in cases of rapidly growing Anglo population? In Arizona, where the Anglo population is exploding, how is retrogression at the local level to be prevented? The issue is very different from statewide retrogression, since local jurisdictions often experience surges of population, as was dramatically the case with both Mesa and Peoria. Is it appropriate, as in Glendale, to leave districts intact in order to meet the benchmark, rather than to strengthen them and risk being unable to meet the benchmark in the future? Could the application of retrogression merely reinforce the status quo? Could a local jurisdiction simply make no changes or make merely cosmetic changes to meet the retrogression test?

Should local districts be drawn with an eye to assisting identified minority candidacies? If they are not, can minorities be elected? And if they should be drawn to assist identified candidates, how is it determined and by whom that they are being drawn in the right place? Where do viable minority candidates come from? Do they necessarily come from the areas of minority concentration? What if minority candidates won in the existing at-large scheme and oppose districts as a threat to their political survival? Should black incumbents be protected in areas of rapidly growing Hispanic population? Should districts be designed to minimize rivalry among minority candidates? How does one accomplish this with candidates of different minorities or with candidates of the same minority without "playing favorites?"

Local jurisdictions must also often face choices among at-large, from-district, and by-district electoral systems. Should at-large schemes be replaced in situations where it is impossible to create single-member districts? Should they be created when the jurisdiction is so small as to make it virtually impossible to create a viable system? Should districts be considered when a legal minority constitutes a majority in a jurisdiction? What about other, alternative schemes of representation: modified at-large systems; cumulative voting; proportional representation? Are they preferable to the imposition of districts for purposes of minority representation, or do they carry problems of their own?

The issues canvassed in our review of the three statewide redistrictings raise much broader questions. In particular, the statewide cases suggest that alternative redistricting authorities (commissions or partisan majorities in state legislatures) differentially affect Hispanic and other minority aspirations. Indeed, in a fundamental sense, the statewide cases point toward questions concerning the future of the federal Voting Rights Act and additional state legislative requirements affecting redistricting.

The 1965 Voting Rights Act was enacted with the support of large majorities of Americans; indeed, even in the South, 49 percent of white voters supported the Act at the time of its passage. The legislation quickly secured its aims as huge numbers of blacks registered to vote for the first time and as the discriminatory practices of southern jurisdictions were overthrown. Nearly four decades later, however, minority voting rights and the political and judicial means of enforcing them in redistricting are a focus of swelling controversy.

One cause of controversy is the political tension between minority activists—seeking to increase the number of ethnically representative districts—and their historic allies in the Democratic Party, both the leaders who seek to increase the number of their party's seats and the incumbents, whose concern is personal political security. In Arizona, this tension was vividly illustrated in the contrasts between the plans authored by the Minority Coalition and the state Democrats. In California, even more strikingly, MALDEF pitted itself against liberal Democrats Howard Berman, Brad Sherman, and Bob Filner.

The outcome of *Cano v. Davis*, a clear victory for the congressional incumbent Democrats, has been seized on by some as a portent of the future of voting rights in redistricting. The *Cano* finding that whites do not vote as a bloc to prevent the election of preferred Hispanic candidates is "old news," according to Edward Blum and Roger Clegg. "Minority candidates have attracted so much white cross-over voting during the last fifteen years that their success at winning does not raise an eyebrow."[27] In this view, which focuses on the numbers of Latinos who now hold office in California, Section 2 and Section 5 enforcement practices are counterproductive to the original conception of the Voting Rights Act, which was intended as "a mechanism to ensure that people are not treated differently according to race when they vote."[28] Blum and Cleggs' judgment is harsh: the effort to assure the right to vote, they claim, has degenerated into a "DOJ-led extortion racket" in which states have to "racially gerrymander to the nth degree in order to receive preclearance."[29]

Perhaps *Cano* is, indeed, the wave of the future; and perhaps the bureaucratic apparatus of preclearance will one day fall to judicial scrutiny. Yet, whatever judges decide, issues of minority representation of the kind discussed in this chapter will remain a focus of political controversy. In particular, the struggle between white and black incumbents on one side and Latino challengers on the other, is likely to continue to be explosive.

The contest between Richard Katz and Richard Alarcon in a state senate primary in California's San Fernando Valley turned into a bruising, racially embittered battle between Jewish and Latino activists. All seven of the white Democratic incumbents in southern California, where Latinos are rapidly approaching majority status, are Jewish. Will Latinos in term-limited legislative districts wait for these Democratic congressional incumbents to retire? Or will they turn to redistricting reform or to congressional term limits to accelerate their removal?[30]

If the federal Voting Rights Act fails to provide a remedy for Latino under representation, activists may well turn to other means. An especially interesting example of such a resort is the California Voting Rights Act (CVRA).[31] Although the act affects only local jurisdictions, it has the potential of enabling the election of scores of Latinos to office in city, county, and special district elections, thereby opening up opportunities for these local officials to gain name ID and become potential state legislative and congressional candidates.

With little fanfare, indeed, practically unnoticed by the public and the media, the CVRA was passed in July 2002 to go into effect in January of 2003. Under the Act, jurisdictions can be sued if they use at-large, from-district, or mixed election systems. A jurisdiction may be vulnerable even if minority candidates have been elected under one of the aforementioned systems. This new law goes well beyond federal voting rights law by stating that, "The fact that members of a protected class are not geographically compact or concentrated may not preclude a finding of racially polarized voting . . . but may be a factor in determining an appropriate remedy."[32] In other words, the first Gingles precondition—"the minority group must be able to demonstrate that it is sufficiently large and geographically compact to constitute a majority in a single-member district"—is not necessary to prove a claim. Moreover, appropriate remedies could include not merely a move to a by-district system but creation of "influence districts" in a district system or even the imposition of alternative systems such as cumulative voting or proportional representation.

Though it will be up to Congress in 2007 to decide the fate of the federal Voting Rights Act, the California state legislature—under pressure from Hispanic activist groups and with the leadership of its own Hispanic members—took matters into its own hands and found a political means of enhancing Hispanic representation. It is an approach that will be watched in many states and jurisdictions of the southwest. Of considerable interest, also, will be the contrast between the results of commission redistrictings, such as in Arizona, and the results of redistrictings run by partisan majorities, such as those in Florida and California. In particular, the drive for incumbent security, which was so obvious in California's sweetheart gerrymander, may be seen to offer many more obstacles to Hispanic aspirations than are presented in the commission form of redistricting.

NOTES

1. Florence Adams, *Latinos and Local Representation* (New York: Garland Publishing, 2000).

2. Adams, *Latinos*.

3. In nearly all the cases on which I provide detail (excepting California which, curiously, is my home state) I served as a political cartographer, intimately involved in the line-drawing process. I was primary linedrawer for all the local districtings; I was involved in the initial Arizona Commission redistricting; and I participated to a much lesser extent in the Florida redistricting.

4. Douglas Johnson, of National Demographics Corporation (*www.ndcresearch.com*), produced the graphics for this article.

5. I use the terms Hispanic and Latino; but very few people get up in the morning, look in the mirror and say, I'm a Latino or I'm a Latina or I'm a Hispanic. More typically, people think of themselves as Mexican Americans, Cuban Americans, Puerto Rican Americans, Guatemalan Americans, and so forth. These distinctions have considerable importance because the different groups tend to act politically with a degree of independence from one another. In Arizona and California, the overwhelming majority are Mexican Americans; in Florida, as we discuss more at length later in the chapter, the traditional dominance of Cuban Americans in the Hispanic community is being increasingly challenged by Puerto Rican Americans and Central Americans, including Mexican Americans.

6. Proposition 106 amended Article IV, Part 2, Section 1 of the *Arizona State Constitution*.

7. *Arizona State Constitution*, Article IV, Part 2, Section 1, (14), A-F.

8. *Arizona State Constitution*, (15).

9. Proceedings of the Arizona Independent Redistricting Commission Meeting, October 14, 2001, 73. A "benchmark" is considered the last legally enforceable redistricting plan in force.

10. Under the watchful eye of court-appointed special master, Bruce Cain, the commission drew interim districts for use in the 2002 elections. The commission then convened again to make final adjustments to the districts in accordance with the DOJ objection. These final districts were precleared by the Justice Department without objection; but the court challenge from the Democrats, in an attempt to force the commission to draw more competitive districts, was argued in Superior Court before Judge Kenneth L. Fields from November to December 2003. At this writing the parties are awaiting Judge Fields' ruling. There were two cases, which were joined: *Arizona Minority Coalition for Fair Redistricting v. Arizona Independent Redistricting Commission*, CV 2002-004380; and *Ricarte v. Arizona Independent Redistricting Commission*, CV 2002-004882.

11. The leaders of the House and Senate Reapportionment Committees, Karen Thurman and Peter Deutsch, carved congressional districts for themselves.

12. The Constitutional Revision Commission of 1978 had proposed an Independent Redistricting Commission, which was supported by Republicans. In 1993, the state senate unanimously adopted a redistricting commission that died in the Democratic-controlled house. In 1998, however, it was Republican leadership pressure that stymied a redistricting reform proposal in the Constitutional Revision Commission of that year.

13. *Martinez v. Bush*, 02-20244-CIV-Jordan and 02-10028-CIV-Jordan, U.S. District Court, Southern District of Florida, Miami Division.

14. "Nesting" is the process of incorporating districts within districts. For example, if a state has 40 senate districts and 80 house districts, each senate district would be made up of two house districts.

15. Senate Redistricting Staff and Consultants, "The Redistricting Dispute," *California Journal* (January 2002): 38.

16. Senate Redistricting Staff and Consultants, "Redistricting Dispute," 38.

17. Mexican American Legal Defense and Education Fund, "The Redistricting Dispute," *California Journal* (January 2002): 40.

18. *Cano v. Davis*, 211 F. Supp. 2d 1208; 2002 U.S. Dist.

19. *Cano v. Davis*, 12.

20. *Cano v. Davis*, 23.

21. *Cano v. Davis*, 28–29.

22. *Federal Register*, Vol. 66, No. 12, Thursday, January 18, 2001, 5412.

23. *Federal Register*, 5413.

24. *Federal Register*, 5413.

25. Maricopa County, Arizona, worked with the U.S. Bureau of the Census to conduct mid-decade censuses in 1985 and 1995.

26. District 1 is largely undeveloped territory that has been annexed to the city. Non-Hispanic population growth in that area could further limit the city's ability to draw even a single majority-minority district in the future.

27. Edward Blum and Roger Clegg, "Color Inside the Lines," *Legal Affairs* (November–December 2003): 4. A very different view of the Voting Rights Act is advanced by Anita Earls in the same issue of *Legal Affairs* in an article titled, "Equal Effects." She claims that the Act remains a vital and necessary part of American democracy.

28. Blum and Clegg, "Color Inside the Lines," 5.

29. Blum and Clegg, "Color Inside the Lines," 3.

30. In the 1990s, California's term limits opened the door to many Latinos. In 1990 only six Latinos held partisan elective office; but by 2000 there were 33.

31. *California Elections Code*, Section 1, Chapter 1.5, 14025-14032.

32. *California Elections Code*, 14028 (c).

III

CASE STUDIES IN THE OLD AND NEW MILLENNIA

8

The Art of the Dummymander: The Impact of Recent Redistrictings on the Partisan Makeup of Southern House Seats[1]

Bernard Grofman and Thomas L. Brunell

Effective gerrymandering can increase/decrease the number of seats captured by a particular party, but gerrymandering cannot produce miracles; it cannot turn water into wine, or Republicans into Democrats. A lifeboat metaphor is useful in understanding districting.

The carrying capacity of any lifeboat is limited. If you try to overload it, the boat may sink, or at least tip over, washing a number of people overboard.[2] The carrying capacity of a party's voting strength is limited. If you try to make it carry too much weight (spread the party's voting strength too thin among too many districts) the lifeboat will probably go under in bad (electoral) weather, even if it is afloat when skies are blue and the ocean calm. Moreover, if some of the logs holding up the lifeboat are going to be knocked away by the waves (i.e., realignment trends are reducing a party's voting strength, key incumbents who play a vital role in holding on to marginal seats are likely to retire), then a party that fails to take such uncomfortable longer-term realities into account will discover that, even if the lifeboat does not sink initially, it is bound to founder later in the decade.

Since blacks are such loyal Democrats, the creation of black majority seats that soak up blacks (and also often have substantial proportions of white Democrats in them, who live in close proximity to black areas) has been blamed for a good part of the Democratic congressional losses after the 1990s round of redistricting. Yet black-majority seats are really not that different from other seats that are packed with Democrats. If you waste Democratic votes in some districts that means that you have to be very careful about how you parcel out the remaining Democratic strength. Especially when margins are thin, the effect of electoral tides on partisan representation is nonlinear. There can be a huge tipping effect in a particular election; a high proportion of those on the lifeboat can be washed away (i.e., if you try cutting the margins too thin, the partisan balance in a state can change *very* rapidly).

Both foresight and ruthlessness are needed. If a party overestimates the carrying capacity of its lifeboat, it risks having it sink, thus ending the (political) lives of all (or most) on board. But recognizing the problem is not enough. Party leaders must be ruthless enough (and have enough political clout) to sacrifice some people (loyal party members, often with years of sterling service) who are desperate to get on board the lifeboat. In Spock-speak: "The good of the many must outweigh the good of the few."

We can illustrate these points with a discussion of congressional districting in the Deep South in the 1990 and 2000 rounds of redistricting, focusing on Alabama, Georgia, Mississippi, North Carolina, and South Carolina. We will argue that, in a number of these states, the result of failing to understand the carrying capacity of the lifeboat on the part of the party controlling the districting process and/or its reluctance or inability to take the appropriate measures, is what we will call a *dummymander*. A *dummymander* is a gerrymander by one party that, over the course of the decade, benefits the other party, and actually looks as if it was designed by that party rather than the party in power.

ALABAMA

The Alabama congressional plan adopted in 1992 was proposed by Republicans and ordered into effect by a federal court. It created a 68 percent black majority in a new 7th district. Barone and Ujifusa blame this district for the subsequent victories of Republicans in two seats, "the once-competitive 2nd and the previously Democratic 6th, from which tens of thousands of blacks had been removed to raise the black percentage in the 7th."[3]

The probable partisan outcomes over the course of the 1990s can be prognosticated by the distribution of the 1992 presidential vote across the seven Alabama House districts shown in table 8.1 (the first two columns).[4] The 1992 plan creates a *very* packed Republican seat in the 6th and a reasonably safe Republican seat in the 2nd, as well as two other likely Republican seats, the 1st and the 4th; the Democrats, in contrast, have the certainty of only one seat, the black majority 7th, and a shot at holding two more of the seven House seats in the state, the 5th and the 3rd. Over the course of the decade, Democratic losses mounted. In 1990 the split was 6D, 1R; in 1992 and 1994 it was 4D, 3R; by 1998 it was 2D, 5R. In 2000 it stayed 2D, 5R, with all incumbents retaining their seats.

In the 2000 round of redistricting the size of Alabama's House delegation remained at seven. Now the Democrats controlled the process. Hop-

Table 8.1. 1992 and 2000 Presidential Results by Congressional District: Alabama

1992 Presidential		*2000 Presidential*	
District	*Clinton Percent-Bush Percent*	*District*	*Gore Percent-Bush Percent*
1	−15	1	−23
2	−18	2	−24
3	−6	3	−5
4	−11	4	−24
5	−3	5	−10
6	−38	6	−49
7	43	7	34

ing to improve on their performance in the 1990s, they passed a congressional redistricting plan that targeted the 3rd congressional district as a possible Democratic pick up by doubling the number of African Americans in that district.[5] Paralleling our analysis for the 1990 redistricting round, we break down the presidential vote from the 2000 election by the new congressional district lines. From the table we can see that the Democrats still have one safe (packed) district, the 7th; however, in 2002 they continued to control the 5th congressional district, even though the district leaned Republican.

From table 8.1 we can also see that Democrats in the 2000 round did not go far enough in reshaping the 3rd congressional district in a Democratic direction in the light of the fact that support for Bush 43 in 2000 was greater than what it had been for Bush 41 in 1992, in that the district was only minusculely less pro-Republican than before (and assuming that the majority of Perot supporters would otherwise have voted Republican). Prior to the 2002 election, Bob Riley, the incumbent in the 3rd, vacated his congressional seat to run for governor. The Republicans ran Mike Rogers, who won the seat with 51.1 percent of the vote. His opponent was Joe Turnham, who is a white Democrat and a long-time Alabama Democratic Party activist. (In 2000, in the old district 3, Riley, the Republican incumbent, had won with no Democratic opposition.)

After the 2002 election, in the 108th Congress, the delegation remained 5 to 2 in favor of the GOP. 2002 was probably the Democrats' best opportunity to pick up a seat, in that Representative Rogers will now, as the incumbent, have an opportunity to increase his visibility in the 3rd, and the 3rd is the only district that might realistically be a pickup for the Democrats. Thus we expect that, over the course of the decade the Alabama delegation will remain with a 5 to 2 Republican edge, although a further loss of one seat for the Democrats is not out of the question in an especially good Republican year.

GEORGIA

Writing before the 1994 Republican takeover of the House, Barone and Ujifusa's discussion of Georgia's 1992 congressional redistricting specifically blames the Voting Rights Act (VRA) for Democratic congressional losses in Georgia in the 1992 election, and anticipates more such losses in the future.[6] They characterize the VRA as "requiring the maximum number of majority-black districts." In Georgia, the Department of Justice insisted that that a third black-majority seat be drawn when the state legislature submitted for preclearance a plan that only had two black-majority seats in it.[7] In Georgia, Barone and Ujifusa assert that the VRA, "required the maintenance of the black majority 5th in Atlanta and the creation of a new black majority 11th, stretching from Atlanta to Savannah, which diverted Democratic voters from the 1st district, subsequently captured by a Republican. It also required the maximization of the black percentage in the 2nd district in southwest Georgia, siphoning off Democratic votes from the 3rd District, which went Republican." They go on to note that, in 1992, "of nine Democratic incumbents, three were reelected, three retired, and three were defeated."

Barone and Ujifusa end their discussion of 1992 congressional redistricting in Georgia with the prescient observation: "All eight of the white-majority districts could conceivably be seriously contested by Republicans some time in the decade."[8] In fact, all eight of these seats went Republican in 1994, so that the partisan balance in Georgia's congressional delegation went from 9D, 1R in 1990 to 7D, 4R in 1992 to 3D, 8R in 1994.[9] It was 3D, 8R again in 1998. The Georgia delegation stayed 3D, 8R in 2000, with all incumbents winning reelection. In 1994 and throughout the rest of the decade, the only Democratic House members in Georgia were African-Americans elected from the three districts that were drawn as black majority in 1992 (albeit two of these were redrawn with considerably lower black percentages later in the decade[10]).

But are the Democratic defeats in Georgia really to be blamed solely on the VRA? Well, in our view, not really. A good part of the blame must be attached to the white Democrats in Georgia who suffered from two psychological ailments common among the young: the belief that because you seem healthy now, you'll never get sick, and the belief that it is good to be as thin as possible as long as you still remain breathing. Democrats doing the congressional redistricting in Georgia may be said to have suffered from what we will call "bulimia-inducing anorexia," i.e., a regurgitation reflex in which districts designed to be won by slim margins (so as to maximize the number of seats under party control) are then tossed into the waiting hands of members of the other party in a year when the electoral tides (or incumbent resignations) run against you.

If you look at the distribution of Democratic support in Georgia's eleven congressional districts (table 8.2) as shown by 1992 election results, you will see that the 1990s Georgia congressional districting plan appears to be a classic *Republican* gerrymander. Based on the presidential vote in 1992, we would expect that three districts would be won by Democrats in a runaway (thus packing the Democratic vote); one seat (held in 1990 by Newt Gingrich) should be a very safe Republican seat; three districts ought to be Republican seats (but with some chance of staying Democratic if there was a popular Democratic incumbent in place and a weak Republican challenger), and four seats should be competitive seats near certain to trend Republican over the course of the decade (although some of these seats might be held onto by the Democrats as long as popular Democratic incumbents are running in them). Yet this districting was not done by Republicans or by a court; it was done in a state with Democrats running both chambers of the legislature and holding the governorship! Thus, in substance, the 1990s Georgia congressional redistricting plan looks like a dummymander—a pro-Republican partisan gerrymander that was actually drawn by Democrats.

Why did this dummymander happen? Well, one reason, but far from the only reason, is that this was a plan subject to the important legal constraint of needing to draw three black-majority seats to obtain DOJ preclearance approval.[11] One way to make sense of this districting from a Democratic perspective is to see it as looking at things from the most optimistic perspective possible—an attempt to hold on to a maximum of 10 seats in the short run and 7 seats in the long run. But such optimism risked the downside possibility of being held to only 3 seats (the black-majority seats) if electoral tides

Table 8.2. 1992 and 2000 Presidential Results by Congressional District: Georgia

1992 Presidential		*2000 Presidential*	
District	*Clinton Percent-Bush Percent*	*District*	*Gore Percent-Bush Percent*
1	−11	1	−29
2	41	2	−2
3	−11	3	−5
4	−6	4	41
5	42	5	42
6	−26	6	−38
7	−8	7	−44
8	−5	8	−40
9	−14	9	−35
10	−8	10	−42
11	43	11	−4
12		12	9
13		13	16

went against the Democrats. With the advantage of hindsight, it is obvious that redistricting as if the 1990s were going to be as good for Georgia Democrats as the 1980s had been was not a smart move! Indeed, it doesn't take hindsight to see the Democrat's folly. Any realistic look at the steady decline in Democratic support among white southerners over the past 40 or so years should have revealed how badly such optimism was misguided.

Georgia Democrats would have been far better off to concede 4 seats to the Republicans (and to pack them with Republicans to the greatest extent possible), and to put as many Democrats as possible in the remaining seven seats. Had they done this they could, in my view, have held on to a 7 to 4 advantage for the rest of the decade. Even if you do not believe that Democratic strength could have sustained 7 seats, it surely was concentrated enough to have sustained 6 seats, keeping a Democratic majority in the delegation.

Why wasn't this "casting pearls before elephants"[12] a feasible strategy for the Georgia Democrats? Well, in a nutshell, they had too many incumbents to protect. Of the nine Democratic incumbents in 1990, only three retired. This meant that Democrats had to try to draw districts to reelect these six incumbents (5 white, 1 black) at the same time as they were putting large numbers of black (and some white) Democrats in the two new black-majority seats. In short, they had to try to draw at least 8 Democratic seats (3 with black-majorities) if they were both to keep their incumbents happy and satisfy the Department of Justice. Yet, as the top-down realignment in the South worked its way down to the level of U.S. House seats, given the partisan trends among white voters, Georgia Democrats simply did not have the electoral support base to hold on to eight (of their previous nine) House seats for ten more years.

And, if they did not have the votes to hang on to eight (of their previous nine) seats, they certainly did not have the votes to hang on to all nine of these seats. And, if they didn't have the votes to hang on to nine seats, they certainly didn't have the votes to hang on to their previous nine seats *and* pick up a new seat as well. Yet, from the distribution of Democratic voting strength across districts, it appears that Democrats attempted not just to hold on to the nine seats they held in 1990, but to give themselves the possibility of picking up a tenth seat. The only seat they truly conceded to the Republicans was the seat held by Newt Gingrich.

The only way to describe the Georgia Democrats' congressional redistricting leading to a dummymander is in terms of "criminal optimism." To return to our lifeboat metaphor, the carrying capacity of the Democratic lifeboat in Georgia was limited. If you tried to overload it, it would eventually tip over. At least one white Democratic incumbent had to be sacrificed of the five running for reelection. If this incumbent were not thrown overboard (i.e., his district made heavily Republican), and if Democratic strength were not concentrated in no more than seven districts, the whole Democratic congressional ship (the U.S.S. Georgia) would eventually sink—and, in 1994, sink it did.

Hoping to recoup some of the losses from their miscalculations of the 1990 round, the Georgia Democrats enacted another ambitious plan for the 2002 elections in which they hoped to pick up four seats (the two new seats Georgia received after apportionment, CD 12 and CD 13, and two seats held by Republicans, CD 3 and CD 11). The Democratic strategy in Georgia was to concede six seats to Republicans (Districts 1, 6, 7, 8, 9, and 10) and draw boundaries that packed white voters into those districts, a tactic some termed "bleaching." This allowed for black voters to be spread more evenly among the remaining districts than they had been in the 1990s plan.

The two Republican incumbents targeted by the Democrats were Bob Barr in the 11th district and Saxby Chambliss in the 3rd district. Both of these incumbents vacated their districts in reaction to the new political landscape that they faced. Of the four targeted seats the Democrats only managed to win two—one new seat, the 13th district, won by David Scott and one seat with a previous Republican incumbent, the 3rd, won by Jim Marshall. Republican Representative Barr, whose new district was the 11th ran in the new 7th district but lost to another Republican incumbent, John Linder, in the primary. Ironically the 11th district was held by the Republicans, with newcomer Phil Gingrey winning by a narrow margin (51.6 percent of the vote). Chambliss ran for the Senate and upset incumbent Max Cleland (D), although the Democrats were able to take Chambliss' vacated congressional district, with Jim Marshall winning by just 1,500 votes.

The 12th district was also created so that a Democrat could win—Al Gore carried the district by 10 percentage points in 2000. However, the Democrats ran Charles Walker Jr., son of a prominent black Georgia state legislator. Walker's campaign was fraught with ethics problems, and Max Burns ended up beating Walker by 10 percent because of these issues.

Going into the 2000 round the delegation was split 8 Republicans and 3 Democrats. The ambitious Democratic plan posited a potential swing of the delegation to 6 Republicans and 7 Democrats, but the actual split after the 2002 election was 8 Republicans and 5 Democrats. Democrats had made gains, but not as many as they had hoped.

From the data in table 8.2 we see that there are four seats "in play"—districts 2, 3, 11, and 12. Over the course of the decade, the Democrats will have their hands full trying to wrestle the additional two seats they planned on getting from the Republicans, but some further gains are not impossible. The key problem for Democrats is that the two most Democratic districts are among the most packed—Gore carried districts 4 and 5 by more than 40 percentage points. These votes could have been spread out more efficiently. The Democrats had their chance in the 2000 round, when they controlled the districting process. It is unlikely that the stars will ever again be in such a favorable alignment for them. Still, in the 2000 round the Democrats did a much better job of packing Republicans to compensate for their own packed seats than they had in the previous decade.

MISSISSIPPI

Writing just after the 1994 elections, Barone and Ujifusa blame the VRA-mandated drawing of a 63 percent black seat (the 2nd, initially held by Mike Espy) for the 1994 Republican win in the 1st congressional district (when Democratic incumbent Jamie Whitten retired), *and* predicted that the concentration of black voting strength in the 2nd could lead to the loss of the three remaining white Democratic House seats in Mississippi later in the decade.[13] Barone and Ujifusa also make an important point about conflicts between black legislators and civil rights groups: "Ironically, Espy wanted to hold down the black percentage in the 2d in the 1991 plan, because he was winning white votes and he wanted more black influence in other districts. But civil rights apparatchiks said no."[14]

Looking at the 1992 presidential vote (table 8.3), we see that the Mississippi congressional redistricting produced two seats that looked as if they should certainly go Republican over the course of the decade, two that leaned Republican, and the black-majority 2nd that should be Democrat until the cows came home. What looked like a Republican gerrymander was drawn by a Democratic legislature intent on protecting its incumbents. When the plan was drawn in 1991 the state still had a Democratic governor. In 1990, the Mississippi delegation was 5D, 0R; in 1992 it was again 5D, 0R, and in 1994 it was 4D, 1R. In 1996, with a party switch by one Democratic incumbent and a retirement by another, it became 2D, 3R. In 1998, with a seat regained by the Democrats it was 3D, 2R. In 2000 it stayed that way, with all five incumbents reelected, each by very considerable margins.

As with Georgia, some have blamed the severity of the two (and, at one point, three) Democratic congressional losses in Mississippi on the VRA. But it is not really the VRA; in fact, in Mississippi, unlike elsewhere in the deep South, we saw relatively far-sighted decisions on the part of white Democrats!

Since Mississippi was one of the most heavily Republican Southern states in presidential voting in 1988 and 1992 and since it had a Republican governor elected in 1991, it helps to think about Mississippi in lifeboat terms. It should have been obvious to Democratic party leaders in the 1990s round of redistricting that there weren't enough loyal Democrats to create five Democratic House seats in Mississippi that would last the decade. And apparently, unlike in Georgia, the obvious actually was obvious to the Mississippi Democrats. In Mississippi the Democrats chose to draw two House seats that

Table 8.3. 1992 and 2000 Presidential Results by Congressional District: Mississippi

1992 Presidential		*2000 Presidential*	
District	*Clinton Percent-Bush Percent*	*District*	*Gore Percent-Bush Percent*
1	−8	1	−20
2	21	2	16
3	−24	3	−30
4	-9	4	−33
5	−22	5	

were clearly going to go to the Republicans (at least once the present incumbents retired), and they concentrated their own voting strength in three districts. Of course, two of those three were still districts that leaned Republican, and one did go Republican in 1996; but, Democrats did capture one of these districts and recapture the other, so that, with the black-majority seat, they retained a majority of the state's congressional delegation in 1998 and 2000— making Mississippi the only state in the seven states of the deep South covered by the Voting Rights Act (Alabama, Georgia, Louisiana, Mississippi, North Carolina, South Carolina, Virginia) where Democrats still controlled a majority of the congressional delegation at the end of the decade.[15]

After the 2000 census Mississippi's congressional delegation was reduced from five seats to just four. Again the Democrats completely controlled the districting in the state but lawmakers could not agree on a plan, with a main bone of contention being how to shape the new district that presumably would merge the area now represented by Mississippi's two freshmen representatives, Charles "Chip" Pickering, a Republican from the 3rd district, and Ronnie Shows, a Democrat from the 4th district. There were sufficient internal rivalries and sectional disputes within the Democratic Party that the party simply could not come to an agreement on a map. As a result, several lawsuits were filed, and a federal court ended up enacting a plan that combined two incumbents, Pickering and Shaw, one of each party, in a district titled 3rd congressional district—i.e., with a Republican incumbent. All three federal judges were Republican appointees. The district that they drew was 30 percent black, but the white composition of the district was such as to leave the district with a clear overall Republican preponderance. Indeed, in 2002, "Chip" Pickering beat Democrat Ronnie Shows by more than 30 points. Thus, the delegation went from a 3 to 2 Democrat advantage in 2000, to a split delegation with two seats controlled by each party, in 2002.

The data in table 8.3 indicate that while one district is safely theirs, the Democrats are lucky to currently hold even two districts in Mississippi. There is a good chance that they will lose one of these districts over the course of the decade, the 4th district, currently represented by Gene Taylor (D), which voted overwhelmingly Republican in the 2000 presidential election. Taylor has represented this district since 1989 and is likely the Democrats best hope of holding on to the seat. The other two districts in the state appear safely Republican.

NORTH CAROLINA

North Carolina in the 1990s round of redistricting is another textbook case of Democrats trying to hold on to more House seats than they had votes, succeeding in the first postredistricting election (with the aid of incumbency and some help from a winning Democratic presidential candidate), and then losing big thereafter. In other words, North Carolina in the 1990s is a textbook dummymander. In North Carolina in the 1990s, as in Georgia in the 1990s, the problem for the Democrats was too many House incumbents and not enough realism. Bowing to the inevitable the Democrats drew the 6th, 9th, and 10th, seats that had previously elected Republicans, as solid Republican districts. But, considering the constraints imposed by the two heavily Democratic black-majority seats that had been drawn under threat of DOJ preclearance denial (one a newly added seat, the 12th), it just didn't makes sense for Democrats to try to hold on to *all* the remaining House seats, even though these seats were previously held by white Democrats. The distribution of the 1992 presidential vote across these 12 districts is shown in table 8.4.

Table 8.4. 1992 and 2000 Presidential Results by Congressional District: North Carolina

1992 Presidential		*2000 Presidential*	
District	*Clinton Percent-Bush Percent*	*District*	*Gore Percent-Bush Percent*
1	32	1	15
2	−5	2	−7
3	−8	3	−30
4	−8	4	8
5	0	5	−33
6	−19	6	−35
7	0	7	−4
8	−2	8	−8
9	−19	9	−27
10	−21	10	−31
11	0	11	−19
12	41	12	15
13		13	0

If the Democrats had created another two really safe Republican seats in which to pack Republican strength, they could have survived the decade with a majority of the North Carolina congressional delegation. As it was, although 7D, 4R in 1990, and 8D, 4R in 1992, in 1994 the North Carolina House delegation shifted to 5D, 7R; and it remained with that partisan complexion in 2000. As to why the Democratic legislature did not concede another one or two Republican seats, can be attributed to the need to protect existing white Democratic incumbents, of whom there were six running for reelection in 1992, and/or to overoptimism. In particular, the Democrats tried to keep the 11th district, a competitive seat in the 1980s (with a Republican incumbent in 1990), as a competitive seat in 1992. In the long run, they should probably have conceded this seat to the Republicans by increasing the proportion of Republican-leaning voters in it (via juggling the boundaries between the 11th and the 9th and 10th districts and other districts), and using the Democrats this freed up elsewhere (e.g., to shore up the Democratic incumbent in the 8th, Bill Hefner, who ended up squeaking through in 1994 with only 52 percent of the vote) in a district that ultimately went Republican.

North Carolina was the beneficiary of the 2000 reapportionment by narrowly besting Utah for the 435th seat in the House of Representatives.[16] The Democrats again controlled the redistricting process in the state and had learned some useful lessons from their 1990s mistakes. Paralleling our earlier results for the 1990 redistricting round, we show in table 8.4 the partisan distribution (based on the 2000 two-party presidential vote) of the thirteen North Carolina House seats redrawn after the 2000 census.

From table 8.4 we see that the Democrats packed the Republicans more heavily than in the prior round of districting—districts 3, 5, 6, 9, and 10, and to a slightly less extent, district 11, all voted Bush by very large margins in 2000. By packing these seats, and conceding them to the Republicans, Democrats gave themselves some chances in the remaining seats. In particular, Democrats created the new 13th district to lean Democratic, and were able to win that seat in the 2002 election. The Democrats also targeted the 8th congressional district, where Robin Hayes (R) had been the incumbent since 1998, but in 2002 Representative Hayes managed to hold on to the seat.

Republicans now hold a 7 to 6 seat advantage in the North Carolina House delegation, but that is still an improvement for Democrats over the 7 to 5 result from 2000. Since there are a few seats potentially in play in the state, it is hard to prognosticate which party will hold the majority of the North Carolina delegation in 2010 (although if we were forced to bet, we would bet on the Republicans); what can be safely said is that the Republicans are very unlikely to fall below six of the thirteen seats at any time over the remainder of this decade.

SOUTH CAROLINA

Barone and Ujifusa's observe that the creation of a black-majority seat in South Carolina in 1992 "made the 1st, 2nd, 3rd, and 5th districts more Republican."[17] They regarded South Carolina in the 1990s as pretty much a lost cause for the Democrats once that black-majority House seat had been drawn.

A look at the distribution of the 1992 presidential vote in South Carolina's congressional districts (table 8.5) shows that they were quite right. There was really one seat, the black-majority district, which Democrats could have expected to win with any certainty in the districts created in the 1990s redistricting round. In 1990, the South Carolina House delegation was 4D, 2R; in 1992 it was 3D, 3R; but by 1994 it was 2D, 4R; in 1998 and again in 2000 the results were again 2D, 4R. In 1994, while a popular white Democratic incumbent in District 5 was holding on to that district by the skin of his teeth, the retirement of another popular white Democratic incumbent cost the Democrats District 3. Barone and Ujifusa (2000) attribute the ability of the Democrats to hold on to District 5 throughout the decade of the 1990s, sometimes even winning it by large margins, to the popularity of the incumbent Democrat (and his superb campaigning skills); but no incumbent can live forever.[18]

For the 2000 round of redistricting, there were no changes in the size of South Carolina's House delegation. Going into the 2002 election the delegation was 4 to 2 in favor of the Republicans. The Republicans in the state legislature drew a congressional map that Democratic Governor Jim Hodges vetoed. With the state deadlocked, a federal panel of judges then drew a map that was very similar to the plan inked by the Republican state legislators.

One major change from the 1990s plans was to Representative Jim Clyburn's (D) 6th district. He is the only African American representative in the congressional delegation from South Carolina. The district was trimmed

Table 8.5. 1992 and 2000 Presidential Results by Congressional District: South Carolina

1992 Presidential		*2000 Presidential*	
District	*Clinton Percent-Bush Percent*	*District*	*Gore Percent-Bush Percent*
1	−20	1	−21
2	−16	2	−20
3	−16	3	−29
4	−21	4	−32
5	−23	5	−12
6	31	6	18

of some of its African American voters. It went from being 65 percent black VAP to 54 percent. Representative Clyburn was not too displeased with this, even going to far as saying that he could "live with 43 percent." The court gave as its reason for the reduction in African American voters the need to make the district more compact by smoothing out the edges of the district. Representative Clyburn, like each of the other incumbents in South Carolina, did not have any trouble holding on to his seat in 2002.

Paralleling our data for the 1990 redistricting round, we show in table 8.5 the partisan distribution (based on the 2000 two-party presidential vote) of the six South Carolina House seats. From this data we see that the Democrats most optimistic scenario under the present plan is to remain at the present 4R to 2D split. The 6th district is still very safe, confirming Representative Clyburn's intuition about his ability to hang on to his seat even after the black percentage in it was lowered, but Representative John Spratt (D) is winning a seat that leans to the Republicans. That seat might shift to the Republican column. Indeed, even breaking up the present black-majority seat and using blacks as sandbags, it is hard to see how Democrats could win more than two (or at most three) of the House seats in South Carolina. When it comes to federal elections, there just are not that many Democratic-voting whites in the state!

DISCUSSION

The potential political consequences attributable to congressional redistricting have increased greatly in the last round of redistricting over what was found in earlier redistricting periods. This greater importance of redistricting stems from a combination of three factors.

The first factor is the nearly even partisan balance nationwide, demonstrated, for example, by the vote in the presidential election of 2000, and, since 1994, by the unusually close partisan balance (by historical standards) between Republicans and Democrats in the House. The second factor is the small number of competitive seats in the U.S. House of Representatives left after the redistricting that followed release of the 2000 Census data—accentuating a trend that was already readily visible following the last several reapportionment cycles. The third factor is the dramatic rise in ideological polarization between the parties.[19] This development greatly increases the perceived stakes in control of Congress. The growing partisan rancor and decline in bipartisan compromise observed in Congress over the past decade means that the difference between a party's winning 49 percent and 51 percent of House seats is now vast. Given the absence of a "moderating center" in either party, the party that is in the minority is truly the "out" party, having little or no influence on outcomes. A minority party in the House can be effectively shut out of the political process.[20]

Because the consequences of districting have risen, more attention than ever has been paid to the redistricting process both from a scholarly and a journalistic perspective. In this essay we have focused on the 1990s and 2000 rounds of redistricting in five deep southern states. The popular view of the partisan consequences of U.S. redistricting in the 1990s is that Republican gains in the House were concentrated in the Deep South, where the "affirmative gerrymandering" that was supposedly forced on states covered by Section 5 of the VRA by a Department of Justice insistent on "max-black" plans created black-majority districts in which Democrats had been packed, and in the process, "bleached" the remaining districts of enough loyal black Democrats that white Democratic candidates could no longer stand up against the onrushing Republican tide. Many activists and many journalists (and some academics) have blamed the Democrats' loss of control of the U.S. House of Representatives in 1994 on VRA-related districting. However, we believe that picture is too simplistic.

First, even without strict VRA enforcement, Democratic strength in the South was on the wane. Given the conservatism of most white Democratic voters, the "Solid (Democratic) South" made little sense. It was entirely an artifact of the Civil War. When the North finally won the Civil War, in 1964 and 1965, when the Second Reconstruction (most notably, the passage of the Civil Right Act of 1964 and the Voting Rights Act of 1965[21]) put an end to Jim Crow practices, as Lyndon Johnson had foreseen,[22] Democratic dominance in the South would be the price the Democrats would have to pay for this victory.[23]

Second, to call something racial gerrymandering only when districts are drawn to *aid* minority representation, or to imply that race was not a major factor in previous redistrictings in the South, is to neglect history. Once blacks were enfranchised in significant numbers, Democrat-controlled legislatures in the South had often deliberately used black voters as "sandbags" to shore up Democratic seats, with care taken that there were enough blacks in the districts to guarantee a Democratic win, but not so many that a black candidate would have a realistic chance to win the Democratic primary. Moreover, even when few blacks were registered, in anticipation of the possibility of future black suffrage gains, black concentrations were often divided among several districts or, at the local level, at-large election methods were put in place to assure the long-run control of white majorities.[24]

Third, Voting Rights Act enforcement in the 1990s by the U.S. Department of Justice did not really follow a max-black strategy,[25] although in a few states (e.g., Georgia), at least at the congressional level, it was hard to call it anything else.[26]

Fourth, Democratic losses in 1994 occurred throughout the country, not just in the Deep South. Still, we argue that the partisan effects of redistricting mistakes made by Democrats in the South alone mattered enough to have affected partisan control of the House later in the decade when the House was even more closely divided between the two major parties.[27]

Fifth, and finally, as we have attempted to show here, for the 1990s, at least for Georgia and North Carolina (and, we suspect, several other states as well), the mistakes made by the Democrats in drawing lines for the U.S. House of Representatives were not compelled by the need to draw additional minority seat. If only the Democrats had been brave enough to seize the nettle and concede a number of seats to the Republicans by making them very safe Republican seats, and then done a better job in distributing the remaining Democratic voting strength they would have been in much better shape. The 1990s congressional plans in these three states were, to a greater or lesser extent, dummymanders. Of the three Deep South states we have examined that were in the 1990s under Democratic control of the redistricting process, only in Mississippi did the Democrats in control of redistricting display any real smarts.[28]

When we turn to the 2000 round of redistricting in these five Southern states we see that Democratic losses of the 1990s largely persist. In South Carolina and Mississippi the Democrats are doing about as well as they could ever hope to do given the changes in political sentiments in those states. In Georgia and North Carolina there were limited Democratic gains, but nothing like a return to the Democratic glory days is ever going to be possible given the new political realities in the South. We would emphasize, however, that Democratic gains in these two states can be attributed in large part to redistricting, with Democrats having learned not to completely repeat the mistakes of their 1990s dummymanders. But, in the next (post–2010 Census) round of redistricting, if the Republicans were to control the redistricting in these states (or a Court that is influenced by Republican-drawn plans does the map drawing), then look to see even these limited Democratic gains reversed.[29]

NOTES

1. An earlier (single-authored) version of this paper was presented at the University of California, Irvine Center for the Study of Democracy Conference on Comparative Redistricting, December 6–8, 2001. The first-named author is indebted to helpful conversations over the years with Chandler Davidson, Lisa Handley, and James Loewen; and to Clover Behrend for bibliographic assistance. We also owe a special thanks to Clark Bensen for help with recent election data.

2. Remember the "Titanic"—the lifeboat scenes in the movie, that is.

3. Michael Barone and Grant Ujifusa, *The Almanac of American Politics* (Washington, D.C.: The National Journal, 1996), 7.

4. We have a table for each state with data from both 1992 and 2000 presidential elections. These are broken down by the congressional districts after the 1990 round and 2000 round respectively.

5. In contrast, the seven House incumbents (5 Republicans and 2 Democrats) endorsed an incumbent protection plan that made as few changes as possible.

6. Barone and Ujifusa, *The Almanac* (1994), 331.

7. Holmes, "Reapportionment Strategies in the 1990s: A Case of Georgia," in *Race and Redistricting in the 1990s*, ed. Bernard Grofman (New York: Agathon Press, 1998).

8. Barone and Ujifusa, *The Almanac* (1994).

9. Georgia gained a House seat in 1990.

10. Holmes, "Reapportionment Strategies."

11. In *Miller v. Johnson*, (515 U.S. 900, 1995) the Supreme Court repudiated the view that Section 5 required the drawing of three black-majority House districts in Georgia.

12. We thank A. Wuffle (personal communication, April 1, 2001) for suggesting this phrase.

13. Barone and Ujifusa, *The Almanac* (1996), 748.

14. Barone and Ujifusa, *The Almanac* (1996), 748.

15. In Texas, the Democrats also managed to keep a substantial majority of the state's congressional delegation.

16. This was a seat allocation that was not without controversy. The Supreme Court heard an appeal from the state of Utah (*Utah v. Evans*).that centered around the imputation of people in the census that gave North Carolina this seat. In 2001, the Court resolved the case in favor of North Carolina.

17. Barone and Ujifusa, *The Almanac* (1996), 1198.

18. Barone and Ujifusa, *The Almanac* (2000).

19. It is our view that the increased demographic and political homogeneity among districts—changes related to redistricting practices developed since *Baker v. Carr*—has contributed substantially both to reduced competitiveness at the district level and to increased polarization in the House. Even if greater political homogeneity is merely a byproduct of a bipartisan gerrymander designed to protect incumbents, it can contribute to partisan polarization. Incumbents representing politically homogeneous constituencies need not appeal to independents or voters of the other party to win reelection and so are free to adopt relatively extreme ideological positions.

20. If, on the basis of the districts as they have been configured, a party can reasonably expect to be in majority control of a legislature for the course of a decade, then almost certainly its leaders will be less inclined to engage in political compromise with members of the other party.

21. J. Morgan Kousser, "The Voting Rights Act and the Two Reconstructions," in *Controversies in Minority Voting,* ed. Bernard Grofman and Chandler Davidson (Washington D.C.: The Brookings Institution, 1992).

22. Chandler Davidson, "The Voting Rights Act: A Brief History," in *Controversies in Minority Voting,* ed. Bernard Grofman and Chandler Davidson (Washington, D.C.: The Brookings Institute, 1992).

23. Of course, the South could never become as solidly Republican in the future as it had been solidly Democratic in the past because of the presence throughout the South of substantial numbers of enfranchised black voters who are loyal Democrats.

24. See various essays in Chandler Davidson and Bernard Grofman, eds., *Quiet Revolution in the South* (Princeton, N.J.: Princeton University Press, 1994).

25. Mark Posner, "Post-1990 Redistrictings and the Preclearance Requirement of Section 5 of the Voting Rights Act," in *Race and Redistricting in the 1990s*, ed. Bernard Grofman (New York: Agathon Press, 1998). And also see Bernard Grofman, "Would Vince Lombardi Have Been Right if He Had Said, 'When It Comes to Redistricting, Race Isn't Everything, It's the Only Thing'?" *Cardoza Law Review* 14, no. 5 (1993): 1237–76.

26. It is also important to point out that the Department of Justice did not see itself as having an obligation to monitor the shape of the districts being created in response to Section 5 concerns. DOJ would not seek to require a jurisdiction to draw an additional majority-minority district unless it felt that such a district could reasonably be drawn, but if, for reasons of its own, the jurisdiction chose to draw the district in a contorted or amoeba-like fashion, that was regarded as none of DOJ's business as long as the district created a realistic opportunity to elect minority candidates of choice. In particular, DOJ cannot be blamed for the peculiar configuration of the North Carolina 12th Congressional district; much of the irregularities were due to concerns to protect the seat of a white Democratic incumbent in a neighboring district. See Grofman, "Vince Lombardi," 1993.

27. Bernard Grofman and Lisa Handley, "Estimating the Impact of Voting-Rights-Act-Related Districting on Democratic Strength in the U.S. House of Representatives," in *Race and Redistricting in the 1990s*, ed. Bernard Grofman (New York: Agathon Press, 1998), 51–67.

28. In Alabama and in South Carolina in the 1990s there was a court-drawn plan. However, in both, the plan tracked Republican proposals.

29. Since the Texas Republicans succeeded in their mid-cycle endeavors to redraw the state's congressional lines, expect to see substantial Republican gains in that state. Redistricting does matter, albeit, as we said in the opening of this chapter; it "cannot turn water into wine, or Republicans into Democrats."

9

The Republicans Take Control: The 2001 Redistricting in Michigan

John R. Chamberlin

Between 1925 and 2002, no member of Congress or state legislator from Michigan was elected from a district whose boundaries were determined by an institution other than a court. That era ended with the elections of 2002 when, in districts drawn by Republicans, Republican candidates won approximately 50 percent of the two-party vote in congressional, state house, and state senate races, but won 60 percent of the 15 congressional seats, 57 percent of the 110 state house seats, and 58 percent of the 38 state senate seats.[1,2] Modern partisan gerrymandering had finally arrived in Michigan, warts and all.

THE HISTORY OF REDISTRICTING IN MICHIGAN

From the mid-1920s through 1962, legislative districts in Michigan were not redrawn at all, and the state's urban citizens suffered the fate of urban citizens around the country—increasing underrepresentation in Congress and their state legislature. In 1962, while Michigan was holding a constitutional convention, the U.S. Supreme Court handed down its decision in *Baker v. Carr*. Since the decision only established the justiciability of redistricting, without specifying criteria by which districting plans would be judged, the constitutional convention continued its deliberations and produced an article in a new constitution that assigned responsibility for state legislative redistricting to an eight-person, bipartisan commission, which was instructed to take into account both population and land area in drawing legislative districts. Congressional redistricting was left in the hands of the state legislature.

The commission deadlocked in its first effort at drawing new state legislative districts and the matter wound up in court. Soon after this, the U.S. Supreme Court handed down its decision in *Reynolds v. Sims*, and the portions of the new Michigan Constitution that conflicted with the principle of one person, one vote were history.

The commission lived on, but it never succeeded in producing a districting plan. It deadlocked 4 to 4 along party lines at every opportunity between 1963 and 1981, with the result that the Michigan Supreme Court determined the boundaries of state legislative districts following each census. In 1982, the Michigan Supreme Court invalidated the entire article of the constitution devoted to redistricting, which left responsibility for state legislative redistricting with the state legislature.[3] In its decision, the court laid the foundations for subsequent redistricting when it noted: "Apart from population and land area, we see in the constitutional history of this state dominant commitments to contiguous, single-member districts drawn along the boundary lines of local units of government which, within those limitations, are as compact as possible."[4]

The legislative process proved no more adept at producing a districting plan than the commission. Due to divided party control of the Michigan state government, the courts ended up drawing the congressional district lines in the 1970s, 1980s, and 1990s. In the 1990s, the state legislature's first try at redistricting the state legislature met the same fate; divided party control produced deadlock and courts had to settle the matter.

Until the most recent round of redistricting, observers did not really expect the legislature and the governor to produce a redistricting plan. While some attention was paid to going through the motions within the legislature, the real efforts were devoted to signing up litigators, making sure the redistricting software was running smoothly, and court shopping for judges who might favor the party that put them in office.

That changed following the 2000 census. Republicans controlled both houses of the legislature and the governorship and they proceeded to do a very skillful job of partisan gerrymandering. The inevitable legal challenges by Democrats were unsuccessful. In a state with an even balance of Republicans and Democrats in recent elections, Republicans succeeded in switching the Michigan congressional delegation from 9 to 7 in favor of the Democrats to 9 to 6 in favor of the Republicans. In addition, they solidified their hold on the state legislature, electing substantial majorities in both houses.

SETTING THE STAGE FOR THE 2001 REDISTRICTING

As Michigan headed into the redistricting process in 2001, four factors loomed large in shaping the outcome: (1) Republican control of the process,

(2) the loss of a seat in the U.S. House, (3) term limits for state legislators, and (4) legislation passed by the state legislature setting standards that redistricting plans for congressional and state legislative districts must meet.

Republican Control

In November 1998, John Engler was reelected governor and twenty-three Republicans were elected to the thirty-eight-member state senate, locking in Republican control of two of the three elements of the redistricting process in 2001.[5] In that year, voters also sent fifty-six Republicans to the 110-member state house, making it likely that one party would control the redistricting process for the first time in seventy-five years. In 2000, the Republicans added to their margin, controlling the house by a fifty-eight to fifty-two margin, and the party prepared to use its power to reshape Michigan's electoral districts.

Reapportionment 2001: Michigan Loses Another Congressional Seat

Michigan's population grew by 7 percent in the 1990s, but that was not enough to stem the continuing erosion of the size of its congressional delegation. Michigan lost one seat following the 1970 census, two more in the 1980s, one in the 1990s, and another one this time around, bringing its delegation to 15 members. This meant that the size of a congressional district went from 580,956 in 1991 to 662,562 in 2001. Once again, Detroit's population declined substantially, meaning that significant shifts in the congressional districts of southeast Michigan became necessary. With none of the incumbents indicating an intention to retire, some political bloodshed was in store for the state regardless of who ended up drawing new congressional district lines, but with Republicans in control, the Democrats were clearly in trouble.

Term Limits

In 1992, Michigan voters approved a constitutional amendment that limits state representatives to three two-year terms and state senators to two four-year terms.[6] Term limits started to have massive effects on the legislature with the 2000 election. That year, 64 of the 110 members of the house were forced out by term limits. In 2002 it was the senate's turn to feel the effect of the constitutional amendment, with only 9 of 38 senators being eligible to run for reelection. Michigan does not have staggered terms in its senate, so the entire body was up for election in 2002. Among other things, this meant that some of the 36 members of the house facing term limits in 2004 gave serious consideration to running for one of the open senate seats in 2002.

Term limits therefore shaped the politics of redistricting in significant ways. The house had very few experienced legislators. The relatively new members lacked solid incumbency histories that could be relied upon in fine-tuning house districts, which made a partisan gerrymander trickier than in pre–term limit days. And most of the senate districts would be open seats because of term limits. In addition, sitting legislators had no experience with the kind of high-stakes political bargaining that characterizes legislative redistricting. Even long-time party leaders had no real history of focusing on a legislative resolution of redistricting, since in prior decades everyone knew that the courts would ultimately decide the matter. Because of the impact of term limits on the senate, a fair number of house members cared more about the senate map than they did the house map. The fact that almost all of the senate's experienced members were being ousted by term limits meant they cared much less than would usually be the case about the details of the senate map. This created a good bit more flexibility for those drawing the senate lines than would have been the case prior to term limits. The usual tension between the controlling party's interest in maximizing its gains and the party's incumbents' interests in their own districts was lessened considerably.

The Apol Standards

Another significant factor in the run up to the 2001 redistricting was the adoption by the Republican state legislature of ground rules to govern the redistricting process and criteria to be met by redistricting plans. In 1996, they passed a bill that set standards for a districting plan for the state legislature.[7] In 1999, they amended this law to assign original and exclusive jurisdiction for any redistricting litigation to the Michigan Supreme Court.[8] In 1999 the legislature also passed two quite similar bills covering congressional redistricting.[9]

One bill in each pair assigned original and exclusive jurisdiction for any redistricting litigation to the Michigan Supreme Court. It also specified a process to be used by the court if the legislature and governor failed to produce a districting plan. The Michigan Supreme Court had at the time a majority of justices who had been nominated by the Republican Party.[10] Thus assignment of original jurisdiction to the Michigan Supreme Court ensured that Republicans would get a sympathetic initial hearing should litigation occur.

The second bill in each pair wrote into law what had become known as the "Apol Standards," named after Bernie Apol, a retired elections official in Michigan who served as a special master for the Michigan Supreme Court in the 1980s and 1990s rounds of redistricting. Apol recommended that the court use these criteria to choose among alternative districting plans, and he helped to produce the plans that the court finally implemented. In order of importance, the Apol standards address:

- Population equality. In the 1980s criterion for state legislative redistricting, this criterion reflected the Mahan decision, requiring that the maximum population deviation among state legislative districts be less than 16 percent. In the 1990s, the standard was stricter—population deviations could be no more than plus or minus 5 percent from the ideal district size—reflecting the belief that such districts would escape judicial scrutiny. The bill addressing congressional districts called for equal population.
- Observance of the Voting Rights Act.
- Observance of local jurisdictional boundaries. A districting plan should cut as few county boundaries "as is practicably possible." Among plans that cut an equal number of county boundaries, the one that cuts the fewest city and township boundaries is to be preferred.
- Contiguity.
- Compactness. This provision is buried rather deep in the provisions, and is subject to some stringent contingencies. Thus, while compactness is well defined, its bite is next to nonexistent

Democrats have never liked the Apol standards, even though a number of observers of redistricting in the 1980s and 1990s had thought that Democrats might have been given the upper hand by the Supreme Court's plans that used them. While some of the Democrats' doubts about the standards definitely stemmed from the fact that Apol was a Republican, their principal concern has always been that the prominence given to county boundaries meant that residents of Wayne County, and in particular the largely Democrat, African American residents of Detroit, would be packed into districts that would dilute their voting power.

Republicans, on the other hand, have usually portrayed this criterion as politically neutral. The outcome of the 2001 redistricting, which mostly honored the criterion, but was nevertheless a partisan gerrymander, testifies to the difficulty of finding a criterion that is both neutral and has bite when it comes to redistricting. However one views the neutrality of this criterion, there is little doubt that the respect it generates for county, city, and township boundaries has played a very significant role in redistricting in Michigan in the last three decades. Compared to districts in many other states with similar levels of partisan competition, districts in Michigan have been relatively undistorted by ham-handed attempts to fine-tune election outcomes. No squashed bugs, no long meandering districts, few obviously funny shapes that could only be explained by intricate attempts at gerrymandering. Michigan's districts in 2001 look less gerrymandered than districts in many other states. The Apol local boundary criterion certainly constrains partisan gerrymandering, but as the 2002 election outcomes in Michigan demonstrate, it proved a sufficiently loose constraint that Republicans could still succeed in their efforts to tilt the electoral playing field to their advantage.

It seems natural to ask why Republicans, almost certain to control redistricting in 2001, would tie their own hands by imposing these redistricting standards in the late 1990s. Possible motivations include:

- The Apol standards provide good political cover (the Apol standards define fairness, they reflect Michigan's redistricting history, they make gerrymandering appear impossible, etc.) while not acting as a significant constraint on partisan gerrymandering. The electoral outcomes are consistent with this motivation.
- The Republicans really believed that the Apol standards define "fairness" in districting. This is certainly what one finds in floor speeches about the standards, but the political stakes were such that it seems unlikely that this was a serious factor in the decision to adopt the standards.
- Republicans believed that the courts would impose the Apol standards in reviewing any plan passed by the legislature, so the adoption of the standards ensured that the legislature's plan would withstand judicial scrutiny. Given the composition of the Michigan Supreme Court, this seems overly cautious behavior.
- The Apol standards are reasonably fair but can be regarded as a loose constraint, since if need be the legislature can argue that an act of a prior legislature cannot bind the current legislature. This is in fact what happened. When the Democrats challenged the Republican plan and presented an alternative districting plan with fewer breaks in county and township lines (by their count), the court found in favor of Republicans who argued that the bill enacting the Apol standards did not bind the 2001 legislature.

The Apol standards have now played an important role in three decades of redistricting in Michigan. Whether, in light of the court decision, anyone will attempt to resurrect them for the 2011 round of redistricting remains to be seen of course. The political cover they provide for gerrymanderers is important, however, and the fact that the Republicans in 2001 came very close to meeting them meant that Michigan's district maps look less gerrymandered than maps in many other states. The 2002 election results, however, are testimony to the fact that a set of districts can look fairly regular and fair without necessarily being so.

THE REDISTRICTING PROCESS IN 2001

The processes used to produce congressional and state legislative maps in 2001 were similar and observers' judgments of them are very highly correlated with partisan affiliation. If one reads floor speeches by Republicans, one would think that once the Apol standards are in place redistricting is little more than a mechanical task, with little room for partisan discretion and that the majority party provided ample opportunities for anyone interested in redistricting to register their views and have them considered by majority legislators whose sole goal was fairness. If one reads speeches by Democrats, on the other hand, one would think that the process that led to the new maps was one of worst offenses to democratic government we've witnessed in our state, with no public hearings, little respect for the Voting Rights Act, sneaky partisan floor maneuvers, and disregard for the Apol standards that the Republicans themselves had put in place.

On the available facts, what can one say about the process? First, it was mostly a secret process, open to Republican Party officials and legislative leaders and their counselors, and to Republican members. The overall shape of the eventual congressional plan contained few surprises, having been previewed in a widely publicized plan floated in January 2001 by EPIC/MRA, a polling firm, and the Michigan Chamber of Commerce. The details of the maps for the state legislature were much more closely held, and this left Democrats in suspense until the very last moment.

Few real opportunities for public discourse were available. Early discussions of a set of forums around the state came to naught. Reasonably short deadlines were announced for the submission of districting plans. Maps to accompany the state legislative plans that were ultimately passed were not made available to Democrats or to members of the public prior to the vote. Shell bills were passed out of committee, with details to be added at the last minute on the floor. In general, Democrats, the media, and the public were kept in the dark as much and as long as possible, and new plans were passed with little legislative debate on the merits of the particular plans (as opposed to high-minded rhetoric from Republicans and outraged rhetoric from Democrats).

This was not a process that had much to do with self-governance by citizens in a democratic society. The process and the outcome demonstrate that redistricting in Michigan in 2001 was an exercise in which one party chose the constituencies it preferred for its members in ways that limit the ability of the citizens of Michigan to play meaningful roles in determining the makeup of their congressional delegation or their state legislature. On the other hand, it didn't offend democratic principles more than partisan redistricting in other states. Nor did Republicans engage in practices that Democrats would have foresworn had they controlled the process. Indeed, as Democratic Senator

Vernon Smith conceded from the senate floor in the debate about enacting the Apol standards, "In our estimation the Republican majority is doing what we probably would do if we were in control."[11] Redistricting is hardball politics. It enables a majority party to tilt the playing field in its favor in a way that can extend for a decade or more and it offers irresistible opportunities to target minority party politicians whom the majority party would love to see return to private life.

THE CONGRESSIONAL REDISTRICTING PLAN

Michigan's population grew in the 1990s but not as fast as the nation as a whole, so it lost a congressional seat in the 1991 reapportionment, reducing its delegation to 15. Detroit continued to lose population, while suburban areas grew. After the 2000 elections, Democrats outnumbered Republicans 9 to 7 in the congressional delegation, with freshman Republican Mike Rogers having won election by only 111 votes, the closest congressional election in the nation. In control of redistricting, Republicans set ambitious goals, including shoring up Mike Rogers' seat, electing two additional Republicans, and creating trouble for Democrats. In the end, they succeeded on all dimensions.

Protecting Mike Rogers

The Eighth District added Republican Clinton County and Republican northern Oakland County and lost a portion of Democratic Washtenaw County. Rogers won easily in 2002 with 69 percent of the two-party vote.

Creating Two New Republican Seats

A new Tenth District in the "thumb" area of Michigan was created for Candace Miller, the term-limited secretary of state. She had carried every county in the state when she was reelected in 1998 and had been touted by many as a Republican candidate for governor to replace the term-limited John Engler (with some observers hoping for a "dream team" race between Miller and Granholm, guaranteeing Michigan's first female governor). But party leaders favored Lt. Gov. Richard Posthumus and crafted a congressional seat for Miller instead. The new Tenth District included much of David Bonior's old district, but not his hometown of Mt. Clemens. Miller, running against a well-known county prosecutor, Carl Marlinga, won with 64 percent of the two-party vote.

The 2001 congressional map also included a new Eleventh District in western Oakland County and northern Wayne County for Thaddeus McCotter, a

State Senator and, not coincidently, vice chair of the Senate Reapportionment Committee. Andrew (Rocky) Raczkowski, a term-limited state representative from the same area, made clear his aspirations to run for Congress, but the party created a district more favorable to McCotter. When the districting plan for the senate also did not contain a favorable district for Raczkowski, the former majority leader found himself out in the cold. In the end, he agreed to take a bullet for the party by opposing Carl Levin for the U.S. Senate. Many believe that the favorable district for McCotter was, at least partially, a reward for his leadership in expelling from the senate a Republican member whose behavior on and off the legislative floor over a number of years had antagonized and embarrassed Republican Party members. In November, McCotter defeated Democratic Senator Kevin Kelley with 59 percent of the two-party vote. This was the closest Republican victory and it seems likely that Democrats will try to contest it in 2004, but by then McCotter will benefit from some incumbency advantage.

Republican Incumbents

Of the six incumbent Republicans, four (Hoekstra (Second), Ehlers (Third), Upton (Sixth), and Smith (Seventh)) saw only minor changes in their districts. All won reelection rather easily. The new districting plan swapped some counties between Stupak's First District and Camp's Fourth District, with no significant effect on either representative. The remaining Republican incumbent, Joe Knollenberg of Oakland County, was significantly affected by the new congressional map. The new Eleventh District was created out of much of Knollenberg's old district, and while he retained the heart of his district, he had to appeal to a significant number of new constituents in the eastern part of Oakland County. In the end, he won relatively easily, with virtually the same percentage (59 percent) of the two-party vote he garnered in 2000.

Wreaking Havoc on Democrats

At the heart of the Republican's gerrymander was the pairing up of six Democratic incumbents. By the time the smoke cleared in November 2002, three of them were out of office: Jim Barcia (5 terms), David Bonior (12 terms), and Lynn Rivers (4 terms).

Barcia's old Fifth District was sliced into four parts—with sections ending up in the new First, Fourth, Fifth, and Tenth Districts. After initial talk that he might challenge Kildee in the new Fifth District, Barcia opted to run for a state senate seat (to which he was elected). Kildee won easy reelection when the Republicans didn't even field a candidate.

For a number of elections Republicans had been claiming that Bonior was too liberal for his district and that surely this would be the year to oust him in favor of a Republican with views more closely matching those of the district's citizens. But each time they failed by considerable margins. This time around, redistricting allowed them to do what they hadn't been able to do via the ballot box. They altered Bonior's Tenth District in ways that left almost all observers believing that Bonior could not win reelection in that district. They moved Bonior's base in Mt. Clemens into the Twelfth District and added three Republican counties in the thumb to the Tenth to create the district for Candace Miller. Faced with running in a primary against Sander Levin, in a district that included much of Levin's old district, Bonior opted out and entered the race for governor. He finished a distant third in the primaries.

Levin thus survived another round of redistricting. Because his district in the northern suburbs of Detroit has a high population density and each decade brings population shifts from Detroit to the suburbs, Levin's district is a perennial candidate to be carved up in the re-creation of the suburban districts. But as he did in the 1990s, he ended up with enough of his old district intact that no Democrat could challenge him, and he cruised to an easy victory in the Twelfth District.

Lynn Rivers did not follow the lead of Barcia and Bonior in abandoning a primary challenge. Her Thirteenth District was split, some of it going into the new Eleventh District and some into John Dingell's district as it moved westward into Wayne and Washtenaw counties. Rivers challenged Dingell in the primary, attracting a lot of nationwide attention for challenging the dean of the house and staying close in the polls during the primary season. But in the end Dingell won by 20 percentage points. He then easily outdistanced an inexperienced Republican challenger in November, winning his 23rd term with 74 percent of the two-party vote.

The Upper Peninsula

Bart Stupak, Democrat from Michigan's Upper Peninsula, whose First District is sufficiently remote that pairing him with another Democrat wasn't possible, nevertheless had to cope with some serious rearrangements to his district. The Traverse City area in northwestern Michigan was removed from his district and replaced by counties further south along the eastern side of the state, in the upper part of Barcia's old district. The First District now encompasses almost half the land area of Michigan (up from about 44 percent in the old district), and the distance from its southernmost point to its westernmost point at the Wisconsin border of the Upper Peninsula is about 550 miles. The new district means more miles on Stupak's car as he covers his district, but he won easy reelection with 72 percent of the two-party vote. In general, he did better in the new counties in his district than he had two years previously in the counties that were removed in the new congressional plan.

The Detroit Districts

The two African American Democrats from Detroit easily won reelection, but in districts that looked considerably different from their districts in the 1990s. The 1990s districts had an east-west orientation, with Conyers representing a horizontal northern slice of the city and Kilpatrick a district to the south. In the new congressional map, the districts run north-south, with Conyers getting the western slice and Kilpatrick the eastern one. The new districts compensated for Detroit's population loss in the 1990s by adding territory in Wayne County that had previously been represented by John Dingell. The results demonstrated that regardless of how one divides the city of Detroit, it's Democratic territory.

A Small Glitch and a Legal Challenge

Soon after the state legislature passed the congressional plan, it was discovered that two census tracts had been omitted from the lists of tracts establishing the new districts and that as a result 4,578 people in southeastern Michigan needed to be added. The Democrats claimed that this required that redistricting be reopened in the legislature; Republicans claimed it was a technical matter that could be cleaned up before the plan went to the governor for his signature. In the end, the governor's signature was delayed by two months as the Republican legislature made sure it made the changes in ways that didn't leave them open to a legal challenge.

Democrats filed suit to block the congressional plan on other grounds, claiming that the Republican plan did not minimize the number of breaks in county and municipal boundaries as required by the 1996/9 statute. Democrats produced a plan that they claimed had fewer breaks. There was considerable debate about how to count such breaks, of the kind that only litigators find very enlightening. In the end the Michigan Supreme Court accepted a Republican argument that regardless of the number of breaks, the 2001 legislature could not be bound by rules promulgated by the legislature in 1999, and that the legislature was free to ignore that standard if it wished.[12] Whatever high ground the adoption of the Apol standards might have represented earlier, when push came to shove the standards were bent a bit to serve the partisan goals of the controlling party.

In the Final Analysis

The outcomes of the November 2002 elections confirmed the quality of the Republican gerrymander. The delegation switched from 9 to 7 Democrat to 9 to 6 Republican. All 13 incumbents who were on the ballot in November were reelected. Republicans gained 60 percent the seats with slightly less than 50 percent of the two-party vote. The average percentage of the two-party vote for Republican winners was 66.1 percent, for Democrats 82.7 percent.[13] Mike Rogers got a safe new district, two new Republicans won, and the other incumbents averted serious challenges. Democrats were effectively packed into 6 districts—with winning percentages ranging from 70 percent (Levin) to 100 percent (Kildee and Kilpatrick) of the two-party vote. Republican votes were spread effectively across districts, with no Republican winning by less than 59 percent or more than 72 percent of the two-party vote.

In contrast, consider the results of the 2000 congressional races. Democrats won 56 percent of the seats with a bit less than 55 percent of the two-party vote. Four Democrats were elected with less than 70 percent of the two-party vote (compared to one in 2002). The average successful Democrat won with 72.4 percent of the vote, the average Republican with 63.4 percent. All in all, the 2002 results confirm a very accomplished Republican gerrymander.

Looking ahead, this gerrymander seems likely to hold. Nick Smith has announced his intention to retire, and it is likely that there will be spirited competition for his Seventh District seat, but Republicans have the edge in the district. The Ninth District seems safe for Joe Knollenberg in the short run, but he turned 70 last year and should he decide to retire, the district would probably generate a competitive race. The Democrats who remain hold even safer seats than before, but that can be no real consolation to a party that finds itself the victim of a partisan gerrymander. Thus, despite the fact that Michiganders in the aggregate have in the last decade shown themselves a bit more inclined to vote Democratic than Republican in congressional races, the chances seem small that the Democrats will regain their majority in the congressional delegation before the 2011 round of redistricting.

THE STATE HOUSE AND SENATE REDISTRICTING PLANS

Republicans went into the 2002 elections holding a 58-42 edge in the house and a 23–15 edge in the senate. In the elections held in the new districts, they boosted their margin by five in the house (the most Republican members in 50 years) and lost one in the senate. The size of these majorities suggests that Democrats will have difficulty wresting control of either body in the near future.

Population shifts within the state necessitated some significant alterations in state legislative districts. In the senate, 13 districts exceeded the +5 percent limit and 12 fell below the −5 percent limit. The smallest district, in Detroit, fell 55,000 voters short of the average size; the largest, in suburban Oakland County, had 45,000 more voters that the target size.

Despite the Republicans willingness to abandon the Apol standards when it was necessary to fend off a challenge in court, they generally honored the boundary cutting constraint in the state legislative plan. Inspection of the plans shows that with the exception of urban areas, where boundary breaks were inevitable, districts are composed of whole counties. The Republican plans were also carefully designed to avoid violating the Voting Rights Act. In most cases, the home bases of incumbents were preserved and the partisan composition of their districts was not substantially altered. As a result, all nine incumbent senators who ran won reelection (3 Democrats, 6 Republicans), as did 57 of the 58 house incumbents who stood for reelection (one Democrat lost).

Some party members complained that within urban areas the legislative plans failed to maximize Republican gains, but party leaders seem to have decided that it was more important to lock in a Republican majority than to gamble on trying to win as many seats as might have been possible. The principal reason to stretch for more Republican victories would have been to achieve a veto-proof legislature (26 senators and 74 representatives). The prospects of pulling this off in the house were exceedingly slim, and emphasizing that goal at the expense of risking downside losses would have betrayed a lack of confidence in the party's ability to hold onto the governorship.

The attention paid to county boundaries did produce a great many changes in districts even if it didn't impact incumbents. Most districts retained an incumbent's core constituency, but it was common for one or two counties to be swapped in or out as redistricters sought to honor both county boundaries and the limit on population deviations across districts. The Apol standards for the state legislature permitted population deviations of ±5 percent and the Republicans ended up using this flexibility in its entirety. In the house the districts ranged in size from −4.97 percent to +4.95 percent of the average size. In the senate, the range was from −4.94 percent to +4.97 percent. Much of this population deviation across districts stems from the constraint on cutting county boundaries rather than partisan motivations. There does not appear to have been a systematic attempt, for instance, to make Democratic districts larger than Republican districts.

When the House Committee met to consider a redistricting bill for the state legislature, the Republicans introduced a shell bill that provided no details about the districts. Democrats offered their bill as a substitute, and to their surprise the Republicans voted to send it to the floor, delaying by several additional days the opportunity for Democrats to see what was in store for them.[14] Both the Democratic Party and the Democratic caucus prepared plans. It is interesting to note that the party claimed that its house plan contained 63 districts with Democratic majorities and the caucus claimed that its plan was balanced, with each party having a likely majority in 55 districts. Although neither ever got the chance to be tested at the polls, if the claims were not wholly implausible, they suggest just how much maneuvering room the line drawers had within the Apol standards to produce partisan plans.

Senate Outcomes

The Republicans lost a seat relative to 2000, but they still ended up with 58 percent of the seats on just over 50 percent of the vote. Races for the senate were considerably closer than the congressional races, with 10 Republicans and 4 Democrats winning with less than 60 percent of the vote. The average winning percentage for Republicans was 60 percent, for Democrats 68 percent, but this difference is greatly affected by the lopsided Detroit districts. The distribution of winning percentages for the two parties look like what you would expect from a gerrymander—more winnable but not safe districts for Republicans and lots of packed districts for Democrats. In the end, 21 state house representatives won seats in the senate in November 2002. The fact that most of the candidates had either incumbency or name recognition working for them should have made senate redistricting easier than house redistricting. Nevertheless, the Republicans lost a senate seat.

House Outcomes

The Republicans picked up five seats in November 2002, winning 57 percent of the seats with just under 50 percent of the total vote. Because almost half of the house races were open seats, it was not as easy to tailor districts to take advantage of name recognition. Nevertheless, the Republicans ended up doing extremely well in the election. The average winning percentages were 63 percent for Republicans and 73 percent for Democrats. A third of Republicans won with less than 60 percent of the vote. For Democrats, that percentage was about 20 percent. As in the senate, the winning percentages have the earmarks of a partisan gerrymander—lots of packed Democratic districts (beyond the inevitable overwhelmingly Democratic districts in Detroit) and more Republicans than Democrats with winnable but not entirely safe districts. In comparison with the 21 house members who won election to the senate, three term-limited senators won house seats.

In the Final Analysis

The Republicans' short-run hold on the state legislature seems secure. Partisan gerrymanders always risk cutting margins too close to the line, and medium-term voter shifts could put one of the houses of the legislature at risk of Democratic control, but it seems likely that the packing of Democrats in the new districts will keep Republicans in control. The governorship, which Democrats retook after 12 years, would seem to be the most likely way to avoid being at the mercy of Republican line drawers a decade from now.

CONCLUSION

In 2001, Michigan Republicans delivered what was arguably the most accomplished Republican gerrymander in the nation. As often happens when one party controls redistricting, opportunities for genuine participation by the public or members of the other party were nil, with ordinary citizens being the raw materials for redistricting rather than its authors. Term limits and the Apol standards made the task of gerrymandering more difficult for Republicans, but in the end they did not serve as barriers to a significant shift in the congressional delegation and to solid majorities in the state legislature. The emphasis in the Apol standards on honoring county, city, and township boundaries continued Michigan's tradition of districting maps that don't look particularly gerrymandered. The maps are also ample testimony to the fact that looks can be deceiving, that districts that look fairly regular and that honor local jurisdictional boundaries can nevertheless tilt the electoral playing field in very significant ways.

NOTES

1. The actual percentages of the statewide (two-party) vote totals were 49.4 percent in congressional races, 50.4 percent in senate races and 50.0 percent in house races. Republican candidates were not on the ballot in two congressional districts; had they offered even a token opponent, their statewide vote percentage would no doubt have been a few points higher.

2. This even partisan balance in Michigan was reflected in several key statewide races. Democrat Jennifer Granholm edged Republican Lt. Gov. Richard Posthumus by 125,000 votes (out of 3 million) to become Michigan's first female governor, while Republican Mike Cox defeated Democrat Gary Peters by 5200 votes to become the first Republican in several generations to hold the attorney general post. Two other statewide races were not close, but each party won one. Veteran Democrat Carl Levin easily won reelection to the U.S. Senate by seven hundred thousand votes and Republican candidate for Secretary of State Terri Lynn Land, aided by personal and family campaign expenditures of several million dollars, won by 370,000 votes.

3. *In re Apportionment of State Legislature*, 413 Mich. 96.

4. 413 Mich. 140.

5. Michigan elects all 38 senators every four years, so the 1998 election determined the party composition of the senate for the 2001 redistricting.

6. The amendment also limited members of Congress to three terms, but that provision was ruled unconstitutional.

7. Michigan Public Act 463 of 1996

8. Michigan Public Act 223 of 1999 (Senate Bill 814)

9. Michigan Public Act 221 of 1999 (Senate Bills 810 and 811)

10. Michigan has the unusual practice of nominating judicial candidates at party conventions and then having them run without party affiliations.

11. *Journal of the Michigan Senate*, October 28, 1999

12. *LeRoux v. Secretary of State*, 465 Mich. 594, 640 N.W.2d 849

13. The 82.7 percent includes two districts with no Republican challenger. If a Republican with a pulse had run in each district, they would probably have garnered at least 10 percent of the vote, which would have reduced the average Democratic victory percentage by several points (and increased the Republican percentage of the statewide two-party vote).

14. Republicans had evidently had the opportunity the night before to inspect the party's plan.

10

All Quiet on the Western Front: Redistricting and Party Competition in California House Elections

Gary C. Jacobson

California's population grew so rapidly during the last half of the twentieth century that the state gained an average of about five House seats after each of the five censuses spanning the period (1950 to 1990; see figure 10.1). Each opportunity to carve out new districts and reconfigure old ones inspired elaborate partisan maneuvering and often fierce partisan conflict. Thus when the 53 House districts allotted to California by the 2000 census were to be drawn, a full-blown Democratic gerrymander seemed the likeliest outcome. With large Democratic majorities in the California Assembly and senate and Democrat Gray Davis in the state house, the only constraint on partisan artistry was the prospect of court intervention if the Democrats overreached. But, according to the consensus of observers in politics and in the press, rather than maximizing Democratic seats, the legislature maximized incumbent protection, effectively reducing the number of competitive House districts to zero for 2002 and, conceivably, for the rest of the decade. The new configuration of districts also promises to reinforce the growing partisan and ideological polarization of the California delegation and therefore of the Congress as a whole. In this chapter, I examine why and how the legislature produced such an unusual configuration of U.S. House districts and consider what its remarkable handiwork portends for national politics in the coming decade.

BACKGROUND: REDISTRICTING WARS, 1950S TO 1990S

It is impossible to understand just how unusual California redistricting politics was after the 2000 census without reviewing the contentious post–World

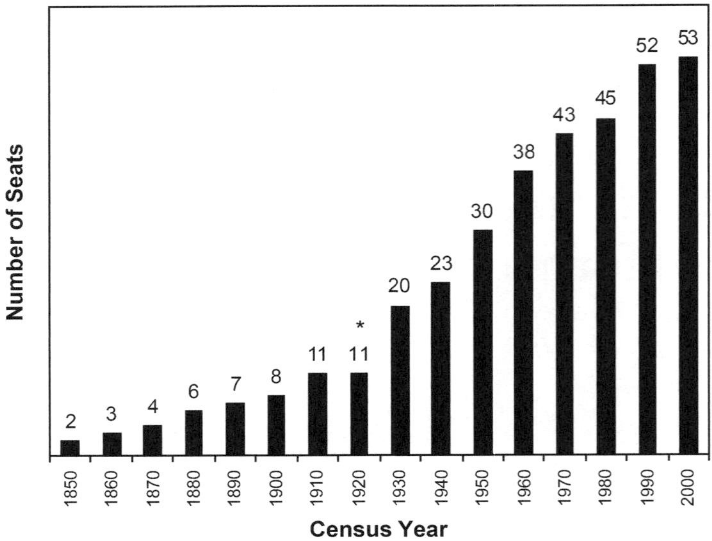

*Districts were not reapportioned after the 1920 census

Figure 10.1. The California House Delegation Since Statehood

War II history of the process. By the 1940s, California's progressive tradition of "nonpartisanship" had become a threadbare cover for continued Republican dominance of a state where Democrats held a twenty-point advantage in party registration. In 1951, the unified Republican government produced a gerrymander that gave Republicans 19 of 30 House seats (63.3 percent) with a district average of 54.0 percent of the major-party vote in 1952, and again 19 of 30 seats when their average vote dropped to 48.5 percent in 1954 (see Table 10.1). Districts were also drawn to maintain Republican control of the state legislature.

The Republicans had, however, given themselves too many marginal districts, which proved costly in the Democratic landslide of 1958. Democrats took a majority of the House delegation, 16 to 14, and, more importantly, they took control of the state government. Thus in 1961 Democrats were able to retaliate in kind, drawing lines that gave their House delegation seven of California's eight new seats.[1] After the 1962 election, the Democrats held a 25 to 13 majority (65.8 percent) while winning only 51.9 percent of the vote. Although Democrats lost seats in 1964 and 1966, the gerrymander limited the damage; in 1966, they won 21 of 38 seats (55.3 percent) with only 46.8 percent of the vote (table 10.1).

In 1967, the California Supreme Court compelled a fresh redistricting to meet the equal population standard set by *Wesberry v. Sanders*.[2] The new lines reflected a bipartisan compromise under divided government (Repub-

Table 10.1. Votes and Seats in California House Elections, 1952 to 2002

Control of Redistricting		*% Democratic Votes*	*% Democratic Seats*	*Difference*
Republicans	1952*	46.0	36.7	−9.3
	1954	51.5	36.7	−14.8
	1956	52.4	43.3	−9.1
	1958	60.0	53.3	−6.7
	1960	53.9	53.3	−0.6
Average, 1952–1960		*52.8*	*44.7*	*−8.1*
Democrats	1962*	51.9	65.8	13.9
	1964	52.9	60.5	7.6
	1966	46.8	55.3	8.5
Average, 1962–1966		*50.5*	*60.5*	*10.0*
Split Party Control	1968*	44.9	55.3	10.4
	1970	50.2	52.6	2.4
Average, 1968–1970		*47.6*	*53.8*	*6.4*
	1972*	52.7	53.5	0.8
Court "Special Masters"	1974*	58.4	65.1	6.7
	1976	55.6	65.1	9.5
	1978	51.8	60.5	8.7
	1980	46.7	51.2	4.5
Average, 1974–1980		*53.1*	*60.5*	*7.4*
Democrats	1982*	50.9	62.2	11.3
	1984*	50.5	60.0	9.5
	1986	51.2	60.0	8.8
	1988	53.7	60.0	6.3
	1990	51.5	57.8	6.3
Average, 1984–1990		*51.7*	*59.4*	*7.7*
Court "Special Masters"	1992*	55.3	57.7	2.4
	1994	49.3	51.9	2.6
	1996	52.5	55.8	3.3
	1998	53.5	53.8	0.3
	2000	54.9	61.5	6.6
Average, 1992–2000		*53.1*	*56.1*	*3.0*
Democrats	2002*	53.7	62.3	8.6

*election following reapportionment

lican Governor Ronald Reagan and a tenuously Democratic legislature) and were aimed at protecting incumbents.[3] The Republican surge that had elected Reagan governor in 1966 continued, and Republicans took control of the assembly in 1968 and the senate in 1969. Expecting to keep control of the legislature in 1970, Republican leaders were clear about their intentions. In a secret memo later acquired and gleefully exposed by the Democrats, Republican Jerry Lewis, then a member of the Assembly Elections and

Constitutional Amendments Committee, wrote, "Our number one criteria [sic] should be a program designed to establish districts in California that will elect the highest possible number of Republicans to the State Legislature and House of Representatives. . . . I believe we have an unusually good opportunity to develop a 'balanced and representative plan,' which in reality is totally designed for partisan purposes."[4] The Republicans never got the opportunity, narrowly losing control of both houses in 1970 despite Reagan's reelection.

The post-1970 redistricting thus took place under divided partisan control of government. A bipartisan scheme backed by all 38 House incumbents had been virtually a done deal when a surprise Republican assembly victory in a special election derailed the entire process. The Republicans demanded assembly district lines be drawn to protect their new incumbent, Democrats refused, and Reagan ended up vetoing redistricting legislation for all three sets of legislative districts, handing the matter off to the state supreme court. The action came so late that the court did not have time to draw lines for 1972, so, for the House elections, it simply endorsed the plan supported by all of the incumbents and left it up to the legislature to draw new lines for 1974.

Another bipartisan plan supported by nearly every incumbent on both sides passed in 1973 but was also vetoed by Reagan. This left the final design to three Special Masters appointed by the state supreme court and charged with drawing up districts designed to meet "good government" criteria of compactness, consistency with other political units, and racial fairness. Imposed by the court, the Special Masters' scheme actually favored Democrats a bit more than the plan vetoed by Reagan.[5] The new districts fully registered the effect of the strong Democratic tide in 1974 (a year of recession and Watergate), and Democrats increased their majority in the California House delegation from 23 to 20 to 28 to 15. Not until the strong Republican surge of 1980 were Democrats reduced to near parity, 22 to 21 (table 10.1).

Partisan conflict over the post-1980 redistricting reached entirely new levels of intensity and rancor. Republicans hoped to lock in their 1980 gains even though Democrats controlled the legislature, state house, and the state supreme court (six of the seven justices were Democratic appointees). The assembly speaker, Democrat Willie Brown, had been elected with both Republican and Democratic votes, and Republicans expected him to take care of them on reapportionment. But Brown had his own party to unite, and stories of flagrant Republican gerrymanders in other states (Indiana, Washington, Colorado) provoked demands from state and national Democrats for retaliation.[6] Republicans sought to split the Democrats by proposing a redistricting plan that would increase the number of seats winnable by Latino Democrats while protecting every Republican incumbent. Democrats trumped this strategy by enacting an artful Democratic gerrymander (brainchild of Congressman Phil Burton, a liberal from San Francisco) that was equally favorable to

Latinos while inflicting far more damage on Republicans. Assemblyman Bob Naylor's reaction typified Republican outrage; he damned the Democrats' redistricting as "the closest thing we have in this country to lining people up against the wall with a firing squad. At least the Ayatollah only does that to his enemies. This plan does that to the Speaker's friends."[7]

The new map also drew criticism from the media and reform groups for the convoluted shapes of many of the districts. For example, the district Burton designed for his brother, John, was composed of three sections connected only by the waters of San Francisco Bay; two parts of one section were linked only by a narrow strip of land underlying some railroad yards. The incensed Republicans put a referendum on the June 1982 primary election ballot that allowed voters to reject each of the three redistricting plans. Voters did so, by more than 60 percent of the vote in every case, but the state supreme court, by a 6 to 1 party line vote, allowed the new districts to be used for the 1982 election. Common Cause, the self-appointed citizen's lobby, joined the Republicans to sponsor another referendum for the November 1982 ballot that would establish a ten-member bipartisan commission to draw future districts. The same electorate that chose Republican George Deukmejian to be governor gave the measure only 45 percent of the vote, so it failed.

After the election but before Deukmejian took over, the legislature passed a revised map, signed by Jerry Brown, the lame duck Democratic governor, that was only cosmetically different from the one rejected by voters in June. The new district lines were drawn under the guidance of Michael Berman, a Democratic consultant with redistricting experience going back to 1973 and brother of Howard Berman, who had just been promoted from the assembly to the U.S. House of Representatives by the 1982 election.[8]

Berman's map remained in force for the remainder of the decade, but not because Republicans had given up fighting it. A conservative Republican assembly member, Don Sebastiani, heir to the winery fortune, mounted an initiative that would have replaced the Democrats' districts with ones designed by a Republican consultant. Governor Deukmejian scheduled a special election for December 13, 1983 for the vote, presumably angling for a low turnout that would yield a more Republican electorate. However, on a 6 to 1 party line vote, the state supreme court disallowed the referendum, mainly on the ground that the state constitution mandated reapportionment only once a decade, and it had already occurred. Deukmejian then proposed for the November 1984 ballot another initiative establishing a commission composed of retired judges that would redraw lines from 1986 onward. After a noisy and expensive campaign, it lost by the same 45 to 55 percent margin as its predecessor.

The struggle continued in federal court as Republicans, in *Badham v. Eu,*[9] sought to have the districts overturned on the ground that they were so strongly biased against Republicans that they violated the Constitution. The Supreme Court had, in *Davis v. Bandemer,*[10] declared that a partisan gerrymander could go so far as to be unconstitutional, but it has yet to see a scheme that crossed this line, including Berman's 1982 design. A three-judge panel sided with the Democrats in district court (again on a 2 to 1 party-line vote), and the Supreme Court affirmed their dismissal of the case in 1989.

The tenacity with which California Republicans sought to overturn Burton and Berman's handiwork is a measure of their enduring anger and frustration. The districts of the 1980s did favor Democrats, albeit to a declining extent over time (table 10.1). Gearing up for the post-1990 redistricting, the Republicans' main objective was to elect Republican Pete Wilson governor so that he could veto anything objectionable the Democrats in the legislature might enact. Two Republican-sponsored propositions regarding redistricting were also on the June 1990 ballot. One would have required redistricting legislation to be passed by a two-thirds vote of both houses, signed by the governor, and approved by voters in a referendum. The other would have established a commission composed of five Democrats, five Republicans, and two independents to choose among plans proposed by interested groups. If both propositions passed, the one receiving the most votes would prevail. Although Wilson won, both propositions failed by 2 to 1 margins—victims of the effective campaign Michael Berman orchestrated against them.[11]

After the election, Democrats in the legislature sought to make a deal with Republicans, designing three sets of redistricting plans as negotiating documents, but Wilson would have none of it. His strategy was to veto all plans, appoint his own rump "Commission" to draw the maps, then turn the issue over to the state supreme court—now with a solid Republican majority[12]—whose appointed Special Masters would use his commission's document as a starting point. When the Commission's product threatened a drastic reduction in minority representation (guaranteeing a Voting Rights Act challenge), another Republican consultant (Joe Shumate, designer of the 1983 Sebastiani plan) was brought in to repair it. The state supreme court duly appointed three retired judges (two Republicans, one Democrat) as Special Masters, who ignored both the legislature's and Shumate's work, producing (with expert assistance) their own district maps drawn without regard, they claimed, to politics. "We had no agenda, no political purpose, and we did not consider any political consequences," said one of the retired judges.[13]

Analysts in both parties initially thought the Masters' maps favored Republicans; Democrats, along with two civil rights groups, the Mexican-American Legal Defense Fund (MALDEF) and the NAACP, sought to overturn them in state and federal court. In each venue they lost "on straight party-line votes, each of the ten judges voting for the party of the person who had appointed him or her."[14] In fact, however, the House districts for the 1990s were comparatively free of partisan bias (table 10.1).

This brief history makes clear just how partisan and contentious the politics of redistricting have traditionally been in California. To be sure, the state's politics have been intensely partisan for decades,[15] but rarely has the naked pursuit of partisan advantage been more transparent than in the redistricting wars. Even judges' decisions routinely favor the party of the person who appointed them, although such bias is scarcely confined to California.[16] The impact of partisan gerrymandering can be exaggerated,[17] but the a glance at the data in table 10.1 suggests that California's partisan gerrymanders (Republican 1952 to 1960, Democratic 1962 to 1966, and 1982 to 1990) have indeed helped the dominant party, providing a substantial increment of seat shares over vote shares.

The results of regression analyses, reported in table 10.2, confirm this suspicion. The first equation, included for comparison, shows that over the entire time period, the relationship between the Democrats' share of House votes and seats was surprisingly weak, although the (imprecisely estimated) coefficient has the expected positive sign and a plausible magnitude. The second equation includes dummy variables distinguishing those elections held under Republican or Democratic gerrymanders from the others. The coefficients indicate that both parties benefited substantially from controlling the process, although Republican more in the 1950s (before *Wesberry v. Sanders*) than Democrats in the

Table 10.2. The Effects of Partisan Redistricting in California, 1952 to 2002

	Equation 1	*Equation 2*	*Equation 3*
Constant	13.92 (21.64)	1.75 (11.15)	13.58 (10.37)
Democrats' percentage of major-party House votes	0.80† (0.42)	1.06** (0.22)	0.83*** (0.20)
Republican gerrymander		−12.99*** (1.95)	−18.75*** (2.66)
Republican gerrymander X time since Republican gerrymander			2.95** (1.08)
Democratic gerrymander		4.23** (1.68)	6.35** (1.88)
Democratic gerrymander X time since Democratic gerrymander			−1.44† (0.77)
Adjusted R^2	.10	.77	.84
Number of cases	25	25	25

Note: The dependent variable is the Democrats' percentage share of House seats; Standard errors are in parentheses.
†p < .10, *p < .05, **p < .01, ***p < .001, two-tailed tests.

1960s and 1980s. Absent partisan control of the process, the share of seats matches the share of votes quite closely (intercept insignificant, coefficient on Democratic votes = 1.06). Controlling for gerrymandering also improves the equation's fit dramatically (the adjusted R^2 grows from .10 to .77). Finally, the third equation adds a counter indicating how long after the last partisan gerrymander the election occurred (the second election after the gerrymander = 1, third = 2, fourth = 3, fifth = 4) which, interacted with the partisan gerrymander dummy, shows that the partisan benefits of gerrymandering decay over time. The coefficients suggest that the nineteen-point increment of seats over votes estimated for Republicans in 1952 had fallen to 6 points by 1960; the 6.4-point Democratic increment estimated for 1984 had nearly disappeared by 1990.[18]

REDISTRICTING AFTER THE 2000 CENSUS

There is little question, then, that partisan gerrymanders of California House districts did work as planned to favor the gerrymandering party, albeit with diminishing returns over time. Thus with motive, means, and opportunity, the California Democrats might have been expected, following the 2000 census, to carve out House districts that decimated Republicans and set off another decade of partisan warfare in court and at the ballot box. Instead, they produced a map endorsed not only by overwhelming majorities of both parties' California House delegations, but also by Karl Rove (G.W. Bush's chief political advisor), the Republican National Committee, House Minority Leader Dick Gephardt, and Representative Martin Frost, chair of the Democratic Congressional Campaign Committee.[19] Not by coincidence, the map they endorsed contained nary a single competitive district. It was designed to give Republicans 20 seats, same as before redistricting, and to increase the Democratic delegation from 32 to 33.

The Democrats controlled the process, so their thinking is central to understanding this surprising outcome. The principal reason they were satisfied with adding only one seat was that they had done so well in 2000—picking up four seats to reach 32, their highest total for the decade—that they already held about as many seats as they could reasonably expect to win without risking too many losses in a down year. Indeed, simply preserving the status quo would lock in a clear net Democratic advantage of seat shares over vote shares (table 10.1). The first priority of the Democratic delegation was, naturally enough, self-preservation. They caucused and agreed to hire veteran redistricting consultant Michael Berman for a reported $600,000—$20,000 each for the 30 or so Democrats who paid up—on the implicit promise that he would design, and obtain from the legislature, safe districts for all of them. The expected return on this investment was high; as Representative Loretta Sanchez put it, "Twenty thousand is nothing to keep your seat. I spend $2 million every election."[20] With safer seats, Democratic incumbents could look forward to weaker opposition and therefore cheaper campaigns. The only Democrat arguably hurt by the plan was Gary Condit, beset by scandal,[21] whose revised district was more Democratic in registration but included a lot of new territory. Condit lost the primary decisively to assembly member Dennis Cardoza, running behind even in the old parts of his district.

Although national Democratic leaders were less concerned with protecting every incumbent Democrat and more with winning the additional seats they would need to take over the House, they, too, were persuaded that Democrats had just about maximized their take in California. They had initially hoped for at least one additional seat but recognized that they would have to fight the delegation to get it and took solace from the money Berman's districts would save the party. As Frost, who was responsible for the House Democrats' redistricting strategy, put it, "The DCCC devoted some money trying to take those seats and now we have them, and we'll use those resources in competitive races elsewhere."[22]

Berman and the Democrats also sought to avoid a Republican legal challenge that might have led to an unwelcome and unpredictable court intervention or yet another Republican ballot initiative that, at best, would be expensive to defeat. They succeeded by protecting every Republican incumbent except Stephen Horn, whose already heavily Democratic district was carved up and distributed into several even more heavily Democratic districts, including a new one, and drawing a second new district in the Central Valley that was a sure Republican bet. Horn, at 70, retired. A few Republicans objected to signing away their chance to add to their current 20 seats, seemingly for the rest of the decade,[23] but most incumbents were relieved that Democrats had not played havoc with their districts but had, instead, given marginal Republicans safer seats. National Republicans concurred, content that, despite full Democratic control of the process, they did not lose any seats. According to *California Journal* reporter Carl Cannon, Karl Rove, "still spooked over Bush's dismal performance in California in 2000, agreed that Republicans should cut their losses and accept Berman's deal—and met with Berman in secret to shake hands on it."[24] The Berman plan was, with a few minor modifications, adopted by the legislature, 70 to 10 in the assembly, 38 to 2 in the senate. Governor Davis signed it into law on 27 September 2001.

THE NEW DISTRICTS

It is easy to see why California's House incumbents would be happy with Berman's handiwork. A district's division of major party registrants is an excellent predictor of election results, even more so now than in previous.[25] Thus we can assess the partisan effects of redistricting by comparing major party registration figures before and after the new lines were drawn. Table 10.3 lists the changes in the Democrat's share of major party registrants between 2000 and 2002 in order of the 2000 district ranking, lowest to highest.[26] The seats that Democrats took from Republicans in the 1996 to 2000 elections are in boldface; Condit's district italicized. The data are displayed graphically in figure 10.2.

All twelve incumbent Democrats whose party's share of registrants had been below 60 percent got a more Democratic district for 2002, with an average gain of 4.4 percentage points. This group included every Democrat who won with

Table 10.3. U.S. House Seats in California Held by Democratic Incumbents

Old District Number (2000)	*New District Number (2002)*	*Old Democratic Registration Percentage*	*New Democratic Registration Percentage*	*Change*
22	**23**	**49.8**	**57.4**	**7.5**
10	**10**	**51.0**	**56.3**	**5.3**
36	**36**	**51.1**	**57.9**	**6.9**
49	**53**	**52.0**	**56.3**	**4.3**
18	*18*	*54.0*	*56.7*	*4.1*
27	**29**	**54.1**	**57.3**	**3.2**
24	27	55.7	60.6	4.9
15	**15**	**56.4**	**59.0**	**2.6**
46	**47**	**56.6**	**58.8**	**2.2**
20	20	57.4	63.5	6.1
1	1	58.8	59.9	1.1
42	43	59.7	64.3	4.6
14	14	60.3	60.1	−0.2
50	51	62.4	61.2	−1.2
17	17	63.7	62.7	−0.9
6	6	64.6	64.8	0.2
5	5	64.7	67.3	2.5
16	16	65.7	64.4	−1.2
13	13	69.0	69.6	0.6
12	12	69.5	68.2	−1.3
29	30	70.7	65.3	−5.3
31	32	71.2	66.7	−4.5
34	38	72.0	72.4	0.4
26	28	73.0	72.7	−0.2
7	7	73.6	70.7	−2.8
30	31	77.6	77.8	0.1
8	8	81.8	82.0	0.2
33	34	83.2	75.1	−8.1
37	37	84.2	77.6	−6.6
9	9	85.1	84.5	−0.6
32	33	85.5	84.1	−1.3
35	35	87.2	83.0	−4.2

Note: Registration percentage is calculated as the percentage of major party (Democrat and Republican) registrants. Districts taken from Republicans 1996–2000 are in **boldface**; Gary Condit's district is *italicized*.

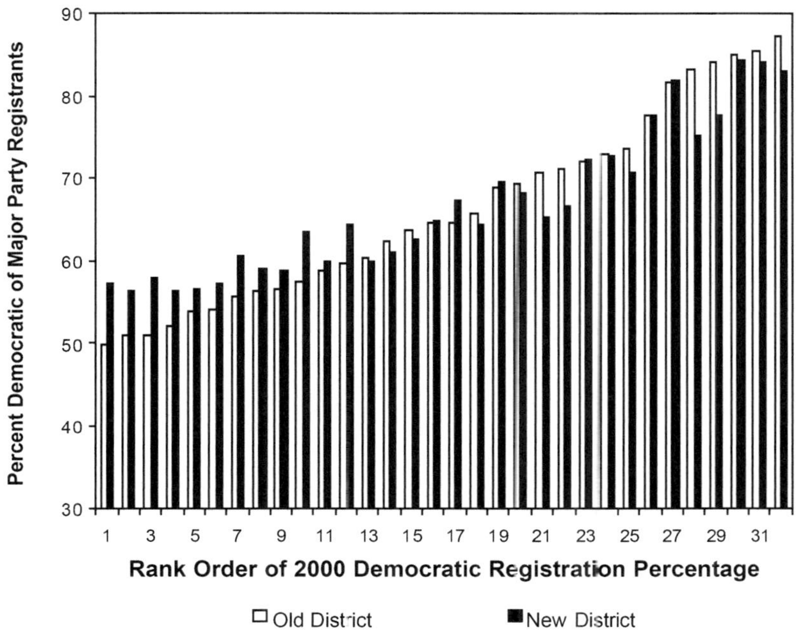

Figure 10.2. Change in Party Registration in U.S. House Districts in California, 2000 to 2002: Democratic Incumbents

less than 55 percent of the major-party vote in 2000 or whose seat had at one time been held by a Republican. The other districts became an average of 1.7 points less Democratic, but in no case did the share of registrants in the new district drop below 59.9 percent, so none was put at risk. The one new district designed for a Democrat (the 39th) was 66.5 percent Democratic.

Marginal Republican incumbents—with the exception of Horn—were treated even better. The registration data in table 10.4 (displayed graphically in figure 10.3) show that all eight Republican incumbents elected in 2000 to districts with less than 54 percent Republican registration gained Republican registrants for 2002. The average gain was a hefty 6.3 percentage points, compared to a average gain of 0.9 points for Republican incumbents in less marginal districts. No Republican incumbent was left with less than 54 percent major party registrants. In addition to the 19 districts held by incumbents, Republicans were guaranteed the new 22nd district (62.3 percent Republican major-party registration).

Not everyone was happy with the results, for by strengthening both parties' marginal incumbents, the 2002 district map virtually eliminated competitive House districts, raising the prospect that no California district would change party hands for the rest of the decade. A comparison of figures 10.4 and 10.5 illustrates this point. Figure 10.4 shows partisan makeup of the 1992 to 2000

Table 10.4. U.S. House Seats in California Held by Republican Incumbents

Old District Number (2000)	*New District Number (2002)*	*Old Republican Registration Percentage*	*New Republican Registration Percentage*	*Change*
3	**3**	**47.5**	**54.1**	**6.6**
11	11	48.5	55.2	6.7
23	24	49.5	56.9	7.5
28	26	49.9	57.5	7.6
41	42	51.7	62.5	10.8
44	45	53.3	56.6	3.2
52	52	53.5	59.0	5.5
25	25	53.8	56.0	2.2
19	19	54.7	54.3	−0.3
2	2	54.8	56.0	1.2
39	40	54.8	58.5	3.7
40	41	55.6	58.1	2.4
4	4	57.5	59.9	2.4
43	44	57.7	59.6	1.9
21	22	59.1	62.3	3.1
45	46	60.7	59.8	−0.9
51	50	61.6	60.2	−1.4
47	48	64.6	65.7	1.1
48	49	65.9	62.6	−3.3

Note: Registration percentage is calculated as the percentage of major party (Democrat and Republican) registrants; the district once held by a Democrat is in **boldface**.

districts rank ordered by their share of Democratic registrants in 2000. It also specifies the party holding the seat throughout the decade or, if both parties held the seat after at least one election, the party holding it after the 2000 election. Republicans dominate where Democratic registration falls below 50 percent. The apparent exception, the Republican district once held by a Democrat with 45 percent Democratic registration in 2000, is only apparent; the Democratic registration in the district was actually 53 percent back in 1992 when the Democrat won the seat. (Registration patterns do change across a decade, an important point discussed below.) From 1992 to 2000, Republicans won every district with less than 47.7 percent Democratic registration.

Democrats prevail when Democratic registration exceeds 56 percent. Horn is the notable exception, holding a solidly Democratic seat throughout the decade. Two other Republicans won seats with more than 56 percent Democratic registration earlier in the decade, but only one remained after 2002, and by then the Democratic registration in his district had fallen to 51.5 percent.

At present, then, a California House district may be considered competitive (potentially winnable by either party) with between 47 and 56 percent Democratic registration. From 1992 through 2000, from 12 to 17 of California's 52 districts fell into this range. As figure 10.5 shows, not a single one re-

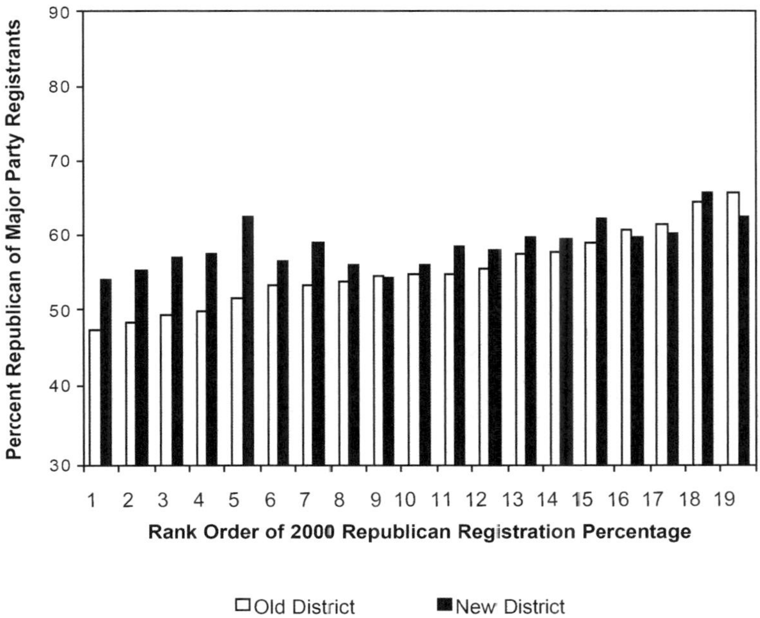

Figure 10.3. Change in Party Registration in U.S. House Districts in California, 2000 to 2002: Republican Incumbents

mained in 2002. There is no district with the Democrats' share of major party registration falling between 45.9 and 56.3 percent. The gentle upward slope created by rank ordering the 2000 districts by Democratic registration percentage in figure 10.4 is interrupted for the 2002 districts by a conspicuous 10 percentage-point escarpment between the twentieth and twenty-first observations. Its visual kinship to the aftermath of an earthquake on a block fault carries the ironic message that the partisan balance of the California House delegation might be insensitive to anything less than the political equivalent of the Big One.

The Berman plan, and similar if a bit less egregious bipartisan gerrymanders for the state assembly and senate seats,[27] drew considerable criticism from editorial writers, good government groups, and academics. Political scientist John J. Pitney, Jr. observed acidly, "It appears that the Legislature has decided to relieve us of the burden of elections."[28] A leader of the League of Women Voters worried that the dearth of competition would depress turnout.[29] The *Wall Street Journal*'s editorial staff, revealing a previously well-disguised affection for ideological moderation, griped that the bipartisan gerrymander not only eliminated competition but also turned moderate Democrats into liberals as they adjusted to new district party balances.[30]

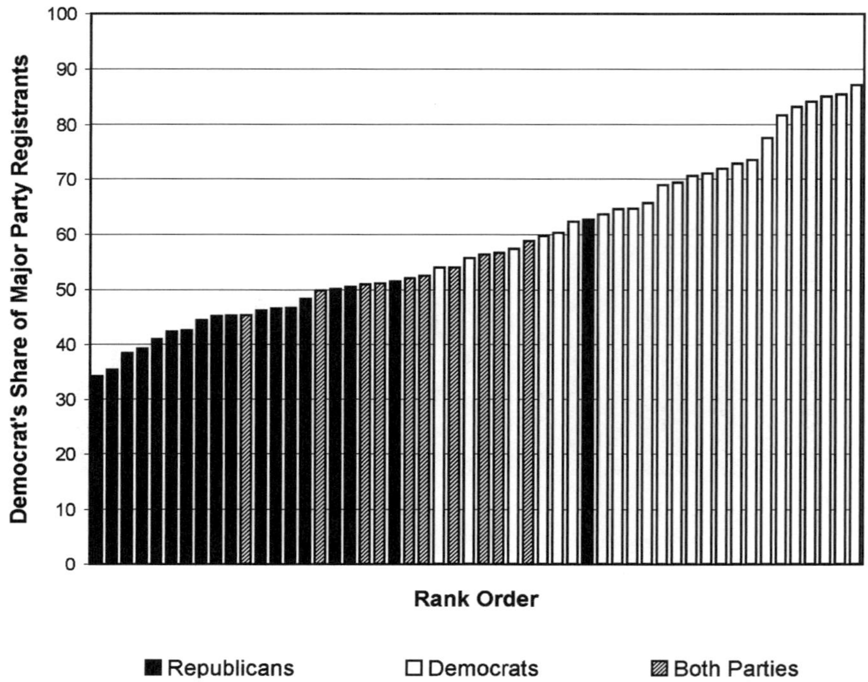

Figure 10.4. Registration and Party Control of California House Seats, 1990s

None of these complaints mattered, because none was justiciable. But the plan was attacked in several lawsuits. Three suits challenged various northern California districts on the ground that the district lines split communities of interest; the state supreme court declined to take up the cases.[31] A more serious challenge was mounted in federal court by MALDEF, which charged that the districts violated the Voting Rights Act of 1965 and the Equal Protection Clause of the Fourteenth Amendment. MALDEF's lawyers argued that Berman could have drawn an additional Latino district in the San Fernando Valley but had instead split Latino areas to protect his brother's seat in the new 28th district. They also objected to the new 51st district, represented by Bob Filner, because although it had a Latino majority, that majority could have been even larger if additional Latino neighborhoods had been included.[32] A three-judge panel of the Ninth Circuit rejected MALDEF's case by summary judgment before trial, mainly on the ground that both districts were winnable by Latinos—indeed, Latinos comprise by a wide margin the largest single ethnic group in both[33]—and thus did not abridge Latino voting rights. It did not help MALDEF's claim of discriminatory intent that 23 of the 26 Latino state legislators had voted for the redistricting legislation.[34]

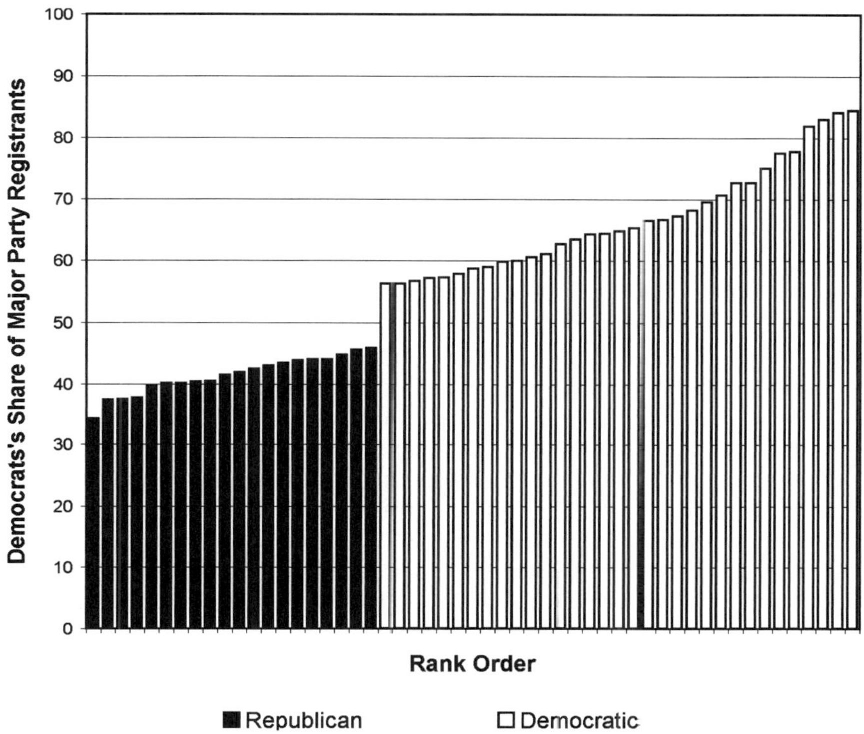

Figure 10.5. Registration and Expected Control of California House Seats, 2002

THE CONSEQUENCES OF CALIFORNIA'S POST-2000 REDISTRICTING

What are the political consequences of the new California House districts likely to be? One obvious and expected consequence is already evident: a decline in competition for House seats—at least in the general election. The 2002 California House elections were unusually quiet for year ending in "2." Indeed, they were unusually quiet compared to almost any year. On average from 1968 through 2000, 12 percent of House incumbents from California faced challengers who had held elective public office (a simple but useful measure of candidate quality).[35] For 1972, 1982, and 1992, reapportionment years, the proportion was higher, 18 percent. For 2002, it was only 4 percent. That is, only two of 50 incumbents faced challengers who had ever won an election. In both cases the office was relatively low profile—local school board and community college trustee.

Remarkably, none of the 38 assembly and senate members forced into retirement by term limits challenged a House incumbent in the general election. The only state legislators to attempt a move to Congress were the two aiming to replace Condit, Republican Senator Dick Monteith and Cardoza, victor over Condit, who squared off in the general election, and two others who sought, unsuccessfully, nominations for the newly created open seats. Clearly, the kind of careerists who typically mount the most formidable challenges but who are also most strategic in their career decisions[36] saw precious little opportunity in the new configuration of California House districts.

Incumbents, in contrast, saw little but opportunity and, with the exception of Horn, none left voluntarily. No fewer than 50 were returned to the House, leaving the California delegation with only three new members, an unusual degree of continuity for a year ending in "2." The 2002 election produced the fewest incumbent departures, the fewest new members, and the greatest proportion (and of course number) of returning incumbents of any postwar reapportionment election year (see table 10.5). The contrast with 1992, when 10 incumbents exited and 17 new members were elected, is particularly striking.

As national party leaders had anticipated, House campaigns were considerably cheaper in 2002 than in 2000, especially for national party committees. In the 1999 to 2000 election cycle, California House candidates had spent \$67.7 million campaigning; in 2001 to 2002, they spent \$47.8 million, a 31 percent reduction. The largest decrease occurred among challengers, whose total spending fell by more than two-thirds, from \$15.9 million to \$5.1 million, between the two elections. The congressional campaign committees' investment in California fell even more dramatically. The Democratic Congressional Campaign Committee and the National Republican Congressional Committee together put only \$436,317 into the 2002 California House races, compared with more than \$10 million in 2000, a decrease of 96 percent.[37]

As always, the expectations that deterred experienced challengers and left the campaigns of those who ran starving financially fulfilled themselves. Indeed, as Figure 10.6 shows, the gap in election results actually exceeded the

Table 10.5. Changes in Redrawn California House Districts, 1952 to 2002

	1952	*1962*	*1972*	*1982*	*1992*	*2002*
Number of Seats	30	38	43	45	52	53
Incumbent:						
Retired	2		1	5	8	1
Lost primary to challenger			2		1	1
Lost primary to incumbent			1			
Lost general to challenger	2	4		1	1	
Lost general to incumbent			1			
Incumbents departing	4	4	5	6	10	2
Incumbents returning	19	26	35	35	35	50
New seats	7	8	5	2	7	1
New members	11	12	8	10	17	3

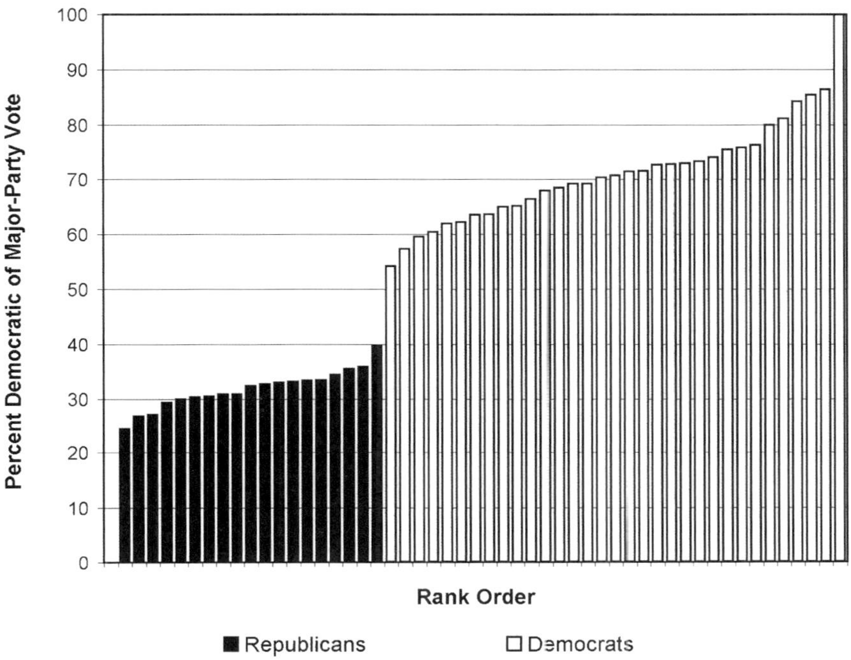

Figure 10.6. The Distribution of the House Vote in California, 2002

gap in registration displayed in figure 10.5. The party with the district registration advantage won all of California's 53 House districts. No Republican won less than 60 percent of the major-party vote. Every Republican won a share of votes larger than the Republican share of registrants in the district; the average increment was 9.6 percentage points. Every Democrat won more than 54.8 percent of the major party vote. All but three won more than 60 percent, and only these three—two of them candidates for open seats—won a share of votes smaller the share of Democratic registrants in their districts. On average, the winning Democrat's share of votes was 3.2 percentage points higher than the Democratic share of district registrants. The 15 percentage-point gap between the least safe Republican and Democrat as measured by the vote was even greater than the 10 percentage point registration gap in figure 10.5. The familiar strategic behavior of potential candidates and contributors thus led to feeble challenges that had the effect of exaggerating the anticompetitive effects of the 2002 House district remap.

The incumbent Democrats who hired Michael Berman certainly got their money's worth. And the Democratic Party as a whole enjoyed the benefit of what turned out to be, in effect, a pro-Democratic gerrymander, as Democrats won 62.3 percent of California's House seats with only 53.7 percent of the total major-party votes cast for House candidates (see table 10.1).

POLARIZED CONSTITUENCIES

In addition to its effect on electoral competition, the 2002 California House redistricting also further polarized the parties' respective electoral constituencies. The registration gap (difference in average Democratic registration percentage) between House districts won by Republicans and Democrats in elections since 1968 is displayed in figure 10.7. Note that from 1968 through 1980, the average registration difference between Republican and Democratic districts was typically less than 15 percentage points. The Burton (1982) and Berman (1984) gerrymanders raised the average difference to about 20 percentage points, a gap maintained by the Special Masters' 1992 to 2000 districts. The 2002 bipartisan map pushed the average registration difference up another 5 percentage points, to 25. As figure 10.8 shows, in both cases, the growing partisan divide between party constituencies is largely a consequence of Republican districts becoming more solidly Republican in registration.[38] Redistricting produced most of this change, and elections did the rest as both parties lost seats with unfavorable registration figures during the 1990s.

The partisan divergence of California House districts shows up not only in registration figures, but also in voting patterns. This is clear from figure 10.9, which displays the difference in the average presidential vote between Democratic and Republican House districts in California since 1952. The notable upward trend is similar to that in figure 10.7, but figure 10.9 also picks up the effects of particular presidential elections; the Reagan-Carter contest of 1980 and the Bush-Gore contest of 2000 were evidently polarizing events all by themselves. Note that, according to the 2000 presidential vote recalculated for the 2002 districts, the parties' constituencies are more divided than ever before. Indeed, by this measure (which permits comparison to states without registration data), California's Republicans and Democrats have more divergent electoral bases than do their counterparts in any other state delegation.

Figures 10.10 and 10.11 suggest some consequences of the widening partisan gap between the parties' constituencies. Figure 10.10 plots the growth of constituency differentiation and the ideological polarization of the California House delegation on a common space. Ideological polarization among House members is measured by the mean party difference in Poole and Rosenthal's DW-Nominate scores. DW-Nominate scores are calculated from all nonunanimous roll call votes cast by House and Senate members; the score locates each member for each Congress on a liberal-conservative scale that ranges from -1.0 to 1.0; the higher the score, the more conservative the member.[39] The trends correspond (the correlation between the two is .87) but not perfectly, as the California House delegation began to move apart ideologically even before the post-1980 redistricting. Figure 10.11 makes a similar comparison but replaces party difference in DW-Nominate scores with party

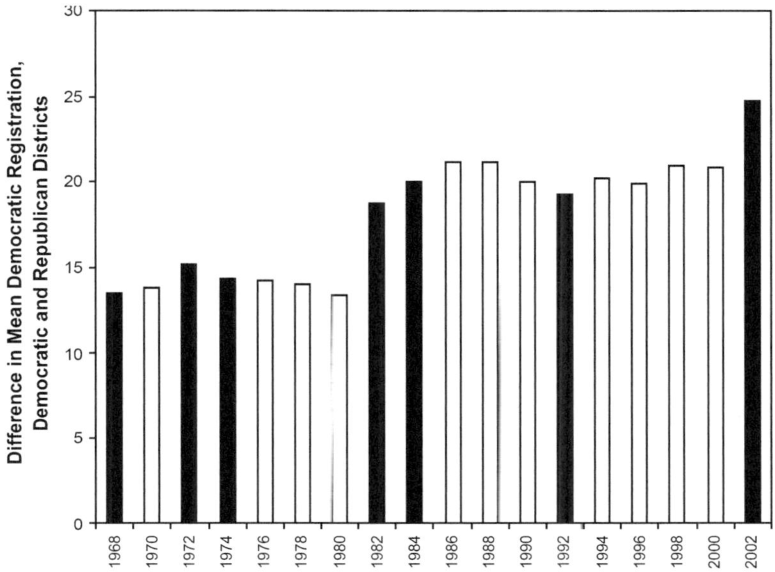

Note: Elections following redistricting are in in black.

Figure 10.7. Partisan Polarization of California House Districts: Registration

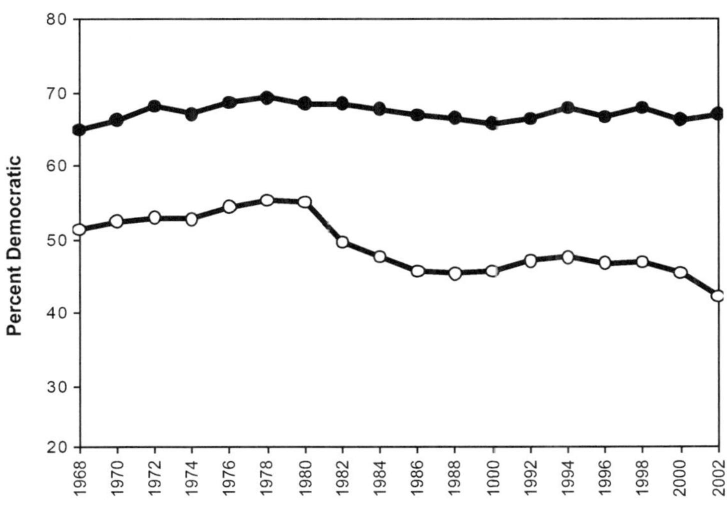

Figure 10.8. Average Party Registration in Democratic and Republican California U.S. House Districts, 1968 to 2002

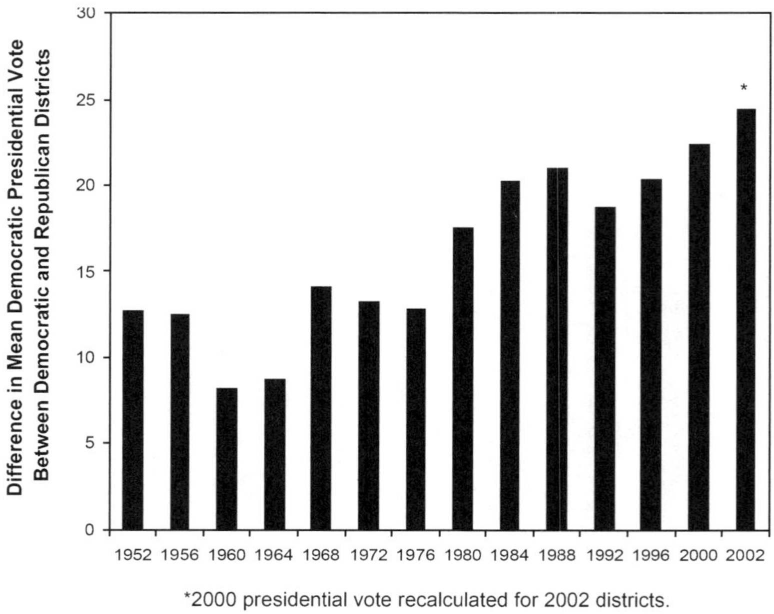

Figure 10.9. The Presidential Vote Gap between Democratic and Republican House Districts

differences in presidential support scores. Presidential support is measured as the percentage of votes for the president's position on conflictual roll calls (defined as those on which less than 80 percent of members in a chamber voted with the president).[40] Again the trends move roughly together (r = .65).

The growth in the gap between the congressional parties' ideological locations and presidential support scores has not been confined to California, to be sure, but neither has the growing distinctiveness of presidential voting patterns in the two parties' respective electoral constituencies.[41] The cross-sectional relationships between district party registration and voting behavior within the California congressional delegation suggest that this conjunction of trends is not merely coincidence. Table 10.6 shows the results from regressing DW-Nominate scores on party registration for California's representatives from the Reagan administration through the Clinton administration. Registration has a statistically significant effect on the roll-call ideology of Democrats and Republicans alike; the higher the Democratic registration, the more liberal the voting pattern. Table 10.7 lists regression estimates of the relationship between registration and presidential support, separating observations by the party of the representative and administration. Again, registration has a statistically significant affect on presidential support (in the expected direction) in every equation, although in this case, the slopes vary. Generally, the effect of district registration is stronger (the slope is steeper) for members who do not share the president's party.

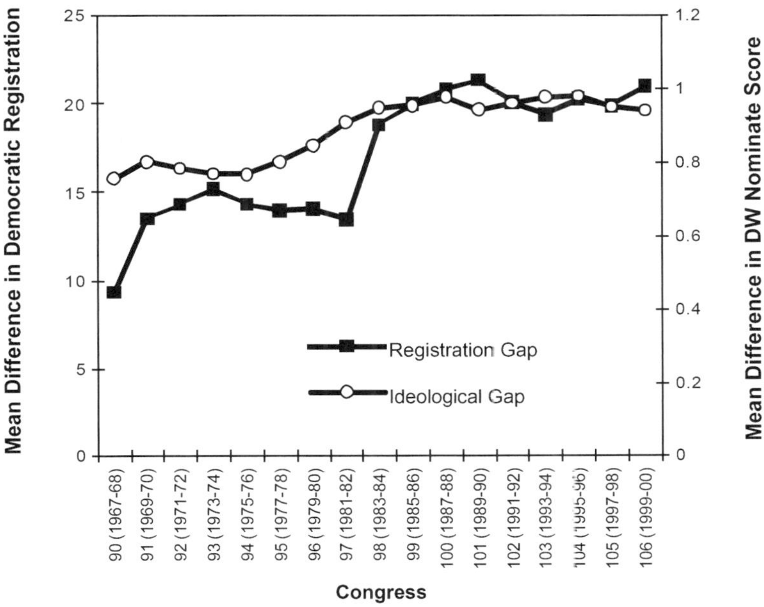

Figure 10.10. Party Registration and Polarization of the California House Delegation

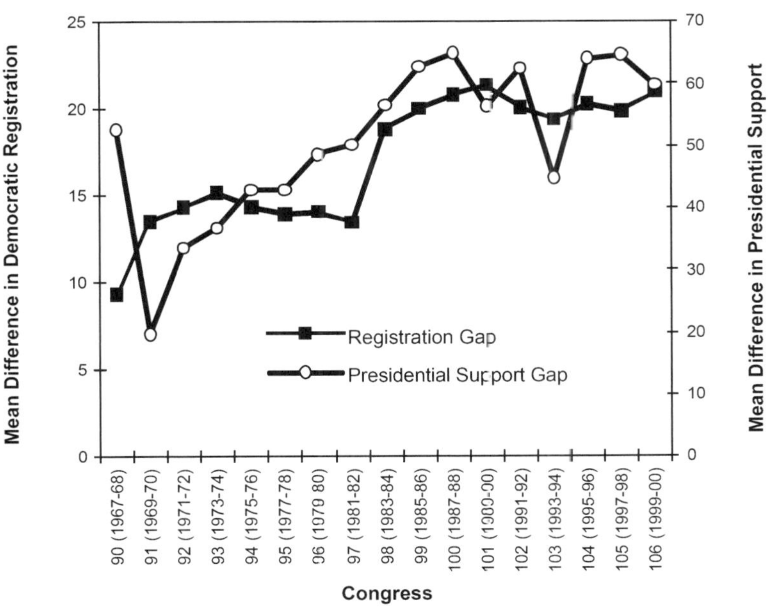

Figure 10.11. Party Registration and Presidential Support in the California House Delegation

Table 10.6. District Party Registration and Roll-Call Ideology

	Democrats' Share of Major Party Registrants	*Constant*	R^2	*Number of Cases*
Democrats	−.0087***	.116	.25	278
	(.0009)	(.061)		
Republicans	−.0077***	.847***		
	(.0013)	(.065)	.13	208

Note: The dependent variable is the member's DW-Nominate score; standard errors are in parentheses.
*p < .05, two-tailed test.
**p < .01, two-tailed test.
***p < .001, two-tailed test.

Although the coefficients of interest are statistically significant at conventional levels, party registration explains only a modest proportion of the variance in either DW-Nominate scores or presidential support scores in these models. The reason for this is suggested by figures 10.12 and 10.13, which plot the predicted levels of roll-call ideology and presidential support (computed from the coefficients in tables 10.6 and 10.7) across the range of actual registration percentages in each equation. Both figures indicate that, although registration does affect voting in Congress, party accounts for the greatest share by far of the variance in roll-call ideology and presidential support.

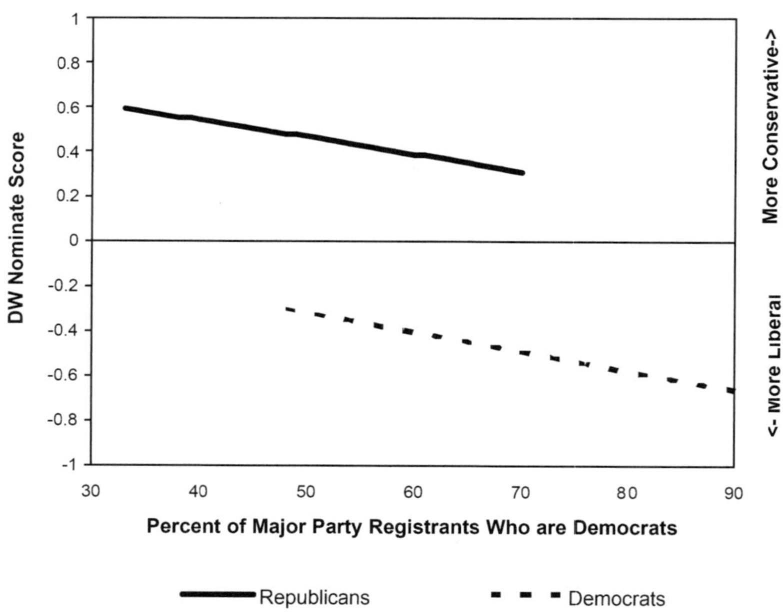

Figure 10.12. Party Registration and Ideology: Administrations from Reagan to Clinton

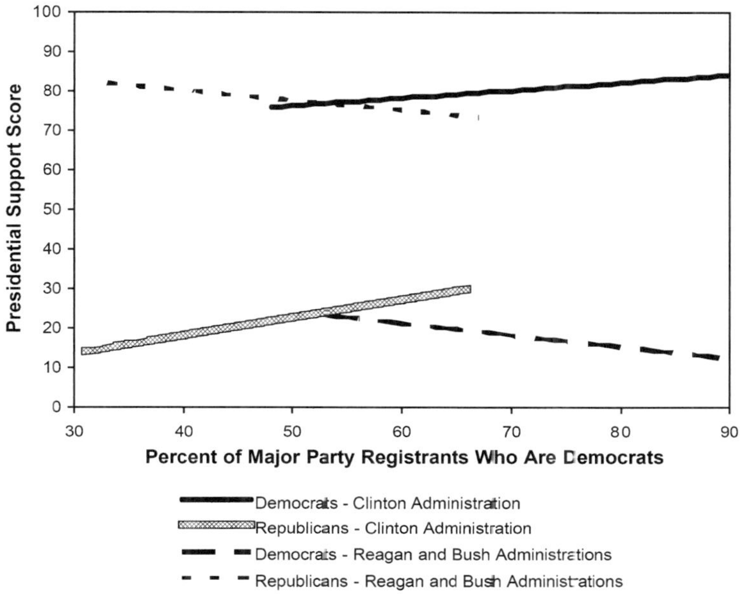

Figure 10.13. Presidential Support: Reagan through Clinton Years

The growing partisan polarization of California's House delegation over the past several decades has, then, reflected the parties' increasingly divergent constituencies. Even before the 2002 redistricting, California's delegation was more widely divided along ideological lines than the delegations of all but three other states.[42] The new districts have given the two parties more divergent constituencies than ever, and the most likely consequence is even greater polariza-

Table 10.7. District Party Registration and Presidential Support in California

	Democrats' Share of Major Party Registrants	*Constant*	R^2	*Number of Cases*
Democrats—Reagan and Bush Administrations	−.296*** (.067)	39.04*** (4.60)	.11	153
Republicans—Reagan and Bush Administrations	−.212** (.095)	90.33*** (4.66)	.05	110
Democrats—Clinton Administration	.196* (.081)	66.57*** (5.50)	.04	106
Republicans—Clinton Administration	.458** (.160)	−.21 (7.61)	.07	93

Note: The dependent variable is the member's presidential support score; standard errors are in parentheses.
*p < .05, two-tailed test.
**p < .01, two-tailed test.
***p < .001, two-tailed test.

tion along party and ideological lines in future congresses, an expectation only reinforced by the departure of the delegation's last moderate Republican (Horn) and most conservative Democrat (Condit).[43] Political scientists who live in California are sometimes asked why the California delegation, unlike delegations from many other states, almost never unites to use the clout inherent in its size to pursue the state's interests. The ideological gulf between the parties supplies a good part of the answer, for it points to the absence of any consensus among California representatives on what the state's interests *are*.

THE COMING DECADE

The Berman plan produced 53 safe seats for California's U.S. representatives. What might upset the delegation's carefully contrived balance of 33 Democrat and 20 Republicans? Condit's fate points to one possibility: scandal. Scandal has sometimes cost a California incumbent his seat (the losers have all been men), but not often. Since 1968, incumbents have lost four primary and three general election contests in which scandal clearly played a part; the average is thus only about one party switch via scandal per decade. Another possibility is that the majority party splits because of a strong third party or independent candidacy, allowing the minority party candidate to win with a plurality vote; but this has occurred only a couple of times in California since 1968.

A strong national tide favoring one of the parties might also push a few of the safe seats into the range where a minority party victory becomes possible. Over the past twenty elections, the average interelection vote swing across California House districts has surpassed 4 percentage points six times and 5 percentage points three times, so a sizable partisan tide during the coming decade is certainly conceivable. But if the partisan configuration of districts remains unchanged, a candidate who rides a tide to victory in a district where the other party maintains a sizable registration advantage will be hard pressed to hold onto it when the tide recedes.

The partisan configuration of districts is, however, unlikely to remain unchanged. Differential population growth and demographic shifts continually redistribute partisans among House districts and can, over a decade, produce consequential changes in their partisan makeup. Figure 10.14 illustrates this point by showing how the party registration balances changed between 1992 and 2000 in the districts drawn for that decade by the court's Special Masters. The balance in one district changed by more than 10 percentage points, in eight, by more than 6 percentage points, and in eleven, by more than 5 percentage points. Changes of this sort are one reason why partisan gerrymanders become less effective over time (table 10.2). Thus unless California's historical pattern of immigration and internal movement is broken, some of Berman's artful work is certain to be undone before the end of the decade. Figure 10.14 shows that in the 1990s, demographic movement made some districts more

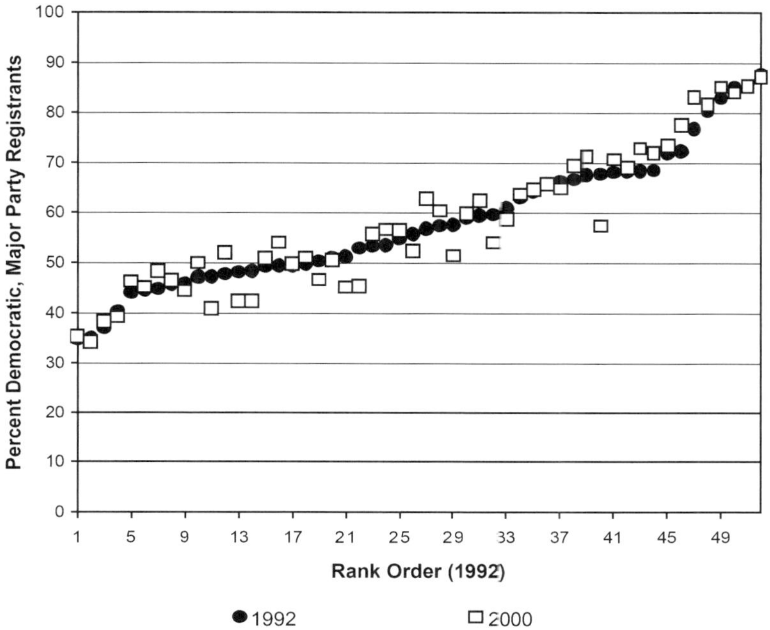

Figure 10.14. Change in Party Registration, 1992 to 2000

competitive, others less so. But because there are *no* competitive districts in the 2002 plan, even random shifts are likely to produce at least a few.

CONCLUSION

Barring major upheavals, California House elections are unlikely to contribute much to changes in the House over the coming decade. They are, however, likely to reinforce the comparatively high levels of partisan polarization that have characterized recent congresses. Nationally, redistricting for 2002 displayed tendencies similar, though less pronounced, to those in California. For example, of the 331 House incumbents from states other than California who ran for reelection in 2002, 73 had, before redistricting, represented districts won by the other party's presidential candidate in 2000. After redistricting, and with the 2000 presidential vote recalculated for the new districts, only 53 represented such districts. Overall, the number of noncompetitive districts (as indicated by a relatively lopsided presidential vote in 2000) grew by 7 or 8. Redistricting is part, if not all, of the explanation for the paucity of competitive races in 2002 that was widely noted, and lamented, in the press. The gap in mean presidential vote between the parties' constituencies also increased slightly, a pattern portending no reduction in partisan polarization.[44] In California and elsewhere, the net effect of redistricting was to reinforce rather than to undermine the status quo, and like the 2000 election,[45] the 2002 midterm thus produced results that continue to reflect with unusual precision the close party balance and clear partisan divide that now characterizes the American electorate.

NOTES

1. Anthony T. Quinn, "California," in *Reapportionment Politics*, ed. Leroy Hardy, Alan Heslop and Stuart Anderson (Beverly Hills, Calif: Sage Publications, 1981), 53–57.
2. 376 U.S. 1.
3. "California Redistricting, Outlook," *Congressional Quarterly Weekly Report*, (May 24, 1968): 1208.
4. Quoted in Morgan Kousser, "Reapportionment Wars: Party, Race, and Redistricting in California, 1971–1992," in *Race and Redistricting in the 1990s*, ed. Bernard Grofman (New York: Agathon Press, 1998), 137.
5. Kousser, "Reapportionment Wars," 144–149.
6. Bruce E. Cain, *The Reapportionment Puzzle* (Berkeley: University of California Press, 1984), 82–83.
7. Quoted in Cain, *Reapportionment Puzzle,* 102.
8. Kousser, "Reapportionment Wars," 154–156.
9. 694 F.Supp. 664 (N.D. Cal., 1988), aff'd mdm 109 S.Ct. 829 (1989).
10. 478 US 109 (1986).
11. Kousser, "Reapportionment Wars," 165–166.
12. Three liberal justices had been voted out in 1986 and had been replaced by Deukmejian with conservative Republicans.
13. Kousser, "Reapportionment Wars," 171.
14. Kousser, "Reapportionment Wars," 174.
15. Gary C. Jacobson, "Partisan and Ideological Polarization in the California Electorate," *State Politics and Policy Quarterly* 4 (Summer 2004): 113–139.
16. Gary W. Cox and Jonathan N. Katz, *Elbridge Gerry's Salamander: The Electoral Consequences of the Reapportionment Revolution* (Cambridge, UK: Cambridge University Press, 2002), 92–95.
17. Kousser, "Reapportionment Wars," 188–89. Amahai Glazer, Bernard Grofman, and Marc Robbins, "Partisan and Incumbency Effects in the 1970s Congressional Redistricting," *American Journal of Political Science* 31 (1987): 702–705.
18. Kousser's analysis of the hypothetical effects of different schemes proposed for the 1990s also demonstrates that partisan gerrymanders can make a difference, of as many as nine seats between the most pro-Democratic and pro-Republican plans (Kousser, "Reapportionment Wars," 177).
19. Carl M. Cannon, "California Divided," *California Journal* (January 2002): 8–14.
20. Cannon, "California Divided," 10.
21. Condit initially denied, then later admitted to a "close relationship" with Chandra Levy, a 24-year-old intern who had disappeared in May 2001 [Adam Graham-Silverman, "California Incumbents Appear Safe Bets in November," *CQW*, (9 March 2002): 638–639]; Levy's body was found a year later in a Washington, D.C. park (Condit is not a suspect).

22. Cannon, "California Divided," 12.
23. Cannon, "California Divided," 11.
24. Cannon, "California Divided," 12.
25. The growth in the proportion of registrants for minor parties or refusing to state has simply taken noises out of the registration data; as the proportion registering other than Republican or Democrat grew from 3 percent to 20 percent between 1966 and 2000, the proportion of the variance in the House vote explained by district registration grew from 55 percent to 88 percent. See Jacobson, "Partisan and Ideological Polarization," 121.
26. The 2000 registration figures are from October and can be found at www.ss.ca.gov/elections/ror/us_cong_10-00.pdf; the 2002 figures are for September and are at www.ss.ca.gov/elections/ror/us_cong_09-06-02.xls.
27. The assembly plan reduced the number of potentially competitive districts by about two thirds (from approximately 18 to about a half dozen), and the senate map included only one reliably competitive district. Both plans were intended to preserve the status quo, a 50 to 30 Democratic majority in the assembly, a 26 to 14 Democratic majority in the senate (Lisa Plendl, "Are Voters Dissed by Redistricting?," *California Journal* (January 2002): 12.
28. Cannon, "California Divided," 10.
29. Plendl, "Voters Dissed?," 13.
30. "Cheating Seating," *Wall Street Journal*, 27 December 2001.
31. *Andal v. Davis* (S101573), *Kennedy v. Davis* (S101719), and *Nadler v. Davis* (S101651).
32. Assemblyman Juan Vargas, the main objector to the 51st district, had tried to knock off Filner in the 1996 primary and evidently wanted a more Latino district to boost his chances of winning a future challenge against the man he once referred to publicly as "that ugly guy" (Cannon, "California Divided," 14.)
33. Latinos comprise 49 percent of the voting age population in both districts.
34. *Cano v. Davis*, 191 F. Supp. 2d 1135 (CD Cal. 2001) (per curiam); I had a minor role as a consultant for the defense in this case.
35. Gary C. Jacobson, "Strategic Politicians and the Dynamics of House Elections, 1946–86," *American Political Science Review* 83 (September 1989): 773–93.
36. Gary C. Jacobson and Samuel Kernell, *Strategy and Choice in Congressional Elections*. 2nd ed (New Haven: Yale University Press, 1983).
37. Party investments include contributions to candidates, coordinated spending on their behalf, and both hard and soft money transfers to state and local parties. The data are from the Federal Election Commission.
38. The observation for 2002 is additional evidence of an effective, if unmarked Democratic gerrymander.
39. For an explanation of their methodology, see Keith T. Poole and Howard Rosenthal, *Congress: A Political-Economic History of Roll Call Voting* (New York: Oxford University Press, 1997). I am obliged to Keith Poole for providing the DW-Nominate data through the 106th Congress.
40. The data were compiled by George C. Edward III and are available at http://bush.tamu.edu/cps/cps/archivedata/index.html. For these charts, the annual scores are averaged for each Congress.
41. Gary C. Jacobson, "Partisan Polarization in Presidential Support: The Electoral Connection," *Congress and the Presidency* 30 (Spring 2003):1–36.

42. The three states are Arizona, Colorado, and Georgia.

43. Horn's career DW-Nominate score was .223; the mean for the remaining Republicans is .527, with none having a score less than .355; Condit's career DW-Nominate score was −.05; no remaining Democrat has a score above −.187.

44. Gary C. Jacobson, "Terror, Terrain, and Turnout: Explaining the 2002 Midterm Election," *Political Science Quarterly* 118 (Spring 2003): 1–22.

45. Gary C. Jacobson, "A House and Senate Divided: The Clinton Legacy and the Congressional Elections of 2000," *Political Science Quarterly* 116 (Spring 2001): 5–27.

11

Family Feud in Massachusetts: How Intraparty Dynamics Influence Redistricting[1]

Barry C. Burden

After learning of the results of the 2000 Census and assessing the political context in the state, one might have expected redistricting in Massachusetts to be completed on autopilot. Most of the conditions that usually lead to contentious districting battles were simply absent in Massachusetts. First, the number of districts was unchanged. Unlike the 1990 Census, which required the state to eliminate a district, small relative changes in population allowed the state to maintain its ten House districts for another decade. Second, district lines were to be drawn by and for Democrats. Democrats dominated the state legislature and the congressional delegation. All ten U.S. House seats were safely held by incumbent Democrats and the party held huge veto-proof majorities in both chambers of the state legislature. Furthermore, no House incumbents faced challenges in the primary election that would have forced party loyalists to choose sides. Third, debates about race have never been particularly salient in Massachusetts. Unlike well-known cases in the South following the 1990 Census, line drawers in the Bay State were not faced with a difficult decision about the representation of blacks or other minorities. Fourth, nearly all participants in the redistricting process publicly agreed to the goal of protecting incumbents. Aside from accommodating modest population shifts that have taken place within the state over the last decade, the redistricting task in Massachusetts should have been easy, subordinate to more important policy issues on the state political agenda.

Compared to the legal battles going on in some other states, redistricting in Massachusetts following the 2000 Census was in fact tame. But it became far more contentious than most analysts would have predicted. The bulk of the strife arose not from traditional racial or partisan cleavages; instead, nearly all of the disagreement occurred within one party, among incumbents, and with few racial overtones. The bumps along the redistricting path were mostly due to conflicts among Democrats, some of them personal, some of them political. This "family feud," which is probably more common than the literature on redistricting recognizes, results from the seemingly innocuous legal provision that *state* politicians determine the jurisdictions in which *federal* candidates must run. The United States is peculiar in having politicians at one level draw lines governing the election of politicians whose seats, according to ambition theory,[2] most of them covet.[3]

Beyond these intraparty disagreements, there were other factors at work in this round of redistricting. Many participants wanted to clean up the unorthodox map put in place after the 1990 reapportionment. The Republican governor wanted to influence the process if only to assert her place in state government, even if her plan would be overridden by the legislature. And racial considerations were not entirely absent. The 2000 Census had showed that Boston had become a majority-minority city for the first time. These and other factors deserve at least some mention in any analysis of the 2000 redistricting.

But in the end nearly all of the difficulty in the redistricting process came from arguments among Democrats who held or sought offices at different levels of government. The federal nature of American government and the requirement that states draw lines for national officeholders allowed for intraparty disputes—particularly between the Speaker of the Massachusetts House and one member of the state congressional delegation over apparently unrelated issues of campaign finance reform—to hinder a process expected to be easy.

The remainder of this chapter documents the issues in play during the latest redistricting round in Massachusetts. First, I provide some background on demographics from the 2000 Census, which set some objective parameters for the new districts. Second, I discuss how debates over campaign finance in both Boston and Washington affect redistricting. Third, I portray the resulting showdown between statehouse Speaker Thomas Finneran and Congressman Marty Meehan. By describing the conflicts between state and federal politicians, this section shows how a family feud erupted in Massachusetts. Fourth, several other redistricting plans are covered to suggest how politicians' goals shaped them. The section indicates how politicians might justify a redistricting plan on grounds other than the ones actually used. The fifth section suggests how the possibility of a majority-minority district was used in this way. The sixth section details how the Finneran plan was eventually put to rest and Massachusetts lawmakers agreed upon a new congressional map. Finally, the conclusion ties these strands together, arguing that intraparty disputes are most likely to arise when conventional debates about race and other factors are minimal. The combination of federalism and progressive ambition suggest that family feuds are more common than the political science literature suggests.

THE 2000 CENSUS

The population of Massachusetts changed modestly during the 1990s. In contrast to the 13 percent growth in the national population, the state expanded by just 5.5 percent, making it 41st out of 50 states in growth since the last census. Even this sub par growth allowed the state to retain all 10 of its House districts. To avoid malapportionment within the state, each new district would need to contain about 636,000 people. The population had shifted its center of gravity to the southeast, so district lines would naturally need to accommodate this intrastate movement.

As in several other states, minority populations grew faster than the nonminority population during the 1990s. The minority share of the state grew from 12 percent in 1990 to 15 percent in 2000. These minorities were far from monolithic, however. They included African Americans and blacks from Haiti and other Caribbean nations, Asians of varying heritage, and a diverse group of Latinos with different countries of origin. Overall, Hispanics are the largest minority block at 6.8 percent, with blacks at 5.4 percent, and Asians at 3.8 percent (the only group above the national average). Minorities had increased their numbers more in Boston and a few other cities, but it was not at all clear that there was a definable minority "interest" that yet warranted a district of its own. Contrary to the experiences in some other states, the 2000 Census results were not dramatic enough to suggest that any serious changes would be made to the state's ten congressional districts. The conflictual nature of redistricting in Massachusetts is therefore attributable to factors other than "packing," "cracking," and other racially motivated techniques aimed at geographically concentrated minorities.[4] Though racial considerations were used to justify the most controversial plan, interpersonal disputes among Democratic politicians were the real source of conflict.

SPILLOVER EFFECTS OF POLICY DEBATES: CAMPAIGN FINANCE

Two years before the 2000 Census would be completed, Massachusetts voters faced a ballot question to create a system of public financing for candidates running for state office. The measure, known as the Clean Elections Law by its proponents, was an initiative aimed at increasing political competition in Massachusetts. Voters passed the Clean Elections Law two to one, a ringing endorsement for a change in the financing of state elections.

The measure affects primarily executive and state legislative offices in Massachusetts. Much like the national system of matching funds for presidential candidates, the law requires that those who wish to be "Clean Elections" candidates gather many small donations in exchange for public funds.[5] To take a concrete example, a gubernatorial candidate running in 2002 who wanted to receive public funding had to raise six thousand contributions of between five and one hundred dollars. In return, the state would augment these funds with those designated by citizens on tax form check-off boxes. Unlike the Federal Elections Campaign Act (FECA) provisions, Massachusetts candidates wishing to bypass these fundraising requirements do not receive public funds for their campaigns yet must still stay below overall spending limits established by the law. In 2002, no gubernatorial candidate—Clean Elections or not—could spend more than three million dollars in hard money. The law thus assists entrepreneurial challengers while constraining what resource-rich candidates can do. Reminiscent of recent changes in the FECA, the law also bans so-called "soft money" altogether.

Despite the message from voters at the ballot box, state legislators were not supportive of Clean Elections. More importantly, it was opposed by the most powerful Democrat in the state: Massachusetts House Speaker Thomas Finneran. Finneran simply derided it as a "frivolous use of . . . precious public dollars."[6] Finneran complained that Clean Elections would "subsidize people who couldn't qualify for 'The Jerry Springer Show'" but "his real gripe, critics say, is that it would underwrite challenges to the Democrats incumbents who provide his power base."[7] Massachusetts has some of the least competitive state legislative elections in the nation, a fact that works to the advantage of incumbents generally but is especially important for the preservation of Speaker Finneran's conservative coalition within the party. He opposed the law because it threatened his hold on state government.

It is not surprising that incumbents prefer the current method of financing campaigns. Just being in office suggests that they benefit from the electoral status quo, which might be little more than an "incumbent protection act."[8] It is perhaps more surprising that they would so openly oppose a measure overwhelmingly favored by voters since they might be penalized for taking the wrong position.[9] Finneran was keenly wedded to the status quo. Facing a weak Republican governor in an overwhelmingly Democratic state, and leading a veto-proof majority in the legislature, Finneran was arguably the most powerful politician in the state.

Meanwhile, U.S. Congressman Martin Meehan of Massachusetts' 5th district was working to advance a campaign finance bill through the U.S. Congress. A sweeping campaign finance plan sponsored by Senators John McCain (R-AZ) and Russell Feingold (D-WI) was introduced in the House by Meehan and his colleague Christopher Shays (R-CT). A version of the McCain-Feingold bill had been introduced in the Senate repeatedly since 1995.

While the bill would not expand the federal program of public financing, it would ban unregulated "soft money" donations to parties and close loopholes in FEC regulations that allow for "issue ads" to be purchased on behalf of candidates. The bill went nowhere in the Senate for several years, but the House version known as Shays-Meehan began to get serious consideration in the late 1990s. The bill actually passed the House on more than one occasion but rarely saw the necessary light of day in the Senate. John McCain later made it a centerpiece of his 2000 presidential campaign against George W. Bush, raising the salience of the issue among voters nationwide. After Bush's election in 2000, the bill finally won passage in both chambers of Congress after long debate in the Senate. The Bipartisan Campaign Reform Act was signed into law by President Bush in March 2002 to the delight of Meehan and his cosponsors.[10]

To remind Bay State legislators of the national initiative, Meehan, Shays, McCain, and Feingold held a joint news conference in Boston celebrating their victory. As he pursued campaign finance reform at the national level, Congressman Meehan simultaneously worked on behalf of Clean Elections in Massachusetts. Just weeks before the election in which the ballot question would be approved, the state's congressional delegation unanimously endorsed the Clean Elections Law at Meehan's request. Meehan made a point of adding that it would "send a clear message to the federal level that the states are interested in reforming the corrupt way we finance our elections."[11] Comments such as these were clearly aimed at Finneran and other state politicians, a kind of sweet revenge for the trouble they caused Meehan over the past nine months. It is to this trouble that I now turn.

THE HOUSE PLAN: MEEHAN VERSUS FINNERAN

In July 2001 Speaker Finneran "rocked the state's political establishment" by presenting a radical redistricting plan.[12] The plan was apparently devised without consulting other Democrats at the state or federal level. It was purposely offered early in the redistricting season to preempt more incremental plans. The Finneran map would have shifted 40 percent of Massachusetts residents into new House districts despite no change in the number of districts apportioned to the state and little population shift. It also would have created a "majority-minority" 8th district centered in Boston. Most importantly, it would have dismantled Meehan's 5th district and reassembled it in the southeastern part of the state. This would force Meehan to run against fellow incumbent Democrat John Tierney for the right to represent the new 6th district.[13]

Finneran justified his harsh proposal on several grounds. Though he opposed Clean Elections, he argued that voters deserve competitive elections and that his map would create an open seat in southeastern Massachusetts. Moreover, the southeast part of the state has been divided across districts for years. It would benefit from being reunited in a single district, especially since Cape Cod grew more quickly that the rest of the state. He also expressed interest in creating a district that would enhance minority representation.[14] The new 8th district, he asserted, would be the first majority-minority district in the history of the state. Finally, he justified elimination of Meehan's district by saying that he expected Meehan to abandon his seat to run for governor in 2002. If one House incumbent needs to be displaced to achieve these goals, he reasoned, why not select one who was departing already?[15] But Meehan was actually far from a serious gubernatorial campaign, devoting nearly all of his time to the McCain-Feingold bill instead.

Like many reformers before him, Marty Meehan is something of a maverick. The bad taste this leaves in some politicians' mouths means that he has few political allies at the state level. When first elected in 1992, he pledged to limit himself to eight years in office. He later broke the promise by running for reelection in 2000, a decision that upset some ambitious local politicians who might have been planning to run for his seat. During his time in Congress he also pushed hard for more state funding for the New England Patriots' football stadium, a move opposed by Speaker Finneran. There were also complaints from state legislators that Meehan failed to serve the depressed cities in his district well by not bringing home federal funds as his predecessor Paul Tsongas had. Instead, state Democrats contended, Meehan spent too much time in Washington, often appearing more frequently on political talk shows to promote his antitobacco and campaign finance agendas than at town meetings in his district.

As a Boston newspaper put it, "Meehan has long been viewed as an overly ambitious loner by his congressional colleagues, bucking the party on key issues and displaying little loyalty to the state's delegation." On multiple occasions he has been critical of the state legislature. One state legislator complained, "Marty Meehan has made a cottage industry of kicking the crap out of the Massachusetts Legislature for all sorts of reasons. He doesn't have a single friend in this state."[16]

It is not mere coincidence that Meehan's district was the only one in the state subject to elimination in the Finneran plan. The 2000 redistricting battle built on the unpleasant history between state legislators and Meehan. It was heightened by the ongoing campaign finance reform proposals, which Meehan championed and Finneran relentlessly opposed. In response to questions about why Meehan was singled out from among ten congressmen, other Democrats made clear that it was not about his potential run for governor. "'Marty made his own bed,' one longtime friend and fellow pol said."[17] While other members of the delegation began discussing the upcoming redistricting among themselves as the 2000 Census loomed, Meehan was too busy advocating his campaign reform bill.[18] Fearing that he would be targeted by Finneran, Meehan might have joined his colleagues in establishing collegial relationships with state legislators. Instead, he alienated state office holders further by working overtime for a policy most of them opposed.

Because of this bad blood, Meehan was sure that Finneran's proposal was designed to do away with him politically. Ideally, it might push him out of the governor's race and perhaps cost him his House seat at the same time.[19] The *timing* of Finneran's presentation was especially keen. Meehan's time in the summer of 2001 was consumed with building a bipartisan coalition to support the McCain-Feingold between the Congress and incoming Bush administration. "'It couldn't have come intentionally at a crueler time,' said one of Meehan's close supporters. 'It was an unbelievable act of cannibalism.'" As one national observer put it, "Meehan is the latest victim of a specialty of Massachusetts politics, the skewering of Democrats by Democrats, especially of reformers."[20] Though Meehan was the target in this instance, Finneran admitted, "I honestly don't lose any sleep over the potential that the congressional delegation might be angry at me."[21]

Fellow Democrats noticed that Meehan had built a serious campaign war chest of roughly two million dollars by 2000. That amount was far more than necessary to retain his House seat, which by most accounts was quite safe. The account was valuable because it might have been quickly transferred into a gubernatorial campaign should Meehan have decided to run for statewide office. To prevent this possibility, Finneran, Senate President Thomas Birmingham, and Republican Governor Paul Cellucci passed a bill to prohibit federal elected officials from using congressional campaign money in state campaigns. This was done quickly during a special session of the state legislature held right after the passage of Clean Elections. "'With all appropriate deliberation, we rushed it through [the Legislature] in about twenty-five minutes, like dry cleaning,' Finneran recalled."[22] Though this "emergency preamble" would effectively hinder any member of Congress from Massachusetts from easily mounting a bid for state office, it was aimed specifically at Marty Meehan. Birmingham and Cellucci both planned gubernatorial campaigns in 2002, so preventing a strong challenge from a popular member of the congressional delegation made electoral sense for them. Indeed, some polls indicated that Meehan was an early frontrunner for governor. Finneran, on the other hand, had no immediate gubernatorial aspirations and merely wanted to target Meehan.

OTHER PLANS

The 2002 gubernatorial race was already taking shape when the 2000 Census numbers were released. Being a heavily Democratic state with a weak

Republican governor, many Democrats were considered possible contenders for the "corner office" on Beacon Hill. As already noted, Speaker Finneran defended the disintegration of Meehan's district in his plan under the guise that Meehan would vacate his seat to run for governor.

A more committed gubernatorial candidate was Senate President Thomas Birmingham. Birmingham, also a Democrat, raised an enormous campaign war chest early on and was immediately viewed as a frontrunner. In building a statewide coalition to support his campaign, Birmingham would naturally want support from the state's congressional delegation. In what was brewing to be a bloody intraparty competition for the gubernatorial nomination, making fellow Democrats angry would not be a wise move on Birmingham's part.[23] Unlike Meehan, Birmingham was single-mindedly focused on the governor's race.

As senate president, Birmingham naturally helped shape the redistricting plan produced in the upper chamber. Though the house and senate are both dominated by Democrats, their plans had little in common. Perhaps the only notable point of agreement between them was the idea of moving toward a minority district centered in Boston. While the Finneran plan emanating from the house would have radically redrawn state lines, the senate proposal would keep 85 percent of Massachusetts voters in their current districts. More importantly, Marty Meehan's district would remain intact and other districts would be altered slightly to accommodate population shifts. As one media account put it, "Unlike the House plan, the Senate map only tinkers with the edges of the state's 10 US House districts."[24] The senator chairing the Joint Redistricting Committee explained that the senate "decided to do only incremental changes" and "emphasize continuity."[25] The differences between the house and senate plans thus reflected the interests of their leaders. Finneran and the house took dead aim at Meehan while Birmingham, who already had conspired to hinder Meehan's fundraising capabilities, chose to appease the congressional delegation.

The Republicans also felt obligated to offer a redistricting plan. Their goal was not so much to win approval of their plan—an unlikely prospect given the huge majorities held by Democrats in the state legislature—but to provide a reasonable alternative that might reveal cracks in the Finneran plan. Acting Governor Jane Swift also needed to demonstrate that she was a player in state policymaking. She had recently been the subject of a number of personal and financial scandals and had become governor only because of the resignation of Paul Cellucci in April 2001 to become Ambassador to Canada. Swift was also viewed by the media and public as a political amateur, being a thirty-seven-year-old woman who was juggling one-year-old twins and a 150-mile commute to the state capital from her home in the extreme western part of the state. Offering a sensible redistricting plan was thus one of many necessary steps for the fragile Republican governor to take, if only to create a sense of relevancy.

One thing the Swift and Birmingham plans had in common was protection of the ten congressional incumbents. Birmingham might have done this for predictable reasons, mainly to keep fellow Democrats happy prior to a statewide campaign. Swift might have done it to begin building bridges with congressional Democrats or simply to spite Finneran, who often caused her difficulty.[26] Republicans and senate Democrats were explicit about the fact that their plans protected incumbents. Senate President Birmingham admitted, "There's no reason to pit two incumbent Democrats against one another . . . it doesn't advance the common interest of Democrats."[27] And the chair of the Senate redistricting committee was equally blunt. "It is possible to help Southeastern Massachusetts without necessarily pitting two incumbent congressmen against each other."[28]

The main justification from senate Democrats for maintaining the status quo was influence in Washington. Though Birmingham might have personally wanted just to make incumbent House members happy, in public he emphasized the ability of incumbents to attract federal resources to the state. Beyond all of the other factors that arise in redistricting, Birmingham pointed out that "the clout of the delegation in Washington is an important consideration as well."[29]

This standard idea of "clout" was spun in unorthodox ways by others. Republicans like Swift reasoned that voters wanting to have influence in Washington might elect Republicans who could work with the Republican House and Bush administration. This point was not argued vigorously and in the end Swift supported the existing Democratic delegation. Finneran contended that a new incumbent might be a smart move in the 5th district since Meehan has spent more time doing national talk shows than serving the residents of the Merrimack Valley.[30] A more junior member who cultivated the district might be superior to a more senior incumbent pursuing goals unrelated to his constituent's interests.

But both of these rationales are weak compared with the motivation to retain existing incumbents. Journalist Thomas Oliphant observed as much when he condemned Finneran's map. He marveled, "as of today I have not heard of a single instance in American history where a state has discarded its congressional representation structure when it was not required to—either by the census-caused addition or elimination of seats or, more recently, by some significant population variation within districts in the nearly forty years since the one person, one vote principle was first applied by the U.S. Supreme Court to House elections."[31] In the summer of 2001 it looked as though Massachusetts might be the first.

Republican support for Democratic incumbents might be surprising to those who read the redistricting literature. The coalition to protect incumbent

Democrats was heavily Republican while the plan that axed the district of one incumbent Democrat originated in the most heavily Democratic institution in the state. Though the Republican plan might have been an insincere effort to win the favor of some politicians and confront others, the same could have been said of the Finneran plan. Both provided political cover for their decisions. In addition to arguing that his plan tidied up the 1990 map by creating more compact districts, Speaker Finneran also made an appeal for better racial representation to rationalize his proposal.

PROSPECTS FOR A MINORITY DISTRICT

In addition to the divisions that arose around partisanship, incumbency, and personal disputes, race and ethnicity played a role in the redistricting process, though a somewhat unexpected one.

Massachusetts is one of the most Democratic and socially liberal states in the nation.[32] The Bay State gave Gore 60 percent of the vote of the 2000 presidential election, ranking only behind Rhode Island and Washington, D.C. in its Democratic support. And Democratic voter registration outnumbers Republican almost three to one. Yet despite the diversity of the majority party, all 10 of its House members, both of its U.S. Senators, and all statewide elected officials were non-Hispanic Caucasians. Elected officials remained demographically homogeneous despite the fact that the 2000 Census showed that Anglo white population had shrunk to just half of Boston.[33] The growth of minorities in Boston and other communities had not been reflected in congressional representation, Boston mayor Thomas Menino argued, because the state lacked a "Boston district." The city was divided—cracked, some would say—by the 8th and 9th districts. This relegated minorities, who theoretically could have controlled a city-wide district, to small shares of the population in each of the House districts that included part of the city. Mayor Menino half-heartedly argued that the new plan ought to move the city into a single district to give minorities in Boston more voice and a better chance at "descriptive" representation.[34]

Creating the state's first majority-minority district would require real alterations to existing districts. Finneran's plan provided for some changes in Michael Capuano's historic 8th district by swapping some areas outside of the city for areas inside of it.[35] Capuano, only a second-term member and thus the most junior in the state's delegation at the time, seemed to accept this change to his district.[36]

The Finneran plan made just enough adjustments to create a new district that would be 51.49 percent minority according to his estimates. Not all agreed with Finneran's calculations. "One thing [Finneran's plan] doesn't do, all the hype to the contrary, is create a 'majority-minority' district. The redrawn 8th District would be 54.6 percent white."[37] More importantly, whether minorities constituted a literal majority or not, they were far from forming a cohesive voting bloc. "Of course, though the new 8th would be less than 50 percent white and more than half people of color, the ethnic minorities are so diverse—African-American, Caribbean, Asian-American, Hispanic—and often so politically inactive that a dream of a minority rep still seems far away."[38] Moreover, if one acknowledges the turnout disparities between whites and minorities, a higher threshold than 50 percent would be required.[39] Despite these issues, it remains surprising in some ways that racial and ethnic considerations were handled with so little controversy[40] and that other factors would be pivotal.

DÉNOUEMENT

Finneran's map had the effect of pushing Meehan out of rather than into the governor's race in Massachusetts. Within two weeks, Meehan had met with Finneran and announced that he would seek reelection to the House, asking for support from fellow Democrats to retain the district. Having lost his justification for eliminating the 5th, Finneran was forced to compromise with more reasonable senate Democrats in forging a map that would be acceptable to both.[41] The September 11 terrorist attacks also took attention from the matter.[42] Negotiations behind closed doors were hurried along in hopes that a joint plan could be approved before adjournment at the end of the year. Leaders failed to do that and returned to pass the plan in January. Acting Governor Swift rejected the legislature's plan in mid January and suggested the alternative map recommended by Republicans. She was soon overridden by the Democratic legislature and new districts were put into place for the 2002 elections. All in all, it was a quiet and rather anticlimactic ending to a surprisingly contentious redistricting season in Massachusetts.

The 2002 elections resolved some matters but only pushed others further into the future. Among members of the state congressional delegation, only Meehan faced a notable challenge. In the end he kept his House seat, though with a mere (by Massachusetts standards) 60 percent of the vote on Election Day, the lowest percentage among the state's ten representatives. In the end, Finneran's fears about Clean Elections seemed minor since only a few candidates even qualified for funding, and none of them was victorious. In the tight fiscal environment, the public financing system fell under attack. A Finneran-backed ballot measure allowed a majority of Massachusetts voters to express their displeasure with spending tax money on political campaigns. The gubernatorial race overshadowed this maneuver. The Democrats saw a contentious primary in which Birmingham finished third behind Shannon O'Brien, who was Finneran's preferred Democrat. O'Brien lost a spirited race to outsider Republican Mitt Romney in November, continuing divided government in the Bay State for a few years more.

Though redistricting was settled for another decade and a number of related issues were sewn up by Election Day, the Finneran-Meehan conflict remains unresolved. Both politicians are likely to remain key actors in Massachusetts politics and are likely to meet on redistricting or other matters in the future. For now Finneran remains the most powerful Democrat on Beacon Hill and will not immediately abandon the speakership. Meehan is likely to seek a U.S. Senate seat when Ted Kennedy retires in 2006 or when John Kerry seeks the presidency in 2004.[43] In short, federalism and intraparty battles are likely to continue mixing until the next round of redistricting following the 2010 census.

CONCLUSION

An important point to be taken from this case is that while the *effects* of districts are systematic and well understood, the factors that *cause* particular district lines to be drawn are less predictable. Political scientists can foresee with some certainty what kind of candidate will be elected from a particular district knowing just a few facts about the demographics of its residents, as Canon's (1999) distinction between the supply and demand of candidates makes clear. It is more difficult to explain how district lines will be drawn in the first place, even with a wealth of information at hand.

The case of Massachusetts is instructive because it shows that even the broad sets of categories thought to define redistricting debates are sometimes overshadowed by other idiosyncrasies. Raw data about the number of people living in various communities is essential for knowing how district lines might be drawn because the legal requirements for avoiding malapportionment are so strict in the United States. And one might expect racial or ethnic considerations to come in to play frequently because of the desires of interest groups, political parties, and courts to either heighten or diminish minority influence on national politics. Parties themselves compete for control of district lines. One can anticipate in most states how the Democratic and Republican redistricting plans might differ, and that the losing party might challenge the result. Finally, incumbents seek to protect themselves by minimizing changes in their districts, at least those that might make the district more hostile to their reelection. When a state loses one or more districts following reapportionment, at least one incumbent must depart in the next election.

Massachusetts saw few of these common themes at work. The state neither lost nor gained seats. One party—the Democrats—had veto-proof control of both chambers of the state legislature, making the Republican governor nearly irrelevant. It is hard to imagine a cozier relationship than an essentially one-party legislature drawing lines to protect a one-party delegation.

Nearly all of the players in Massachusetts are of the same party and even religion (Catholic); often ethnicity (generally Italian or Irish) and gender are the only factors distinguishing politicians from one another.[44] Though the growth of minority populations in Boston and elsewhere might have prompted the creation of a majority-minority district, there was little serious movement in that direction. In short, redistricting should have been easy.

Despite all of these factors working in favor of speedy and uncontroversial redistricting, serious disagreements appeared. This "family feud" erupted not *despite* the absence of friction on standard fronts of conflict but *because* the Massachusetts 2000 case lacked conflict on these other, more conventional dimensions.[45] The dearth of "big issues" such as loss of a seat, racial considerations, or partisan disputes allowed for some unexpected factors to come into play. In particular, the intersection of campaign finance reform efforts at the state and national levels elevated the friction between one member of Congress and the Speaker of the Massachusetts House. The absence of traditional districting cleavages left a vacuum in which federalism, ambition, and personal conflicts surfaced. Few academic accounts in the literature on redistricting would have predicted that the McCain-Feingold legislation would have lead to a radical map proposal from the Massachusetts House of Representatives. The 2002 gubernatorial race, which was to feature Senate President Birmingham and perhaps Congressman Meehan, was part of the story as well. All of these items fall under the heading of "unanticipated consequences."

Redistricting is fascinating because it pits conflicting goals against one another. Legal standards such as compactness are often difficult to reconcile with minority representation. A frequent trade off—that was also important in Massachusetts—is the coherence of district identities versus retaining incumbent clout. Any serious effort to protect incumbents likely undermines community representation. Finneran justified jeopardizing Meehan's place in Congress by unifying southeastern Massachusetts in a single district. Thus, one region's clout competes with the influence of a particular representative in Washington. Trade-offs like these are widely recognized and are thus not too surprising in this case. But the Massachusetts case demonstrates that the range of goals in conflict is wider than previous acknowledged. Most obvious are the unexpected side effects of federalism. In this case it was manifest as personal and policy disagreement between state and federal office holders. These disagreements—particularly between Speaker Finneran and Representative Meehan—spilled over to the redistricting process, perhaps because there are few other outlets for such conflicts to expose themselves. Disagreements over campaign finance laws among other factors provided

Finneran with the motivation to elevate an interpersonal dispute to a full-fledged family feud. The combination of vesting state politicians with the power of redistricting, federalism, and widespread progressive ambition makes this possible.

It is perhaps ironic that such unexpected conflict in the redistricting process occurred in the backyard of the father of strategic line drawing: Elbridge Gerry. Gerry had been an important part of the American founding as vice president, a member of Congress, and signer of the Declaration of Independence. As has been recounted elsewhere, after being elected governor of Massachusetts in 1810, Gerry drew attention when he proposed an odd looking legislative district around Boston in 1812. An editorial cartoonist added wings and a head to the district silhouette, making it appear as a sort of salamander. The hybrid term "gerrymander" was born. Ironically, many of the communities featured in the original *Boston Weekly Messenger* cartoon are found in Meehan's 5th district today. It is even more poignant that Gerry's great-grandson, Elbridge T. Gerry, passed away at age 90 just as the bickering over Clean Elections was spilling into the upcoming redistricting process. More symbolic is that a portrait of the original Gerry still hangs across from Speaker Finneran's office door.

NOTES

1. The term "family feud" was used in an August 31, 2001 *New York Times* editorial to describe Massachusetts redistricting. It is also the title of a television game show that has been airing almost constantly since the 1970s.

2. Joseph A. Schlesinger, *Ambition and Politics: Political Careers in the United States* (Chicago: Rand McNally, 1966).

3. David Butler and Bruce Cain, *Congressional Redistricting: Comparative and Theoretical Approaches* (New York: Macmillan Publishing, 1992).

4. For example, Bernard, Grofman, ed., *Race and Redistricting in the 1990s* (New York: Agathon Press, 1998).

5. As will be made clear below, the term "matching funds" is misleading. Public funds supplied to Clean Elections candidates far exceed their own fundraising.

6. Scott LeHigh, "Public Funds for Elections Endorsed," *Boston Globe*, 11 October 1998, B1.

7. "Family Feuds in Massachusetts," *New York Times*, 13 August 2001, A16.

8. Gary C. Jacobson, "Practical Consequences of Campaign Finance Reform: An Incumbent Protection Act?," *Public Policy* 24 (Winter 1976): 1–32.

9. R. Douglas Arnold, *The Logic of Congressional Action* (New Haven, Conn.: Yale University Press, 1990) and David R. Mayhew, *Congress: The Electoral Connection* (New Haven, Conn.: Yale University Press, 1974).

10. This ended Meehan's legislative quest, but the battle over campaign finance at the national level did not end there. Senator Mitch McConnell (R-KY) and other opponents of McCain-Feingold immediately launched legal challenges to the measure.

Litigation and court rulings are ongoing today, rendering the future of the Bipartisan Campaign Reform Act unclear.

11. LeHigh, "Public Funds."

12. Glen Johnson and Rick Klein, "Colleagues Back Meehan on Districts," *Boston Globe*, 27 July 2001, A1.

13. It is an ironic fact that Meehan first won his seat in 1992 following a radical redistricting that harmed an incumbent. Representative Chester Atkins' district was redrawn to make him vulnerable.

14. Some insiders seriously doubted these motivations. See Thomas Oliphant, "Finneran's Proposal Is a Loser for the State," *Boston Globe*, 29 July 2001, D7.

15. A more conventional strategy would have been to target the 9th district where long-time incumbent Joseph Moakley was retiring. A new member was to be elected in a special election slated for the fall of 2001.

16. David R. Guarino, "Pols Lend Support to Controversial Finneran Plan," *Boston Herald*, 12 July 2001, 4.

17. Guarino, "Controversial Finneran Plan."

18. Glen Johnson, "Mass. Delegation Drawing a New Map," *Boston Globe*, 27 March 2001, A1.

19. Vincent G. Moscardelli, "Politics, Geography, and the Ghost of Elbridge Gerry: Majority-Minority Districting in Massachusetts in the 21st Century" (paper presented at the annual meeting of the American Political Science Association, Boston, Mass., August 2002).

20. Thomas B. Edsall, "Rep. Meehan Takes a Hit—From Fellow Democrats," *Washington Post*, 22 July 2001, A5.

21. Scot Lehigh and Frank Phillips, "Finneran's Tough Talk Catches Congressmen Off Guard," *Boston Globe*, 21 January 1999, A1.

22. Edsall, "Rep. Meehan Takes a Hit."

23. Support from the party establishment might not matter in a state where one wins the party nomination simply by winning a primary election. In Massachusetts, Democratic candidates must secure the support of at least 15 percent of delegates attending the summer Democratic convention. Delegates are a combination of party elites such as local elected officials and party activists who are nominated in town and city caucuses. The support necessary from inside the party establishment makes it difficult for candidates from outside such as Robert Reich (who earned a meager 15.85 percent at the convention).

24. Frank Philllips, "Minorities Welcome U.S. House Map Plan," *Boston Globe*, 25 September 2001, B2.

25. Shaun Sutner, "Meehan and McGovern Winners in Plan," *Worcester Telegram & Gazette*, 25 September 2001, A1.

26. National Republicans were not as accepting as Swift of a continuing Democratic delegation. Former Massachusetts state legislator and current Bush Chief of Staff Andrew Card complained while touring the state that the delegation was unfairly asking, "Please protect us all." Andrew Miga, "Frank Flips on Meehan Support," *Boston Herald*, 28 July 2001, 4.

27. Philllips, "Minorities Welcome U.S. House Map Plan."

28. Ellen J. Silberman, "Senate Leaders: Meehan's Seat Safe," *Boston Herald*, 10 August 2001, 5.

29. Brian C. Mooney, "Redistricing Fight Renews House-Senate Rivalry," *Boston Globe*, 10 August 2001, B6.

30. Lehigh and Phillips, "Finneran's Tough Talk."

31. Oliphant, "Finneran's Proposal."

32. Gerald C. Wright, John C. McIver, Robert S. Erikson, and David B. Holian, "Stability and Change in State Electorates, Carter through Clinton" (paper presented at the annual meeting of the Midwest Political Science Association, Chicago, April 2000).

33. In fairness, the Census also showed Massachusetts to be 85 percent white, non-Latino. This is about 10 points higher than the national average.

34. Hanna F. Pitkin, *The Concept of Representation* (Berkeley, Calif.: University of California Press, 1967).

35. Over the last half century, only John F. Kennedy, Thomas P. "Tip" O'Neill, and Joseph P. Kennedy had held the seat centered in Cambridge.

36. As noted above, a new member would be elected in the 9th district upon Moakley's departure.

37. Jeff Jacoby, "Finneran's Map Passes the Test," *Boston Globe*, 16 July 2001, A11.

38. Wayne Woodlief, "Remap Plan Makes Sense, Mischief," *Boston Herald*, 12 July 2001, 33.

39. Charles Cameron, David Epstein, and Sharyn O'Halloran, "Do Majority-Minority Districts Maximize Substantive Black Representation in Congress?" *American Political Science Review* 90, no. 4 (December 1996): 794–812. David Lublin, *The Paradox of Representation: Racial Gerrymandering and Minority Interests in Congress* (Princeton, N.J.: Princeton University Press, 1997).

40. Vincent G. Moscardelli, "Politics, Geography, and the Ghost of Elbridge Gerry."

41. Finneran mistakenly thought that only the house was responsible for congressional redistricting. After a reporter corrected the speaker by pointing out that the senate is an equal partner, an embarrassed Finneran apologized, saying, "You are vindicated and I am educated." Mooney, "Redistricting Fight."

42. Some were arguing that redistricting differences should have been papered over to bring political stability in difficult times. Wayne Woodlief, "Stability Has to Come First—Conflict over Redistricting Must End Soon," *Boston Herald*, 30 September 2001, 29.

43. The governor has the power to appoint a replacement should Kerry abandon his seat. When it appeared that Swift would lose the governorship to a Democrat, Meehan might have considered himself a possible appointee. Since Romney won, Meehan would likely have to run against an appointed Republican to hold the seat.

44. Corey Dade, "Ties that Bind," *Boston Globe*, 25 October 2002, B1.

45. The actors involved are a "family" in more ways than one. In addition to all being leaders of the Democratic Party in Massachusetts, nearly all are Roman Catholic, of Irish (or occasionally Italian) heritage, and Baby Boomers.

12

Iowa and the Political Consequences of Playing Redistricting Straight

Peverill Squire

One of the more curious aspects of the 2002 U.S. House elections was that contests in Iowa took center stage on the national scene The state is used to playing a leading role in the presidential nomination process because of its first-in-the-nation caucuses. But with only a handful of seats, House races in Iowa typically get little attention in the rest of the country. In 2002, however, the situation was far different; House races in Iowa were much more competitive than were contests in the rest of the country, and the national press took note. The *Washington Post*, for example, observed, "There are as many competitive seats at play in Iowa's five congressional districts . . . as there are in the 133 districts of Texas, California, Illinois, and New York."[1] A similar appraisal was offered in a story by a prominent *New York Times* reporter, "Iowa has five representatives in the House and three competitive races, more than any other state. California has fifty-three seats and only one remotely competitive race."[2] Clearly, an unusual amount of the nation's electoral action in 2002 was in Iowa.

But why would that be the case? Iowa, after all, has just one percent of the nation's population and, accordingly, just one percent of the seats in the House. Why should Iowa corner the market on competitive House elections? Both the *Post* and the *Times* pointed to the same explanation: the state's unique redistricting system. Only in Iowa are the congressional (and state legislative) district lines drawn by a nonpartisan legislative bureau that by law cannot take into account any information on voting patterns, or even where incumbent legislators live. In virtually every other state partisan information drives the redistricting process, with districts created to either advance the majority party's interests or to protect incumbents. The result is that one party or the other enjoys a distinct advantage in almost every congressional district in the country. But that is not the case in Iowa. Redistricting produces districts where both parties have every reason to think they can win.

In this chapter I explain how Iowa came to adopt a redistricting system that works to produce competitive elections instead of giving either incumbents or parties built-in advantages. I then examine how the process has unfolded in each of the three decades it has been used. Finally, I explore the effects of redistricting on U.S. House races in Iowa in 2002.

THE ADOPTION OF IOWA'S REDISTRICTING PROCESS

How did Iowa come to adopt a redistricting scheme so out of the ordinary? The events leading to the establishment of the novel redistricting process started with the series of U.S. Supreme Court decisions handed down in the 1960s that revolutionized the rules governing how legislative district lines were to be drawn around the country.[3] The series of U.S. Supreme Court's decisions requiring the use of "one-person, one-vote" redistricting standards pushed Iowa to amend its constitution in 1968 to bring the state's redistricting requirements into conformity with the new national rules. In addition to adopting the U.S. Supreme Court's population standard, the constitutional amendments also made several other noteworthy changes in Iowa's redistricting practices. First, it was specified that none of the state's 99 counties could be split between two or more congressional districts.[4] Second, state legislative districts had to be compact and contiguous.[5] Third, the redistricting plan had to be adopted and signed into law by September 15 of the year following the decennial census, or the Iowa State Supreme Court would be charged with producing a plan by December 31 of that year.[6] And finally, the state supreme court retained original jurisdiction for all litigation arising from redistricting and was given the power to produce the redistricting plan if it found the plan produced by the legislature to be unconstitutional.

These changes set the stage for a protracted struggle over redistricting in Iowa following the 1970 census. In 1971, the Republican controlled legislature produced a redistricting plan signed by the Republican governor into law that disgruntled Democrats took to the Iowa State Supreme Court. The state supreme court found that the plan's range ratio—the population difference between the largest population district and the smallest population district—was too large in both the state senate plan and the state house plan, putting each plan in violation of the one-person, one-vote standard. The state supreme court further found that the differences in population across the districts created by the legislature were not as limited as they could have been and that the deviations from numerical equality were driven by the legislature's desire to both "facilitate keeping present members of the legislature in office," and to provide district boundaries that avoided "having such members contest each other at the polls."[7] In addition, the state supreme court concluded that the legislative plan produced districts that were not compact.[8] Thus the state supreme court held that the state legislative district lines had been drawn to meet the needs of incumbent legislators and did not satisfy the standards imposed by the U.S. Supreme Court and the Iowa state constitution.

Having tossed out the redistricting plan adopted by the state legislature, the state supreme court found itself compelled by the state constitution to produce its own plan. This they did with the technical assistance of the state legislature's nonpartisan Legislative Service Bureau. The state supreme court's redistricting plan had much smaller range ratios than the legislative plan and it met other constitutional standards as well.[9] Thus the state legislative lines Iowa lived with during the 1970s were drawn by the state supreme court, not the state legislature.

As the need to redistrict once again drew near in 1979, the partisan rancor that had accompanied the passage of the legislative redistricting plan and the subsequent court battle over it earlier in the decade still lingered. But partisans on both sides of the political divide had come to recognize that the plan produced by the state supreme court had been fair and that neither the Republicans nor the Democrats had enjoyed any electoral advantage under it. Thus there was a desire on the part of some members of the state legislature to devise a method of redistricting that would produce a similar neutral outcome.

Legislation to do just that first germinated in a small subcommittee of the state House of Representative's Committee on State Government.[10] The plan produced by the subcommittee covered redistricting for both U.S. House seats and the state legislature and it contained several essential features. First, it relied on the legislature's nonpartisan Legislative Service Bureau to draw the initial redistricting proposal considered by the legislature.[11] That plan could only be voted up or down by the legislature, no amendments would be allowed. If the first plan failed to pass, the Legislative Service Bureau would produce a second plan. It too could not be amended by the legislature, only voted up or down. If the second plan failed, the Legislative Service Bureau would produce a third plan. Only this plan could be amended by the legislature. The House bill stipulated that in developing its redistricting plans the Legislative Service Bureau was to consult with a special committee composed of legislative leaders.

The idea that the initial drawing of district lines should be taken from the legislature enjoyed considerable support in Iowa political circles. But alternatives to the specific plan developed by the subcommittee soon surfaced. Governor Robert Ray, a popular Republican in his eleventh year in office, wanted a public commission to be charged with drawing the lines. But that proposal generated little interest in the state house because it would completely remove the legislature from the redistricting process. Representatives argued that redistricting was ultimately a responsibility assigned to the legislature and that they should retain that function.

When the subcommittee's plan reached the house floor it enjoyed impressive bipartisan support. There were nine substantive amendments offered to alter the plan and all were rejected by comfortable margins.[12] On final passage the measure received 97 votes in favor and no votes in opposition.

The state senate did not take up the redistricting process bill until the following year. And when it did finally take it up, serious reservations were expressed. Many state senators argued that the house plan would place too much political pressure on the Legislative Service Bureau. They proposed instead to create a five-member redistricting panel and charge it with drawing district lines. Under their counter proposal the majority leader and minority leader in each legislative chamber would appoint one panel member, and the four appointed members together would choose the fifth panel member. The senate's proposal stipulated that lobbyists, elective officeholders, candidates for office, and relatives of incumbents could not serve on the redistricting panel. The senate passed its plan overwhelmingly, 46 votes in favor to only two in opposition.[13]

The competing redistricting process plans were reconciled through compromise. Members of the house strongly opposed the main thrust of the senate's proposal to create a redistricting panel because they feared it would produce plans that represented political trade offs. Negotiators from the house and senate agreed to keep the house's proposal allowing the Legislative Research Bureau to draw the initial set of plans and two subsequent plans if needed. Senators opposed the house's idea of having legislative leaders consult with the Legislative Service Bureau on the drawing of plans and that idea was dropped from the final bill. Instead, the redistricting panel envisioned in the senate's bill was transformed into a Temporary Redistricting Advisory Commission, a body charged with holding hearings around the state to allow opinions on the proposed plans to be expressed in a fashion that would deflect the political heat away from the Legislative Service Bureau. The senate gained one other concession from the house. The house plan was to govern only the redistricting process for the 1980s. The senate prevailed in making the process permanent.[14]

THE MECHANICS OF THE REDISTRICTING PROCESS IN IOWA

Iowa's redistricting process as created by law in 1980 is unusual but relatively straightforward. Once the U.S. Census Bureau releases the census data for Iowa the Legislative Service Bureau takes that information and prepares the initial redistricting plan. The plan must meet the population equality standards established by the federal courts and other requirements in the Iowa law. The latter require that none of the state's 99 counties be split between two or more U.S. House districts, and that House districts be contiguous and compact.[15] Iowa law also states that district lines shall not be drawn to the advantage of a political party or legislative incumbent, or any other person or group. To ensure this the law explicitly states that certain information is not to be used in drawing district lines, including the home addresses of incumbent legislators, party registration data, voting histories, and demographic data other than those required by federal law.

Assuming that the Census Bureau delivers the population data to the state on time, the Legislative Service Bureau is required to submit its first redistricting plan to the state legislature by April 1 of the year following the census. By this point in the process the Temporary Redistricting Advisory Commission has already been appointed, with the majority party and minority party leaders in each house each designating a member, and the four legislative appointees selecting the fifth member. Iowa law states that commission members must be eligible voters in the state, but may not be elective officeholders, employees of the U.S. Congress or state legislature, or related to an employee of either legislative body.

Once the Legislative Service Bureau's first plan is sent to the legislature, the Temporary Redistricting Advisory Commission is required to make information on the proposed lines available to the public and to hold at least three public hearings on the plan. Each hearing is to be held in a different geographic area of the state. Following the end of the scheduled hearings, the commission is required to submit a report to the state legislature. After the commission's report is submitted, the state legislature must bring the initial redistricting plan up for a vote in one of the chambers expeditiously after a mandatory seven-day wait. If the plan passes in the first chamber, the second chamber must deal with it promptly. A constitutional majority is required in both houses to pass the plan. No amendments are allowed to the plan.

Should the first plan fail to pass in either chamber, the Legislative Service Bureau is required to develop and submit the second plan. In devising the second plan, the Legislative Service Bureau may take into account whatever reasons the state senate or house of representatives gives for rejecting the first plan, assuming those reasons do not conflict with federal or state law. The second plan must be submitted to the state legislature within twenty-one days after the first plan fails to pass the legislature, or May 1, whichever date is later. The Temporary Redistricting Advisory Commission is not required to hold hearings on the second plan. As with the first plan, the state legislature is expected to take up the second plan quickly—seven days after its submission. And again, the legislature must vote the plan up or down; no amendments are allowed.

Should the second plan fail, the Legislative Service Bureau is required to develop a third plan. This plan must be submitted by June 1, or within 21 days after the second plan failed to pass, whichever date is later. Again, the legislature must wait seven days after the plan has been submitted before bringing it up for a vote. Unlike the first two plans, however, the third plan can be amended by the legislature until a plan garnering a constitutional majority in each house is achieved. The governor must sign any redistricting plan that passes the legislature.

THE EXPERIENCE WITH REDISTRICTING IN IOWA IN THE 1980S AND 1990S

How has Iowa's redistricting process worked in practice? The first two plans developed by the Legislative Service Bureau in 1981 failed to pass the GOP-controlled state legislature for partisan reasons. The first plan placed two Republican U.S. House incumbents in the same district; the second plan split the two incumbents but gave one of them a district with strong Democratic leanings. Republicans were careful, however, to couch their rejection of the plans in nonpartisan language, citing a very small deviation in population across the districts as justification for the negative responses. The third plan developed by the Legislative Service Bureau also raised the ire of the GOP because they calculated that under it another of their U.S. House incumbents would have a difficult time winning reelection. But Republicans feared that the public would not look favorably on their party if it tinkered with the third plan and they passed it without amendment.[16]

What were the political consequences of the 1981 redistricting plan as it played out over the five elections it covered? During the 1980s not a single U.S. House incumbent from Iowa failed to win reelection. So from that perspective, the Legislative Service Bureau plan that was finally adopted by the state legislature might look like an incumbent protection plan. But during the decade four incumbents retired from the House, and in three of those cases the opposing party won the open seat. And in the fourth case, the winning candidate who held on to the seat for his party—Republican Jim Nussle—did so by only 1,642 votes, or just 1 percent of all the votes cast.

In 1991, the second time the process was employed, redistricting went more smoothly, even though the basic task facing the state was much more challenging. Because Iowa's population declined during the 1980s, the state lost a seat in the U.S. House in the 1990 reapportionment, dropping to five seats from six seats. The state legislature, now under the control of the Democrats, approved the first plan submitted by the Legislative Service Bureau with overwhelming bipartisan majorities.[17] The plan greatly shuffled U.S. House district lines in Iowa, but neither party calculated that they would be greatly disadvantaged. The most conspicuous outcome of the plan was that two incumbents—Republican Nussle and Democrat Dave Nagle—were forced into the same district. Nussle again squeaked through to victory, this time by 2,966 votes, again just 1 percent of the votes cast. Despite having to introduce themselves to many new constituents, the other four incumbents were reelected.

Over the rest of the decade of the 1990s the redistricting plan had much the same partisan consequences as had the 1980s plan. Although most U.S. House contests in the state were competitive, only one incumbent was defeated by a challenger—in the 1994 GOP landslide Democrat Neal Smith, an eighteen-term House veteran lost to his Republican challenger, plastic surgeon Greg Ganske. But once again open-seat contests offered the out party a chance to claim a seat. While a Republican replaced one Republican incumbent who retired from the House, a Democrat replaced the other retiring Republican.

REDISTRICTING IN 2001

The redistricting process in Iowa began routinely in 2001. The Legislative Service Bureau delivered the initial redistricting plan to the state legislature on April 12. The Temporary Redistricting Advisory Commission then held its three required public hearings on the plan in different parts of the state: Sioux City, Iowa City, and Des Moines. The Commission's report on the hearings was turned over to the state legislature on April 25.

The district lines for the U.S. House in the first plan generated considerable partisan anxiety on the part of Republicans because two GOP incumbents, Jim Leach and Jim Nussle, were placed in the same district. State legislators also had their own concerns about the plan because the lines for the state house and state senate districts placed 70 of the 150 state legislators in districts with other incumbents.[18] Generally, Democrats supported the lines, but the Republican majority opposed them.

On April 30, the state house committee assigned to review the plan passed it on to the full chamber without a recommendation, signaling that it was likely to fail. On May 2, however, the state senate beat the house to the punch and rejected the plan on a 27 to 21 vote. Only one Republican voted for the plan.[19] The Senate vote obviated the need for the house to vote on the plan.

In rejecting the first redistricting plan the senate took the opportunity to advise the Legislative Service Bureau of its reasons for doing so. Most of the senate's stated objections revolved around claims that the population deviation across the districts in the first plan strayed too far from the ideal population standard. The senate then went on to criticize the first plan for failing to "reflect urban and rural interests in our state to the extent consistent with the Iowa Code," claiming that the proposed lines "regionalized Iowa at the Congressional level."[20] Republicans voiced particular concerns that the first plan created a western Iowa district that encompassed thirty-two mostly sparsely populated counties and stretched from the Minnesota border in the north to the Missouri border in the south. The worry was that the large district would isolate the western third of the state.

The Legislative Service Bureau's second plan was delivered to the state legislature on June 1. The new plan responded in part to the concerns expressed by the senate on the first plan. Population deviations were further reduced from the already low deviations in the first plan as the senate had requested. But the Legislative Service Bureau noted in presenting the second plan that Iowa law makes no provision for considering urban and rural interests in devising district lines. In addition, the Bureau observed that the Senate's "resolution provided no definition of 'regionalized' and provided no guidance as to why the first plan failed in this regard or how this concept is consistent with the requirements of [the law]."[21]

The congressional district lines in the second plan did differ from those in the first plan. But, for the most part, the GOP's major reservations about the initial set of lines were not removed by the second plan. Republican incumbents Nussle and Leach were still placed in the same district. And, although some counties were shuffled out of the large district in western Iowa, others were shuffled in, and the lines still encompassed thirty-two counties and still stretched from Minnesota to Missouri. But the GOP's ability to campaign against the second set of lines was greatly reduced by the Legislative Service Bureau's success in reducing the population deviations. As table 12.1 shows, the overall range for the second U.S. House plan—the population difference between the most populous and the least populous districts—was only 134 people. Given that the ideal district population size was 585,625 people, being off at most by forty people too many or ninety-four people too few was a remarkable achievement, especially with the constraint that each of the state's ninety-nine counties had to be wholly contained within a House district. That the population deviations were so small was a testament to both the Legislative Service Bureau's skill in devising the plan and the fact that many of Iowa's counties contain so few residents that shifting them around allowed the Bureau to create five districts with virtually identical population sizes.

Although there was some grumbling about the second set of district lines—one Democrat in the state house characterized them as "bizarre, awkward, crazy, embarrassing"—both state legislative chambers passed them easily and with bipartisan support. The vote on June 19 was seventy-eight to eighteen in favor in the house, and thirty-seven to thirteen in support in the senate. Some legislators were reconciled to the lines, rationalizing that they were "as good as we're likely to see." Others were more supportive of the process, with the

Table 12.1. Iowa House 2001 Redistricting Plan and Its Political Consequences in the 2002 U.S. House Elections

District Number	*Total Population in District*	*Percent Deviation from Ideal District Population*	*Deviation From Ideal District Population*	*Percent District Vote for Gore in 2000 Election*	*Percent Vote for Winner in 2002 House Election*
1	585,302	0.006%	37	52.2	57.2 Nussle (R)
2	585,241	−0.004%	−24	53.1	52.2 Leach (R)
3	585,305	0.007%	40	49.0	53.4 Boswell (D)
4	585,305	0.007%	40	48.0	54.8 Latham (R)
5	585,171	−0.016%	−94	39.8	62.1 King (R)

Sources: Iowa Legislative Service Bureau, "Second Redistricting Plan," June 1, 2001, as corrected on June 18, 2001; Iowa Secretary of State, Official Canvas Summary, December 2, 2002; National Committee for an Effective Congress, "Iowa: New Congressional Districts for 2002."

Republican chair of the House State Government Committee, Janet Metcalf, commenting, "No one political party can grab the process and write a plan that gives it a disproportionate advantage."[22]

THE EFFECTS OF REDISTRICTING IN THE 2002 ELECTION

Was the redistricting plan as politically neutral in the 2002 elections as supporters of the process might claim? Adoption of the plan certainly had immediate consequences for two of Iowa's incumbent members of the U.S. House. As soon as the congressional lines passed the state legislature, Representative Jim Leach changed his residency from his lifelong home in Davenport to Iowa City, thereby changing House districts and avoiding a contest against his fellow Republican Jim Nussle. Shortly thereafter, the lone Democrat in the House delegation, Leonard Boswell, announced that he too would move. His home in Davis City was located in the large and very Republican 5th district in the western part of the state. He opted to move to Des Moines where the new 3rd district was open because GOP Representative Greg Ganske, who would have run in the district, chose to run instead for the U.S. Senate. (Many state legislators faced similar dilemmas; the new lines placed sixty-four of them into districts with other incumbents, forcing many of them to move, retire, or face a bruising electoral battle.)[23]

District lines that are drawn without regard to partisan considerations should produce more competitive races. As the 2000 presidential vote in each of the new House districts given in table 12.1 demonstrates, four of the five districts were closely divided between the two parties. Only the 5th district was heavily tilted in favor of one party, in this case the Republicans. In the other four districts both parties could easily envision a scenario where they could capture the seat. But every district, save for the 5th, was being contested by an incumbent. The challenge in those districts was for the out party to recruit a quality challenger.

By most measures, several of the challengers who took on Iowa's incumbent representatives in the 2002 elections were not the politically experienced candidates usually associated with competitive races. The contest in the 2nd district, for example, pitted the thirteen-term GOP incumbent Jim Leach against Julie Thomas, a Cedar Rapids pediatrician. Des Moines lawyer Stan Thompson took on Democratic incumbent Leonard Boswell in the 3rd district. The Democratic challenger to Republican incumbent Tom Latham in the 4th district was John Norris, a former chair of the state party and chief of staff to the governor. None of these challengers had ever held elective office. Only in the 1st district, where Republican Representative Jim Nussle faced Bettendorf Mayor Ann Hutchinson did an incumbent face a high-quality challenger by most political science measures.

Although, on paper, Iowa's House challengers did not appear to be among the stronger candidates running for office in 2002, the fact that they were among the few running in districts that were not gerrymandered in favor of an incumbent or a party gave them credibility with campaign contributors. All four of the House challengers in Iowa were able to run serious campaigns, as their fundraising totals demonstrate. In a campaign year where the median House challenger raised a bit less than $62,000, the lowest sum raised by an Iowa challenger was Republican Thompson's $900,829. Each of the three Democratic challengers raised over $1 million, with Thomas leading the way with $1,346,597. Thus, House challengers in Iowa, Republican and Democrats alike, had more than enough money to finance competitive races.

In the end, even with their vast financial war chests, none of Iowa's challengers won. This outcome was, of course, the same for virtually all of their counterparts throughout the country. But Iowa's races were competitive. As shown in the final column in table 12.1, several of Iowa's House races were very close and none could even remotely be called a landslide for the incumbent.

CONCLUSIONS

The political consequences of playing redistricting straight in Iowa are subtle but important. Using a redistricting process that avoids maps gerrymandered to serve the interests of a party or incumbents does not result in dramatically different election outcomes, at least superficially. The system does not imperil incumbents; in the eleven elections in which lines drawn by Iowa's redistricting process have been used, U.S. House incumbents have won fifty-one races and lost only one.[24] Thus, in terms of election outcomes, incumbency advantages clearly trump Iowa's redistricting scheme. But, House races in the state are competitive and challengers generally get access to the resources they need to run credible campaigns. The real benefits of playing redistricting straight, however, appear in open-seat contests. Since the introduction of Iowa's redistricting system there have been eight open-seat races for the House. Of those contests, five resulted in a change in party control of the seat, a far higher percentage than found in the rest of the country.[25] In the final analysis, Iowa's redistricting system creates legislative elections where the desires of the electorate determine election outcomes rather than having them ordained in advance by the cartographical machinations of parties and politicians.

NOTES

1. "It All Comes Down to This," *Washington Post*, 6 October 2002, 3(B).

2. Adam Clymer, "The Nation: Democracy in Middle American; Why Iowa Has So Many Hot Seats," *New York Times*, 27 October 2002, 4(1).

3. The Legislative Service Bureau of the Iowa General Assembly has produced a very useful redistricting guide on which I rely heavily in this section. See Iowa General Assembly—Legislative Service Bureau, December 2000, "Legislative Guide to Redistricting," <http://www.legis.state.ia.us/Central/LSB/Guides/redist.htm> 12 June 2003.

4. Iowa Constitution, Article 3, section 37.

5. Iowa Constitution, Article 3, section 34.

6. Iowa Constitution, Article 3, section 35.

7. *In re Legislative Districting of General Assembly*, 193 N.W. 2d at 789 (Iowa 1972).

8. *In re Legislative Districting*, at 791.

9. The court's plan is given in *In re Legislative Districting of General Assembly*, 196 N.W. 2d 209 (Iowa 1972), and corrected in part in *In re Legislative Districting of General Assembly*, 199 N.W. 2d 614 (Iowa 1972).

10. The subcommittee had three members: Republicans Nancy Shimanek of Monticello and James Anderson of Brayton, and Democrat Jean Lloyd-Jones of Iowa City. Lloyd-Jones had been a plaintiff in the court case that had resulted in the 1971 legislative redistricting plan being declared unconstitutional. She was later elected to the Iowa House of Representatives.

11. The story of the development of the redistricting process bill on the House side is taken from the House Journal and from Charles Bullard, "House OKs Non-Partisan Plan for Reapportionment by 1981," *Des Moines Register*, 29 March 1979, 4A.

12. Backers of the redistricting process bill did accept three amendments that corrected minor problems with their original proposal.

13. See the account in Bonnie Wittenburg, "Senate Wants Panel to Draw New Districts," *Des Moines Register*, 10 April 1980, 4A.

14. See "Fair Redistricting," *Des Moines Register*, 9 May 1980, 18(A).

15. Iowa Code 42.4, subsection 4 provides a description of a compact district and two measures of compactness.

16. See the discussion in Phil Duncan, "New Iowa Map: No Gerrymandering Allowed," *Congressional Quarterly Weekly Report*, 19 September 1982, 1798–1801.

17. The state senate passed the plan on a 39 to 10 vote and the House followed the next day with a 93 to 7 vote in favor. See Rhodes Cook, "Iowa Remapping Goes Smoothly as Six Districts Become Five," *Congressional Quarterly Weekly Report*, 18 May 1991, 1306.

18. Jonathan Roos, "Remap Plan Expected to Fail in House," *Des Moines Register*, 1 May 2001.

19. Jonathan Roos, "senate Rejects Redistricting Plan," *Des Moines Register*, 3 May 2001.

20. Senate Resolution 50 as quoted in Iowa Legislative Service Bureau, "Second Redistricting Plan," 1 June 2001 as corrected on 18 June 2001.

21. Iowa Legislative Service Bureau, "Second Redistricting Plan."

22. The quotes and vote totals are from Lynn Okamoto and Jennifer Dukes Lee, "Lawmakers OK New Map," *Des Moines Register*, 20 June 2001.

23. See Okamoto and Lee, "Lawmakers OK New Map," and Lynn Okamoto, "Redistricting Gives Legislators Opportunities, Tough Choices," *Des Moines Register*, 21 June 2001.

24. This calculation does not count the Nussle and Nagle, incumbent versus incumbent race in 1992.

25. See Norman J. Ornstein, Thomas E. Mann, Michael J. Malbin, *Vital Statistics on Congress 1999–2000* (Washington, D.C.: AEI Press, 2000), 45.

IV

REDISTRICTING IN THE NEW MILLENNIUM: PROBLEMS AND SOLUTIONS

13

Redistricting in Texas: Institutionalizing Republican Ascendancy

Seth C. McKee and Daron R. Shaw

The growth of Republicanism in Texas is striking. The GOP currently holds the governorship, the two U.S. Senate seats, and both the Texas senate and house. They have not lost a single statewide election since 1998. According to exit polls, the Republicans enjoy a party identification advantage of about three points. Nonetheless, there is a notable exception to GOP hegemony: Democrats currently hold half of Texas' thirty-two U.S. House seats.[1]

This chapter seeks to explain why the Republican Party was unable to attain majority status in the Texas U.S. House delegation before the 2004 elections. In particular, we focus on the electoral impact of redistricting on partisan competition in Texas congressional elections over the past decade—from 1992 to 2002. The main argument is simple: after the 1990 Census, Texas Democrats countered a Republican electoral tide by crafting a highly effective partisan gerrymander. Thus, despite Republican gains in Texas congressional contests, the redistricting plan and incumbency advantage enabled the Democrats to hold onto a majority of the Texas delegation up through the 2002 elections.

We also contend that contradictory legal rulings have produced a tendency for redistricting plans to replicate the broad contours of existing districts to (1) gain the support of incumbent office holders, and (2) satisfy voting rights mandates. This tendency was initially evident in redistricting in Texas in 1992 and after the 2000 Census, but is now under siege. In the wake of the 2002 elections, Texas legislators passed a new redistricting map that will increase the number of Republican congressional districts. In fact, Republican Governor Rick Perry called for multiple special sessions of the legislature in order to redraw the state's congressional map. Since early May of 2003, redistricting news has been plentiful and this chapter makes an effort to note and contextualize the key developments leading up to the Republican plan enacted for the 2004 elections.

Our analyses proceed as follows: first, we provide a primer on redistricting that identifies the precedents defining the legal parameters for Texas redistricting plans. Second, we review and evaluate the partisan impact of redistricting in Texas, starting with the districts in place before the 1990 Census. Third, we provide a summary of the current redistricting fight, which began in earnest when Republican lawmakers proposed a bill that would have redrawn the districts to benefit their candidates. Fourth, we analyze the likely electoral effects of the enacted Republican plan whose earlier incarnations provoked first House and then Senate Democrats into leaving the state in parliamentary maneuvers designed to deny the Republicans legislative quorums necessary to instate new congressional district lines. Finally, we conclude with a brief discussion on the role of race in Texas politics and mention the broader implications of the Republican plan enacted for the 2004 elections.

LEGAL PARAMETERS FOR TEXAS REDISTRICTING

Interestingly, there are no legal requirements prescribed for congressional districts in the Texas Constitution.[2] This means that only federal law is germane with respect to redistricting. Consequently, in this section we discuss several federal legal precedents[3] that shape congressional redistricting in the state of Texas.[4] More specifically, we discuss (in turn) the equal population rule, the Voting Rights Act (VRA) and subsequent court decisions, and the limited precedent with respect to partisan gerrymandering.

Equal Population Requirement

In the landmark case of *Baker v. Carr* (1962), the Supreme Court determined that the judiciary had a role to play in regard to malapportionment—the unequal distribution of the number of voters in districts.[5] In this decision the Court "held that federal courts have jurisdiction over claims that state legislative apportionments violate the Fourteenth Amendment, that such claims are justiciable . . . and that residents of malapportioned districts have standing to sue."[6] However, the Court did not establish the one-person, one-vote standard for congressional districts until its 1964 ruling in *Wesberry v. Sanders*.[7] More recent case law has made it clear that there are very few conditions where a violation of the one-person, one-vote principle is permissible.[8] Furthermore, given the precision of contemporary computer technology, even miniscule deviations from population equality (based on the official census data) evoke considerable suspicion. A state must demonstrate a compelling interest for failing to meet the one-person, one-vote rule. Furthermore, if this justification passes judicial scrutiny, it must accomplish the state's objective with the smallest (compared to other plans) deviation from population equality.[9]

According to the 2000 Census, the 2002 Texas congressional redistricting plan (1151C) contains individual district deviations indistinguishable from zero (0.00 percent). The ideal congressional district population for Texas is 651,619.[10] Under plan 1151C, the actual deviation from the ideal population of any district is never more than one person and no district is below the ideal population.

The Voting Rights Act and Subsequent Court Decisions

The Voting Rights Act (VRA) of 1965 reaffirmed the franchise to Southern blacks who had long been denied the vote through state-enforced legal impediments.[11] In particular, sections 2 and 5 of the VRA provide limitations on the state's discretion in crafting redistricting plans. Section 2 "prohibits a state or a political subdivision of a state from using any 'standard, practice, or procedure,' including a redistricting plan, 'which results in denial or abridgement of the right of any citizen of the United States to vote on account of race or color' or membership in a protected language minority group." In short, the original purpose of Section 2 was to enforce the "Fifteenth Amendment to the U.S. Constitution."[12] With the tremendous increase in voter registration among Southern blacks following passage of the VRA, however, many states in the South[13] used redistricting as a means to dilute the votes of its black citizens.[14] A revision, or at least a reinterpretation of Section 2 was therefore necessary to prevent minority vote dilution.[15]

The courts provided such a reinterpretation by ruling that a challenge to redistricting plans that purportedly weakens the voting strength of minority groups does not have to establish a discriminatory intent. Rather, a much lower evidentiary threshold has to be met—a districting plan will be held in violation of Section 2 if it is proven that the *effect* of the plan would result in minority vote dilution.[16] Using the Texas Legislative Council's definition, minority vote dilution is:

> the creation of districts that either (1) divide members of a racial or ethnic minority group among several districts, artificially reducing the group's opportunity to influence elections . . . or (2) place extraordinarily high percentages of members of a racial or ethnic minority group in one or more districts, so that minority voting strength is artificially limited to those districts and is minimized in neighboring districts.[17]

The case of *Thornburg v. Gingles* (1986) set a three prong test that must be satisfied in order to contest a redistricting plan on the grounds that it "results in members of a racial or language minority group having less opportunity than the general electorate to elect representatives of their choice:[18]

1. the minority group submerged in the multimember district is sufficiently large and geographically compact to constitute a majority in at least one single-member district;
2. the minority group is politically cohesive and votes as a bloc; and
3. the majority in the multimember district votes sufficiently as a bloc to enable it to usually defeat the minority group's preferred candidates in the multimember district.[19]

In addition to meeting the three-part threshold in *Gingles*, it is necessary for plaintiffs to "demonstrate that, based on the totality of the circumstances, the challenged election structure denied them an equal opportunity to participate in the political process and to elect candidates of their choice." As a legal matter, it has been a virtual foregone conclusion that if the *Gingles* test is satisfied, then a plan will be found to violate Section 2.[20]

As applied to Texas, in accordance with legal precedent set by the Fifth Circuit Court (which has jurisdiction over Texas, Louisiana, and Mississippi), under the first prong of the *Gingles* test a minority population must be geographically compact and able to constitute a majority "of the voting-age citizen population" in order to create a majority-minority district.[21] For congressional districts, this standard is high considering the large population of noncitizen Hispanics and the more compact, comparatively smaller black voting-age populations located in the urban cores of Houston and the Dallas-Fort Worth Metroplex. Under the congressional boundaries valid for the 1990s, the combined voting-age populations of Hispanics and blacks in the above-mentioned urban areas, however, have enabled the creation of several districts (the 18th and 24th in the Metroplex and the 25th, 29th, and 30th in Houston) that are majority-minority because their Hispanic and black populations vote as a bloc and are thus politically cohesive.[22]

Ironically, Texas was not subject to Section 5 of the VRA until 1975, "when Congress expanded the scope of the act beyond race and color to include language minorities."[23] Section 5 of the VRA requires certain states, including Texas, to submit districting plans to the Department of Justice (DOJ) and/or the U.S. District Court for the District of Columbia in order to get approval for the plan before it takes effect. This requirement under Section 5 is commonly referred to as preclearance. There are two options under the preclearance requirement—and the state of Texas must exercise one of the options prior to enacting a new plan:

1. obtain a declaratory judgment from the U.S. District Court for the District of Columbia that the voting change does not violate the substantive standards under Section 5; or

2. submit to the justice department a voting change to which the department does not interpose an objection.[24]

With respect to its impact on minority voting rights, the legal standard for meeting the preclearance requirement under Section 5 is considerably less than the precedent established by Section 2. In *Beer v. United States* (1976), the Supreme Court "held that changes in election laws are entitled to preclearance unless they 'lead to a retrogression in the position of racial minorities with respect to their effective exercise of the electoral franchise.'"[25] In other words, the Court allows for preclearance of plans that do not leave minority groups *worse* off under the new districting plan compared to the last binding plan (referred to as the benchmark).

Furthermore, "even if the change [under the new plan] perpetuates existing discrimination, it is entitled to preclearance unless it actually increases the degree of discrimination."[26] This precedent was upheld in subsequent cases including *Reno v. Bossier Parish School Board* (*Bossier I*, 1997). The Court thus made it clear that retrogression was the only legal objection for a denial of preclearance under Section 5. This ruling was important because the DOJ had denied preclearance for the Bossier Parish School Board's redistricting plan on the grounds that the plan was in violation of Section 2. The Court overruled the position of the DOJ by affirming the district court's opinion, finding that a Section 2 inquiry is not appropriate ". . . because the two sections were designed to 'combat different evils' and to adopt the view that preclearance must be denied whenever a covered jurisdiction's plan violates Section 2, would . . . abandon the retrogression standard under Section 5."[27]

In the 1990s round of redistricting, at the behest of the DOJ, legislators were informed, "'the Voting Rights Act requires you to create as many minority controlled districts as physically possible.'"[28] This was questionable advice and, beginning with *Shaw v. Reno* (*Shaw I*, 1993), the Court invalidated several majority-minority districts because they constituted racial gerrymanders in violation of the Equal Protection Clause of the Fourteenth Amendment.[29] In *Shaw I*, the Court held that race-based districting would be subject to strict scrutiny and majority-minority districts would have to be 'narrowly tailored' to meet a 'compelling state interest.'[30] Race could no longer be the predominant factor in designing majority-minority districts. This ruling was fine-tuned and elaborated in the subsequent cases of *Miller v. Johnson* (1995), *Bush v. Vera* (1996), and *Shaw v. Hunt* (*Shaw II*, 1996).

In *Miller*, the Court stated that the shape of a district did not by itself invalidate a district and thus a district may have a shape that does not raise suspicions and still be unconstitutional if race was the primary justification for creating the district.[31] In *Vera*, the Court declared three Texas congressional districts (the 18th, 29th, and 30th)[32] unconstitutional racial gerrymanders because race was the predominant factor in designing these districts despite the state's admission:

> that its foremost districting principles were to seek partisan advantage and to protect incumbents. It routinely ignored compactness and respect for political subdivisions when necessary to further these "higher" principles.[33]

In *Shaw II*, the Court was willing to allow "compliance with section 2 [to] be a compelling state interest but concluded that the challenged district was not narrowly tailored to accomplish that objective."[34]

In the most recent and relevant redistricting decision, *Hunt v. Cromartie* (*Cromartie II*, 2001), the Court indicated that in the absence of an admission that race was the overriding purpose in creating a district, it will be more difficult for challengers to prove race was the predominant factor. In this case, the Court "concluded that . . . race and political affiliation were so highly correlated."[35] This is an important clarification by the Court because, as Butler points out:

> As a practical matter, *Cromartie II* modifies *Vera*'s holding that race cannot be used as a proxy to accomplish other objectives. The distinction between the *impermissible* use of race in *Vera* and the *permissible* use in *Cromartie II* appears thin.[36]

In sum, the Court has provided a very narrow legal space for redistricting plans with majority-minority districts. As Butler puts it, "legislators can be justifiably anxious that they will be 'damned by the Constitution' if they consider race and 'damned by the Voting Rights Act' if they do not . . . and their best efforts may yet be undone by the change of a single vote on the Court."[37] Nonetheless, the ruling in *Cromartie II* provides some flexibility in defense of race-based redistricting because the Court acknowledges the difficulty in separating race from party affiliation, and if the overriding rationale of a districting plan furthers a partisan as opposed to racial purpose, it is likely that the plan will survive strict scrutiny.

Turning our attention back to the Lone Star State, the court-ordered plan for the 2002 Texas congressional elections was on safe ground with respect to issues of minority vote dilution because it preserves the integrity of the majority-minority districts established under the last binding plan (1000C). In the opinion of the three-judge panel (U.S. District Court for the Eastern District of Texas, *Balderas v. Texas*, 2001) that drew the lines for the 2002 congressional districts:

> We have endeavored to ensure that the plan complies with the goals of sections 2 and 5 of the Voting Rights Act.
>
> Our plan works no retrogression. We have maintained intact the existing districts, and, to the extent the boundaries have changed, as we "zeroed out" the

plan, the minority populations have been either enhanced or not diminished in any meaningful way (i.e., by mere fractions of percentages).[38]

Partisan Gerrymandering

The main point on partisan (political) gerrymandering is simple: the courts have not been willing to uphold plaintiffs' claims of voter discrimination. In the 1986 case of *Davis v. Bandemer*, "the Supreme Court expressly held that claims by members of a political party that a redistricting plan discriminates against them in violation of the Equal Protection Clause were justiciable."[39] More instructively, a plurality of the Court issued a two-part test plaintiffs would have to meet in order to prove a partisan gerrymander in violation of Equal Protection:

1. an intent to discriminate against a political group; and,
2. an actual discriminatory effect on that group.[40]

Meeting the first requirement—intent to discriminate—has not been difficult. The Court has considered direct evidence, such as statements "by those in control of the redistricting process," as well as circumstantial evidence (i.e., shape of districts, greater protection of the majority party's incumbents, etc.), as proof of "partisan intent to discriminate."[41] In several cases, both types of proof have yielded considerable evidence of partisan gerrymanders.

Passing the second part of the test, a discriminatory effect, has thus far been insurmountable. In *Badham v. March Fong Eu* (1989) a federal district court delineated a two-prong test to establish discriminatory effect:

1. a history of disproportionate results; and,
2. strong evidence that the plaintiffs lacked political power and were denied fair representation.[42]

The problem here for plaintiffs is that the courts have taken an extremely broad view of the second prong. Similar to cases involving minority vote dilution, "'unconstitutional discrimination occurs only when the electoral system is arranged in a manner that will consistently degrade . . . a group of voters' influence on the political process as a whole.'"[43] Even the most blatant examples of partisan gerrymandering have not met this "virtually unattainable standard of proof for success."[44] Butler concludes that, "it appears . . . the only practical limitations on partisan gerrymandering are those imposed by state law and legislative self-restraint."[45] In a recent decision regarding partisan gerrymandering in Pennsylvania, *Vieth v. Jubelirer* (2004), the opinion of the Court cast strong doubt that any districting plan could exhibit a politically motivated gerrymander so severe as to warrant legal redress.[46] The ruling in *Vieth* suggests Texas' 2004 congressional map will pass Supreme Court scrutiny.

REDISTRICTING AND ELECTORAL OUTCOMES: THE CASE OF TEXAS, 1990 TO 2002

Against this legal backdrop, the 1991 Texas redistricting plan (C657) was an unabashed Democratic gerrymander.[47] Richard Niemi and Alan Abramowitz point out that, "in Texas . . . the Republicans had a 5.8 percent higher average vote in 1992 than in 1990 but won virtually the same proportion of seats (29.6 percent in 1990, 30.0 percent in 1992)."[48] This plan remained in effect until the *Vera* ruling invalidated three districts (18th, 29th, and 30th) as racial gerrymanders, and forced the state to reconfigure the lines of thirteen districts.[49] In its plurality opinion in *Vera*, the Court acknowledged that Texas' districting plan amounted to "a mixed motive case" because race and incumbency protection were both stated goals. But the Court avoided taking on the issue of partisan gerrymandering and instead focused on the use of race in drawing districts 18, 29, and 30. Contending that race was the "predominant factor," the Court ruled the plan unconstitutional.

The dissent's opinion in *Vera*, however, makes a stronger case (in our view) that the racial motivation was subordinated to the Texas Democrats' intention to create a partisan gerrymander, and that this partisan motivation accounts for the "bizarre" shapes of districts 18, 29, and 30. These districts could have been made more compact, but only at the risk of weakening the Democratic vote in neighboring districts presided over by Anglo Democratic incumbents (i.e., Metroplex Representatives Martin Frost in District 24 and John Bryant in District 5).[50]

For redistricting after the 2000 Census, it is important to keep in mind that there is a residual partisan bias favoring the Democrats because the last effective plan (1000C)[51] kept in place many of the district lines from the 1991 plan.[52] More specifically, race-based redistricting was a means to further the partisan ends of Texas Democrats after 1990,[53] and so "any plan [for the 2002 congressional elections] necessarily begins with a Democratic bias due to the preservation of protected majority-minority districts, all of which contain a high percentage of Democratic voters."[54]

Partisan Effects of Race-Based Redistricting

The 1990s round of redistricting deserves partial credit for bringing about the Republican House majority in the Congress after the 1994 elections.[55] In the South, race-based redistricting has generally had the effect of aiding the electoral prospects of Republican candidates. The insistence on the part of the Department of Justice (DOJ) to require states to maximize the number of majority-minority districts[56] benefited Republicans because black populations were packed into majority-minority districts. Put another way, substantially greater percentages of blacks were drawn into these districts than was necessary for them to elect a representative of their choice.[57] The flipside of this is that large portions of black votes were wasted because they were not needed to elect the preferred candidate of the minority population. These excess or surplus votes would have been better used in neighboring districts to aid the election campaigns of Anglo Democrats.

As it turned out, several of the districts adjacent to majority-minority districts favored Republican candidates because the reduction in their black voting-age populations resulted in constituencies that were more disposed to vote Republican.[58] There was "a realization on the part of Republicans that creating majority-minority districts tended to substitute a black Democrat for a white one, and to enhance the election of Republicans in the now 'whiter' surrounding districts."[59] The reduction in the number of white Democrats was most evident and pronounced in the Deep South[60] states where modest population growth after the 1990 Census resulted in a net gain of zero seats and the creation of five new majority-black districts. For white Democrats in the Deep South, the lack of additional seats[61] following the 1990 reapportionment made it more difficult to create majority-minority districts and, at the same time, limit the harmful electoral effects of reducing the black populations in surrounding districts. In short, the combination of a lack of population growth and the creation of several majority-black districts made white Democrats in the Deep South states susceptible to electoral defeat.[62]

The packing of minority voters in the 1990s through the creation of majority-minority districts was a departure from the typical method of vote dilution employed by Southern line drawers. In the days of the Democratic Solid South, cracking (or fragmenting) was the preferred redistricting technique that Southern white Democrats used to disfranchise black voters—especially after passage of the VRA.[63] Cracking is accomplished by drawing district lines in a way that fragments and disperses votes across multiple districts.[64] Historically, in Southern states like Texas, Anglo Democrats fragmented voting districts to dilute minority votes, and hence foreclose the possibility of electing black or Hispanic candidates.[65] But in the 1990s, with the rise of the Republican Party in Southern congressional elections, these same redistricting methods (packing and cracking) were used to effectuate partisan gerrymanders.[66]

Texas Is Different: Democrats Use Race to Their Partisan Advantage

Texas was the exception that proved the rule of majority-minority districts resulting in Republican seat gains. As mentioned previously, because of its booming population, Texas gained three seats following the 1990 reapportionment, increasing its total to thirty. Compared to the rest of the Southern states, Texas has the smallest percentage of blacks and the largest percentage of Hispanics. The significantly higher growth rate of Texas' minority population[67] provided a much-needed buffer that enabled Texas Democrats to comply with the DOJ's majority-maximization decree and at the same time further a Democratic gerrymander.[68]

With Texas' black population confined mainly to the urban cores of Houston and the Dallas-Fort Worth Metroplex (smaller concentrations of black populations are scattered in East Texas), the 1991 plan (C657) configured Districts 18 (Houston) and 30 (Dallas) for the purpose of electing black candidates. The plan accomplished this goal with less than majority-black voting-age populations (BVAPs) in both districts (48.6 percent BVAP in the 18th and 47.1 percent BVAP in the 30th), although adding their respective Hispanic voting-age populations (HVAPs) brought the minority voting-age populations of these districts to more than 60 percent. Less than 7 percent (2/30) of Texas' congressional districts were designed to elect black candidates. The relatively small percentage of the black populations (compared to majority black districts created in the rest of the South) in these districts and their dense urban locations foreclosed the possibility of a ripple effect of reduced minority populations in surrounding districts thought to be promising for Republican candidates. As the dissenting opinion argues in the *Vera* case, these districts—along with the 29th, a majority Hispanic district with an Anglo Democratic representative (Gene Green)—had tortured shapes because the intention was to satisfy both the majority-minority maximization position of the DOJ as well as to further a Democratic gerrymander.

The state's large Hispanic population proved advantageous to Texas Democrats because Texas' Hispanic voters favor the Democratic Party. Under the 1991 plan, out of the seven Hispanic majority districts, Democratic incumbents represent six. In the twenty-one Anglo-majority districts, the Democrats packed Republican voters in suburban growth areas where it was clear the Democrats could not win and protected "white urban Democrats, long dependent on black votes, [by giving them] . . . districts where Democratic rural counties were substituted for urban black neighborhoods."[69] Packing was the preferred method used to dilute Republican votes under plan C657. In the words of Earl and Merle Black:

> Texas Democrats had packed most Republican voters into a small number of metropolitan/suburban districts, creating safe havens for a handful of Republican incumbents. Just as concentrating black voters into a few districts reduced the Democratic vote in neighboring districts, so also conceding Republican victories in a few seats benefited Democratic prospects in adjacent districts. . . . Likely Republican voters were concentrated into eight districts that had "voted

at least 68 percent for Bush in 1988," a tactic that helped make Republican congressional candidates uncompetitive in many other districts. Far from destabilizing the Texas delegation, reapportionment and redistricting enabled Texas Democrats to perpetuate their traditional advantage for another decade.[70]

The Importance of Race and Evidence of Republican Vote Dilution, 1992 to 2002

In this section we present evidence that points to the enduring effectiveness of the Democratic plan (C657) instated for the 1992 elections. We argue that race, with the exception of party identification, remains the most reliable indicator of vote choice[71] in Texas congressional elections. Moreover, we show how race has shaped the contours of political competition[72] and contributed to the dilution of the Republican vote.

Table 13.1 provides summary statistics on many key aspects of Texas U.S. House races from 1990 through 2002. Clearly, even with the addition of five seats through reapportionment between 1990 and 2002, there is a Republican trend. The number of Republican representatives increases from eight in 1990 to fifteen following the 2002 election. Incumbent defeats have been extremely rare; only four (three Democrats and one Republican) have occurred over these seven elections. Open seat pickups from the other party have been even more uncommon. Perhaps less obviously, by looking at the average vote margin and the average two-party winning percentage for Democrats and Republicans, it is evident that more Republican votes have been wasted. Victorious Republicans have consistently won by much greater margins in contested elections and hence their corresponding winning percentages have remained higher throughout these election years.

Data on the changing racial composition of Texas congressional districts tell another, more complex story. For Democratic members, the Anglo voting-age population was 58 percent in 1992—by 2002 it was reduced to 46 percent. By contrast, the Hispanic voting-age population increased 10 percentage points (26.5 percent to 36.5 percent) for Democratic districts between 1992 and 2002, while the black voting-age population has held fairly constant. In GOP-held districts, the average percent of the African American and Hispanic voting-age populations are substantially lower, but note that these minority proportions have steadily increased because of the higher rate of minority population growth. On its face, it appears then that the Republican trend is relatively stronger than the concomitant increase in Texas's minority population, since Republican candidates have fared better in more recent elections (at least as gauged by Republican votes).

A simple and common way to assess the impact of race on partisan outcomes is to regress the party vote on a district's racial composition.[73]

Table 13.1. Vital Statistics on Congressional Districts in Texas U.S. House Elections, 1990 to 2002

Election	*1990*		*1992**		*1994*		*1996*		*1998*		*2000*		*2002*	
Party	D	R	D	R	D	R	D	R	D	R	D	R	D	R
Incumbents	18	8	18	8	16	9	12	9	16	13	17	12	16	12
Newly Elected	1	0	3	1	3	2	5	4	1	0	0	1	1	3
Contested Seats Won	10/14	4/14	18/25	7/25	19/25	6/25	17/29	12/29	11/19	8/19	11/21	10/21	12/23	11/23
[a]Defeated Incumbents	0	0	1	0	2	0	0	1	0	0	0	0	0	0
[b]Open Seats Won	0	0	0	0	0	0	0	2	0	0	0	0	0	0
[c]AVAP % (avg.)	77.7	87.8	57.9	77.7	56.3	76.8	55.3	75.1	47.7	67.5	46.8	66.3	46.0	67.0
[d]HVAP % (avg.)	22.1	9.5	26.5	15.2	28.0	14.7	28.5	15.9	35.9	21.3	35.9	21.3	36.5	20.9
[e]BVAP % (avg.)	13.1	6.4	14.2	4.1	14.2	5.8	14.7	6.6	14.5	7.6	14.6	7.7	14.9	7.2
[f]Vote Margin % (avg.)	20.4	41.6	25.0	44.1	22.2	33.8	25.7	39.5	22.0	32.8	28.2	33.9	25.1	38.5
[g]Win % (avg.)	60.2	70.8	62.5	72.0	61.1	66.9	62.8	69.7	61.0	66.4	64.1	67.0	62.5	69.2
N	**19D**	**8R**	**21D**	**9R**	**19D**	**11R**	**17D**	**13R**	**17D**	**13R**	**17D**	**13R**	**17D**	**15R**

Notes: The authors compiled the data from *The Almanac of American Politics (1991–2001)*, the 1990 and 2000 U.S. Censuses, the Texas Legislative Council, the Texas Secretary of State, and *CQ's Congressional Elections (1998)*.

*Texas gained three House seats following the 1990 reapportionment and two House seats after the 2000 reapportionment.

[a] Defeated Incumbents = incumbents who were defeated by candidates of the opposing party.

[b] Open Seats Won = open seats won by candidates of the party opposite the previous incumbent.

[c] AVAP = Anglo voting-age population; one race only for 2000 Census data (1998, 2000 and 2002 elections). In 1990 Anglo voting-age population includes Hispanic voting-age population.

[d] HVAP = Hispanic voting-age population; not confined to a racial classification.

[e] BVAP = Black voting-age population; one race only for 2000 Census data (1998, 2000 and 2002 elections).

[f] Vote Margin = the average margin of victory for each party for contested seats (two-party percentage).

[g] Win = the average percentage of the two-party vote for contested seats won by each party.

Table 13.2 estimates the probability of electing a Democratic representative (1 = Democrat, 0 = Republican) in Texas congressional elections from 1990 through 2002 as a function of the percentage of a district's African American and Hispanic voting-age populations. The data indicate that the percentage of blacks has a noticeably stronger positive effect than the percentage of Hispanics on the likelihood of a Democratic member. This difference is rendered even more interpretable in table 13.3, which presents the probabilities (derived from the logit estimates from table 13.2) of electing a Democrat based on selected Hispanic and black district percentages.

Given the importance of race on election outcomes, it is hardly surprising that the most vulnerable incumbents are those whose party affiliation is out of step with the racial composition of their districts. After the 2002 elections, seven Anglo Democrats represented districts with majority Anglo populations, and one Hispanic Republican resided in a majority Hispanic district. Based on presidential voting behavior in these districts, several of these representatives appear to be marginal. In the short-term, however, incumbency has proven to be sufficient to get several of these members reelected to the House. As we demonstrate later, the 2004 plan (1374C) endorsed by Republican U.S. House Majority Leader Tom DeLay, seeks to increase the GOP's share of the Texas delegation by slicing up the districts of Anglo Democrats who represent majority Anglo constituents.

Even without addressing the fundamental importance of race in shaping political strategy and deciding elections, the simple pattern of votes in Texas congressional elections from 1990 to 2002 sheds light on the ingenuity of the Texas Democrats.[74] First, by isolating contested districts (Democrat vs. Republican) we can classify votes as effective, surplus, and wasted.[75] And second, using the more common measure of seats to votes ratio, we can show the extant Democratic bias in Texas congressional elections.

Table 13.2. Likelihood of a Democratic Representative, 1990 to 2002

Independent Variables	*Coefficient (se)*	*t*
Black Voting-Age Population	25.07*	6.01
	(4.17)	
Hispanic Voting-Age Population	5.92*	6.00
	(0.99)	
Intercept	−3.28*	−6.08
	(0.54)	
N	209	
Log Likelihood	−95.61	
Pseudo R^2	.32	

Source: Unless otherwise stated, all data for tables and figures (and throughout this study) are from the authors' data set, which was constructed from the sources cited in Table 1.

*$p < .000$; coefficients are logit estimates with standard errors in parentheses. Dependent variable is coded 1 = Democrat, 0 = Republican.

Table 13.3. Probabilities of a Democratic Representative, 1990 to 2002

HVAP (%)	*BVAP (%)* 0	*5*	*10*	*15*	*20*	*25*	*30*
0	.04	.12	.32	.62	.85	.95	.99
5	.05	.15	.38	.68	.88	.96	.99
10	.06	.19	.45	.74	.91	.97	.99
15	.08	.24	.53	.80	.93	.98	.99
20	.11	.30	.60	.84	.95	.98	>.99

Note: Probabilities derived from logit estimates in Table 13.2.

By definition, we classify effective votes as those that count toward winning an election. In other words, effective votes constitute the simple majority (50 percent plus one) and thus are only cast in a contest the party wins. Surplus votes are a party's votes that exceed the simple majority (effective votes) won by the party. Wasted votes are all votes cast for the party that loses the election. By sorting votes into these categories, we expect that the Texas Democrats should have substantially more effective votes (and fewer wasted votes) than the Republicans. The expectation for surplus votes is not as clear. On the one hand you have majority-minority districts, which are dominated by Democratic representatives and should have large surpluses. On the other hand, you have Republican members controlling a few districts that were packed with Republican voters under the 1991 plan.

Figures 13.1, 13.2, and 13.3 present the data for effective, surplus, and wasted votes by party. As expected, the Democrats have a much greater per-

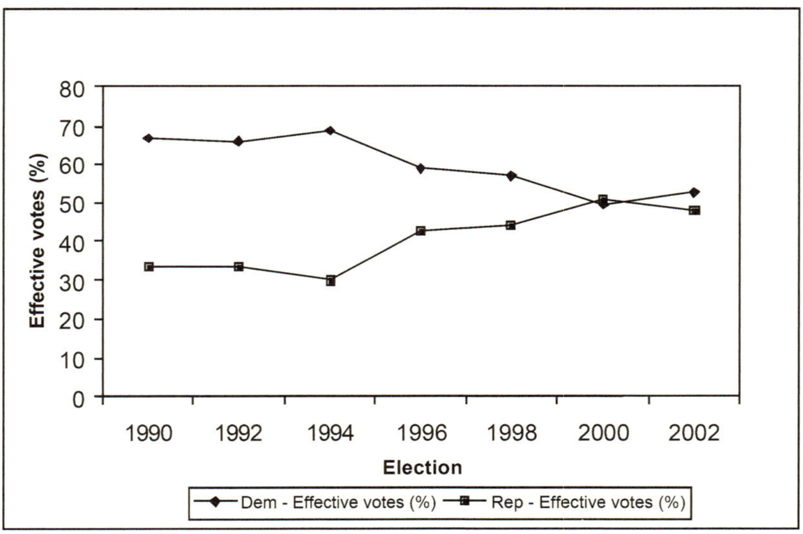

Figure 13.1. Effective Votes by Party, 1990 to 2002

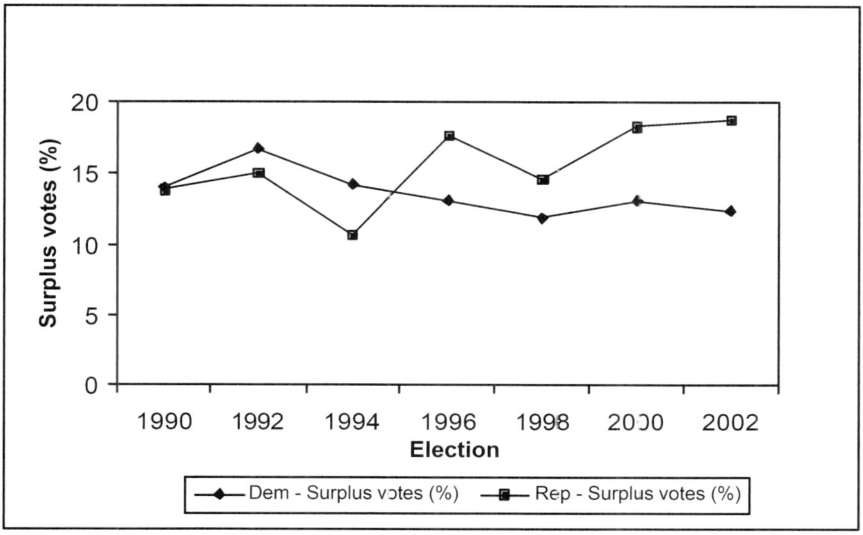

Figure 13.2. Surplus Votes by Party, 1990 to 2002

centage of effective votes. The Republican trend is evident in later elections as the gap narrows (the GOP actually received more effective votes in 2000, 51 percent vs. 49 percent). Democrats have a slim lead in surplus votes until 1996, when Republicans henceforth win contests with more votes to spare than their Democratic counterparts. Part of the frustration among Republicans is the large portion of surplus votes that would, of course, be more

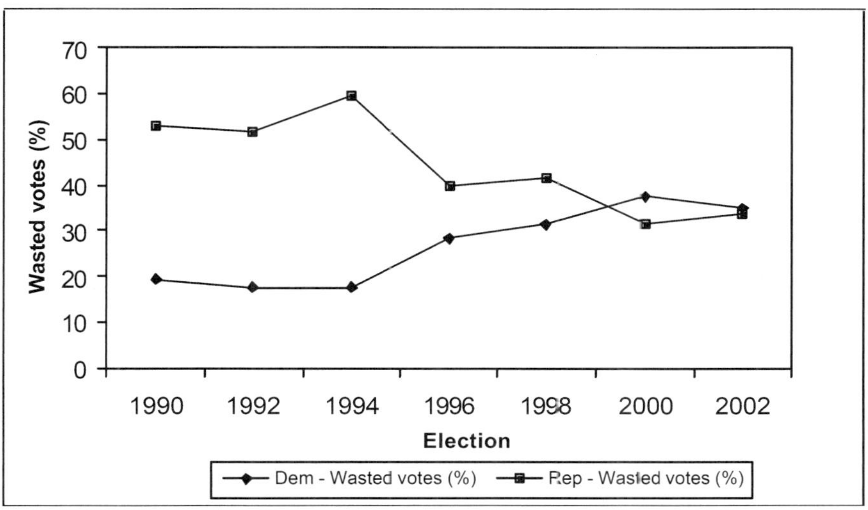

Figure 13.3. Wasted Votes by Party, 1990 to 2002

effective with favorable redistricting. With respect to wasted votes, Republican candidates have fared much worse than Democrats, but again the trend favors the GOP. Republicans received proportionally fewer wasted votes in the last two elections (31 percent vs. 38 percent in 2000, and 33 percent vs. 35 percent in 2002).

Another way to assess the structure of party competition is to calculate the seats to votes ratio. If the percentage of seats is greater than the accompanying portion of votes (> 1), the party is exceeding expectations. Or, in more colloquial language, the party is getting more bang for its electoral buck. Although there is inherent bias in a single-member, simple plurality system because the percentage of seats rarely matches the percentage of votes won, when this ratio is markedly different from one, there is strong evidence of partisan bias.

Figure 13.4 presents the seats to votes ratio for the Democratic Party for (a) all seats and (b) contested seats. Remember, if the ratio is greater than one, then a party is winning more seats than votes. The data indicate a strong Democratic bias in districting. For instance, in 1994—an exceptionally bad year for Democrats across the board—Texas Democratic candidates received only 43 percent of the two-party vote, but won 63 percent of the congressional seats. Among contested races in 1994, Democratic candidates won 52 percent of the vote and 76 percent of the seats. Still, despite this evidence of an effective Democratic gerrymander, the Republican trend is evident in the decline in the seats to votes ratio for more recent elections.

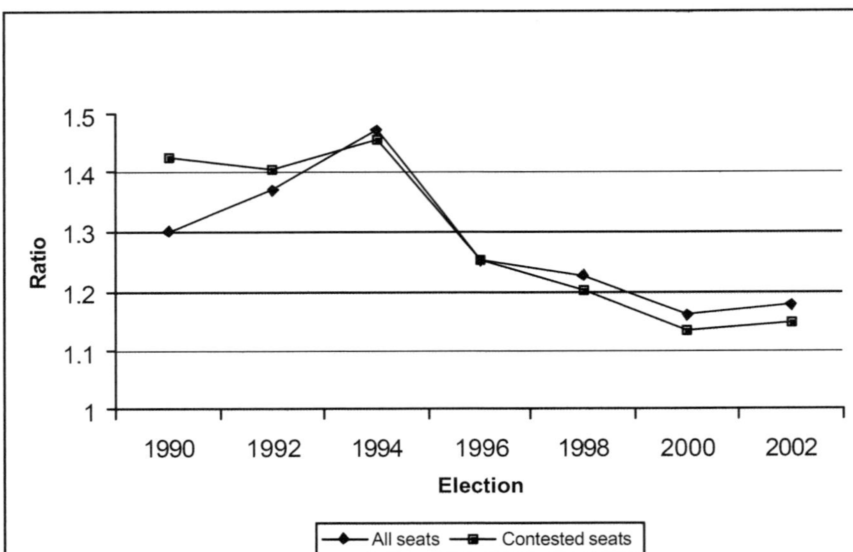

Figure 13.4. Democratic Seats to Votes Ratio, 1990 to 2002

Redistricting and At-Risk Seats

In 1990 there were twelve Anglo Democrats representing majority Anglo districts. In these districts, the average of the 1992 and 1996 Republican presidential vote (two party) was 50.8 percent.[76] After the 1992 election, there were thirteen Anglo Democrats in majority Anglo districts and yet the average GOP presidential vote (1992 to 1996) declined to 49.6 percent. This finding further suggests the effectiveness of the Democratic redistricting. The number of Anglo Democrats with majority Anglo districts was eleven in 1994, 9 in 1996, and seven from 1998 to 2002. It took until the 1998 elections for the average Republican presidential vote to return to over 50 percent in the majority Anglo districts represented by Anglo Democrats.

As mentioned earlier, because of the importance of race in Texas politics, Anglo Democrats from districts that voted for Republican presidential candidates (so-called "split results" districts[77]) are politically vulnerable.[78] Some of these Anglo Democrats are particularly at-risk given that the number of Anglo Democrats representing majority Anglo districts has declined considerably since 1990. In fact, the GOP has targeted split-result districts across the country and, not surprisingly, this is where the party has had its most success.[79] Under the 2002 map, only one Republican had a split-result district, Henry Bonilla (District 23), whose district has a 63 percent Hispanic voting-age population. In 2002, the average Democratic presidential vote (1992 to 1996) in Bonilla's district was 51 percent.

Table 13.4 presents a comparison of the number of Democratic and Republican candidates in at-risk and safe seats based on the average presidential vote (1992 and 1996 elections) of the party that corresponds to the political affiliation of the representative (e.g., the Democratic presidential vote for Democratic members).[80] These data indicate the Democrats have more at-risk members. If we consider all members whose party garnered less than 52 percent of the presidential vote, five out of seventeen (29.4 percent) Democrats and only one out of fifteen (6.6 percent) Republicans (Rep. Bonilla) were vulnerable in 2002. Of course this analysis is not surprising—there should be more at-risk Democrats. Not only because of a general pro-Republican trend, but also because the Democratic gerrymander in 1991 was expansive in terms of increasing the electoral opportunities for Democrats and packing Republican voters.

The redistricting that occurred in 1996 in compliance with the ruling in *Vera* altered the lines of thirteen districts.[81] Overall, the change in the racial compositions of these districts was minimal. There was, however, partisan turnover in districts 5 and 9 in the 1996 elections. Republican Pete Sessions won the 5th district in an open-seat contest (Democratic incumbent John Bryant lost in the primary). The changes to the 5th before the election increased the Anglo voting-age population from 68 percent to 72 percent (the BVAP went from 15.3

Table 13.4. At-Risk and Safe House Seats by Party, 1990 to 2002

Average District Presidential Vote for Winner's Party (1992–1996 Presidential Elections)	*1990*	*1992*	*1994*	*1996*	*1998*	*2000*	*2002*
Less than 48%							
Democrats	5	5	4	3	3	3	3
Republicans	0	1	2	1	1	0	0
TOTAL	5	6	6	4	4	3	3
48%–52%							
Democrats	2	2	2	1	1	1	2
Republicans	1	0	0	2	1	3	1
TOTAL	3	2	2	3	2	4	3
More than 52%							
Democrats	12	14	13	13	13	13	12
Republicans	7	8	9	10	11	10	14
TOTAL	19	22	22	23	24	23	26

percent to 14.5 percent, while the HVAP went from 15.3 percent to 12.4 percent). There was hardly any change in the racial composition of the 9th district, a Democratic leaning district whose controversial freshman incumbent, Republican Steve Stockman, ended up losing to Democrat Nick Lampson.[82]

The court-ordered plan (1151C) in effect for the 2002 elections protected incumbents of both parties because it strayed very little from the last effective plan (1000C) in place for the 2000 elections. Under plan 1151C (excluding the two new seats added through reapportionment), the average percent of each district that remained from plan 1000C is 84 percent, with a standard deviation of 14 percent (the median district retained 89 percent of its old territory). The two newly created districts, 31 and 32, amounted to guaranteed Republican pickups because they were created from heavily Republican areas.[83]

The U.S. District Court for the Eastern District of Texas, the court that drew the boundaries and ordered into effect plan 1151C, commented on its intention to help incumbents:

> We asked if the resulting plan was avoidably detrimental to Members of Congress of either party holding unique, major leadership posts. We looked at three Democrats and three Republicans, consensus members of this limited group, each with substantial leadership positions in the Congress. It was plain that these members were not harmed in their reelection prospects by this plan and that, indeed, no incumbent was paired with another incumbent or significantly harmed by the plan. . . . Doubtlessly some may see any such weighting as an incumbency factor since congressional leadership so directly correlates with seniority. This view is not without force.[84]

Without incumbent effects, Republican gains would be concentrated in those districts with majority Anglo populations formerly represented by Anglo Democrats. In 2002, there are seven districts with majority Anglo populations represented by Anglo Democrats (Districts 1, 2, 4, 9, 10, 11, and 17). In the 2000 presidential election George W. Bush averaged 63 percent of the two-party vote in these districts. He failed to win only District 10 (53.1 percent in favor of Al Gore), a Democratic outlier containing the University of Texas and most of Austin (the eastern half of Travis County).

Because the court-ordered plan (1151C) for the 2002 elections had a strong incumbency bias, it protected several at-risk Anglo Democrats who would otherwise have faced potential defeat. After the 2002 elections, Texas Republicans won majorities in both chambers of the state legislature and retained the governorship. In 2003, multiple special sessions were called for the purpose of drawing a new congressional map with the intention of increasing the number of Republicans. There is no doubt that Anglo Democrats were at the top of the Republicans' most-wanted list.

Redistricting Revisited: Partisan Conflict Erupts[85]

As early as December of 2002 there were rumblings of an attempt by the GOP to redraw the congressional map.[86] U.S. House Majority Leader Tom DeLay spearheaded the effort to introduce a plan to increase the number of Republicans in the Texas congressional delegation. At present, the United States House of Representatives has 229 Republicans, 205 Democrats, and 1 Independent. Given the GOP's narrow majority in the U.S. House, DeLay summed up his thoughts for another round of Texas redistricting: "I'm the majority leader, and we want more seats."[87]

Since the three-judge panel's plan (1151C) effective for the 2002 congressional elections maintained the political status quo, DeLay maneuvered for a new plan that would increase the number of Republicans. The likelihood of passing a new plan improved substantially after the 2002 elections because the Republican Party became a majority in the Texas House for the first time in over 130 years. They increased their number in the 150-member delegation from sixty-two to eighty-eight. With control of the governorship and both chambers[88] of the state legislature, it appeared DeLay would get his wish of a new GOP map.

With DeLay applying the pressure, the Texas House Committee on Redistricting approved plan 1180C on May 6, 2003. State Rep. Phil King (R-Weatherford) drafted the plan with the assistance of Jim Ellis, an aide to DeLay and the executive director of Americans for a Republican Majority.[89] The plan sparked an outcry among Democrats who condemned it as a blatant attempt to kill off veteran Anglo Democrats and the fragmenting of communities of interest—like Austin, which would be parceled into four districts.[90]

The House scheduled a vote on the plan for Monday, May 12, but to the surprise of most Republicans, fifty-eight Democrats were no shows. This prevented a vote, because at least one hundred members are needed to constitute a quorum for conducting business. It was later discovered that fifty-one of the fifty-eight Democrats had fled to Ardmore, Oklahoma, to avoid the possibility of being arrested under Texas law for intentionally busting a quorum.[91] In an allusion to the legendary Killer Bees of 1979—fourteen state senators[92] who hid out to prevent a quorum on a bill by Lt. Gov. Bill Hobby that would have created a separate Republican presidential primary—these renegade Democrats were instantly dubbed the "Killer D's."[93] The Killer D's put the bill to rest by staying away until the end of Thursday's session, the last day to consider the plan during the regular session of the legislature which ended June 2.

Nonetheless, the Killer D's triumph proved to be temporary. On Wednesday, June 18, two days after consulting with DeLay, House Speaker Tom Craddick, and Lt. Gov. David Dewhurst, Gov. Perry called for a June 30 special legislative session to redraw Texas' congressional boundaries.[94] The first special session allowed the house to produce a revised redistricting plan, which largely adhered to the contours of plan 1180C.

After failing to hammer out a consensus bill in the first special legislative session, Lt. Gov. Dewhurst hinted that he would waive the traditional requirement that two-thirds of senators (twenty-one of thirty-one) must agree to bring a bill to the floor for a simple majority vote during the second special session.[95] This prompted the exodus of eleven senate Democrats to Albuquerque, New Mexico, effectively denying the GOP leadership a quorum to do business. After exhausting the second session, Senator John Whitmire (District 15) finally broke ranks on September 2 and returned to his Houston district. Governor Perry responded by reiterating his pledge to call a third session, which began on September 15. The house and senate passed different plans resulting in a house-senate conference undertaken to draw a final map. The sticking point was an intraparty dispute over West Texas. Republicans had to craft a compromise plan acceptable to Speaker Craddick (R-Midland) and Senator Robert Duncan (R-Lubbock), who tussled over the configuration of districts in West Texas.

Finally, on October 10, 2003, the house passed plan 1374C on a seventy-six to fifty-eight vote. Two days later the senate approved the plan on a 17 to 14 vote. Governor Perry signed the bill into law on October 13. Given the partisan nature of the plan, it was obvious that the Democrats would seek to have the courts overturn the plan. Several lawsuits were brought forth and the primary argument for striking down the plan hinged on its being a violation of the Voting Rights Act. Specifically, Texas Democrats argued that the plan packs minority voters and thereby dilutes their votes, a violation of Section 2 of the VRA. Further, it was contended that the plan commits retrogression, a violation of Section 5 of the VRA, because it leaves minority voters worse off than under plan 1151C. A secondary argument was that it was unlawful to institute another redistricting plan mid-decade if there was already a plan enacted after the 2000 Census. The GOP countered that race was used as a proxy to further a partisan gerrymander—the same argument used by Texas Democrats in *Vera*.

On December 19, 2003, the Department of Justice precleared plan 1374C—finding no violation of Section 5 of the VRA. The last hurdle that stood in the way of the plan becoming effective for the 2004 elections was the decision issued in *Walter Session et al. v. Rick Perry et al.* (2004). The plaintiffs proposed four objections to plan 1374C:

1. Texas may not redistrict mid-decade;
2. the Plan unconstitutionally discriminates on the basis of race;
3. the Plan is an unconstitutional partisan gerrymander; and
4. various districts in Plan 1374C dilute the voting strength of minorities in violation of Section 2 of the Voting Rights Act.[96]

On January 6, 2004, the same court that drew the 2002 plan, the U.S. District Court for the Eastern District of Texas, upheld the plan. The court rejected all four of the plaintiffs' claims, basically agreeing with the justification offered by Texas Republicans, stating that, "politics, not race, drove Plan 1374C."[97] In the next section we evaluate plan 1374C.[98]

EVALUATING THE 2004 MAP (PLAN 1374C)

What will be the likely electoral impact of plan 1374C? In this section, we assess the probable effect that the 2004 map will have on the 2004 elections. Of course, the primary objective of the plan is to increase the number of Republicans. Plan 1374C seeks to fulfill this goal by executing three interdependent strategies:

1. targeting Anglo Democrats by dismantling their constituencies,
2. pitting incumbents against each other, and
3. fortifying its sole at-risk member, Republican Henry Bonilla.

Targeting Anglo Democrats

As noted, the most at-risk Democrats are those in split-result districts. These are the members the 2004 plan targets for defeat. In addition, two Anglo Democrats representing majority-minority districts under the 2002 map were also targeted. The largest remaining portion of District 25 (46.5 percent), represented by Chris Bell in 2002 was made into a new district (District 9 in plan 1374C) with a plurality black voting-age population (36.5 percent). The largest remaining segment of Martin Frost's District 24 (26.5 percent) under the 2002 plan was made part of a new Anglo majority district (District 24 with a 67.1 percent Anglo voting-age population). So it appeared that Chris Bell would be susceptible to defeat in the Democratic primary at the hands of an African American challenger. This is in fact what happened. In the case of Frost, the largest segment of his old district formed a heavily Republican district. Only Anglo Democratic incumbent Gene Green was spared under 1374C. He retains 80.6 percent of his majority Hispanic constituency. Under plan 1374C, the incumbency advantage[99] that many of these Anglo Democratic members have used to scare off strong Republican challengers[100] is considerably weakened by ridding these members of large portions of their traditional constituencies.

Taking the largest percent[101] of each incumbent's district that remains intact under the 2004 plan and classifying incumbents into three categories: (1) Anglo Democrats, (2) Minority Democrats, and (3) Republicans, shows that the greatest changes were made to districts represented by Anglo Democrats. Table 13.5 presents the average and median percent of the largest remaining portion of districts represented by Anglo Democrats, minority (Hispanic and African American) Democrats, and Republicans after the 2002 elections. On average, Anglo Democratic incumbents represented districts in which only half of their constituencies were preserved in new districts under the 2004 map. The median percentage is slightly less at 47 percent. By comparison, the average and median portions that remain under plan 1374C for districts represented by minority Democrats and Republicans are substantially greater.

Multivariate analysis confirms the relatively greater reduction of the constituencies of Anglo Democrats. Table 13.6 presents a regression of the per-

Table 13.5. What Remains under Plan 1374C

Representative	*% Old (2002 plan)*
Anglo Democrats (n = 10)	Average = 50.04
	Median = 47.10
Minority Democrats (n = 7)	Average = 75.83
	Median = 78.80
Republicans (n = 15)	Average = 61.57
	Median = 62.50
All Districts (n = 32)	Average = 61.08
	Median = 60.20

Note: The percent old refers to the average and median percent of the largest portion of each district that remains for each incumbent under the 2004 map. This does not mean that incumbents chose to run for reelection in 2004 in those districts that contain the greatest share of their old constituencies.

Table 13.6. Dismantling the Districts of Anglo Democrats under Plan 1374C

Independent Variables	*Coefficient (se)*	*t*
Anglo Democrats	−0.158*	−2.869
	(0.055)	
Number of Districts the Old District Is Split into	−0.052*	−2.829
	(0.018)	
Black VAP (%)	0.290	1.090
	(0.266)	
Hispanic VAP (%)	0.212	1.567
	(0.135)	
Intercept	0.788**	7.305
	(0.108)	
N	32	
Adjusted R^2	0.412	

Note: Coefficients are OLS estimates with standard errors in parentheses. Dependent variable is the largest percentage of the district (from plan 1151C) that remains under plan 1374C.
$^{**}p < .001$; $^{*}p < .01$

centage of the old district (the largest percentage of each district in plan 1151C that remains under plan 1374C) on the black voting-age population (BVAP), the Hispanic voting-age population (HVAP), the number of districts that the old district is now included in, and a dummy variable for Anglo Democratic incumbents under plan 1151C (after the 2002 elections).

After controlling for all the other factors in the model, the ten Anglo Democrats are significantly more likely to have their constituencies reduced; more specifically, there is a reduction of 15.8 percent compared to all other representatives. By greatly reducing the constituencies of these Anglo Democrats, the bond of incumbency is weakened because so many "new" voters have little familiarity with these members and less incentive to vote for them.[102] Furthermore, many of these new voters are located in heavily Republican areas.[103]

Pitting Incumbents against Each Other

The second strategy is to pair incumbents against each other. In the case of the 2004 map, however, it is highly unlikely that several of these Democrats would run in the districts where they are paired against fellow incumbents. First, in Texas there is no district residency requirement. Second, for those incumbents (Green and Turner) who are paired in districts that retain just a trace of their old constituents, staying put would amount to political suicide.

Based on their district residences, the 2004 map pits incumbents against each other in four districts: Districts 2, 6, 7, and 19. District 2 pairs Democratic incumbents Gene Green and Nick Lampson against each other. Representative

Green, who currently represents a majority Hispanic district, would have little chance here because the district includes just 1.1 percent of his old constituency (compared to 47.7 percent of Lampson's old district). The larger question is whether Lampson could win the general election in this split-result district and this is contingent on the quality of the Republican challenger.

District 6 places three incumbents against each other, two Democrats: Representatives Martin Frost and Jim Turner, and one Republican: Joe Barton. Under this scenario, either Democrat would certainly lose in this Republican district[104] to a strong Republican incumbent who retains 66.4 percent of his old district (21.6 percent for Frost and 4.4 percent for Turner). District 7 pairs a Republican with a Democrat: Republican John Culberson (in his second term) versus freshman Democrat Chris Bell. This also would be a landslide in favor of Culberson; he keeps 51.8 percent of his constituents to Bell's 18.8 percent, and the district gave George W. Bush 69 percent of the vote in 2000.

The last paired district is the 19th, which would have veteran Democrat Charles Stenholm square off against newly elected Republican Randy Neugebauer.[105] At first glance it would appear the conservative Democrat could win in this district, but a closer look suggests the contrary. First, Stenholm was the most at-risk Anglo Democrat in 2000, winning with only 52 percent of the two-party vote against a quality Republican challenger (Abilene City Councilman Rob Beckham). Second, Stenholm would have 30.9 percent of his old constituency while Neugebauer would hold onto 57.5 percent of his previous district, with the remaining 11.7 percent coming from the old 13th district (represented by Republican Mac Thornberry). The constituency edge thus goes to Neugebauer, but more importantly the district partisanship is heavily Republican. The average Republican presidential vote for the 1992 and 1996 elections would have been 64 percent and George W. Bush would have carried this district with 75 percent.

It turns out that the 2004 elections will be run with incumbents paired against each other in two districts. Stenholm and Neugebauer will indeed face each other in District 19, and Martin Frost chose to seek reelection in District 32 against Republican Pete Sessions who is considered the prohibitive favorite. In the new 32nd district, Sessions retains 52.3 percent of his old constituency versus 20.4 percent for Frost. George W. Bush carries the district with 64 percent of the 2000 presidential vote.

By slicing up old districts and pairing incumbents, plan 1374C accomplishes candidate displacement.[106] In other words, under plan 1374C the alteration of district boundaries is done to leave several Democratic incumbents in the predicament of running for reelection in new districts where they may lose (in the primary or general) versus running in other districts where they have no chance of winning.

Protecting an At-Risk Republican

Recall that the only at-risk Republican in 2002 was Henry Bonilla. In 2002, Bonilla faced a strong challenge from Democrat Henry Cuellar (ex-Secretary of State and ex-State Rep., D-Laredo), garnering only 52 percent of the two-party vote. The 2004 map removes the Democratic threat by reducing the percentage Hispanic voting-age population from 63 percent to 51 percent and increasing the percentage Anglo voting-age population from 33 percent to 45 percent (the BVAP increases from 2 percent to 5 percent). In 2000, George W. Bush captured 59 percent under the old 23rd, and would have received 64 percent in the new district. Under plan 1374C, Bonilla's only electoral threat is in the Republican primary (a likely possibility given racially polarized voting).

The Forecast for the 2004 Elections

The 2004 map shook up the electoral landscape before a single vote was cast in Texas' Democratic and Republican primaries. Ralph Hall switched parties in early January, leaving the Texas U.S. House delegation evenly divided between sixteen Democrats and sixteen Republicans. In addition, prior to Hall's switch, Democratic incumbent Jim Turner opted for retirement. Democrat Lloyd Doggett, as displacement would have it, abandoned the new Republican Tenth and chose to seek reelection in District 25, a new majority Hispanic district that runs from southeast Austin to the Mexico border. Doggett won the Democratic primary and is thus assured reelection in this heavily Democratic district. Incumbent Democrat Chris Bell lost to African American Al Green in the primary for District 9, a plurality black district. Incumbent Democrat Ciro Rodriguez appears to have lost to Henry Cuellar in the primary for District 28, although the outcome has been disputed and there remains one last legal appeal.

In table 13.7 we offer our assessment for the 2004 elections based on election data current at the time of the 2004 primaries. The table summarizes what we consider the number of guaranteed districts for Texas Democrats and Republicans and the toss-up districts under plan 1374C. We expect Republicans to maintain their current sixteen seats and add three open Anglo majority seats (Districts 10, 11, and 24). Incumbent Democrats win eight majority-minority seats and pick up two open majority-minority seats (Districts 9 and 28). The toss-up seats are of course, those split-result Anglo majority districts with Anglo Democratic incumbents (Districts 1, 2, and 17). In sum, under plan 1374C, Republicans win between nineteen and twenty-two of Texas's thirty-two seats, and Texas' minority delegation (excluding Republican Henry Bonilla) goes from seven to eight (one more African American).

Table 13.7. Guaranteed Republican, Democratic, and Toss-Up Districts in 2004

Republicans	*Democrats**	*Toss-Ups (All Anglo Democrats)*
3—Sam Johnson	9—*Al Green*	1—Nick Lampson
4—Ralph Hall	15—Ruben Hinojosa	2—Max Sandlin
5—Jeb Hensarling	16—Silvestre Reyes	17—Chet Edwards
6—Joe Barton	18—Sheila Jackson Lee	
7—John Culberson	20—Charlie A. Gonzalez	
8—Kevin Brady	25—Lloyd Doggett	
10—*Michael T. McCaul*	27—Solomon P. Ortiz	
11—*Mike Conaway*	28—*Henry Cuellar*	
12—Kay Granger	29—Gene Green	
13—Mac Thornberry	30—Eddie Bernice Johnson	
14—Ron Paul		
19—Randy Neugebauer		
21—Lamar Smith		
22—Tom DeLay		
23—Henry Bonilla		
24—*Kenny Marchant*		
26—Michael Burgess		
31—John Carter		
32—Pete Sessions		
N = 19 (18 Anglos, 1 Hispanic)	N = 10 (5 Hispanics, 3 African Americans, 2 Anglos)	N = 3

*Two defeated Democrats: Martin Frost loses in District 32 and Charles W. Stenholm loses in District 19. Non-incumbents in italics.

DISCUSSION

Over a half-century ago Texas had one-party politics dominated by a conservative Democratic faction that warred against a weaker liberal/progressive wing.[107] Compared to its Southern neighbors, Texas' politics focused more on economics than race, the conservative "haves" versus the liberal have nots.[108] As a peripheral South state, Texas lacks a high black population and therefore racial conflict has never been as significant as in the case of its Deep South sisters.

But like the rest of the South, with the advent of genuine two-party competition made possible by the national parties taking clear positions on civil rights,[109] race has become more salient and the Anglos who once aligned with the conservative wing of the Democratic Party have become Republicans.[110]

Indeed, today Texas politics is inextricably linked to race because political ideologies now cleave along racial lines. V. O. Key thought (and hoped) the politics of race would eventually fade away and be replaced by modified class politics that drew political lines chiefly around struggles between the "haves" and "have nots" (sort of like the old Texas politics). This vision has not come to pass because substantial numbers of lower-class Anglos have re-aligned with the Republican Party.[111] Race has, in a sense, trumped class in Texas politics. This is not necessarily because of extant racial concerns; rather it is because ideological conservatism was born out of the politics of race. Put another way, the conservatism of the Texas Republican party is not dependent on the politics of race. It is a conservatism that has instead managed to flourish in the absence of any substantial racial threat.

But the coincidence of race, ideology, and party means that race looms large in the politics of redistricting. In the 1990s, with substantial realignment having taken place among Texas voters, Democrats knew their only chance of holding off a Republican takeover was through the implementation of a partisan gerrymander. This gerrymander sustained Democratic control of the congressional delegation through the 2002 elections, but now the tables have turned. Democrats were wise to play every card they had to thwart the passage of a new redistricting plan. The Republican plan enacted for the 2004 elections, in a sense, returns the favor. Instead of packing minorities in order to increase the number of Republican members, a strategy fraught with legal complications, the 2004 map achieves its purpose by dismantling the districts of Anglo Democrats.[112] After all, the GOP has contended for years that incumbency accounts for the reelection of Democrats in districts that appear to be Republican according to reliable measures (e.g., the district presidential vote and racial makeup). In Texas, the new congressional map for the 2004 elections provides an historic opportunity to see if the Republican argument is valid.

NOTES

1. Democrats had a seventeen to fifteen advantage until Representative Ralph Hall switched parties in January 2004.

2. Texas Legislative Council (hereafter abbreviated as TLC): *State and Federal Law Governing Redistricting in Texas* (Austin: Texas Legislative Council, 2001), 140.

3. Due to space limitations and the scope of this study, we do not discuss the establishment of a benchmark plan and complications that arise from the retrogression standard under Section 5 of the VRA (for a review of these issues see Katharine Inglis Butler, "Redistricting in a Post-*Shaw* Era: A Small Treatise Accompanied by Distrcting Guidelines for Legislators, Litigants, and Courts," *University of Richmond Law Review* 36 (2002): 171–95). Furthermore, because Texas has no legal requirements that stipulate adherence to traditional redistricting criteria (i.e., compactness, contiguity, preserving communities of interest, preserving political subdivisions, etc.), we do not discuss these concepts in detail.

APPENDIX

Table 13.8. Important Events in the 2003 Redistricting Dispute

Date	*Session*	*Event*
6/30/03	1st	First special session convenes.
7/8/03	1st	House passes plan 1268C, 83-62 vote.
7/14/03	1st	Republican Senator Bill Ratliff joins 10 Democrats in signing pledge opposing consideration of redistricting plan (move blocks redistricting by denying 2/3s of Senate to consider a plan). Lt. Gov. Dewhurst responds by suggesting he will drop 2/3s rule for second special session.
7/23/03	1st	Senate Jurisprudence Committee passes plan 1327C on 4-3 party line vote.
7/27/03	1st	Intra-party dispute surfaces among GOP over drawing districts in West Texas. Speaker Tom Craddick wants a separate district drawn for his hometown of Midland. Craddick is opposed by Republican Senator Robert Duncan who wants to keep Midland in a single district that includes Lubbock (Duncan's hometown).
7/28/03	1st	Eleven Democratic Senators (dubbed the "Texas 11") deny Republicans a quorum (2/3s present for a quorum) by going to Albuquerque, New Mexico. Senators' boycott is done in anticipation of second session that would waive 2/3s rule for debating a plan.
7/28/03	2nd	Second special session convenes at 3:15 P.M. (Texas 11 are already gone).
7/29/03	2nd	House passes plan 1268C, 75-26 vote.
8/7/03	2nd	Republicans file suit with Texas Supreme Court to compel Texas 11 to attend session. Democrats file suit in Travis County Court to rule against a special session conducted for the purpose of redistricting, claim suspension of 2/3s rule is a violation and seek ruling that prevents their arrest if they return to Texas.
8/12/03	2nd	16 Republican Senators vote (unless the Texas 11 return in 48 hours) to fine each boycotting senator $1,000 a day, doubled each day, but no more than $5,000 a day for the duration of their absence (amounts to $57,000 per senator if gone the entire session).

8/15/03	2nd	Additional impositions placed on Texas 11 if fines aren't paid: "a ban on purchases, travel, use of Capitol conference rooms, parking for senators and their staffers, subscriptions, printing privileges, cell phones and floor passes for missing members' aides" (Herman 2003d).
8/20/03	2nd	Democrats file a federal suit in a Laredo Court claiming they can boycott the session under their right to free speech and therefore they should not have to pay fines or be arrested.
8/26/03	2nd	Second special session ends.
9/2/03	Not in session	Democratic Senator John Whitmire, one of the Texas 11, returns to Texas—effectively ending the 37-day boycott and thus giving the Senate a quorum to debate redistricting.
9/10/03	Not in session	The rest of boycotting Democrats return to Texas.
9/12/03	Not in session	Democrats' lawsuit is dismissed.
9/15/03	3rd	Third special session convenes at noon.
9/17/03	3rd	House passes plan 1268C, 76-43 vote.
9/18/03	3rd	In 13-10 vote, Republican Senators place Texas 11 on probation (until regular session convenes in 2005), dismissing fines and sanctions unless members are gone over 72 hours "while the Senate is under 'call,' the procedure used when senators try to break the quorum" (Herman 2003e).
9/22/03	3rd	Gov. Perry presents a partial map that creates separate West Texas districts in an effort to resolve conflict between Craddick and Duncan.
9/24/03	3rd	Senate passes plan 1362C, by 18-12 vote (plan doesn't resolve West Texas dispute because Midland and Lubbock are in the same district).
9/25/03	3rd	House-Senate conference committee (5 Representatives and 5 Senators, includes 1 Democrat from each chamber) is appointed to hash out a final map.
10/10/03	3rd	House passes plan 1374C, 76-58 vote.
10/12/03	3rd	Senate passes plan 1374C, 17-14 vote and 3rd special session ends.
10/13/03	Not in session	Gov. Perry signs H.B. 3, plan 1374C into law.

4. In this section we rely heavily on a law review article by Butler, "Redistricting in a Post-*Shaw* Era,"137–270, and a pamphlet published by the TLC, *State and Federal.*

5. Malapportionment almost always refers to the case of a voter residing in a district with substantially more residents relative to other districts. Such a person's vote is diluted (assuming all other factors, such as turnout, are held constant). Prior to the equal population requirement, the South was infamous for malapportionment because it allowed rural elites to maintain their hold over political power in the face of urban growth.

6. Butler, "Redistricting in a Post-*Shaw* Era," 147–48.

7. According to Butler, "[t]he equal population requirement for congressional districts comes not from the Fourteenth Amendment, but from Article I, section 2 of the Constitution, which mandates that representatives to Congress be chosen 'by the People of the several States.'" Butler, "Redistricting in a Post-*Shaw* Era," 149–50.

8. See Butler, "Redistricting in a Post-*Shaw* Era," 149–52.

9. Butler, "Redistricting in a Post-*Shaw* Era," 151. TLC, *State and Federal Law*, 24–31.

10. Ideal population = 20,851,820 (2000 Texas population) / 32 (number of U.S. House seats) = 651,619.375.

11. See Chandler Davidson, *Minority Vote Dilution* (Washington, D.C.: Howard University Press, 1984). Frank R. Parker, *Black Votes Count* (Chapel Hill: University of North Carolina Press, 1990). C. Vann Woodward, *The Strange Career of Jim Crow* (New York: Oxford University Press, 2002).

12. TLC, *State and Federal Law*, 47.

13. Throughout this study the South is defined as the eleven states of the Confederacy: Alabama, Arkansas, Florida, Georgia, Louisiana, Mississippi, North Carolina, South Carolina, Tennessee, Texas, and Virginia.

14. See Frank R. Parker, "Racial Gerrymandering and Legislative Reapportionment," in *Minority Vote Dilution*, ed. Chandler Davidson (Washington, D.C.: Howard University Press, 1984).

15. Section 2 of the VRA as amended in 1982 "render[ed] illegal any electoral device whose intent *or result* denied or abridged the voting rights of racial or language minorities" (Davidson, *Minority Vote Dilution*, 18).

16. Although we do not discuss at length the Constitutional protection (applied under the Fourteenth Amendment of the Equal Protection Clause, but also justiciable under the Fifteenth Amendment) against minority vote dilution that falls outside the purview of the VRA, suffice it to say that the standard to prove a violation is much more stringent because one must demonstrate evidence of a plan's discriminatory effect and discriminatory intent with "the invidious purpose of diluting the voting strength of members of a racial or ethnic group" (TLC, *State and Federal Law,* 90). Also, whereas the VRA case law deals with suits brought overwhelmingly by minorities, the *Shaw* rulings and subsequent cases we discuss are brought mainly by white plaintiffs who claim their voting rights have been compromised (denial of Equal Protection under the Fourteenth Amendment) as a result of living in a district designed for the purpose of electing a minority representative. This is basically the flip side of the complaint leveled by minorities under the VRA.

17. TLC, *Guide to 2001 Redistricting* (Austin: Texas Legislative Council, 2000), 26. The first definition of vote dilution forbids "cracking" the minority vote and the sec-

ond definition prohibits "packing" the minority vote. In the next section of the chapter we discuss some of the redistricting techniques that serve to dilute the votes of minority groups and the votes of supporters of one of the major political parties.

18. Although the *Gingles* case involved a multimember district, it has been interpreted to apply to single-member districts (hence congressional districts are subject to the *Gingles* decision). Butler, "Redistricting in a Post-*Shaw* Era."; TLC, *State and Federal Law*, 49.

19. TLC, *State and Federal Law*, 50.

20. See Butler, "Redistricting in a Post-*Shaw* Era."; TLC, *State and Federal Law.*

21. TLC, *State and Federal Law*, 54.

22. TLC, *State and Federal Law*, 55.

23. TLC, *State and Federal Law*, 70.

24. TLC, *State and Federal Law*, 70.

25. Butler, "Redistricting in a Post-*Shaw* Era," 171.

26. Butler, "Redistricting in a Post-*Shaw* Era," 171.

27. We must note that "Section 5 preclearance does not bar a subsequent challenge to the new plans under other law, such as the federal constitution or Section 2 of the Voting Rights Act" See TLC, *State and Federal Law*, 75–76, 83.

28. Butler, "Redistricting in a Post-*Shaw* Era," 141.

29. Butler, "Redistricting in a Post-*Shaw* Era."

30. Butler, "Redistricting in a Post-*Shaw* Era," 197.

31. Butler, "Redistricting in a Post-*Shaw* Era." TLC, *State and Federal Law.*

32. As stated in Congressional Quarterly, *Congressional Elections: 1946–1996* (Washington, D.C.: Congressional Quarterly Inc., 1998), 324, footnote 6:

> In July 1996 a panel of federal judges declared that three Texas districts [18th, 29th, and 30th] were unconstitutionally drawn. The three districts and an additional ten surrounding ones were redrawn, invalidating the March 1996 primary results for the districts. In November, candidates in the thirteen districts ran in open primaries, with only those capturing a majority of the vote winning outright. Special runoff elections were held in December for the top two finishers in the districts where no candidate received a majority of the votes cast.

33. Butler, "Redistricting in a Post-*Shaw* Era," 204.

34. Butler, "Redistricting in a Post-*Shaw* Era," 205–206.

35. Butler, "Redistricting in a Post-*Shaw* Era," 216.

36. Butler, "Redistricting in a Post-*Shaw* Era," 216–17.

37. Butler, "Redistricting in a Post-*Shaw* Era," 143.

38. Found on page 11.

39. TLC, *State and Federal Law*, 107.

40. TLC, *State and Federal Law*, 109

41. TLC, *State and Federal Law*, 110

42. Butler, "Redistricting in a Post-*Shaw* Era," 169.

43. TLC, *State and Federal Law*, 113.

44. James E. Lennertz, "Back in their Proper Place: Racial Gerrymandering in Georgia," *Political Geography* 19 (2000): 168.

45. Butler, "Redistricting in a Post-*Shaw* Era," 169.

46. David E. Rosenbaum, "Justices Bow to Legislators in Political Gerrymander Case," *New York Times*, 29 April 2004, A.

47. See Michael Barone and Grant Ujifusa, *The Almanac of American Politics: 1994* (Washington, D.C.: National Journal, 1993), 1209. Earl Black and Merle Black, *The Rise of Southern Republicans* (Cambridge: Harvard University Press, 2002), 344–46. Richard Murray and Sam Attlesey, "Texas: Republicans Gallop Ahead," in *Southern Politics in the 1990s,* ed. Alexander P. Lamis (Baton Rouge: Louisiana State University Press, 1999), 315–16, 321.

48. Richard G. Niemi and Alan I. Abramowitz, "Partisan Redistricting and the 1992 Congressional Elections," *Journal of Politics* 56 (1994): 814.

49. Under plan C746, TLC, *Guide to 2001 Redistricting.*

50. The dissent also pointed out that the three new seats added through reapportionment, Districts 28 (Tejeda, D-San Antonio), 29 (Gene Green, D-Houston), and 30 (Johnson, D-Dallas, chair of the Texas Senate Committee on Redistricting), were all won by former state senators who each had a hand in designing the districts they won in the 1992 congressional elections. Barone and Ujifusa, *Almanac of American Politics: 1994.*

51. Plan 1000C (used for the 2000 elections) involved rather minor adjustments to the previous plan (C746) based on the updated 2000 census data (personal communication with Charles H. Eckstein, research specialist for the Texas Legislative Council).

52. In comparison to the 1991 plan, according to Murray and Attlesey, "Texas: Republicans Gallop Ahead," 336: "[t]he court-ordered plan [C746] smoothed out the boundaries of affected districts and reduced minority populations in the Eighteenth, Twenty-Ninth, and Thirtieth Districts, but did not drastically alter the partisan makeup of the redrawn electoral units."

53. On this point see Butler, "Redistricting in a Post-*Shaw* Era," 204–205.

54. Balderas v. Texas, 2001, 9.

55. Charles S. Bullock, III, "Affirmative Action Districts: In Whose Faces Will They Blow Up?" *Campaigns & Elections* (April 1995): 22–23. Kevin A. Hill and Nicol C. Rae, "What Happened to the Democrats in the South?: US House Elections, 1992–1996," *Party Politics* 6 (2000): 5–22. David Lublin and D. Stephen Voss, "Boll-Weevil Blues: Polarized Congressional Delegations into the 21st Century," *American Review of Politics* 21 (Winter 2000): 427–50.

56. See Maurice R. Cunningham, *Maximization, Whatever the Cost: Race, Redistricting and the Department of Justice* (Westport, Conn.: Praeger, 2001).

57. David Epstein and Sharyn O'Halloran, "A Social Science Approach to Race, Redistricting, and Representation," *American Political Science Review* 93 (1999): 187–91; David Epstein and Sharyn O'Halloran, "Measuring the Electoral and Policy Impact of Majority-Minority Voting Districts," *American Political Science Review* 43 (1999): 367–95.

58. Kevin A. Hill, "Does the Creation of Majority Black Districts Aid Republicans? An Analysis of the 1992 Congressional Elections in Eight Southern States," *Journal of Politics* 57 (1995): 384–401. John R. Petrocik and Scott W. Desposato, "The Partisan Consequences of Majority-Minority Redistricting in the South, 1992 and 1994," *Journal of Politics* 60 (1998): 613–33.

59. Butler, "Redistricting in a Post-*Shaw* Era," 218.

60. The Deep South states are: Alabama, Georgia, Louisiana, Mississippi, and South Carolina.

61. Georgia gained one seat, Louisiana lost a seat, and Alabama, Mississippi, and South Carolina broke even.

62. Seth C. McKee, "Majority Black Districts, Republican Ascendancy, and Party Competition in the South, 1988–2000," *American Review of Politics* 23 (Summer 2002): 123–39.

63. Parker, *Black Votes Count.*

64. See Parker, "Racial Gerrymandering," 89–92, and also Donald Ostdiek, "Congressional Redistricting and District Typologies," *Journal of Politics* 57 (1995): 534. Although it is not discussed here, stacking is another redistricting technique. As explained by Parker, "Racial Gerrymandering," 89–92: "[s]tacking is the racial gerrymandering technique in which a large minority population concentration is put together with a larger white population with the purpose or effect of depriving minority voters of a voting majority." It is easy to see why this technique would be just as effective for crafting a partisan gerrymander.

65. Black and Black, *Rise of Southern Republicans.*

66. We do not claim that these redistricting plans were necessarily designed to advance the electoral opportunities of Republicans. In fact, most of the Southern states had Democratic legislatures (AR, FL, GA, NC, TN, TX, and VA), and the rest were divided between the two parties (AL, LA, MS, SC) during the initial redistricting following the 1990 census. See Niemi and Abramowitz, "Partisan Redistricting," 813. What advantaged the Republicans was the creation of majority-minority districts, which essentially packed black voters into a few districts. The unintended consequence, at least from the vantage point of Democratic line drawers, was the increase in Republican voting in the districts adjacent to the newly created majority-minority districts. see Petrocik and Desposato, "Partisan Consequences."

67. According to census data, the Texas Anglo population increased 10 percent from 1980 to 1990, 6 percent from 1990 to 2000 (17 percent from 1980–2000). Contrast this with an increase in the African American population of 18 percent from 1980 to 1990, 19 percent from 1990 to 2000 (41 percent from 1980 to 2000). Most striking has been the tremendous growth of Texas' Hispanic population: 45 percent between 1980 and 1990, 54 percent from 1990 to 2000, and over 123 percent from 1980 to 2000.

68. Bob Mansker, an aide to Congressman Martin Frost (Dallas-Fort Worth), "one of the most endangered Democratic incumbents," developed "[t]he award-winning plan" (Murray and Attlesey, "Texas Republicans Gallop Ahead," (1999, 316). According to Richard Murray and Sam Attlesey:

> the task of . . . Bob Mansker was to design realigned districts that the twenty-seven incumbents, including eight Republicans, could sign off on. Ironically, he could do this only by using the districting procedures the Justice Department was promoting for other reasons. So the odd shaped districts created in Texas not only increased minority representation, but also preserved incumbent interests—a very different result from what had occurred in Georgia and North Carolina. (1999, 316)

69. Barone and Ujifusa, *Almanac of American Politics: 1994,* 1209; Black and Black, *Rise of Southern Republicans,* 345; Murray and Attlesey, "Texas: Republicans Gallop Ahead," 316.

70. Black and Black, *Rise of Southern Republicans,* 344–45.

71. Texas does not have party registration. At the individual level (using American National Election Study data for Texas, 1988–2000) there is a significant difference in the congressional voting behavior of Texas Anglos and blacks, even when controlling for income, party ID, and incumbency (results not shown, but we will provide upon request).

72. See Earl Black, "The Newest Southern Politics," *Journal of Politics* 60 (1998): 591–612.

73. See David Lublin, "The Election of African Americans and Latinos to the U.S. House of Representatives, 1972–1994," *American Politics Quarterly* 25 (1997): 269–86; Epstein and O'Halloran, "Social Science Approach," 187–91; Epstein and O'Halloran, "Measuring the Impact," 367–95; David Epstein and Sharyn O'Halloran, "Majority-Minority Districts and the New Politics of Congressional Elections," in *Continuity and Change in House Elections,* ed. David W. Brady, John F. Cogan and Morris P. Fiorina (Stanford: Stanford University Press, 2000).

74. It is important to note that for the 1991 redistricting, line drawers had access to racial data down to the block level (the lowest unit of aggregation with 100 percent data on the American population). In particular, Texas' "REDAPPL" redistricting software provides racial composition (Anglo, black, Hispanic, black plus Hispanic, and other) at the block level. Ironically, the technology available to Texas mapmakers was looked upon with suspicion by the Court in the *Vera* case. In its opinion, the Court found it curious that the REDAPPL program did not provide data (election data in particular) other than race at the block level. This was further evidence in the opinion of the Court that race was the predominant factor in the drawing of Districts 18, 29, and 30 under plan C657. But, as we have pointed out, race is a reliable predictor of voting behavior and it would thus make sense for Texas Democrats to rely on racial data in promulgating a partisan gerrymander.

75. Ron Johnston, "Manipulation Maps and Winning Elections: Measuring the Impact of Malapportionment and Gerrymandering," *Political Geography* 21 (2002): 1–31.

76. We exclude the 2000 presidential vote from this discussion because the candidacy of native-son George W. Bush most likely inflates Republican strength.

77. See James E. Campbell, "The Presidential Pulse and the 1994 Midterm Congressional Election," *Journal of Politics* 59 (1997): 830–57.

78. Under the 2002 map, several of these districts were heavily rural (especially Districts 1, 2, 4, 11, and 17) and have been represented by ideologically conservative/populist "Boll Weevil" Democrats. See Barone and Ujifusa, *Almanac of American Politics: 1994.*

79. See Alan I. Abramowitz, "The End of the Democratic Era? 1994 and the Future of Congressional Election Research," *Political Research Quarterly* 48 (1995): 873–89; Black and Black, *Rise of Southern Republicans*; Campbell, "The Presidential Pulse"; Gary C. Jacobson, "The 1994 House Elections in Perspective," *Political Science Quarterly* 111 (1996): 203–23; Gary C. Jacobson, "Reversal of Fortune: The Transformation of U.S. House Elections in the 1990s," in *Continuity and Change in House Elections,* ed. David W. Brady, John F. Cogan and Morris P. Fiorina (Stanford: Stanford University Press, 2000).

80. This analysis is similar to Jacobson, "Reversal of Fortune," 15–16.

81. The 13 districts with new boundaries were: Districts 3, 5, 6, 7, 8, 9, 18, 22, 24, 25, 26, 29, and 30.

82. The racial composition (percent) of the 9th District before and after redistricting was: 69.9 to 69.8 AVAP, 19.8 to 19.9 BVAP, and 8.5 to 8.4 HVAP. In 1994, Stockman won in an upset over 16-term Democratic incumbent Jack Brooks (Michael Barone and Grant Ujifusa, *The Almanac of American Politics 1998* (Washington D.C.: National Journal, 1997), 1360.

83. Also, Republican incumbent Pete Sessions left the 5th district to run in District 32. District 31 was created from Districts 5 (3.8 percent), 7 (23.5 percent), 8 (28.1 percent), 14 (17.2 percent), and 21 (27.3 percent) under the 2000 plan. Republican incumbents represented all of these districts. District 32 was created from Districts 3 (18.7 percent), 5 (15.7 percent), 6 (0.0 percent), 26 (62.6 percent), and 30 (3.0 percent) under the 2000 plan. A Democrat represented only District 30. Voters in Districts 31 and 32 voted 62 percent for Dole in 1996.

84. *Balderas v. Texas,* 2001, 8.

85. This condensed account hardly scratches the surface of the events surrounding the redistricting controversy. A case in point is the evidence that the Texas Department of Public Safety (DPS) destroyed records relating to their search for the Killer D's after it came to light that the DPS called upon agents at the Department of Homeland Security to search for a "missing" plane. It turns out the plane was that of former House Speaker and State Rep. Pete Laney (D-Hale Center), one of the Killer D's who camped out at the Holiday Inn in Ardmore, Oklahoma (Eunice Moscoso, "Feds were sent looking for Laney's 'Lost' Plane," *Austin American-Statesman,* 16 May 2003; David Pasztor, "Democrats Fume after DPS Destroys Killer D Records," *Austin American-Statesman*, 22 May 2003; Kate Zernike, "Texas Deleted Documents about Search for Democrats," *New York Times,* 22 May 2003). Several books could be penned (and will be) on this historic episode in Texas politics.

86. Dave McNeely, "GOP May Try to Redraw District Map," *Austin American-Statesman,* 12 December 2002. Like most states, the Texas state legislature is responsible for redistricting (in the absence of a court-enforced plan) (David Butler and Bruce Cain, *Congressional Redistricting: Comparative and Theoretical Perspectives* (New York: MacMillan, 1992).

87. David M. Halbfinger, "Across U.S., Redistricting as a Never-Ending Battle" *New York Times,* 1 July 2003, 1.

88. There are 19 Republicans and 12 Democrats in the 31 member Texas Senate.

89. Ken Herman, "Revised District Map is Coming," *Austin American-Statesman,* 6 May 2003; Laylan Copelin, "GOP Redistricting Plan Raises Fuss," *Austin American-Statesman,* 4 May 2003.

90. Ken Herman, "District May Be Linked by a Thread," *Austin American-Statesman,* 12 May 2003.

91. Ken Herman, "AWOL Deomcrats Found," *Austin American-Statesman,* 13 May 2003.

92. Twelve of the "Killer Bees" holed up in a west Austin apartment garage (Dave McNeely, "Killer D's Echo 1979 Killer Bees," *Austin American-Statesman,* 13 May 2003).

93. McNeely, "Killer D's." Speaker Tom Craddick labeled these absentee Democrats "Chicken D's" (Dave McNeely, "Redistricting only widens House Divide," *Austin American-Statesman,* 22 May 2003).

94. Laylan Copelin and Michele Kay, "D.C. Keeps Eye on Special Session," *Austin American-Statesman,* 19 June 2003. Under Texas law, the governor can call

continuous 30-day special sessions for the purpose of dealing with any specific topic of his/her choosing.

95. Laylan Copelin, "Tallying Senate Redistricting Votes Is Tricky," *Austin American-Statesman,* 11 June 2003. Laylan Copelin and Ken Herman, "Senate Impasse may Kill new Map," *Austin American-Statesman*, 15 June 2003.

96. *Session v. Perry* 2004, 1.

97. *Session v. Perry*, 27.

98. See Table 8 in the appendix for a more detailed account of the events that took place during the 2003 redistricting.

99. See John A. Ferejohn, "On the Decline of Competition in Congressional Election," *American Political Science Review* 71 (1977): 166–76; Morris Fiorina, *Congress, Keystone of the Washington Establishment* (New Haven: Yale University Press, 1989); Andrew Gelman and Gary King, "Estimating Incumbency Advantage without Bias," *American Journal of Political Science* 34 (1990): 1,142–64; Andrew Gelman and Gary King, "Systemic Consequences of Incumbency Advantage in United States House Elections," *American Journal of Political Science* 35 (1991): 110–38; Gary C. Jacobson, *The Politics of Congressional Elections,* 5th ed (New York: Addison- Wesley, 2001); David Mayhew, *Congress: The Electoral Connection* (New Haven: Yale University Press, 1974).

100. Since 1998, only Representative Stenholm has faced a Republican opponent with prior elective experience (he has faced an experienced Republican in each of the last three elections). Representative Doggett has not faced a Republican opponent since 1996.

101. We use "percentage of constituency" and "percentage of the district" interchangeably. This percentage is measured in terms of district population, not geographic area.

102. John H. Alford and David W. Brady, "Partisan and Incumbent Advantage in U.S. House Elections," in *Congress Reconsidered*. 4th ed., ed. Bruce I. Oppenheimer and Lawrence D. Dodd (Washington, D.C.: CQ Press, 1989); Petrocik and Desposato, "Partisan Consequences," 613–33. Scott W. Desposato and John R. Petrocik, "The Variable Incumbency Advantage: New Voters, Redistricting, and the Personal Vote," *American Journal of Political Science* 47 (2003): 18–32.

103. For instance in District 10 under plan 1180C, except for the 38.2 percent of the district that remains from the old district and a sliver of District 18 (136 persons = 0.0 percent) under plan 1151C, the rest (61.8 percent) of the district is created from Republican districts in plan 1151C: Districts 7 (2.2 percent), 8 (3.7 percent), 14 (23.9 percent), 21 (11.7 percent) and 31 (20.2 percent). The lowest percentage of the 2002 statewide Republican vote in these five Republican sections was 60.4 percent (District 14) and the highest was 73.7 percent (District 31).

104. George W. Bush wins 66 percent of the 2000 presidential vote in this district.

105. Randy Neugebauer won a special runoff election (6/3/03) against Republican Mike Conaway to replace veteran Republican Larry Combest, who announced his intention to resign shortly after winning the 2002 general election. Neugebauer, a real estate developer, has political experience as a former Lubbock City Councilman (Hastings Wyman, *Southern Political Report,* no. 605 (26 May 2003), 6.

106. Bruce E. Cain, "Assessing the Partisan Effects of Redistricting," *American Political Science Review* 79 (1985): 320–33.

107. George Norris Green, *The Establishment in Texas Politics: The Primitive Years, 1938–1957* (Westport, Conn.: Greenwood Press, 1979).

108. V.O. Key Jr., *Southern Politics in State and Nation* (Knoxville: University of Tennessee Press, 1996).

109. Edward G. Carmines and James A. Stimson, *Issue Evolution* (Princeton N.J.: Princeton University Press, 1989).

110. Kevin P. Phillips, *The Emerging Republican Majority* (New Rochelle, N.Y.: Arlington House, 1969).

111. Black and Black, *Rise of Southern Republicans.*

112. There are 21 majority Anglo districts in both the 2002 (1151C) and 2004 (1374C) plans. In these districts, the average Anglo voting-age population is 70.0 percent in plan 1151C and 70.2 percent in plan 1374C. Among the 11 majority-minority districts under each plan, the average majority-minority voting-age population (black plus Hispanic) goes from 68.1 percent in plan 1151C to 68.5 percent under plan 1374C. By contrast, there is little doubt that the plan that sparked the redistricting battle, plan 1180C, would be struck down because of its blatant use of packing minority voters to ensure Republican gains. Plan 1180C includes 22 majority Anglo districts with an average Anglo voting-age population of 70.4 percent. And for the ten majority-minority districts in plan 1180C, the average majority-minority voting-age population is 73.7 percent.

14

Missing the Target: The Supreme Court, "One Person, One Vote," and Partisan Gerrymandering

Richard L. Engstrom

The delineation of the geographical districts used to elect members of the United States House of Representatives, state legislatures, and local legislative bodies has become an embarrassing aspect of American democracy. The purpose of this delineation, according to the U.S. Supreme Court, is to provide people with "fair and effective representation" within these bodies.[1] Unfortunately, however, that goal is often ignored by those designing and adopting districts, and the results of the process often miss that target by a wide margin. The politically driven process we employ to do this is especially conflictive and litigious compared to those used to designate electoral districts in other democracies.

Especially disappointing is the fact that, when the target is badly missed, the American judiciary rarely requires any corrective measures. The courts' approach to this problem is to emphasize one constraint, the basic equal population principle, well beyond the point of satiety, while largely washing its hands of what is now a much more fundamental problem—equipopulous gerrymandering. This misalignment in judicial priorities has created a redistricting climate ripe for manipulation by those much more interested in political gain than fair and effective representation for all the people.

This chapter will identify how we have arrived at this point, and also propose a way out of this political thicket through restructuring how we arrange electoral competition. The replacement of our current winner-take-all district systems with semiproportional arrangements such as limited, cumulative, and preference voting would greatly reduce the critical impact that district lines have on election outcomes. Geographically based districts can be retained in these arrangements and the resulting electoral outcomes will better reflect the diversity in political preferences among voters. Despite the rhetoric of some of their opponents, these semiproportional arrangements are not "proportional representation" systems. And their adoption in this country will not, by itself, result in numerous political parties gaining seats in legislative bodies, coalition governments, and political gridlock that American commentators so often associate with the more fully proportional systems.

PARTISAN REFERENTS FOR DISTRICT BOUNDARIES

The goal of fair and effective representation requires periodic revisions in district boundaries. This has been a decennial task, following the enumeration of the country's population, which happens every year that ends in zero. The round of redistricting following the 2000 census has been called "the most contentious ever."[2] The previous round was itself thought to have set records for the amount of conflict it generated, with the disputes over lines lasting into the second half of the decade in many settings, and into the next decade in some.[3]

When it came to statewide districting plans, the post-2000 round entailed more instances of the unabashed use of party referents in decisions concerning where to draw the district lines than ever before. The public battles in the previous decade centered more on the treatment of minorities protected by the Voting Rights Act, primarily African Americans and Latinos, than explicitly on political parties. There were numerous racial gerrymandering complaints, usually brought by minority voters but sometimes by white or Anglo voters, alleging that the lines discriminated against them. Concerns about party benefits were certainly in the background of many of these disputes, but rarely were they at the center of the rhetoric. In the post-2000 round things were different. The battles have been more explicitly partisan, with the complaints focusing on the partisan bias of the plans. Not only did party leaders and loyalists complain, so did minority voters. While the issues were more overtly partisan, minority voters alleged that they were reduced to pawns in the redistricting battles, with both Democrats and Republicans placing them where it advantaged the respective party the most. In some settings, leaders of a party that had control of the post-2000 redistricting process were unashamed to articulate their partisan motivations. Indeed, it has been noted that "While redistricters typically recoil from even the mildest accusation of *racial* motivation, they willingly confess if confronted with the starkest accusations of *partisan* motivation."[4]

A new issue arose in the post-2000 round of redistricting, that of partisan re-redistricting. The expression "re-redistricting" had been used previously to refer to additional changes made in new districting arrangements in response to the judicial invalidation of plans.[5] The term has taken on a new referent in the latest round of redistricting however. It became applied to an extraordinary phenomenon—replacing a new plan that had been found constitutionally sound by a court with another plan more favorable to the party that was in control of the government.

Two states, Texas and Colorado, chose to revise their congressional lines again after elections were held under new lines in 2002. The districts used in the 2002 election had been adopted in each state by courts after the state legislatures could not agree on new districts. The Republicans gained control of the redistricting process as a result of the subsequent state elections, and proceeded to adopt a second plan more favorable to their party. While re-redistricting required by the judicial invalidation of plans has been common, re-redistricting not required by a court has not been. The partisan motivations in redrawing the district lines a second time were obvious. This phenomenon caused great alarm, creating a fear that a controlling party could revise districts after every election in an effort to retain, or enhance, its majority status.[6] Colorado's second revision was invalidated by the state's supreme court as a violation of the state's constitution.[7] The Texas plan, however, which was projected to switch the thirty-two-member state delegation from 17 Democrats and 15 Republicans to 10 Democrats and 22 Republicans after the 2004 election, and help the Republicans maintain control of the House, was approved by a federal district court that found re-redistricting was not a violation of federal law. The Texas dispute was before the U.S. Supreme Court in 2004.[8]

JUDICIAL PRIORITIES

The intense partisan dimension to the post-2000 round of redistricting was not surprising. Partisan polarization in Washington[9] and the tight partisan division in the U.S. House—221 Republicans to 212 Democrats and two independents following the 2000 congressional elections—had made congressional districting a particularly sensitive matter. State legislative redistricting in states with competitive two-party systems was also frequently contentious. And computer-assisted redistricting made the manipulation of district boundaries easier. But equally important, if not more, was the widely held perception that the courts would not intervene in partisan gerrymandering disputes. While the Supreme Court had held in 1986 in *Davis v. Bandemer*,[10] that partisan gerrymandering was a violation of the Equal Protection Clause of the Fourteenth Amendment to the U.S. Constitution, no districting plan had ever been invalidated on that basis. It was widely assumed that the judicial reticence to be involved in this issue would continue.

As noted above, if the goal of redistricting is fair and effective representation, judicial priorities are missing that target. These perverse priorities could not be better illustrated than by one of the first federal court decisions reviewing new districts following the 2000 census, *Vieth v. Commonwealth of Pennsylvania* (2002).[11] The case involved congressional districts in Pennsylvania. The number of U.S. House seats allocated to Pennsylvania was reduced from 21 to 19 as a result of the census. There were two basic complaints about the new districts in this case. One was that the districts violated the one person, one vote standard, the other was that the plan was a blatant political gerrymander.

The state asked for summary judgment in its favor on both issues. Under this standard, "the court must accept the facts alleged in the complaint as true, and draw all reasonable inferences in favor of the plaintiff."[12] In short, even if all of the plaintiffs' factual allegations are correct, they would still lose under the law.

The population equality complaint was based on the plaintiffs' factual allegation that the largest and smallest districts in the plan differed by *nineteen* people. The least populous district in the plan, as of April 1, 2000, had 646,361 people in it, while the most populous district had 646,380.

The gerrymandering complaint alleged that the new plan was "designed to ensure that Republicans would win at least thirteen of the nineteen congressional seats."[13] The plan was adopted by a majority Republican legislature and signed by a Republican governor after, it was alleged, "prominent national figures in the Republican party," including Dennis Hastert, the Speaker of the U.S. House of Representatives, and Karl Rove, the high profile political advisor to President George Bush, pressured them to adopt a plan very favorable to Republicans "as a punitive measure against Democrats for having enacted apparently pro-Democratic redistricting plans in other states."[14] The state's Democratic legislators, it was further alleged, had "no input" into how the lines were drawn.[15] The Republican bias in the plan (thirteen of nineteen seats), the plaintiffs contended, was a gross deviation from the state's partisan make up. The two major parties were described as having "nearly equal support" in the state.[16] Major party voter registration was 53.6 percent Democratic and 46.4 percent Republican. The November 2000 congressional elections resulted in Democrats winning 50.6 percent of the two-party vote and ten of the twenty-one seats at that time, while the Republicans won 49.4 percent of the votes and 11 of the seats. The parties also split the two-party vote for five statewide contests in that November election by 50.1 percent to 49.9 percent in favor of the Democratic candidates.[17]

The outcome of the summary judgment motions left many political observers not versed in the law in disbelief. The court granted the motion on the partisan gerrymandering complaint, but denied the one concerning the deviations from perfect population equality. In a decision consistent with Supreme Court precedents, the gerrymandering claim was dismissed because the plaintiffs had failed to allege facts "indicating that they have been shut out of the political process."[18] The court noted specifically that plaintiffs had made:

> no allegations that anyone has ever prevented, or will ever prevent, Plaintiffs from: registering to vote; organizing with other like-minded voters; raising funds on behalf of candidates; voting; campaigning; or speaking out on matters of public concern.[19]

The plaintiffs were not allowed to have a full trial on the gerrymandering issue because they had not alleged discrimination on *matters unrelated to district lines*.[20] Two days of trial, however, were held subsequently on the nineteen-person population deviation, after which the court found this to violate the one person, one vote rule.[21] The plan was then revised by the state to bring the population deviation down to one person, which was as close to perfect equality as possible (each district contained either 646,371 or 646,372 people). This plan, a minimal revision that was of no consequence to the partisan complexion of the plan, was approved by the court.[22]

Viewed from the perspective of fair and effective representation, the alleged blatant partisan bias in the plan was, needless to say, a much more significant issue than that of a nineteen-person deviation across a set of districts with populations that exceed 646,000. This decision cannot be dismissed as the work of judges whose behavior is deviant from that of their brethren. In terms of the applicable case law, it was not a ludicrous decision. It was, as noted above, consistent with applicable Supreme Court precedents. In terms of the goal of fair and effective representation, however, it reflects how ludicrous the judicial priorities have become. The following identifies how we have arrived at a situation in which judges review trivial population deviations and ignore serious allegations of partisan gerrymandering.

POPULATION EQUALITY

The revision of election districts, as noted above, has been a decennial task. The process begins again after every census. Districts used to elect members of the U.S. House of Representatives, state legislatures, and local governing bodies are revised in order to bring them into compliance, prior to the next election, with the "one person, one vote" rule.[23]

U.S. House Districts

The application of the population equality rule to U.S. House districts is based on Art. I, Sec. 2 of the Constitution, which states in part "The House of Representatives shall be composed of Members chosen every second Year by the People of the several States." As interpreted in *Wesberry v. Sanders* (1964), this requires that districts be equal "as nearly as is practicable."[24] This requirement was implemented in an increasingly demanding manner by subsequent Supreme Court cases. The major Supreme Court precedent concerning population equality in congressional districts as the post-2000 round of redistricting started, and the one that the federal court in the *Vieth* case relied on to reject Pennsylvania's nineteen-person deviation, was that of *Karcher v. Daggett* (2003).[25]

In *Karcher* the Supreme Court rejected, in a 5 to 4 decision, a 1982 plan for congressional districts in New Jersey. The largest district in the plan contained 527,472 people, whereas the smallest contained 523,798. Expressed in percentage terms, the largest was 0.2682 percentage points above the average district size (526,059), and the smallest -0.4298 below the average, for a combined deviation of 0.698. These were extremely small deviations for congressional districts at the time.

The Court rejected the plan because these deviations did not result from a "good-faith" effort to achieve precise equality, and had not been justified as necessary to achieve a "legitimate state objective." The state argued that the deviations should be considered *de minimis* and therefore acceptable because they were smaller than the undercount of the population in the census. It also attempted to justify them based on the objective of maintaining African-American voting strength in the Trenton and Camden areas. These arguments were not found to be persuasive. The good-faith standard was not satisfied because other plans had been presented to the legislature that had "appreciably smaller population deviations"[26] and because it was possible to reduce the deviations in the plan "merely by shifting a handful of municipalities from one district to another."[27] The objective of preserving minority voting strength was rejected as a justification for the deviations because the Court found no link between this goal and the size of the deviations.[28]

The standard for congressional districts, as expressed in *Karcher*, is "there are no *de minimis* population variances, which could practicably be avoided, but which nonetheless meet the standard of Art. I, Sec. 2, without justification."[29] Those challenging a plan on one person, one vote grounds must establish the lack of "good faith," and if successful, the state must justify the deviations based on a "legitimate objective." The Court provided some illustrative objectives that might justify deviations, which were "making districts compact, respecting municipal boundaries, preserving the cores of prior districts, and avoiding contests between incumbent Representatives."[30] When attempting to justify deviations, the Court held that a state must "show with some specificity that a particular objective required the specific deviations in its plan, rather than simply relying on general assertions."[31] The Court did provide judges with considerable discretion in making these determinations, however, stating further that the standard was "flexible depending on the size of the deviations, the importance of the State's interest, and the availability of alternatives that might substantially vindicate those interests yet approximate population equality more closely."[32]

A trial was held in the *Vieth* case, as noted above, on the nineteen-person deviation in Pennsylvania's congressional districts. The court, in a two to one decision, held that that the districts failed to satisfy the *Karcher* test. The fact that the deviation concerned only nineteen people was not disputed by the state. The court held, however, that this deviation did not result from a "good-faith effort" because the person drawing the map was instructed by Republican party leaders to stop after the deviation had been lowered to nineteen.[33] The state attempted to justify the deviation by asserting a goal of not splitting precincts; only six of the 9,427 precincts around the state had been split. And the court did state that such a goal could serve to justify the small deviation. The justification, however, was found by the court to be "a mere pretext,"[34] as it had been demonstrated by the plaintiffs that a plan with only a one person deviation, the lowest possible, could be drawn without splitting any precincts. The deviations, therefore, were avoidable.

State and Local Legislative Districts

There is more flexibility in the one person, one vote rule when the districts at issue are for state and local legislative bodies. The application of the population equality rule to these districts is based on the Equal Protection Clause of the Fourteenth Amendment to the federal Constitution.

The law concerning state and local districts sounds similar to that for congressional. The responsible government is supposed to make "an honest and good faith effort to construct districts . . . as nearly equal in population as is practicable."[35] And deviations from precise equality are permissible as long as they are based on "legitimate considerations incident to the effectuation of a rational state policy."[36] In application, however, these levels of government are not held to the same standards as those applied to congressional districts.

When it comes to state and local governments, the Supreme Court has established a "10 percent rule" for allocating the burden of proof in population equality disputes. This rule evolved over a number of cases during the 1970s and 1980s, during which the Supreme Court distinguished state and local districting from congressional, and held that some deviations at these lower levels would be considered minor and therefore not in need of justification unless the plan reflected a less than good faith effort to attain precise equality.[37] The 10 percent threshold is used as a decision rule that determines which party, those challenging the plan or the state or local government responsible for the plan, has the initial burden of proof in a one person, one vote case, rather than a rule that determines who wins on that issue, as some have interpreted it.

The threshold concerns the combined values of the deviations from the average district population of the most populous and least populous districts within a plan. These deviations are each expressed as a percentage of the average, and these absolute values added together. If the largest district is over the average by 5.0 percentage points, for example, and the smallest is under by 5.0 percentage points, then the combined or total deviation equals 10.0. If the combined deviation exceeds 10.0, then the government responsible for the plan must justify the deviations as resulting from a rational policy or policies concerning districting. When the number is 10.0 or less, the plan is considered presumptively constitutional, at least in terms of population equality, and the burden falls on the challengers to show that a good faith effort to achieve equality had not been made. If they are successful, then the state or local government has the burden to justify the deviations.

It was a widely held view that keeping the combined deviations under 10 percentage points was a "safe harbor" for governments. Recent decisions, however, have made it clear that it is not. In the latest round of redistricting two federal district courts have invalidated plans in which the combined deviations were close to, but yet under, that threshold. Both decisions might be called "backdoor" invalidations of partisan gerrymanders, an expression that applies to invalidating a gerrymander on grounds other than gerrymandering,[38] as both courts stressed, when rejecting the districts, the partisan processes through which the plans had been adopted and/or the partisan features of the plans themselves.

"Backdoor" Invalidations of Partisan Plans

One case, *Larios v. Cox* (2004),[39] concerned state house and senate districts in Georgia. The most and least populous districts in the plan for each chamber had deviations of 4.99 percent and -4.99 percent. The total deviation, therefore, was 9.98. The state adopted redistricting guidelines that emphasized keeping all districts within 5.0 percentage points, viewing this as a safe harbor on population equality. This was not viewed by the court as a good faith effort to reach precise equality, however, as it was possible to reduce the maximum deviations to a single person. The state attempted to justify the deviations through two policies. One was the minimization of the loss in representation for the rural, southern portion of the state and the inner city of Atlanta. Districts in those areas, which have been losing population, consistently had population deviations under the average, many exceeding 4.0 percentage points. This minimization came at the expense of the fast growing suburbs north of Atlanta, in which districts were consistently overpopulated, with deviations often over 4.0 percentage points. Given voting patterns in Georgia, this had the effect of underpopulating the districts of Democratic incumbents and overpopulating those of Republicans. A regional preference was not found to be a legitimate state policy, and in this case, the court found the preference was impossible to separate from a partisan preference.[40]

The second policy cited by Georgia was the protection of incumbents. But this policy was found to be applied in a selective manner—Democratic incumbents were being protected, Republican incumbents were not. In the House plan, half of the Republican incumbents (thirty-seven of seventy-four) were placed in districts with another incumbent, usually another Republican. Only nine of the 105 Democratic incumbents were placed in districts with other incumbents. On the senate side, these respective figures were ten of twenty-four Republicans and two of thirty-two Democrats. The court noted that "the protection of incumbents is a permissible cause of population deviations only when it is limited to the avoidance of contests between incumbents and is applied in a consistent and nondiscriminatory manner."[41] Georgia's policy, the court concluded, was "overexpansive" and "blatantly partisan"[42] and therefore not a legitimate justification.[43] The court had earlier, however, dismissed the plaintiffs' complaint that the plans were partisan gerrymanders by granting summary judgment to the state on that issue,[44] just as the *Vieth* court did in Pennsylvania.

In another case, *Hulme v. Madison County* (2001),[45] a combined deviation of 9.3 percentage points in districts for a county board in Illinois was found to violate the one person, one vote requirement. Republican plaintiffs complained that the process through which the plan was adopted was "tainted with arbitrariness and discrimination."[46] The board consisted of 24 Democrats and five Republicans, and the court found that the process was not conducted in good faith. The court concluded that the entire process was designed to pursue the political agenda of one person, the Democrat who chaired the committee assigned to deal with redistricting. His goal on the population equality issue was to keep the total deviation within the 10 percent limit, rather than try to get deviations closer to precise equality. His political agenda, however, was "to create districts that would not simply disadvantage Republican members of the Board, but 'cannibalize' their districts to the greatest extent possible."[47] The process, the court found, was "characterized by threats, coercion, and bullying."[48] Indeed, the court even quoted this person as telling a Republican member of the Board who had proposed an alternative map, "We are going to shove it [the map] up your f—— ass, and you are going to like it, and I'll f—— any Republican I can."[49] The court held that if this individual's agenda had not dominated the process, the board could have adopted a plan with much lower population deviations. The county's only defense was that the total deviation required no justification because it was less than 10.0 percent.

PARTISAN GERRYMANDERING

Much of the rhetoric in redistricting debates focuses on population deviations. When a plan has a lower total deviation than another plan, that deviation is frequently cited by legislators and litigants as a reason to favor that plan over the other. These deviations, however, are rarely the real reason for the disputes over lines. It is hard to believe that "zeroing out" a nineteen-person maximum deviation in a set of congressional districts, or lowering deviations already under 10 percentage points in a plan for a state legislature or a city council, will affect the quality of representation provided the residents of a state or locality. It is the perceived political consequences of different plans that are the real issue in redistricting. These consequences may concern the reelection prospects of incumbent legislators, the projected ability of African Americans, Latinos, Native Americans, and other groups to elect representatives of their choice, and of course in governmental jurisdictions with competitive political parties, the partisan consequences of the plans. The equipopulous requirement does not reduce the options to a single plan; rather, numerous plans with vastly different political consequences can normally satisfy that requirement.

The courts readily acknowledge that "politics and political considerations are inseparable from districting and apportionment."[50] But they decline to police even blatant political abuses that result from the process, including those that are discriminatory toward protected minority groups, provided they can be attributed to partisan rather than racial motives.[51] Supreme Court decisions, as a former justice of that court warned, have given the "constitutional green light" to politically biased districting plans.[52] Indeed, an expression that some might find an oxymoron, "constitutional political gerrymandering," is now an expression used with no sense of contradiction by Supreme Court justices themselves.[53]

The *Vieth* case in Pennsylvania was not an isolated example of the judiciary's unfortunate focus on minor deviations in population equality while ignoring the more serious issue of partisan gerrymandering. One of the "pro-Democratic" congressional plans that the Republican action in Pennsylvania was allegedly in retaliation to was that in Georgia. Georgia was apportioned two new seats in the U.S. House as a result of the 2000 census, bringing the total number of seats to 13. Republican plaintiffs maintained, in *Larios v. Perdue* (2003),[54] that the state's plan for these 13 seats was an effort "to maximize the political advantage of the Democratic party." The plan allegedly was designed to turn the state's delegation to the House from eight Republicans and three Democrats to seven Democrats and six Republicans.[55] They also maintained, as did the Democratic plaintiffs in Pennsylvania, that the deviations from precise population equality in the plan violated the "one person, one vote" rule. The most populous district in Georgia was thirty-five people above the average, while the least populous was thirty-seven people below. This combined deviation of seventy-two people constituted, in percentage terms, a deviation of about .0001 percent from the average district.[56] The federal court in Georgia, like that in Pennsylvania, granted summary judgment to the state on the partisan gerrymandering claim but proceeded to trial on the population equality issue, despite acknowledging that these deviations were "exceedingly minute."[57] Summary judgment was also granted to the state, as noted above, on the issue of partisan gerrymandering in Georgia's state house and senate. All partisan gerrymandering claims during the post-2000 round of redistricting have been dismissed, including complaints against congressional districts in Florida,[58] Michigan,[59] Maryland,[60] and Texas.[61]

Davis v. Bandemer

The reason that plaintiffs have had such a difficult time with their partisan gerrymandering claims has been a Supreme Court precedent that held that partisan gerrymander is unconstitutional under the Equal Protection Clause yet, at the same time, established a burden of proof for plaintiffs that made this prohibition "virtually unenforceable."[62] In fact the burden imposed on plaintiffs had *nothing to do with gerrymandering*, but required proof that the supporters of a major political party were being discriminated against in aspects of the political process having nothing to do with the way district lines are arranged.

The precedent was *Davis v. Bandemer*, a 1986 Supreme Court decision concerning state legislative redistricting in Indiana.[63] The plans were adopted by a Republican controlled legislature and signed into law by a Republican governor. The Democrats complained that the plans were a Republican gerrymander, and the district court agreed. The Supreme Court recited the lower court's findings that the plans were:

> an intentional effort to favor Republican incumbents and candidates and to disadvantage Democratic voters. This was achieved by "stacking" Democrats into districts with large Democratic majorities and "splitting" them in other districts to give Republicans safe but not excessive majorities in those districts.[64]

The Court never disagreed with this finding, and Republican witnesses openly admitted to the partisan motivations behind the plans.[65]

The Supreme Court response was very divided. Three members of the Court held that partisan gerrymandering was a "nonjusticiable political question" with which courts should not even be involved.[66] Two other justices concluded that the plans were "a paradigm example of unconstitutional discrimination."[67] A four-member plurality held that partisan gerrymandering, if found, would be unconstitutional under the Fourteenth Amendment's Equal

Protection Clause, but it did not agree with the district court that the plans in Indiana rose to that level. The districts therefore were allowed to stand.

The plurality opinion in *Bandemer* has been followed by the lower courts. It established a two-part test for unconstitutional partisan gerrymandering, holding that the burden on plaintiffs alleging partisan gerrymandering includes proof of a purpose to discriminate and also "an actual discriminatory effect."[68] This first part of the test has not been a problem for plaintiffs. Indeed, acknowledging the pervasive role that politics can play in redistricting, the plurality stated, "As long as redistricting is done by a legislature, it should not be very difficult to prove that the likely political consequences of the reapportionment were intended."[69] The effects part of the test, however, has presented plaintiffs with an impossible burden of proof. It requires, as noted above, more than proof of gerrymandering. It requires proof that "the election system is arranged in a manner that will consistently degrade a voter's or a group of voters' influence on *the political process as a whole*."[70]

This effects prong was modeled after earlier cases involving racial discrimination in multimember legislative districts, where proof of minority exclusion from many aspects of the political process, including voter registration and subsequent election participation, and participation in party slating and more formal nomination processes, played a central role.[71] A finding of unconstitutional partisan gerrymandering, the *Bandemer* plurality held, "must be supported by evidence of continued frustration of the will of a majority of the voters or effective denial to a minority of voters of a fair chance to influence the political process."[72] In short, evidence of "stacking" and "splitting" one party's voters within and across districts, the classic tools of gerrymandering, had nothing to do with the constitutional test for the existence of that phenomenon.

While multiple parties appear on some ballots, such as presidential ballots, the United States in effect has a two-party system. The effects portion of the *Bandemer* test, which concerns *the political process as a whole*, is impossible for the supporters of one of the two major parties to meet. It is easy to look at the impact of this test and conclude that "In *Davis v. Bandemer* the Court essentially found political gerrymandering to be constitutional."[73] This was the prevailing view of the law when the post-2000 round of redistricting started, as no partisan gerrymandering allegation had ever been successful under that standard.[74]

Vieth v. Jubelirer

The *Bandemer* decision was revisited by the Supreme Court in 2004. The medium was the *Vieth* decision that granted summary judgment to the state on the partisan gerrymandering complaint against Pennsylvania congressional districts.[75] In another badly divided decision, *Vieth* survived, at least in the outcome, but *Bandemer*'s test did not.

Four justices voted, in *Vieth v. Jubelirer*,[76] to overrule *Bandemer*, holding that partisan gerrymandering was a "political question" that courts should avoid deciding. The eighteen years after *Bandemer*, they concluded, had demonstrated that there are no "judiciary discoverable and manageable standards" for resolving the issue.[77] Four other judges voted to continue the primary holding in *Bandemer* that partisan gerrymandering violates the Fourteenth Amendment, but interpreted the eighteen-year experience differently, and more accurately, by noting that the search for such standards had been impeded by lower courts following precedent, i.e., the effects test established by *Bandemer*'s plurality. These judges voted to vacate the lower court decision in *Vieth* and remand the case for further consideration of the partisan gerrymandering complaint. But they provided little clear guidance, offering among them three different tests for identifying unconstitutional partisan gerrymandering.[78] The ninth justice, Anthony Kennedy, took a middle position. He stated that it was premature to conclude that a manageable test could not be devised, and expressed the fear that "if courts refuse to entertain any claims of partisan gerrymandering, the temptation to use partisan favoritism in districting in an unconstitutional manner will grow."[79] He also provided no clarity on the issue of how to identify the practice, however, rejecting all of the tests proposed by the plaintiffs and other justices. He did suggest that the freedoms of speech and association protected by the First Amendment, however, may be a more effective source of a test than the Fourteenth Amendment.

After *Vieth*, partisan gerrymandering remains unconstitutional in theory, but still not in fact. The door may be open to find a standard through which to police the practice, but with four justices preferring to relieve the courts of any such responsibility, there is not great cause for optimism. *Vieth* leaves "the business of rigging elections" intact for now,[80] and more partisan conflict and costly litigation can be expected, even before the next census if re-redistricting becomes a more frequent practice.

Other recent Supreme Court decisions involving race and redistricting have demonstrated considerable judicial tolerance of partisan considerations as well. In the Court's last redistricting decision prior to the 2000 round of redistricting, *Easley v. Cromartie* (2001),[81] it held that states could defend against allegations of unconstitutional "racial gerrymandering," in this instance intended to help rather than hurt the reelection chances of an African American Democratic congressman, by showing that the motive in drawing the district was partisan rather than racial. The Court found in this particular case that it was not possible to determine from the evidence whether the North Carolina congressional district at issue was designed primarily for a racial or a partisan purpose, and therefore declined to examine the gerrymandering allegation for compliance with the Fourteenth Amendment.

Likewise, in a case involving the preclearance requirement of Section 5 of the Voting Rights Act, the Court in *Georgia v. Ashcroft* (2003)[82] concluded that it was a legitimate choice for Georgia to disperse African American voters across a number of state senate districts. While this would reduce their ability to elect representatives of their own choice, i.e., other African Americans,[83] it would allow for the creation of more so-called "influence districts," in which white Democrats are likely to be elected. Influence districts were intended to help Democrats maintain a majority of the chamber and presumably enhance the overall responsiveness of that legislative body to the African American position on issues before it. Structuring electoral competition to enhance partisan prospects, it is clear, still has the "green light" in American jurisprudence.

ALTERNATIVE ELECTION SYSTEMS

Fair and effective representation, though the goal of redistricting according to *Reynolds v. Sims*, is not the goal pursued by the courts when overseeing this process and its products. The courts have chosen to emphasize that which is easily measured, population equality, to the point of extremely diminished, sometimes counterproductive, returns. The more serious, and admittedly more difficult, problem of partisan gerrymandering, however, remains, and judicial protection against it is only theoretical. Four Supreme Court justices even declared, in *Vieth*, that for them "'Fairness' does not seem to us a judicially manageable standard."[84] If partisan considerations are not to become "the be-all and end-all in apportioning representatives,"[85] relief will have to come from another source. A popular reform proposal is to place the responsibility for drawing district lines with an independent or bipartisan commission, rather than with legislative bodies themselves. But as long as districts are embedded in an election system in which they are winner-take-all electoral units, the location of district lines will be politically sensitive, regardless of who decides where they are placed. Conflict and litigation over lines is likely to continue, as Arizona has experienced with the post-2000 district revisions performed by its new Independent Redistricting Commission.[86] It has even been said that, when it comes to redistricting conflict and litigation, "You are not going to avoid it unless Christ himself came down to draw the lines."[87]

Another approach would be to adopt election systems in which districts will not be so outcome determinative.[88] As noted above, the replacement of our current winner-take-all district systems with semiproportional arrangements such as limited, cumulative, and preference voting would greatly reduce the critical impact that district lines have on election outcomes. Geographically based districts can be retained in these arrangements and the resulting electoral outcomes will better reflect the diversity in political preferences, including partisan preferences, among voters. These systems can be used with multimember geographical districts. They vary from the typical multiseat elections held in this country, however, in that the rules concerning how votes may be cast are different. The voting rules usually employed in multiseat elections are (1) every voter is allowed to cast as many votes as there are seats to be filled, but (2) only one of those votes may be cast for any particular candidate. The winners of the seats are then determined by a plurality vote rule; the N candidates receiving votes from the most voters win the N available seats.

Limited Voting

Limited voting makes the simplest change in the voting rules. In this system each voter in a multiseat election is provided with a number of votes that is less than the number of seats to be filled. For example, if five people are to be elected at large across an entire political jurisdiction or from a geographical district, each voter in that electoral unit may be limited to casting only a single vote. The limitation could also be set at two, or three, or even four. The defining characteristic of limited voting is simply that the number of votes be less than the number of seats. Voters are still restricted to casting only one vote for any particular candidate. Winning candidates are determined by a simple plurality rule; the top N vote recipients are elected to the N seats at issue.

Cumulative Voting

Under cumulative voting rules, each voter may continue to be provided with as many votes as there are seats to be filled, but the restriction that only a single vote may be cast for any particular candidate is removed. Voters may still, if they wish, provide several candidates with one vote apiece. But they also have the option to cumulate their votes behind fewer candidates than there are seats being filled. Generally, the only restriction in distributing votes among the candidates is that the votes be cast in whole units. In a five-seat, five-vote election, for example, voters retain the option of voting for five different candidates, giving each a single vote. But if a voter prefers some candidates more intensely than the others, he or she may cast the five votes for fewer than five candidates. A voter with a strong preference for two particular candidates, for instance, could cast two votes for each of them and another vote for a third candidate, while a voter who strongly prefers the election of one particular candidate could cast all five of his or her votes for that candidate (a practice known as "plumping").[89] As with limited voting, winning candidates are determined by a simple plurality rule.

Preference Voting

The third modified multiseat system receiving attention is preference voting, also know as choice voting and as the single transferable vote (STV). It is like the one vote limited system in that every voter is allocated a single vote. Under preference voting, however, voters are allowed to indicate more than just their first choice among the candidates. Voters may also, if they wish, rank order candidates to reflect their relative preferences among them. In other words, a voter may rank his of her first choice as "1," second choice as "2," third choice as "3," etc., until the voter no longer cares to distinguish among the remaining candidates.

Candidates are rank ordered in a preference voting election because votes that would be "wasted" on one candidate can be transferred to another candidate. A vote is wasted in either of two ways. It could be cast in support of a losing candidate, or it could be a "surplus" vote cast in support of a candidate who would win without it. Rather than have the vote wasted in these situations, preference voting allows that vote to be transferred to another candidate, provided the voter has specified a subsequent preference. Preference voting is a system designed to increase the proportion of voters in an election whose vote will ultimately contribute to the election of a candidate.

The winning candidates in a preference voting election are those whose votes equal or exceed a specified number. This number is usually based on the *Droop quota*, which is the lowest number of votes that can be required for election and yet limit the number of individuals elected to the number of seats to be filled. This quota is 1 more than the quotient obtained when the total number of votes cast in an election is divided by 1 plus the number of seats to be filled. If 3 seats are to be filled and 1,000 votes are cast, for example, the quota will be 251, the value that results from dividing 1,000 by (3 + 1), and then adding 1.

The first step in counting the votes in a preference voting election is to allocate to each candidate the ballots on which he or she is listed as the first preference. If none of the candidates has a number of first preferences equal to or exceeding the quota, then the candidate with the fewest first preference votes is considered defeated and the votes received by that candidate transferred to the candidates listed as the second preference on those ballots. Each candidate's votes are then recounted. If a candidate exceeds the quota, however, then that candidate is declared elected and any surplus votes (above the quota) received by the candidate are redistributed to the candidates listed as the next preference. Whereas transferring the votes of a defeated candidate is straightforward (all of that candidate's votes are transferred to the next most preferred candidates among the remaining candidates), transferring surplus votes is more complicated. Several methods are available for transferring surplus votes. The simplest is to declare a candidate elected once his or her vote matches the quota and then transfer all of the subsequent ballots that go to that candidate. Another method, used in Ireland where preference voting is employed to elect the Dail, the lower (and most significant) house of parliament, is to select randomly a number of ballots equal to a candidate's surplus and transfer those ballots to the next available preference. A third method, probably the most preferable now that computers can be used to count votes, is to redistribute the surplus in a proportional manner. Each remaining candidate (not already elected or eliminated) would be given a share of the surplus votes equal to the proportion of the ballots on which he or she was the next choice of the voters.[90]

A count of the ballots in a hypothetical preference voting election involving five candidates competing for three seats is contained in table 14.1. It assumes that 2,000 votes are cast, so the Droop quota is 501. The first preferences of the voters are distributed as reflected in the column labeled First Count. Candidate C1 receives 480 first preference votes, candidate C2 receives 470, C3 450, C4 350, and C5 250. Given that none of the candidates has met the quota, the lowest vote recipient, C5, is eliminated and his votes redistributed. Most of C5's voters, 200, identified C4 as their second preference, and therefore C4 receives 200 votes via transfer from C5. The other candidates receive only a few of C5's votes, 15, 25, and 10 respectively for C1, C2, and C3. When the second preferences are added to the first preferences, reflected in the column labeled Second Count, C4's new vote total is 550, which exceeds the quota. C4 is therefore declared elected and his 49 surplus votes redistributed. If these surplus votes are transferred proportionally, and C1 is the next preference among the remaining candidates on 281 of C4's ballots, C2 the next preference on 224 of them, and C3 the next preference on 45, then the C1 would receive 25 of the surplus votes, C2 20, and C3 only four. When these votes are added to the candidates' totals, the results, reported in the column labeled Third Count, put C1 and C2 over the quota. C1 and C2 are therefore declared elected to the two remaining seats and the counting of the votes concluded.

Table 14.1. A Hypothetical Preference Voting Election for Three Seats

Candidate	*First Count*	*Transfer*	*Second Count*	*Transfer*	*Third Count*
C1	480	+15	495	+25	520 *elected*
C2	470	+25	495	+20	515 *elected*
C3	450	+10	460	+4	464
C4	350	+200	550 *elected*		
C5	250 *eliminated*				

Preference voting, as noted above, is like limited voting when the number of votes is limited to one. This reduces the ability of a cohesive plurality to win all of the seats. In addition, the transfer feature allows a group to transfer what would otherwise be wasted ballots among more than one candidate preferred by its voters, a feature that makes intragroup competition less likely to cause the defeat of candidates preferred by the group.

All three of these modified multiseat systems satisfy the basic "one person, one vote" rule, or individual voter equality requirement, because every voter has the same number of votes and the same options through which to cast them. Every voter, in short, is treated equally.[91]

SEMIPROPORTIONAL OR SEMIPLURALITY SYSTEMS

These election systems are called semiproportional, or semiplurality,[92] systems because they open up the opportunity for more than one group, including the supporters of a political party, to elect a representative within a district. It is easier to comply with traditional districting criteria in the larger multimember districts. For example, it is easier to make multimember districts contiguous and more compact than are the single-member districts in use today. It is also easier to keep local governments and even voting precincts intact within these larger districts, and to use their boundaries as parts of district boundaries as well. And these larger districts facilitate keeping "communities of interest" intact within districts. These are considerations often thought to improve the representation that people receive through districting arrangements, and that are, with the exception of contiguity, often trumped by political considerations in the design of single member districts.

Threshold of Exclusion

When combined with the usual plurality rules used in this country, multimember districts often function as "winner-take-all" arrangements for the largest party or group in the district. The tendency for the leading political party, or largest racial group, to sweep all of the seats in multi-member districts has been well documented.[93] When the voting rules identified above are used with multimember districts, however, this sweep effect is typically eliminated. These arrangements can provide groups of voters that do not constitute the plurality in a district an opportunity to elect one, or some, of the district's representatives.

These opportunities can be demonstrated theoretically through a coefficient known as the *threshold of exclusion*.[94] This coefficient identifies the percentage or proportion of a district that a group's voters must exceed in order to elect a candidate of its choice *regardless of how the rest of the voters vote*. This coefficient is based on a set of worst case assumptions, from that group's perspective, about the behavior of the other voters. Expressed in partisan terms, concerning Party A, these assumptions are:

1. the voters in favor of Party B cast all of the votes available to them, but
2. none of these votes are cast for the candidate or candidates preferred by party A's voters, but rather are
3. concentrated entirely on the candidates of Party B, for which the number of candidates equal the number of seats to be filled, and are
4. divided evenly among Party B's candidates.

The other voters, in short, are assumed to cast their votes as efficiently as possible in a multiseat election.

The value of the threshold of exclusion for limited voting systems depends on both the number of seats to be filled and on how limited the vote is. The formula for calculating this threshold for limited voting, expressed as a percentage, is:

$$[V/(V + S)] * 100$$

where V = number of votes and S = number of seats.

If the vote is limited to one, for example, the threshold value for a three-seat election is [1/(1+3)]100, or 25.0 percent. In other words, if 251 voters out of 1000 (25 percent+1) all voted for a particular candidate of Party A, then that candidate must be elected to one of the three seats. Even if the other 749 voted according to the worst case assumptions, casting all of their votes for the three candidates for Party B, with candidate B1 receiving 250, B2 also receiving 250, and candidate B3 249, the candidate of Party A would be the highest vote recipient and therefore win a seat. If the Party B voters did not vote according to the worst case assumptions, but instead cast their votes unevenly so that B1 received 260 and B2 255, for example, then the most that B3 can receive is 234 and the Party A candidate still wins one of the three seats.

Illustrative values of the threshold for limited voting, for various seat and vote combinations, are reported in table 14.2. For any number of seats, the more limited the vote is, the lower will be the value of the threshold. Likewise, for any number of votes, the larger the number of seats, the lower the threshold value. The threshold for a two-vote, three-seat election, for example, is 40.0 percent, while that for a one-vote, five-seat election is 16.7 percent.

Table 14.2. Threshold of Exclusion Values

Number of Seats	*Cumulative and Preference Voting*	*Limited Voting*		
		1 Vote	*2 Votes*	*3 Votes*
2	33.3	33.3	—	—
3	25.0	25.0	40.0	—
4	20.0	20.0	33.3	42.9
5	16.7	16.7	28.6	37.5
6	14.3	14.3	25.0	33.3
7	12.5	12.5	22.2	30.0
8	11.1	11.1	20.0	27.3
9	10.0	10.0	18.2	25.0

The formula for calculating the threshold of exclusions value for cumulative voting systems, expressed as a percentage, is:

$$[1/(1 + S)] * 100$$

where S = number of seats.

This is the same as that for limited voting when the number of votes is one. In the three-seat cumulative context, for example, the threshold is again 25.0 percent. In other words, if those 251 voters out of 1,000 (25 percent+1) each "plumped" all three of their votes for Party A's candidate, giving him 753 votes, then A again must win one of the seats. The other 749 voters could distribute their 2,247 votes evenly across only three candidates, so that B1, B2, and B3 each receive 749, and Party A's candidate would still be a winner. Again, if Party B's voters deviated from the worst case assumptions, giving more votes to two of their choices, their third choice would have fewer votes than 749 and therefore Party A's candidate would still win a seat with 753 votes. As with the one vote limited context, the more seats at issue the lower will be the value of the threshold for cumulative voting. Illustrative values of the threshold for the cumulative context, for different numbers of seats, are also reported in table 14.2.

If the Droop quota used with preference voting systems, which identifies the number of votes a candidate must receive in order to be elected, is expressed as a percentage of votes, it is also the same as the threshold of exclusion (plus 1 vote) for a one vote limited system or a cumulative system. As noted above, the Droop quota for a three-seat election with 1,000 voters is 251. This is the result of dividing 1,000 by (3+1), and adding 1. Any group of party voters, in short, that can provide a candidate with at least 25 percent plus one of the votes can elect that candidate to one of the three seats in a preference voting election, just as in a one vote limited or cumulative voting election. The threshold values for preference voting therefore also vary inversely with the number of seats, just as in the other systems.

The threshold of exclusion, it must be remembered, identifies the percentage of the voters in a particular election that a group sharing the same candidate preference must exceed in order to elect that candidate with no assistance whatsoever from the other voters. If the behavior of other voters deviates in any way from the worst-case assumptions, then a group of voters may be smaller and/or less cohesive in its preferences and still have a realistic opportunity to elect a candidate or candidates of its choice through one of these voting systems.

The opportunities provided by these alternative systems are not limited to political parties and protected minorities. They are especially helpful for groups that share interests that are not based on, or strongly associated with, geography. Geographic proximity is certainly not a necessary condition for shared interests. Many of the most salient interests of people are not place related. Ideological beliefs, religious values, and ethnic identities are just some sources of shared political interests that are rarely distributed in a geographically compact fashion. Voters concerned with particular clusters of issues, such as gender discrimination, gay rights, or environmental protection, do not all share neighborhoods.[95] Alternative voting systems allow voters to determine which interests are most important to them and to vote accordingly. Voters concerned with place-related interests can vote based on those interests. But those who find other interests of greater importance can vote based on those concerns. The effectiveness of a person's vote, therefore, will not be so dependent on where they happen to live.[96]

AMERICAN EXPERIENCE WITH ALTERNATIVE SYSTEMS

About one hundred local units of government currently conduct elections under limited or cumulative voting. These governments have adopted these systems primarily in response to complaints of minority vote dilution.[97] The recent experience with these systems has resulted in more African American, Latinos, and Native Americans being elected,[98] and also candidates of the smaller of the two major parties in an area.[99] Their use has also been found to have increased electoral competition, mobilized groups, and increased voter turnout.[100]

The opponents of these systems have essentially regurgitated the complaints one hears in this country about proportional representation systems. They raise concerns about multiple political parties, the election of extremists, coalition governments, and legislative gridlock. They raise the specter of the factionalized political systems of Israel and Italy being exported to the United States. While these generalizations about the experience abroad with proportional systems are themselves subject to dispute,[101] their application to the semi proportional systems proposed in the United States ignores the critical difference in the number of seats proposed to be allocated to districts in these systems. The proponents of these systems almost invariably recommend that only a few seats be allocated to each district, rather than the large number typically found in proportional systems. When district magnitudes are low, such as three to five, the tendency toward serious fractionalization is greatly reduced.[102] Indeed, when Illinois used cumulative voting in three-member districts to elect the lower house of its legislature from 1870 to 1980, the state had a thriving two-party system the entire time.[103]

CONCLUSION

The rules under which the districting game is governed certainly do not demand that "fair and effective" representation be a high priority. Indeed, the opposite is the case. While population equality requirements are pushed beyond any concern for representation by the courts, the serious issue of partisan gerrymandering is, in effect, ignored. The courts seem little inclined to deal with the political referents in line drawing. Indeed, one commentator has even suggested that when it comes to political referents in districting plans, "even deals with the devil, it seems, are legally binding and will be enforced by the courts."[104]

A remedy for blatant partisan gerrymandering is not likely to be found through the courts. A much better approach to the problem will be to adopt election arrangements in which the location of district lines will have less impact on election outcomes. Semiproportional election systems like limited, cumulative, and preference voting are such arrangements. These systems take the emphasis off a party or group constituting a majority within a district, and provide electoral opportunities for those that receive substantial but less than majority support within a district. They also can provide electoral opportunities for groups that share salient interests that are not geographically based. These systems would also facilitate compliance with traditional districting criteria that are widely viewed as facilitating quality representation. They are also likely to make elections much more competitive than are elections today. Less reliance on the courts, and more on structural revisions in our election systems, will make fair and effective representation a more achievable goal.

NOTES

1. *Reynolds v. Sims*, 377 U.S. 533, 565–566 (1964).
2. Kenneth Jost, "Redistricting Disputes," *CQ Researcher*, 14 (May 12, 2004), 236.

3. See Richard L. Engstrom, "The Post-2000 Round of Redistricting: An Entangled Thicket within the Federal System," *Publius: The Journal of Federalism*, 32 (4, 2002): 51–70.

4. Reply Brief in Support of Application for a Stay or Injunction Pending Appeal, *Jackson v. Perry*, No. 03A581, in the Supreme Court of the United States, at 8–9 (emphasis in original), 2004.

5. See Engstrom, "Post-2000 Round," 56, and Jeffery C. Kubin, "The Case for Redistricting Commissions," *Texas Law Review*, 75 (March 1997): 837–72.

6. It has been reported that reredistricting for partisan reasons has been considered in at least five other states. Republicans in Georgia and Ohio have considered it, as have Democrats in California, Illinois, and Oklahoma (Mitchell Berman, "Putting Fairness on the Map: The High Court Has a Chance to Ease Flagrant Partisan Gerrymandering," *Los Angeles Times*, May 28, 2004).

7. *People ex rel. Salazar v. Davidson*, 79 P. 3d 1221 (2003), cert. denied, *Colorado General Assembly v. Salazar*—U.S.—(June 7, 2004).

8. *Jackson v. Perry*, No. 03A581. The re-redistricting process in Texas attracted nationwide attention due to the flight of Democratic state legislators from the state in an effort to block legislative consideration of the Republican's plan. Democratic members of the state house were the first to leave, encamping in a hotel in Ardmore, Oklahoma. Later, Democratic state senators retreated to a hotel in Albuquerque, New Mexico. For details of the Texas experience, see James W. Riddlesperger, "Redistricting Politics in Texas, 2003," paper presented at the 2004 Annual Meeting of the Southern Political Science Association, New Orleans, LA, January 8–9.

9. See, e.g., Brief of Political Scientists Bernard Grofman and Gary Jacobson as *Amici Curiae* in Support of Neither Party. *Vieth v. Jubelirer*, United States Supreme Court, No. 02-1580, 2003.

10. 478 U.S. 109.

11. 188 F. Supp. 2d 532 (M.D. Penna. 2002).

12. *Ibid.*, at 538.

13. Quoted in *id.*, at 536.

14. Quoted in *id.*, at 535.

15. *Id.*, at 535.

16. *Id.*, at 536.

17. *Id.*

18. *Id*, at 547.

19. *Id.*

20. The Pennsylvania Supreme Court dismissed the partisan gerrymander complaint for essentially the same reason (see *Erfer v. Commonwealth of Pennsylvania*, 2002 Pa. Lexis 482, 22–23).

21. *Vieth v. Commonwealth of Pennsylvania*, 195 F. Supp. 2d 672 (M.D. Pa. 2002).

22. *Vieth v. Commonwealth of Pennsylvania*, 241 F. Supp. 2d 478 (M.D. Pa. 2003).

23. See *Wesberry v. Sanders*, 376 U.S. 1 (1964), *Reynolds v. Sims*, 377 U.S. 533 (1964), *Avery v. Midland County*, 390 U.S. 474 (1968), and *Hadley v. Junior College District of Metropolitan Kansas City*, 397 U.S. 50 (1970).

24. *Wesberry*, infra. note 20, at 7–8.

25. 462 U.S. 725. *Karcher* reaffirmed and expanded upon previous precedents concerning congressional districting. For the pre-*Karcher* developments in the law, see Richard L. Engstrom, "Post-Census Representational Redistricting: The Supreme Court, 'One Person, One Vote,' and the Gerrymandering Issue," *Southern University Law Review* 7 (Spring 1981): 173–226.

26. *Ibid.*, at 728.

27. *Id.*, at 739.

28. *Id.*, at 742–744.

29. *Id.*, at 734.

30. *Id.*, at 741.

31. *Id.*

32. *Id.*

33. *Vieth*, infra note 18, at 676.

34. *Ibid.*, at 677.

35. R*eynolds*, infra note 1, at 577.

36. *Ibid.*, at 579.

37. See Engstrom, "Post-Census Representational Redistricting," 173–226, and *Brown v. Thomson*, 462 U.S. 835 (1983).

38. See Robert G. Dixon, Jr., *Democratic Representation: Reapportionment in Law and Politics*, (New York: Oxford University Press, 1968), 492–496, and Engstrom, "Post-Census Representational Redistricting," 212.

39. 300 F. Supp. 2d 1320 (N.D. Ga. 2004).

40. *Ibid.*, at 1,352.

41. *Id.*, at 1,338.

42. *Id.*, at 1,347–48.

43. The district court's decision in *Larios* was summarily affirmed by the Supreme Court (see *Cox v. Larios*, 542—U.S.—June 30, 2004).

44. *Larios*, infra note 39, at 1322, 1351).

45. 188 F. Supp. 2d 1041 (2001).

46. *Ibid.,* at 1045.

47. *Id.*, at 1051.

48. *Id.*, at 1044.

49. *Id.*, at 1051.

50. *Gaffney v. Cummings*, 412 U.S. 735, 753 (1973).

51. Minority groups protected by the Voting Rights Act include African Americans, Latinos, Native Americans, Asian Americans, and Native Alaskans.

52. *Davis v. Bandemer*, 478 U.S. 109 (1986) (Powell, J., dissenting).

53. See *Bush v. Vera*, 517 U.S. 952, 968 (1996) and *Hunt v. Cromartie*, 562 U.S.541, 552 (1999).

54. 306 F. Supp. 1190, 1195 (2003).

55. Jost, "Redistricting Disputes," 236.

56. *Ibid.*, at 1204 n.5 and 1205 n.6.

57. *Id.*, at 1195.

58. *Martinez v. Bush*, 234 F. Supp 2d 1275 (S.D. Flda. 2002).

59. *O'Lear v. Miller*, 222 F. Supp. 2d 850 (E.D. Mich. 2002) and 222 F. Supp. 2d 862 (E.D. Mich. 2002).

60. *Duckworth v. State Board of Elections*, 213 F. Supp. 543 (D.C. Md. 2002).

61. *Session v. Perry*, 298 F. Supp. 2d 451 (E.D. Tx. 451).
62. *Ibid.*, at 474.
63. *Davis v. Bandemer*, 478 U.S. 109 (1986).
64. *Ibid.*, at 166–77.
65. See the quotations from witness depositions, *Id.*, at 117n5.
66. *Id.*, at 144 (O.Connor, J., concurring).
67. *Id.*, at 185 (Powell, J., concurring in part and dissenting in part).
68. *Id.*, at 127.
69. *Id.*, at 129.
70. *Id.*, at 132 (emphasis added).
71. See especially *Whitcomb v. Chavis*, 403 U.S. 124 (1971) and *White v. Regester*, 412 U.S. 755 (1973).
72. *Bandemer*, infra note 58, at 133.
73. Michael A. Smith, "Minority Representation and Majority-Minority Districts after *Shaw v. Reno*: Legal Challenges, Empirical Evidence and Alternative Approaches," *Politics and Policy,* 29 (June 2001): 245.
74. See also *Badham v. Eu*, 694 F. Supp. 664 (N.D. Calf. 1988), *Illinois Legislative Redistricting Commission v. La Paile*, 782 F. Supp. 1272 (N.D. Ill. 1992) *Pope v. Blue*, 809 F. Supp. 392 (W.D. N.C. 1992), *The Fund for Accurate and Reformed Representation v. Weprin*, 796 F. Supp. 662 (N.D. N.Y. 1992), *Terrazas v. Slagle*, 821 F. Supp. 1162 (1993), and *Marylanders for Fair Representation v. Schaefer*, 849 F. Supp. 1022 (D.D. Md. 1994).
75. The case before the Supreme Court, *Vieth v. Jubelirer*, concerned the plan adopted by Pennsylvania that reduced the total deviations from 19 people to a single person. This was "essentially the same redistricting plan" as the previous one and did not differ from it in its partisan implications. The partisan gerrymandering claim registered against this plan was dismissed for the same reasons as the complaint against the first plan [see *Vieth v. Commonwealth of Pennsylvania*, 241 F. Supp. 2d 478, 485 (M.D. Pa. 2003)].
76. 541 U.S.—(April 28, 2004).
77. *Ibid.*, Scalia, J., an opinion, joined by Chief Justice Rehnquist and Justices O'Connor and Thomas.
78. *Id.*, Stevens, J., dissenting, Souter, J., dissenting, joined by Justice Ginsburg, and Breyer, J., dissenting.
79. *Id.*, Kennedy, J., concurring, sl. op. at 7–8.
80. *Id.*, Kennedy, J., concurring, sl. op. at 12, quoting a North Carolina state legislator.
81. *Easley v. Cromartie*, 532 U.S. 234 (2001).
82. 539 U.S. 461 (2003).
83. See, e.g., Richard L. Engstrom, *Revised Research Report*, *Georgia v. Ashcroft*, United States District Court for the District of Columbia, 2002, and more generally Katherine Tate, *Black Faces in the Mirror: African Americans and Their Representatives in the U.S. Congress* (Princeton, N.J.: Princeton University Press, 2003).
84. *Vieth*, infra note 76, Scalia, J., an opinion, sl. op. at 22.
85. *Ibid.*, Stevens, J., dissenting, sl. op. at 24.
86. See, e.g., the recitation of events in *Navajo Nation v. Arizona Independent Redistricting Commission*, 230 F. Supp. 2d 998 (DC. Ariz. 2002), and *Arizona Minority*

Coalition for Fair Redistricting v. Arizona Independent Redistricting Commission, Superior Court of Arizona, Maricopa County, (CV2002-004882, January 16, 2004. For continuing developments, see Paul Davenport, "Appeal Says Redistricting Order 'Predetermined,'" Associated Press State and Local Wire, July 21, 2004.

87. Christopher Buchanan, "States Seek Ways to Make Redistricting less Partisan," *Congressional Quarterly Weekly Report*, November 26, 1977, 2482.

88. The discussion of these alternative election systems draws heavily from Richard L. Engstrom, "The Political Thicket, Electoral Reform, and Minority Voting Rights," in Mark E. Rush and Richard L. Engstrom, *Fair and Effective Representation? Debating Electoral Reform and Minority Rights*, (Lanham, Md.: Rowman and Littlefield Publishers, Inc., 2001).

89. It is not necessary that voters cast votes in whole units. In Peoria, Illinois, for example, a five-vote cumulative system has been adopted whereby voters simply identify up to five candidates they wish to vote for, and then their five votes are allocated evenly among those candidates. If a voter votes for only one candidate, five votes are allocated to that candidate. If a voter votes for two candidates, then two and one-half votes are allocated to each. If a voter votes for three, four, or five candidates, then one and two-thirds votes, one and one-fourth votes, or one vote, respectively, are allocated to each of the chosen candidates.

90. Voters are not necessarily required to rank all of the candidates on a preference voting ballot. When they do not, some ballots may become nontransferable, resulting in the quota not being obtained by the required number of candidates. When this happens, the remaining seat(s) may be filled by applying a simple plurality rule after the final set of transfers.

91. As one court has stated about cumulative voting, "By allowing each voter the same number of votes, cumulative voting subscribes to the one person, one vote requirement with numeric exactness" [*McCoy v. Chicago* Heights, 6 F. Supp. 2d 973, 984 (N.D. Ill. 1998); see also *Kaelin v. Warden*, 334 F. Supp. 602 (E.D. Pa. 1971), *LoFrisco v. Schaffer*, 341 F. Supp. 743 (D. Conn. 1972), and *Orloski v.* Davis 564 F. Supp. 526 (M.D. Pa. 1983).

92. See Arend Lijphart, "Trying to Have the Best of Both Worlds: Semi-Proportional and Mixed Systems," in Arend Lijphart and Bernard Grofman (eds.), *Choosing an Electoral System: Issues and Alternatives* (New York: Praeger, 1984), 207.

93. See, e.g., Richard G. Niemi, Simon Jackman, and Laura R. Winsky, "Candidates and Competitiveness in Multimember Districts," *Legislative Studies Quarterly*, 16 (February 1991): 102–103, and Michael D. McDonald and Richard L. Engstrom, "Minority Representation and City Council Election Systems: A Black and Hispanic Comparison," in Anthony M. Messina, Luis R. Fraga, Laurie A. Rhodebeck, and Frederick D. Wright (eds.), *Ethnic and Racial Minorities in Advanced Industrial Democracies* (New York: Greenwood Press, 1992), 138–39.

94. See Douglas W. Rae, Victor Hanby, and John Loosemore, "Thresholds of Representation and Thresholds of Exclusion: An Analytic Note on Electoral Systems," *Comparative Political Studies*, 3 (January 1971): 479–88.

95. See, e.g., Darren Rosenblum, "Geographically Sexual? Advancing Lesbian and Gay Interests through Proportional Representation," *Harvard Civil Rights—Civil Liberties Law Review*, 31 (Spring 1996): 199–251), and Stephen Bloch, "Cumulative Vot-

ing and the Religious Right: In the Best Interests of Democracy?," *Journal of Contemporary Law*, 24 (1998): 1–34.

96. Mary A. Inman, "C.P.R. (Change through Proportional Representation): Rescuing a Federal Election System," *University of Pennsylvania Law Review*, 141 (May 1993): 1991–2053.

97. Preference voting is used only in Cambridge, Massachusetts to elect the city council and school board.

98. See, e.g., Richard L. Engstrom, Delbert Taebel and Richard L. Cole, "Cumulative Voting as a Remedy for Minority Vote Dilution: The Case of Alamogordo, New Mexico," *Journal of Law and Politics*, 5 (Spring 1989): 469–97; Richard L. Cole and Delbert Taebel, "Cumulative Voting in Local Elections: Lessons from the Alamogordo Experience," *Social Science Quarterly*, 73 (March 1992): 194–201; Richard L. Engstrom and Charles J. Barrilleaux, "Native Americans and Cumulative Voting: The Case of the Sisseton Wahpeton Sioux," *Social Science Quarterly*, 72 (June 1991): 388–93; Robert R. Brischetto and Richard L. Engstrom, "Cumulative Voting and Latino Representation: Exit Surveys in 15 Texas Communities," *Social Science Quarterly*, 78 (December 1997): 973–91; and Richard L. Engstrom, Jason F. Kirksey, and Edward Still, "One Person, Seven Votes: The Cumulative Voting Experience in Chilton County, Alabama," in Anthony Peacock (ed.), *Affirmative Action and Representation:* Shaw v. Reno *and the Future of Voting Rights*, (Durham, N.C.: Carolina Academic Press, 1997).

99. Engstrom, Kirksey, and Still, "One Person, Seven Votes."

100. See Shaun Bowler, Todd Donovan, and David Brockington, *Electoral Reform and Minority Representation: Local Experiments with Alternative Elections* (Columbus, Ohio: Ohio State University Press, 2003).

101. See Arend Lijphard, *Patterns of Democracy: Government Forms and Performances in Thirty-Six Countries* (New Haven: Yale University Press, 1999), Matthew Soberg Shugart, "The Jenkins Paradox: A Complex System Yet Only a Timid Step towards PR," *Representation* 36 (Summer 1999): 143–47; and Ben Reilly and Andrew Reynolds, *Electoral Systems and Conflict in Divided Societies*. (Washington D.C.: National Academy Press, 1999).

102. For more detail on the experience with these systems, criticisms of them, and the response thereto, see Engstrom, "The Political Thicket, Electoral Reform, and Minority Voting Rights," 44–58.

103. See Charles W. Wiggins and Janice Petty, "Cumulative Voting and Electoral Competition: The Illinois House," *American Politics Quarterly*, 7 (July 1979): 345–65; James Kuklinski, "Cumulative and Plurality Voting: An Analysis of Illinois Unique Electoral System," *Western Political Quarterly*, 26 (December 1973): 726–46; Charles W. Dunn, "Cumulative Voting Problems in Illinois Legislative Elections," *Harvard Journal of Legislation*, 9 (May 1972): 627–65; George S. Blair, *Cumulative Voting: An Effective Electoral Device in Illinois Politics* (Urbana, Ill.: University of Illinois Press, 1960); and more generally, Lani Guinier, *Lift Every Voice: Turning a Civil Rights Setback into a New Vision of Social Justice* (New York: Simon and Schuster, 1998), 266–68.

In one of the few places in the United States where an alternative system has been applied to a partisan ballot in recent years, Chilton County, Alabama, Republicans were elected for the first time, to both the county commission and the school board, under cumulative voting [Edward Still "Cumulative and Limited Voting in Alabama, in Wilma Rule and Joseph F. Zimmerman (eds.), *United States Electoral Systems: Their Impact on Women and* Minorities, (New York: Greenwood Press, 1992), 187–90]. This happened in the first and subsequent seven-vote cumulative voting elections there [Engstrom, Kirksey, and Still, "One Person, Seven Votes," 187–190, and Richard H.Pildes and Kristen A. Donoghue, "Cumulative Voting in the United States," *University of Chicago Law Forum* (1995): 274–75], and of course was a boost rather than a threat to any two-party system in that county. No candidates affiliated with parties other than the Democrats and Republicans, nor independent candidates, have been elected in any of that county's cumulative voting contests.

104. Frank del Olmo, "Getting Away with a Blatant Gerrymander," *Los Angeles Times*, June 16, 2002.

Selected Bibliography

Abramowitz, Alan I. "The End of the Democratic Era? 1994 and the Future of Congressional Election Research." *Political Research Quarterly* 48 (1995): 873–89.

Ackerman, Bruce. *Bush v. Gore: The Question of Legitimacy*. New Haven: Yale University Press, 2002.

Adams, Florence. *Latinos and Local Representation*. New York: Garland Publishing, 2000.

Alford, John H., and David W. Brady. "Personal and Partisan Advantage in U.S. Congressional Elections." Pp. 153–69 in *Congress Reconsidered*. 4th ed., edited by Bruce I. Oppenheimer and Lawrence C. Dodd. Washington, DC: CQ Press, 1989.

Alford, John, Holly Teeters, Daniel S. Ward, and Rick K. Wilson. "Overdraft: The Political Cost of Congressional Malfeasance." *Journal of Politics* 56, no. 3 (August 1994): 788–801.

Ansolabehere, Stephen, Alan Gerber, and James Snyder. "Equal Votes, Equal Money: Court-Ordered Redistricting and Public Expenditures in the American States." *American Political Science Review* 96, no. 4 (December 2002): 767–93.

Ansolabehere, Stephen, James M. Snyder, Jr., and Charles Stewart, III. "Old Voters, New Voters, and the Personal Vote: Using Redistricting to Measure the Incumbency Advantage." *American Journal of Political Science* 44, no.1 (2000): 17–34.

Arnold, R. Douglas. *The Logic of Congressional Action*. New Haven, CT: Yale University Press, 1990.

Ball, Howard. "Racial Vote Dilution: Impact of the Reagan DOJ and the Burger Court on the Voting Rights Act." *Publius: The Journal of Federalism*, 16 (1986): 29–48.

Ballard, Gregory G. "Application of Section 2 of the Voting Rights Act to Runoff Primary Election Laws." *Columbia Law Review* 91 (1991): 1145–57.

Banducci, Susan A., and Jeffrey A. Karp. "Electoral Consequences of Scandal and Redistricting in the 1992 House Election." *American Politics Quarterly* 22, (January 1994): 3–26.

Barone, Michael, and Grant Ujifusa. *The Almanac of American Politics.* Washington, DC: National Journal, Bi-annual Publication.

Bartells, Larry M. "Partisanship and Voting Behavior." *American Journal of Political Science* 44, no. 1 (2000): 35–50.

Bauer, Monica, and John R. Hibbing. "Which Incumbents Lose in House Elections: A Response to Jacobson's 'The Marginals Never Vanished.'" *American Journal of Political Science* 33, no. 1 (1989): 262–71.

Berman, Mitchell. 2004. "Putting Fairness on the Map: The High Court Has a Chance to Ease Flagrant Partisan Gerrymandering." *Los Angeles Times*, (May 28).

Black, Earl. "The Newest Southern Politics." *Journal of Politics* 60 (1998): 591–612.

Black, Earl, and Merle Black. *The Rise of Southern Republicans.* Cambridge: Harvard University Press, 2002.

Blair. George S. *Cumulative Voting: An Effective Electoral Device in Illinois Politics.* Urbana: University of Illinois Press, 1960.

Bloch, Stephen. "Cumulative Voting and the Religious Right: In the Best Interests of Democracy?" *Journal of Contemporary Law* 24: 1–34, 1998.

Blum, Edward and Roger Clegg. "Color Inside the Lines." *Legal Affairs* (November-December 2003): 18–20.

Blumstein, James F. "Defining and Proving Race Discrimination: Perspectives on the Purpose v. Results Approach from the Voting Rights Act." *Virginia Law Review* 69 (1983): 633–714.

———. "*Shaw v. Reno* and *Miller v. Johnson*: Where We Are and Where We Are Headed." *Cumberland Law Review* 26 (1996): 503–13.

Books, John, and Charles Prysby. *Political Behavior and the Local Context.* New York: Praeger, 1991.

Bowler, Shaun, Todd Donovan, and David Brockington. *Electoral Reform and Minority Representation: Local Experiments with Alternative Elections.* Columbus: Ohio State University Press, 2003

Brace, Kimball, Bernard Grofman, and Lisa Handley. "Does Redistricting Aimed to Help Blacks Necessarily Help Republicans?" *Journal of Politics* 49, (1987): 143–56.

Brischetto, Robert R., and Richard L. Engstrom. "Cumulative Voting and Latino Representation: Exit Surveys in 15 Texas Communities." *Social Science Quarterly* 78 (1997): 973–91.

Buchanan, Christopher. "States Seek Ways to Make Redistricting Less Partisan." *Congressional Quarterly Weekly Report* (November 26, 1977).

Bullock, Charles S. III. "Redistricting and Congressional Stability, 1962–1972." *The Journal of Politics* 37, no. 2 (1975): 569–75.

———. "Affirmative Action Districts: In Whose Faces Will They Blow Up?" *Campaigns & Elections* (1995): 22–23.

Butler, David, and Bruce Cain. *Congressional Redistricting: Comparative and Theoretical Perspectives.* New York: MacMillan, 1992.

Butler, Katharine Inglis. "Redistricting in a Post-*Shaw* Era: A Small Treatise Accompanied by Districting Guidelines for Legislators, Litigants, and Courts." *University of Richmond Law Review* 36 (2002): 137–270.

Bybee, Keith. *Mistaken Identity: The Supreme Court and the Politics of Minority Representation.* Princeton, NJ: Princeton University Press, 1998.

Cain, Bruce E. "Assessing the Partisan Effects of Redistricting." *The American Political Science Review* 79, no. 2 (1985): 320–33.

———. *The Reapportionment Puzzle*. Berkeley: University of California Press, 1984.

Cain, Bruce, John Ferejohn, and Morris Fiorina. *The Personal Vote*. Cambridge: Harvard University Press, 1987.

Cameron, Charles, David Epstein, and Sharon O'Halloran. "Do Majority-Minority Districts Maximize Substantive Black Representation in Congress?" *American Political Science Review* 90 (1996): 794–812.

Campbell, James E. "The Presidential Pulse and the 1994 Midterm Congressional Election." *Journal of Politics* 59 (1997): 830–57.

Campbell, James E., John R. Alford, and Keith Henry. "Television Markets and Congressional Elections." *Legislative Studies Quarterly* 9 (1984): 665–78.

Cannon, Carl M. "California Divided." *California Journal* (2002): 8–14.

Canon, David T. *Race, Redistricting, and Representation: The Unintended Consequences of Black Majority Districts*. Chicago: The University of Chicago Press, 1999.

———. "Race and Parties in Congressional Redistricting," in *Representation, Redistricting, and Congressional Policy Making*, edited by Neil Pinney and George Serra, forthcoming.

Carmines, Edward G., and Robert Huckfeldt. "Political Behavior: An Overview." Pp. 223–54 in *A New Handbook of Political Science,* edited by Robert E. Goodin and Hans-Dieter Klingemann. Oxford: Oxford University Press, 1996.

Carmines, Edward G., and James A. Stimson. *Issue Evolution*. Princeton, NJ: Princeton University Press, 1989.

Carson, Jamie, and Michael H. Crespin. "Comparing the Effects of Legislative, Commission, and Judicial Redistricting Plans on U.S. House Elections, 1972–2002." Paper presented at the annual meeting of the Western Political Science Association, Portland, Oregon, March 11–13, 2004.

Citizens Research Council of Michigan. *Legislative Apportionment in Michigan*. Report No. 303, December 1991.

Clarke, Peter, and Susan H. Evans. *Covering Campaigns: Journalism in Congressional Elections*. Stanford: Stanford University Press, 1983.

Cole, Richard L., and Delbert Taebel. "Cumulative Voting in Local Elections: Lessons from the Alamogordo Experience." *Social Science Quarterly*. 73 (1992): 194–201.

Congressional Quarterly. *Congressional Elections: 1946–1996*. Washington, DC: Congressional Quarterly Inc., 1998.

Congressional Research Service. "CRS Report for Congress: Black Members of the United States Congress, 1789–1989." Washington, DC: Library of Congress, 1989.

Cook, Rhodes. "Iowa Remapping Goes Smoothly as Six Districts Become Five," *Congressional Quarterly Weekly Report* (18 May 1991): 1306.

Cox, Gary W., and Jonathan Katz. *Elbridge Gerry's Salamander: The Electoral Consequences of the Reapportionment Revolution*. Cambridge, UK: Cambridge University Press, 2002.

Cranor, John D., Gary L. Crawley, and Raymond H. Scheele. "The Anatomy of a Gerrymander." *American Journal of Political Science* 33, no. 1 (1989): 222–39.

Cunningham, Maurice T. *Maximization, Whatever the Cost: Race, Redistricting and the Department of Justice*. Westport, CT: Praeger, 2001.

Davidson, Chandler. *Minority Vote Dilution*. Washington, DC: Howard University Press, 1984.

———. *Race and Class in Texas Politics*. Princeton, NJ: Princeton University Press, 1990.

———. "The Voting Rights Act: A Brief History." Pp. 7–51 in *Controversies in Minority Voting: The Voting Rights Act in Perspective,* edited by Bernard Grofman and Chandler Davidson. Washington, DC: The Brookings Institution, 1992.

Davidson, Chandler, and Bernard Grofman, eds. *Quiet Revolution in the South: The Impact of the Voting Rights Act, 1965–1990.* Princeton, NJ: Princeton University Press, 1994.

Days, Drew S. III. "Section 5 Enforcement and the Justice Department." Pp. 52–65 in *Controversies in Minority Voting: The Voting Rights Act in Perspective*, edited by Bernard Grofman and Chandler Davidson. Washington, DC: The Brookings Institution, 1992.

Desposato, Scott W.,and John R. Petrocik. "The Variable Incumbency Advantage: New Voters, Redistricting, and the Personal Vote." *American Journal of Political Science* 47 (2003): 18–32.

Dixon, Robert G., Jr. *Democratic Representation: Reapportionment in Law and Politics.* New York: Oxford University Press, 1968.

Duncan, Phil. "New Iowa Map: No Gerrymandering Allowed," *Congressional Quarterly Weekly Report* (19 September 1982): 1798–1801.

Dunn, Charles W. "Cumulative Voting Problems in Illinois Legislative Elections." *Harvard Journal of Legislation* 9 (1972): 627–65.

Earls, Anita. "Equal Effects." *Legal Affairs* (November-December 2003): 22–23.

Eisgruber, Christopher L. "Ethnic Segregation by Religion and Race: Reflections on *Kiryas Joel* and *Shaw v. Reno.*" *Cumberland Law Review* 26, (1996): 515–26.

Elliot, Ward E.Y. *The Rise of Guardian Democracy: The Supreme Court's Role in Voting Rights Disputes, 1845–1969.* Cambridge, MA: Harvard University Press, 1974.

Ely, John. "Standing to Challenge: Pro-Minority Gerrymanders." *Harvard Law Review* 111 (1997): 576–95.

Engstrom, Erik J., and Nathan W. Monroe. "Throwing in the Cards: Term Limits, Strategic Retirement, and the Incumbency Advantage." Paper presented at the annual meeting of the American Political Science Association, Boston, MA, August 28–September 1, 2002.

Engstrom, Richard L. "Post-Census Representational Redistricting: The Supreme Court, "One Person, One Vote," and the Gerrymandering Issue." *Southern University Law Review*, 7 (1981): 173–226.

———. "Voting Rights Districts: Debunking the Myths." *Campaigns and Elections* (April 1995): 24–46.

———. "The Political Thicket, Electoral Reform, and Minority Voting Rights." In *Fair and Effective Representation? Debating Electoral Reform and Minority Rights.* Ed. Mark E. Rush and Richard L. Engstrom. Lanham, MD: Rowman & Littlefield Publishers, Inc, 2001.

———. "The Post-2000 Round of Redistricting: An Entangled Thicket within the Federal System." *Publius: The Journal of Federalism*, 32 (2002): 51–70.

Engstrom, Richard L. and Charles J. Barrilleaux. "Native Americans and Cumulative Voting: The Case of the Sisseton Wahpeton Sioux." *Social Science Quarterly* 72 (1991): 388–93.

Engstrom, Richard L., Jason F. Kirksey, and Edward Still. "One Person, Seven Votes: The Cumulative Voting Experience in Chilton County, Alabama." Pp. 285–313 in *Affirmative Action and Representation;* Shaw v. Reno *and the Future of Voting Rights*, edited by Anthony A. Peacock. Durhan, NC: Carolina Academic Press, 1997.

Engstrom, Richard L., Delbert Taebel, and Richard L. Cole. "Cumulative Voting as a Remedy for Minority Vote Dilution: The Case of Alamogordo, New Mexico." *Journal of Law and Politics* 5 (1989): 469–97.

Engstrom, Richard N. "Electoral District Compactness and Voters." *American Review of Politics* 21 (2000): 383–96.

Epstein, David, and Sharyn O'Halloran. "A Social Science Approach to Race, Redistricting, and Representation." *American Political Science Review* 93 (1999): 187–91.

———. "Measuring the Electoral and Policy Impact of Majority-Minority Voting Districts." *American Journal of Political Science* 43 (1999): 367–95.

———. "Majority-Minority Districts and the New Politics of Congressional Elections." Pp. 87–109 in *Continuity and Change in House Elections*, edited by David W. Brady, John F. Cogan, and Morris P. Fiorina. Stanford: Stanford University Press, 2000.

Fenno, Richard F. *Home Style: House Members in Their Districts*. New York: Harper Collins Publishers, 1978.

Ferejohn, John A. "On the Decline of Competition in Congressional Elections." *American Political Science Review* 71 (1977): 166–76.

Fiorina, Morris. *Congress, Keystone of the Washington Establishment*. New Haven: Yale University Press, 1989.

———. *Divided Government*. 2nd ed Needham, Ma: Allyn & Bacon, 1996.

Gelman, Andrew, and Gary King. "Estimating Incumbency Advantage without Bias." *American Journal of Political Science* 34 (1990): 1142–64.

———. "Systemic Consequences of Incumbency Advantage in United States House Elections." *American Journal of Political Science* 35 (1991): 110–38.

Gilbert, Eric. *A Brief History of Reapportionment Reform in Michigan*. Common Cause in Michigan, May 1982

Glazer, Amahai, Bernard Grofman, and Marc Robbins. "Partisan and Incumbency Effects in the 1970s Congressional Redistricting." *American Journal of Political Science* 31 (1987): 680–707.

Goffman, Erving. 1963. *Stigma: Notes on the Management of Spoiled Identity*. New York: Simon & Schuster.

Graham, Hugh Davis. "Voting Rights and the American Regulatory State." Pp. 177–96 in *Controversies in Minority Voting*, edited by Bernard Grofman and Chandler Davis. New York: Oxford University Press, 1990.

———. *The Civil Rights Era: Origins and Development of National Policy, 1960–1972*. New York: Oxford University Press, 1990.

Green, George Norris. *The Establishment in Texas Politics: The Primitive Years, 1938–1957*. Westport, CT: Greenwood Press, 1979.

Grofman, Bernard. "Criteria for Districting: A Social Science Perspective." *UCLA Law Review* 33 (1985):77–184.

———. "Would Vince Lombardi Have Been Right if He Had Said 'When It Comes to Redistricting, Race Isn't Everything, It's the Only Thing?'" *Cardozo Law Review* 14 (1993):1237–76.

———. "*Shaw v. Reno* and the Future of Voting Rights." *PS: Political Science and Politics* 28 (1995): 27–36.

Grofman, Bernard, ed. *Race and Redistricting in the 1990s*. New York: Agathon Press, 1998.

Grofman, Bernard, and Lisa Handley. "Estimating the Impact of Voting-Rights-Act-Related Districting on Democratic Strength in the U.S. House of Representatives."

Pp. 51–67 in *Race and Redistricting in the 1990s*, edited by Bernard Grofman. New York: Agathon Press, 1998.

Grofman, Bernard, Lisa Handley, and Richard G. Niemi. *Minority Representation and the Quest for Voting Equality*. Cambridge: Cambridge University Press, 1992.

Grubert, Jeanmarie K. "The Rehnquist Court's Changed Reading of the Equal Protection Clause in the Context of Voting Rights." *Fordham Law Review* 65, (1997): 1819–54.

Guinier, Lani. "The Triumph of Tokenism: The Voting Rights Act and the Theory of Black Electoral Success." *Michigan Law Review* 89 (March 1991): 1077–154.

Guinier, Lani. *Lift Every Voice: Turning a Civil Rights Setback into a New Vision of Social Justice*. New York: Simon & Schuster, 1998.

Hacker, Andrew. *Congressional Districting: The Issue of Equal Representation,* rev. ed. Washington, DC: Brookings Institution, 1964.

Herrnson, Paul S. *Congressional Elections: Campaigning at Home and in Washington*. Washington, DC: Congressional Quarterly, 1995.

Hess, Stephen. *Live From Capitol Hill!* Washington, DC: Brookings Institution, 1991.

Higgs, Robert. *Crisis and Leviathan: Critical Episodes in the Growth of American Government*. New York: Oxford University Press, 1987.

Hill, Kevin A. "Does the Creation of Majority Black Districts Aid Republicans? An Analysis of the 1992 Congressional Elections in Eight Southern States." *The Journal of Politics* 57 (1995): 384–401.

Hill, Kevin A., and Nicol C. Rae. "What Happened to the Democrats in the South?: US House Elections, 1992–1996." *Party Politics* 6 (2000): 5–22.

Hirsch, Sam. "The U.S. House of Unrepresentatives: What Went Wrong in the Latest Round of Congressional Redistricting." *Election Law Journal*, 2 (2003): 179–216.

Holmes, Robert A. "Reapportionment Strategies in the 1990s: The Case of Georgia." Pp. 191–228 in *Race and Redistricting in the 1990s*, edited by Bernard Grofman. New York: Agathon Press, 1998.

Inman, Mary A. "C.P.R. (Change through Proportional Representation): Rescuing a Federal Election System." *University of Pennsylvania Law Review*, 141 (1993): 1991–2053.

Issacharoff, Samuel. "Groups and the Right to Vote." *Emory Law Journal* 46, (1995): 869–83.

Issacharoff, Samuel, and Richard A. Pildes. "Politics as Markets: Partisan Lockups of the Democratic Process." *Stanford Law Review*, 50 (1998): 643–717.

Jacobson, Gary C. "Practical Consequences of Campaign Finance Reform: An Incumbent Protection Act?" *Public Policy* 24 (Winter 1976): 1–32.

———. "Strategic Politicians and the Dynamics of House Elections, 1946–1986." *American Political Science Review* 83 (September 1989): 773–93.

———. "The 1994 House Elections in Perspective." *Political Science Quarterly* 111 (1996): 203–23.

———. *The Politics of Congressional Elections*, 4th ed. New York: Longman, 1997.

———. "Reversal of Fortune: The Transformation of U.S. House Elections in the 1990s." Pp. 10–38 in *Continuity and Change in House Elections*, edited by David W. Brady, John F. Cogan, and Morris P. Fiorina. Stanford: Stanford University Press, 2000.

———. "A House and Senate Divided: The Clinton Legacy and the Congressional Elections of 2000." *Political Science Quarterly* 116 (Spring 2001): 5–27.

———. "Congress: Elections and Stalemate." Pp. 185–209 in *The Elections of 2000*, edited by Michael Nelson. Washington, DC: Congressional Quarterly, 2001.

———. *The Politics of Congressional Elections*. 5th ed. New York: Addison-Wesley, 2001.

———. "Terror, Terrain, and Turnout: Explaining the 2002 Midterm Election." *Political Science Quarterly* 118 (Spring 2003): 1–22.

———. "Partisan and Ideological Polarization in the California Electorate." *State Politics and Policy Quarterly* 4 (Summer 2004): 113–39.

Jacobson, Gary C., and Samuel Kernell. *Strategy and Choice in Congressional Elections*. Second Edition. New Haven: Yale University Press, 1983.

———. *Strategy and Choice in Congressional Elections*. New Haven: Yale University Press, 1996.

Johnston, Ron. "Manipulating Maps and Winning Elections: Measuring the Impact of Malapportionment and Gerrymandering." *Political Geography* 21 (2002): 1–31.

Jost, Kenneth. "Redistricting Disputes." *CQ Researcher*, 14 (2004): 221–47.

Kairys, David. "Unexplainable on Grounds Other than Race.' *American University Law Review* 45, (1996): 729–49.

Karlan, Pamela S., and Dayrl J. Levinson. "Why Voting Is Different." *California Law Review* 84 (1996): 1201–86.

Karlan, Pamela S., and Peyton McCrary. "Without Fear and Without Research: Abigail Thernstrom on the Voting Rights Act." *Journal of Law and Politics* 4, (1988): 751–77.

Key, V. O., Jr. *Southern Politics*. New York: Vintage, 1949.

Key, V.O., Jr. *Southern Politics in State and Nation*. Knoxville: University of Tennessee Press, 1996.

King, Gary, and Robert X. Browning. "Democratic Representation and Partisan Bias in Congressional Elections." *American Political Science Review* 81, no. 4 (December 1987): 1251–73.

Kousser, J. Morgan. "The Voting Rights Act and the Two Reconstructions." Pp. 135–76 in *Controversies in Minority Voting*, edited by Bernard Grofman and Chandler Davidson. Washington DC: The Brookings Institution, 1992

———. "*Shaw v. Reno* and the Real World of Redistricting and Representation." California Institute of Technology Working Paper #915, 1995.

———. "Estimating the Partisan Consequences of Redistricting Plans-Simply." *Legislative Studies Quarterly* 21, no. 4 (1996): 521–41.

———. "Reapportionment Wars: Party, Race, and Redistricting in California, 1971–1992." Pp. 134–90 in *Race and Redistricting in the 1990s*, edited by Bernard Grofman. New York: Agathon Press, 1998.

———. *Colorblind Injustice: Minority Voting Rights and the Undoing of the Second Reconstruction*. Chapel Hill, NC: University of North Carolina Press, 1999.

Kubin, Jeffrey C. "The Case for Redistricting Commissions." *Texas Law Review* 75 (1997): 37– 872.

Kuklinski, James. "Cumulative and Plurality Voting: An Analysis of Illinois Unique Electoral System." *Western Political Quarterly* 26 (1973): 726–46.

Larson, Bruce, Suzanne Globetti, and Marc J. Hetherington. "The Redistricting Cycle and Strategic Candidate Decisions in U.S. House Races." Paper presented at the annual meeting of the American Political Science Association, Washington, DC, August 31–September 4, 2000.

Lazarus, Jeff. "Challengers Are People Too: How the Strategic Action of Political Challengers Affects House Races." Ph.D. diss., University of California, San Diego, 2003.

Lennertz, James E. "Back in Their Proper Place: Racial Gerrymandering in Georgia." *Political Geography* 19 (2000): 163–88.

Lijphart, Arend. "Comparative Perspectives on Fair Representation: The Plurality-Majority Rule, Geographical Districting, and Alternative Electoral Arrangements." Pp. 143–59 in *Representation and Redistricting Issues*, edited by Bernard Grofman, Arend Lijphart, Robert McKay, and Howard Scarrow. Lexington, MA: Lexington Books, 1982.

———. "Trying to Have the Best of Both Worlds: Semi-Proportional and Mixed Systems." Pp. 207–13 in *Choosing an Electoral System: Issues and Alternatives*, edited by Arend Lijphart and Bernard Grofman. New York: Praeger, 1984.

———. *Patterns of Democracy: Government Forms and Performance in Thirty-Six Countries*. New Haven, CT: Yale University Press, 1999

Lockerbie, Brad. "The Sophomore Surge: Conversion, Mobilization, or Abstention?" *Political Research Quarterly* 47, (December 1994): 961–68.

Lowenstein, Daniel H. "Race and Representation in the Supreme Court," Pp. 49–81 in *Voting Rights and Redistricting in the United States,* edited by Mark E. Rush. Westport, CT: Greenwood Press, 1998.

Lowi, Theodore J. *The End of Liberalism: The Second Republic of the United States*, 2nd ed. New York: W.W. Norton & Company, 1979.

Lublin, David. "Racial Redistricting and Public Policy in the U.S. House of Representatives." Paper presented at the annual meeting of the Southern Political Science Association, Tampa, FL, Nov 1–4, 1994.

———. *The Paradox of Representation: Racial Gerrymander and Minority Interests in Congress*. Princeton, NJ: Princeton University Press, 1997.

———. "The Election of African Americans and Latinos to the U.S. House of Representatives, 1972–1994." *American Politics Quarterly* 25 (1997): 269–86.

Lublin, David, and D. Stephen Voss. "Boll-Weevil Blues: Polarized Congressional Delegations into the 21st Century." *American Review of Politics* 21(2000): 427–50.

Lyons, Michael, and Peter F. Galderisi. "Incumbency, Reapportionment, and U.S. House Redistricting." *Political Research Quarterly* 48 (December 1995): 857–71.

Mann ,Thomas E.. *Unsafe at any Margin: Interpreting Congressional Election*. Washington, DC: American Enterprise Institute for Public Policy Research, 1978.

Martis, Kenneth C. *The Historical Atlas of United States Congressional Districts, 1789–1983*. New York: Free Press, 1982.

Mayhew, David. *Congress: The Electoral Connection*. New Haven: Yale University Press, 1974.

McCubbins, Mathew D., and Thomas Schwartz. "Congress, the Courts, and Public Policy: Consequences of the One Man, One Vote Rule." *American Journal of Political Science* 32, no. 2 (May 1988): 388–415.

McCue, Kenneth F. "California Statewide Election/Registration Data Merged to Census Data, 1990–1992." Institute for Government Studies. University of California, Berkeley, 1994.

McDonald, Michael D., and Richard L. Engstrom. "Minority Representation and City Council Election Systems: A Black and Hispanic Comparison." Pp. 127–42 in *Ethnic and Racial Minorities in Advanced Industrial Democracies*, edited by Anthony M. Messina, Luis R. Fraga, Laurie A. Rhodebeck, and Frederick D. Wright. New York: Greenwood Press, 1992.

McDonald, Michael D. "The How and Why of Compact Districts." *American Review of Politics* 17 (1996): 329–43.

McDonald, Michael P. "Redistricting, Dealignment, and the Political Homogenization of Congressional Districts." Ph.D. diss., University of California, San Diego, 1999.

McKee, Seth C. "Majority Black Districts, Republican Ascendancy, and Party Competition in the South, 1988–2000." *American Review of Politics* 23 (2002.): 123–39.

McKinney, Cynthia. "The Politics of Geography." *Emerge*, (Dec/Jan 1996): 62–66.

Mexican American Legal Defense and Education Fund. "The Redistricting Dispute." *California Journal* (January 2002): 39–41.

Michigan Legislative Research Bureau. *Michigan's Apportionment Puzzle.* Research Report Vol. 19, No. 2. March 2003.

Moscardelli, Vincent G. "Politics, Geography, and the Ghost of Elbridge Gerry: Majority-Minority Districting in Massachusetts in the 21st Century." Paper presented at the annual meeting of the American Political Science Association, Boston, August 2002.

Murray, Richard, and Sam Attlesey. "Texas: Republicans Gallop Ahead." Pp. 305–42 in *Southern Politics in the 1990s*, edited by Alexander P. Lamis. Baton Rouge: Louisiana State University Press, 1999.

Niemi, Richard G., and Alan I. Abramowitz. "Partisan Redistricting and the 1992 Congressional Elections." *Journal of Politics* 56 (1994): 811–17.

Niemi, Richard G., Bernard Grofman, Carl Carlucci, and Thomas Hofeller. "Measuring Compactness and the Role of a Compactness Standard in a Test for Partisan and Racial Gerrymandering." *Journal of Politics* 53 (1990): 1155–79.

Niemi, Richard G., Simon Jackman, and Laura R. Winsky. "Candidacies and Competitiveness in Multimember Districts." *Legislative Studies Quarterly*, 16 (1991): 91–109.

Niemi, Richard G., Lynda W. Powell, and Patricia L. Bicknell. "The Effects of Congruity between Community and District on Salience of U.S. House Candidates." *Legislative Studies Quarterly* 11 (1986): 187–201.

O'Rourke, Timothy G. "The 1982 Amendments and the Voting Rights Paradox," Pp. 85–113 in *Controversies in Minority Voting,* edited by Bernard Grofman and Chandler Davison. Washington, DC: Brookings Institution, 1992.

Ornstein, Norman J., Thomas E. Mann, Michael J. Malbin. *Vital Statistics on Congress 1999–2000.* Washington, DC: AEI Press, 2000.

Ostdiek, Donald. "Congressional Redistricting and District Typologies." *Journal of Politics* 57 (1995): 533–43.

Owen, Guillermo and Bernard N. Grofman. "Optimal Partisan Gerrymandering." *Political Geography Quarterly* 7, no. 1 (1988): 5–22.

Palmquist, Bradley. "The Extended Beta Binomial Model in Political Analysis." Paper presented at the Annual Meeting of the Southern Political Science Association Meeting, 1998.

Parker, Frank R. "Racial Gerrymandering and Legislative Reapportionment." Pp. 85–118 in *Minority Vote Dilution*, edited by Chandler Davidson. Washington, DC: Howard University Press, 1984.

Parker, Frank R. *Black Votes Count: Political Empowerment in Mississippi after 1995.* Chapel Hill: University of North Carolina Press, 1990.

Peacock, Anthony A. "The Voting Rights Act and the Politics of Multiculturalism: The Challenge to Commercial Republicanism at Century's Turn," Pp. 167–95 in *Courts and the Culture Wars,* edited by Bradley C.S. Watson. Lanham, MD: Lexington Books, 2002.

Peterson, Paul E. "A Politically Correct Solution to Racial Classification." Pp. 3–17 in *Classifying by Race,* edited by Paul E. Peterson. Princeton, NJ: Princeton University Press, 1995.

Petrocik, John R. "An Expected Party Vote: New Data for an Old Concept." *American Journal of Political Science* 33, no. 1 (1989): 44–66.

Petrocik, John R., and Scott W. Desposato. "The Partisan Consequences of Majority Minority Districting, 1992–1994". *The Journal of Politics.* 60 (1998): 613–33

———. "Incumbency and Short-Term Influences on Voters." Political Research Quarterly 57, no. 3 (September 2004): 363–73.

Phillips, Kevin P. *The Emerging Republican Majority.* New Rochelle, NY: Arlington House, 1969.

Pildes, Richard H., and Kristen A. Donoghue. "Cumulative Voting in the United States." *University of Chicago Law Forum* (1995): 241–313.

Pitkin, Hanna F. *The Concept of Representation.* Berkeley: University of California Press, 1967.

Plendl, Lisa. "Are Voters Dissed by Redistricting?" *California Journal* (January 2002): 12–14, 35.

Poole, Keith T., and Howard Rosenthal. *Congress: A Political-Economic History of Roll Call Voting.* New York: Oxford University Press, 1997.

Posner, Mark. "Post-1990 Redistrictings and the Preclearance Requirement of Section 5 of the Voting Rights Act." Pp. 80–117 in *Race and Redistricting in the 1990s,* edited by Bernard Grofman. New York: Agathon Press, 1998.

Pritchard, Jack. "*United States v. Hays*: A Winnowing of Standing to Sue in Gerrymandering Claims," *Mercer Law Review* 47 (1996): 955–65.

Quinn, T. Anthony. "California." Pp. 53–57 in *Reapportionment Politics,* ed. Leroy Hardy, Alan Heslop, and Stuart Anderson. Beverly Hills, CA: Sage Publications, 1981.

Rabkin, Jeremy. *Judicial Compulsions: How Public Law Distorts Public Policy.* New York: Basic Books, 1989.

Rae, Douglas W., Victor Hanby, and John Loosemore. "Thresholds of Representation and Thresholds of Exclusion: An Analytic Note on Electoral Systems." *Comparative Political Studies* 3 (1971): 479–88.

Ragsdale, Lynn, and Jerrold G. Rusk. "Who Are Nonvoters? Profiles From the 1990 Senate Elections." *American Journal of Political Science* 37 (1993): 721–46.

Reilly, Ben, and Andrew Reynolds. *Electoral Systems and Conflict in Divided Societies.* Washington, DC: National Academy Press, 1999.

Riddlesperger, James W., Jr. "Redistricting Politics in Texas, 2003." Paper presented at the Annual Meeting of the Southern Political Science Association, New Orleans, LA, January 8–10, 2004.

Rosenblum, Darren. "Geographically Sexual? Advancing Lesbian and Gay Interests through Proportional Representation." *Harvard Civil Rights–Civil Liberties Law Review* 31 (1996): 99–154.

Rosenstone, Steven J., Donald R. Kinder, Warren E. Miller, and the National Election Studies. NATIONAL ELECTION STUDIES, 1996: PRE- AND POST-ELECTION

STUDY [dataset]. 3rd release. Ann Arbor, MI: University of Michigan, Center for Political Studies [producer and distributor], 1998.

Rosenstone, Steven J., Warren E. Miller, Donald R. Kinder, and the National Election Studies. NATIONAL ELECTION STUDIES, 1994: POST-ELECTION STUDY [dataset]. Ann Arbor, MI: University of Michigan, Center for Political Studies [producer and distributor], 1995.

Rush, Mark E. *Does Redistricting Make a Difference: Partisan Representation and Electoral Behavior*. Baltimore: Johns Hopkins University Press, 1993.

Sapiro, Virginia, Steven J. Rosenstone, and the National Election Studies. NATIONAL ELECTION STUDIES, 1998: POST-ELECTION STUDY [dataset]. Ann Arbor, MI: University of Michigan, Center for Political Studies [producer and distributor], 1999.

Scher, Richard K, Jon L. Mills, and John J. Hotaling. *Voting Rights and Democracy: the Law and Politics of Districting*. Chicago: Nelson-Hall, 1997.

Schlesinger, Joseph A. *Ambition and Politics: Political Careers in the United States*. Chicago: Rand McNally, 1966.

Schockley, Evelyn Elaine. "Voting Rights Act Section 2: Racially Polarized Voting and the Minority Community's Representative of Choice." *Michigan Law Review* 89 (1991): 1038–67.

Schumpeter, Joseph A. *History of Economic Analysis*. New York: Oxford University Press, 1954.

Senate Redistricting Staff and Consultants. "The Redistricting Dispute." *California Journal* (January 2002): 38, 41–42.

Senate. Voting Rights Act Extension, Report of the Subcommittee on the Constitution of the Committee on the Judiciary. Senate report 97–417, 97 Congress, 2nd session, Washington, DC: Government Printing Office, 1982.

Shugart, Matthew Soberg. "The Jenkins Paradox: A Complex System Yet Only a Timid Step towards PR." *Representation* 36 (1999): 143–47.

Singh, Robert. *The Congressional Black Caucus: Racial Politics in the U.S. Congress*. Thousand Oaks, CA: Sage Publications, 1998.

Smith, Michael A. 2001. "Minority Representation and Majority-Minority Districts after *Shaw v. Reno*: Legal Challenges, Empirical Evidence and Alternative Approaches." *Politics and Policy* 29 (June): 239–63.

Sniderman, Paul M., and Thomas Piazza. *The Scar of Race*. Cambridge, MA: Belknap Press of Harvard University Press, 1993.

Still, Edward. "Cumulative and Limited Voting in Alabama." In Wilma Rule and Joseph F. Zimmerman (eds.), *United States Electoral Systems: Their Impact on Women and Minorities*. New York: Greenwood Press, 1992.

Stone, Walter J. and L. Sandy Maisel. "The Not-So-Simple Calculus of Winning: Potential U.S. House Candidates' Nomination and General Election Chances." Paper presented at the Annual Meeting of the American Political Science Association, Atlanta, September 2–5, 1999.

Strong, Donald. *Negroes, Ballots, and Judges: National Voting Rights Legislation in the Federal Courts*. [au: need city]: University of Alabama Press, 1968.

Swain, Carol M. *Black Faces, Black Interests: The Representation of African Americans in Congress*. Cambridge, MA: Harvard University Press, 1993.

Tate, Katherine. *Black Faces in the Mirror: African Americans and Their Representatives in the U. S. Congress*. Princeton, NJ: Princeton University Press, 2003.

Teixeira, Ruy A. *The Disappearing American Voter*. Washington, DC: Brookings Institution, 1992.

Texas Legislative Council. *Guide to 2001 Redistricting*. Austin: Texas Legislative Council, 2000.

Theriault, Sean M. "Moving Up or Moving Out: Career Ceilings and Congressional Retirement." *Legislative Studies Quarterly* 23, no. 3 (1998): 419–33.

Thernstrom, Abigail M. *Whose Votes Count? Affirmative Action and Minority Voting Rights*. Cambridge, MA: Harvard University Press, 1987.

Thernstrom, Abigail. "More Notes from a Political Thicket." *Emory Law Journal* 44 (1995): 911–41.

Valelly, Richard M. "National Parties and Racial Disenfranchisement." Pp. 188–216 in *Classifying by Race*, edited by Paul Peterson. Princeton, NJ: Princeton University Press, 1995.

Wiggins, Charles W. and Janice Petty. "Cumulative Voting and Electoral Competition: The Illinois House." *American Politics Quarterly* 7 (1979): 345–65.

Woodward, C. Vann. *The Strange Career of Jim Crow*. New York: Oxford University Press, 2002.

Wright, Gerald C., John C. McIver, Robert S. Erikson, and David B. Holian. "Stability and Change in State Electorates, Carter through Clinton." Paper presented at the annual meeting of the Midwest Political Science Association, Chicago, April 2000.

Wyman, Hastings. *Southern Political Report*, No. 605, 26 May 2003: 6.

Yarbrough, Tinsley E. *Race and Redistricting: The Shaw-Cromartie Cases*, Lawrence: University Press of Kansas, 2002.

Yiannakis, Diana E. "The Grateful Electorate: Casework and Congressional Elections." *American Journal of Political Science* 25, (1981): 568–80.

Zaller, John R. "Politicians as Prize Fighters: Electoral Selection and Incumbency Advantage." Pp. 128–85 in *Party Politics and Politicians*, edited by John Geer. Baltimore: Johns Hopkins University Press, 1998.

Index

Contributors

Florence P. Adams
Rose Institute of State and Local Government, Claremont McKenna College

Barry C. Burden
Harvard University

Thomas L. Brunell
The University of Texas at Dallas

Bruce Cain
University of California, Berkeley

David T. Canon
University of Wisconsin

John R. Chamberlin
University of Michigan

Gary W. Cox
University of California, San Diego

Scott W. Desposato
University of Arizona

Richard L. Engstrom
University of New Orleans

Richard N. Engstrom
Georgia State University

Peter F. Galderisi
Utah State University

Bernard Grofman
University of California, Irvine

Gary C. Jacobson
University of California, San Diego

Seth C. McKee
The University of Texas at Austin

Anthony A. Peacock
Utah State University

John R. Petrocik
University of Missouri

Daron R. Shaw
The University of Texas at Austin

Peverill Squire
The University of Iowa